# MAKING SUBURBIA

# MAKING SUBURBIA

*New Histories of Everyday America*

John Archer, Paul J. P. Sandul, *and*
Katherine Solomonson, *Editors*

*Afterword by* Margaret Crawford

UNIVERSITY OF MINNESOTA PRESS
MINNEAPOLIS • LONDON

Portions of chapter 7 were previously published in Paul J. P. Sandul, *California Dreaming: Boosterism, Memory, and Rural Suburbs in the Golden State* (Morgantown, W.V.: West Virginia University Press, 2014); copyright 2014 West Virginia University Press. An early version of chapter 21 was published as Beverly K. Grindstaff, "Making the Great Outdoors Better: The Outdoor Kitchen and the Changing Design of American Luxury," *IDEA Journal*, special issue, *Interior Territories: Exposing the Critical Interior,* ed. Gini Lee (2009): 121–33.

Published by the University of Minnesota Press
111 Third Avenue South, Suite 290
Minneapolis, MN 55401–2520
http://www.upress.umn.edu


Library of Congress Cataloging-in-Publication Data
Making suburbia: new histories of everyday America / John Archer, Paul J. P. Sandul, and Katherine Solomonson, editors; afterword by Margaret Crawford.
Includes bibliographical references and index.
ISBN 978-0-8166-9296-5 (hc)
ISBN 978-0-8166-9299-6 (pb)
1. Suburban life—United States. 2. Suburbs—United States—History.
I. Archer, John. II. Sandul, Paul J. P. III. Solomonson, Katherine.
HT352.U6M34 2015
307.740973—dc23
2015000050


Printed in the United States of America on acid-free paper

The University of Minnesota is an equal-opportunity educator and employer.

20  19  18  17  16  15          10  9  8  7  6  5  4  3  2  1

# CONTENTS

# Making, Performing, Living Suburbia

JOHN ARCHER, PAUL J. P. SANDUL, AND
KATHERINE SOLOMONSON

Suburbia is so varied that it is impossible to define it in any one way. It is not a single place. It is not even a singular kind of place. Suburbia is a complex and richly textured physical and social fabric, multiple terrains of varied and vital places, practices, and identities. Geographically, architecturally, historically, demographically, politically, socially, and in many other dimensions suburbia is as heterogeneous as the lives of those who reside there.

Even so, stereotypes of suburbia—often as bland and maladaptive—abound. These, more often than not, overlook the multiplicity of suburban forms and ignore the lives of suburbia's inhabitants. Entering "suburbia" in a Google image search, for example, inundates the screen with eerily unpopulated views of post-1945 subdivisions.[1] Those that come up first are mostly aerial views, with curving streets, culs-de-sac, and splashes of turquoise that spread rhythmic patterns across the landscape. Others are set down amid emerald lawns unfurling from houses that are (almost, if not quite) all the same. At first glance, it appears this set of images could have been specially curated to accompany the song "Little Boxes" (1962) by Malvina Reynolds or the opening sequence of the television series *Weeds* (2005–12), which visually exemplifies the antisuburban anthem that "they all come out the same." But the images have been, of course, generated for us by a Google algorithm that draws on Web content produced for various purposes by countless geographically dispersed individuals: scholars, photographers, journalists, cultural critics, bloggers, and many others with varying agendas. Those that come up in the top tiers of this search have the greatest number of sites linked to them, according to Google's algorithm. Most used, most linked, most viewed, and so on: an ongoing, self-reinforcing yet constantly changing process, demonstrating one way innumerable individual actors, human and nonhuman, produce suburbia—in this case, particular representations of suburbia. Indeed, the Google process simply replicates the broader processes by which public knowledge often is propagated.

The version of suburbia described above has become a stereotype frequently enlisted to illustrate, or castigate, the state of suburbia in general. Often characterized as monotonous, homogeneous, and alienating, suburbia also provides a field against which images of deviance play, whether they be the pot-selling mom in *Weeds* or the shot of marching punks from the film *Suburbia* (Penelope Spheeris, 1983) that Google inserts among the subdivision views. While stereotypes serve deliberate purposes for those deploying them, they are too distant from their object to recognize the logics and values that inform quotidian lives in progress. Photographs from a thousand feet up tell us little about the people who live on those curving streets, the aspirations they pursued in buying those houses, or the lives they lead there. Malvina Reynolds may have been appalled at the rows of tract houses going up in Daly City in the early 1960s, but far from being "all the same," as she put it in her well-known song, those "little boxes," and the people who have occupied them, never have been.[2]

Although suburbia is perhaps most easily understood as a place, at a more fundamental level it is both an artifact and an aspect of the lives people are living there. Whether regarded as a set of institutions, a place, a visual type, or even a state of being, suburbia is (and always has been) in a constant state of production. Stereotypes abound—homogeneous, conformist, boring, and many others come to mind—yet they also tend to obscure the multiplicity of landscapes, processes, and cultures that constitute American suburbs. They disregard suburbia's long and varied histories and the ways people have inhabited, revised, and reinterpreted suburban areas over time. Most significantly, in the context of this volume, suburban stereotypes elide the many ways suburbia is, and has been, continuously produced through the actions of those who conduct their lives there—how they live, what they value, and what they do. Everything that people do in suburbia, and everything that contributes to the circumstances of these actions, is part of the process of making suburbia what it is at any given moment, and of remaking it into what it will be thereafter. Inextricable from this process is the participation of human and non-human agents. Without them, there is no suburbia. In the United States, on which this volume focuses, the people who live in suburbia, how they live and what they do, and how they articulate and engage the culture at large are as varied as all of America. The goal of this volume, then, is to look closely at processes of *making* by examining the actions and circumstances that produce what the actors—whether residents, visitors, or observers—know as suburbia.

Over the past three decades, scholarship in such fields as suburban history and suburban studies has developed a range of approaches and perspectives that assess and portray the terrain of suburbia in ways that increasingly engage its diversity and particularity.[3] Suburban history and suburban studies arguably emerged as subfields in the mid-1980s. Pioneering work such as Kenneth Jackson's *Crabgrass Frontier* (1985) and Robert Fishman's *Bourgeois Utopias* (1987) plotted the historical trajectories by which the geographic, social, and ideological formation of suburbia unfolded. Over the next two decades, scholars sharpened and refocused the inquiry, concentrating more closely on particulars of local conditions and practices. Margaret Marsh's *Suburban Lives* (1990) and essays by Mary Corbin Sies analyzed the particulars of dwelling design and household customs and practices in shaping the daily lives and gendered identities of suburbia's residents. Richard Harris, in works such as *Unplanned Suburbs: Toronto's American Tragedy* (1996), has been another leader in this effort, focusing in particular on the growth of working-class suburbs. Others, such as Becky M. Nicolaides's *My Blue Heaven: Life and Politics in the Working-Class Suburbs of Los Angeles, 1920–1965* (2002) and Andrew Wiese's *Places of Their Own: African American Suburbanization in the Twentieth Century* (2004), have further demonstrated the signal importance of class and race in relation to particulars of locality—and thus the understanding of suburbia as quintessentially local, a product at least as much of immediate circumstances and conditions as of national and global trends. Maintaining close attention to particulars of locality, *The New Suburban History* (2006), edited by Kevin M. Kruse and Thomas J. Sugrue, brought out the importance of understanding suburbs in terms of their vital interconnections with specific metropolitan regions.[4] Parallel to such work in suburban studies, academic inquiries in other fields, ranging from political science and art history to policy, planning, and design, have evolved a vibrant discourse on suburbia.[5] Even popular media, ranging from film and television to advertising and marketing, which have consistently been the biggest purveyor of suburban stereotypes and caricatures, have nevertheless increasingly acknowledged that suburbs are all constellations of particular circumstances and, notably, sites of personal consumption that are almost infinitely variable (and thus subdivisible) in terms of demographic marketing categories and equally individualized in terms of personal tastes and practices.[6]

A common element in all these trajectories—academic, professional, and popular—has been an ever closer focus on the conditions and circumstances contributing to the production of suburbia. Social theorists have shown that this process of making and remaking is recursive: what we produce, whether ephemeral or durable, whether material or symbolic, continually shapes and informs us and our successors and in turn serves as the apparatus afforded to actors in the next round of making.[7] Henri Lefebvre's analysis of space as social product makes it clear that the constituent components of suburbia, as with all other spaces, function as instruments of production on multiple scales: beyond the scale at which local actors fashion their world in suburban terms, their product, suburbia, serves as an apparatus by which societal institutions and political regimes establish and sustain themselves on ever larger scales.[8]

Still, as Michel de Certeau and others make clear, although this institutional-spatial apparatus may well constitute a powerful regime, it is not sovereign over daily life. From the standpoint of "ordinary practitioners of the city," individual pedestrians and residents, the daily encounter with the built landscape is one of deliberately performed spatial actions. De Certeau casts these in terms of "pedestrian speech acts" and "pedestrian rhetoric," describing the individual's engagement with given locales as discursive performances of bodily and verbal tactics and syntaxes, or "spatial stories."[9] Casting the day-in, day-out performing of daily life as story making, de Certeau highlights the crucial role of narrative not simply for the pedestrian-flaneur but in almost any dimension of everyday activity. De Certeau also makes it clear that agency is critical to the performance of daily life: in examining the process of daily life in terms of multiple and diverse acts of appropriation, he casts the social actor engaging with his or her world as a vital and prolific small-scale poacher: "Everyday life invents itself by *poaching* in countless ways on the property of others."[10]

There is of course more to everyday life than this; in varying degrees the narrative also involves communication, accumulation, and transfer. Stories, including "spatial stories," are a form of communication that in turn exploit their sites of production and reception as well as the qualities of the media in which they are transmitted. To the extent that actors acquire and deploy objects and materials throughout the fabric of space via the diverse media available, they engage in complex acts of accretion, consumption, and signification. Objects, materials, and the spaces they engage are simultaneously instruments (for example, household furniture and appliances facilitate daily practices of living) and signs (those same objects, depending on their style and quality, may also establish symbolic capital, express class status, and convey an ambiance of welcome or formality). Much of this involves actors continually fashioning and refashioning the objects and spaces they engage. De Certeau discusses this in terms of bricolage (which encompasses such everyday activities as tinkering, or do-it-yourself projects); alternatively, it may be understood in terms of embroidery, in that daily lives in many respects are tantamount to a fabric woven through space.

The point is that these spatial-rhetorical, -accretive, -signifying, -bricolage, -embroidery practices constitute dialogues with the actors' context: the physical, social, and cultural fabric (landscape as well as ethnoscape) that people both employ and produce as part of their practices of everyday living. These practices, and this fabric, are essential means by which people fashion their lives in multiple dimensions—as individuals, families, neighbors, friends, and citizens; as entrepreneurs, workers, believers, teammates, playmates, gardeners, cooks, readers, acquaintances, buddies, lovers, networkers, performers, audience members, tastemakers, enemies, activists, and leaders; as homosexual, African, Asian, or other Americans; as adherents of particular religious and political perspectives; and as connected to history and heritage. To engage in all these dimensions of everyday living necessarily requires that on a daily basis people engage in a nearly unlimited array of signifying and materially productive practices: from making home improvements, choosing decor, and arranging family photographs to cooking, working in the garage, gardening, doing paid work, commuting, telecommuting, shopping, visiting with neighbors, attending a potluck, hanging out with friends, using the playground or basketball court, walking the dog, praying, listening to music, or just sitting in a favorite chair. In all these respects, the always ongoing process of making, apprehending, and reproducing the suburban fabric is instrumental in the practice—indeed the very definition—of everyday life.

Thus, as architect Peter Kellett details in his 2003 examination of barrios and other informal settlements—in a manner that applies just as readily to suburbia—all the physical attributes of home, assembled from whatever materials may be available, become part of the dweller's purposeful everyday shaping of self and social relations: these materials, and what the user does with them, all "relate to issues of identity, economic and social positions: in short, a person's place in society." "Through the processes of occupation, construction and habitation," Kellett writes, the dweller "is actively reconstructing her place in the world."[11] In *Ordinary Affects* (2007), an anthropological and ethnographic inquiry that includes suburbia in its scope, Kathleen Stewart examines ordinary quotidian practices as part of a continuous process of fashioning, signifying, and reproducing, characterizing actors' lives in terms of "a practiced possibility, emergent in projects like home remodeling, shopping, straightening up the house, rearranging furniture, making lists, keeping a diary, daydreaming, or buying lottery tickets."[12] And a passage in Colson Whitehead's novel *John Henry Days* (2002) that vividly portrays the role of furniture in defining and contesting personal relations demonstrates the dynamic capacity of objects as signifiers:

> Putting clothes in any old drawer feels like a political act because recently in the Miggses' household, 1244 Violet Lane, there has unfolded a cold war over spaces. It happens in every household of course, someone picks out a favorite chair or side of the couch; over time someone comes to a choice, or all at once—on the first day the new chair arrives in the house and is claimed. In Alphonse's home the usual pattern of domestic boundary erection has attained the aspect of warfare, with the attendant gamesmanship of posturing, deployment, arcane strategy.[13]

Almost by definition, each and every society constitutes a context, a material, social, and discursive apparatus at large, operating on scales ranging from the global to the local, in which everyone operates. That apparatus necessarily has rules, boundaries, and barriers that shape what people can and cannot do; such is part of society's very raison d'être. The various conditions thus established serve in effect as a menu of opportunities and limitations. That these apply differentially to different individuals and in different places—indeed, there is really no such thing as "equality of opportunity"—means that in substantive ways everyone's life, and thus everyone's suburbia, is different. Given all these conditions and disparities, everyday life amounts to the narrative of the step-by-step, choice-by-choice process by which each and any person, or group, navigates, avoids, selects, contests, transgresses, subverts, and performs them. All of these actions and practices, in turn, once performed, contribute to the constant articulation and recursive instantiation of suburbia and simultaneously articulate the role and relationship of suburbia within the larger social nexus.

From some perspectives, perhaps most notably those of Frankfurt School critics Theodor Adorno and Max Horkheimer, writing in the 1930s and 1940s, and New York intellectuals such as Dwight Macdonald and Irving Howe in the 1950s, the ever-increasing standardization, commodification, and corporatization of American culture has effectively limited the range of possible activities and practices to those defined and prescribed by the system. Critics of suburbia have often implicitly adopted such a perspective when pointing to "ticky-tacky" construction, commodified tract houses, mass-produced furnishings, and the like as necessary evidence of the social and cultural impoverishment of suburbia. But despite such bleak presumptions, people do not become puppets or prisoners of the system simply by virtue of the means by which their material resources were once, or continue to be, produced. For although Adorno and Horkheimer lamented that "the diner must be satisfied with the menu"[14]—in effect must be its prisoner—the variety of ways in which any actor may acquire and deploy the vast array of available commodities affords an endlessly diverse array of quotidian narratives.

At the beginning of the twentieth century the work of Émile Durkheim and Marcel Mauss recognized the fundamental importance of commodities, through gift exchange, in sustaining social structures. More recently Pierre Bourdieu's book *Distinction* (1979) vastly extended our understanding of commodity consumption as instrumental to the specific tastes and aesthetic practices that people employ in articulating positions for themselves vis-à-vis others in the various levels and echelons of society.[15] Indeed, as Dick Hebdige has shown, people construct lives from ensembles of commodities.[16] Perhaps more than any other, anthropologist Daniel Miller's work on consumption has broadened understanding of the role of commodities in the social positioning of the self. In a suburban context such commodities can include everything from the choice of trim packages and finish materials in new house construction to furniture, bedding, electronics, toys, landscaping, patio equipment, clothes, and food; these all become, in Miller's words, "dimensions through which the particular social position of the intended individual is experienced."[17] Commodity consumption, in other words, is not necessarily the badge of dishonor that the critics try to pin on suburbia; rather, in suburbia as everywhere else, it is instrumental in the fashioning of selfhood and society.

Making everyday lives and places, in suburbia as elsewhere, is a matter of commodities and consumption, but it is also at least as much a matter of performing and how that inflects and articulates space. The actor, in effect, enunciates a spatial and bodily script in material, discursive, and symbolic terms. To reiterate: actors are not scripted by institutions or authorities; rather, they fashion their own scripts in terms that necessarily acknowledge the conditions in which the performers act—the streetscape; the reigning economic, political, and legal systems; the linguistic and symbolic vocabularies and conventions that are present; and so forth—but avail the performers of opportunities and means to ignore, contradict, and diverge from the prevailing narrative. As Allen Feldman has shown, even under the harshest of prison regimes, prisoners can fashion spaces on their own terms that controvert and transgress the authority of the institution and the state.[18] Likewise Margaret Crawford, following Nancy Fraser, has shown that local quotidian practices by various individuals and groups may articulate and constitute counterspaces, not by physically altering sites in the built environment but by means of what the actors singly and collectively make and do at those sites. Examples range from appropriating fences around commercial properties as display racks for small-scale retailing to turning shopping mall parking lots into informal sites for car maintenance and repair to food trucks transforming thoroughfares into dining emporiums.[19] A brief example demonstrates the point: houses come with garages, which are purposefully designed to shelter cars and to facilitate their entry and exit. Such is the official bill of fare. Yet it is widespread practice that garages are partially or even entirely taken over for other purposes, such as home businesses, hobbies, gaming, or storage. More to the point, such is the case with the entire range of objects and materials across all of suburbia: the multitudinous ways in which uses are adapted, invented, and combined bespeak the inhabitants' appetite and capacity for original and diverse modes of living.

Everyday lives in suburbia sometimes do tend to the transgressive or counterhegemonic: for example, hip-hop music blaring from a teenager's automobile audio system or house remodeling that flouts neighborhood conventions of scale or design. Any aspect of daily life is performed somewhere on a continuum from outright transgression to absolute conformity. Whatever each actor does, and how it is done, in whichever manner of daily practice—shopping, gardening, playing or making music, entertaining, home decorating, playing with the kids, going to church, and so forth—constitutes another voice in the conversation, another strand of production, all of which as an aggregate of daily lives constitute the suburb itself at any moment in time, as well as over time.[20] Doreen Massey thus argues for an understanding of place in terms of relations: "Both social phenomena and space [are] constituted out of social relations."[21] We would add that those relations are performed, daily, in the rituals and practices of everyday life, the shaping and reshaping of everyday contexts, the ongoing reproduction of suburbia, its people, and its culture. Still, as bell hooks has shown, neither the site nor the conditions of the site necessarily define us. Writing of the radical potential that people have for using their homes to recast social relations on the most local scale, she recounts how "black women resisted by making homes where all black people could strive to be subjects, not objects, where we could be affirmed in our minds and hearts despite poverty, hardship, and deprivation." More ambitiously, she characterizes home as "that place which enables and promotes varied and everchanging perspectives, a place where one discovers new ways of seeing reality, frontiers of difference." From here, one is energized to "move beyond boundaries."[22]

Much of the discussion so far still raises a challenging question: What is suburbia? The very notion of suburbia is central to understanding the everyday lives and practices of those who live, work, and visit there. In nearly every case one's immediate notion of suburbia conditions to some degree whatever one does, and that in turn continues to replicate and evolve what suburbia is. It may be best to start with a short (but not necessarily simple) proposition: suburban is as suburban does. The point is not to invite the facile notion that merely declaring that something is suburban makes it so. Rather, the point is to direct attention to the doing—the making, the living, the performing—and then to the contexts in which or terms under which that is done. These terms and contexts may very well be informed by broad-scale definitions and conventions that commonly signify suburbia, such as boundaries of municipal entities surrounding cities, planning terminology, or certain types of housing stock, such as single-family tract houses. Yet adhering too closely to such definitions and conventions—which is to say, trying to find a clear and rigorous definition of suburbia, and abiding by it—is like assessing a neighborhood based on photographs taken from a thousand feet up. Doing so all too easily overlooks the daily lives being fashioned amid the social and physical apparatus of suburbia.

Attempting to articulate what is "suburban" about what people do, or where they do it, can be a vexing task. On one hand, what suburbanites do is often undifferentiable from what people elsewhere do: whatever is done in suburbia, or in the name of suburbia, is not necessarily exemplary of suburbia. A better index, though a more complex one to discern, may be the discursive, symbolic, and/or material terms in which any actor's doings are cast. For example, many American cities have neighborhoods that visually and demographically are indistinguishable from adjacent suburbs. At the time when many of these were built, their locales were in fact suburbs, outside the city limits, only later becoming part of the city through municipal annexation. From a categorical perspective, it is ambiguous whether these neighborhoods count as suburban. From a performative perspective, however, there are rich (if complex) answers in the terms in which daily lives are carried on. As bell hooks would remind us, and essays in this volume by Charity R. Carney, Trecia Pottinger, Jodi Rios, and Stacie Taranto demonstrate, it is the sub-urbanites' "ways of seeing reality," and how they construct and perform their lives, that make those lives suburban. What is suburban, then, may be defined by external and/or uniform criteria, but it is also necessarily contingent on how people live their lives, the material context in which they do so, and the symbolic and discursive context in which people articulate what they are doing and where they are doing it. As Bruno Latour argues, "You have 'to follow the actors themselves,' that is try to catch up with their often wild innovations in order to learn from them what the collective existence has become in their hands, which methods they have elabo-rated to fit it together, which accounts could best define the new associations that they have been forced to establish."[23] In other words, suburbanites themselves are the arbiters of what is suburban.

Focusing thus on *instances* of suburbia, as produced by specific actors, in a spe-cific material and discursive manner, affords an understanding of the terms in which people individually recognize their own circumstances to be framed, the means they choose for proceeding and how they deploy them, and the terms of valua-tion that they apply. As detailed in several essays in this volume (see Bailey, Dines, Lang, Sandul, Smiley, and Wlodarczyk), discursive constructions are central to the definition and practice of suburbia. Often the appropriation of specific tropes and paradigms is instrumental in the conduct of commerce and articulation of commu-nity (Lung-Amam, Nicolaides, Pottinger, and Rios), political organizing (Retzloff, Sellers, and Taranto), religion (Bugglen and Carney), and shaping domestic space (Andrzejewski, Friedman, Grindstaff, Harris, Lasner, and Waksman). A crucial fac-tor in such instances is that the given trope or paradigm that is enlisted affords those who deploy it the means to identify as, and participate in, the *suburban*: materially and discursively, actors define, value, and live their lives in terms of their choosing that constitute themselves, what they do, and where they are as suburban and simul-taneously contribute to the ongoing definition and construction of suburbia at large. In this manner suburbia is produced and propagated via discourse, concretized in built environments, performed with objects, and embedded in topographies.

Instead of defining suburbanites in terms of the conditions under which they live (e.g., municipal boundaries, mass-produced houses, demographic profiles, tastes, automobile lifestyles), this approach demands close attention to local conditions, individual choices, specific discourses, daily activities, and particular places. Singly and collectively, these are the making of suburbia. Still, just as the social superstructure cannot and does not prescribe any person's actions or life as "suburban," this is not an argument that suburbia is arbitrary or ephemeral. To be understood as suburban requires more than an arbitrary declaration to that effect; the understanding arises from the material and discursive relations that any given actor has with others and with the broader culture. In lifestyle, music, politics, religion, and many other respects, as demonstrated in the essays in this volume, actors constantly declare, shape, and perform what it is to be suburban. Whatever medium in which the material or discursive product results—housing style, political engagement, sexual orientation, musical performance, religious faith, retail space, landscape design, community organization, and so forth—the suburban is constantly produced, reinterpreted, reasserted, and reproduced. This is quintessentially a local process, in terms that Arjun Appadurai helps to inform. In a manner complementary to the discussion above of suburbia as understood in terms of material and social relations, Appadurai describes locality as "primarily relational and contextual rather than . . . scalar or spatial." It is "constituted by a series of links between the sense of social immediacy, the technologies of interactivity, and the relativity of contexts," added to which, here, is attention to the daily activity of making, performing, and living these links. A central concern for Appadurai is to focus on "the production of what we might call *local subjects,* actors who properly belong to a situated community of kin, neighbors, friends, and enemies." He notes that that there are many "ways [for actors] to embody locality," noting that "local subjects engage in the social activities of production, representation, and reproduction." This volume concentrates on those activities and how, by means of which, local actors produce and reproduce their subjectivities and their relations to others. The locality that results is "a structure of feeling, a property of social life, and an ideology of situated community."[24] Such is the suburbia, or rather, such are the suburbias, all of which are localities, addressed in this volume.

The essays that follow are presented under four headings, each of which addresses a distinct aspect, one part of the spectrum, of the ways in which suburbia is lived and made: mobilizing changes, constructing narratives, defining communities, and producing spaces. In each case, the heading is deliberately constructed as a gerund, in order to focus attention on the making and doing of suburbia, its daily and local production, its role as a site that suburban actors shape and are shaped by in their quotidian pursuits. Taken together, the four headings hardly encompass the range of activities, pursuits, and circumstances that constitute all of suburbia; such is necessarily, and (one might well argue) happily, an impossible task. Nevertheless, taken together such as they are, they do serve to illuminate two central characteristics of the making of suburbia: that suburbia as a social artifact is never solely the consequence of the circumstances and interests in which it was first formed, but rather it is continually refashioned by those who live and work there, often in radically different ways; and that those who live and work in suburbia have a central role in defining and debating the terms in which suburbia is made and experienced.

The essays in Part I, "Mobilizing," examine ways in which suburban locales serve not only as sites but also as instruments and media through which residents pursue changes, often in the very terms in which their lives are constituted—terms that include race, class, gender, sexual orientation, ecology, and more. Part II, "Representing," focuses on discursive techniques through which suburbanites fashion the terms in which suburbia will be understood and in which dwellers' roles will be laid out. Part III, "Gathering," examines ways in which suburbanites may shape and deploy their built surroundings as instruments for articulating community identity in terms of qualities such as race, ethnicity, age group, and religion. The essays in the final part, "Building," identify and analyze ways in which residents articulate the spaces of home as instruments of personal and family assimilation and differentiation within the complex, interwoven strata of taste, class, politics, domesticity, family, and selfhood in suburban society.

Opening Part I, Becky M. Nicolaides's essay details shifts over time in the manner in which the diverse populations of postwar Pasadena, California, utilized public and private spaces as fields of civic engagement. As Nicolaides shows, the securely segregated landscape of the 1950s and 1960s afforded whites and blacks alike the opportunity for robust civic engagement, in part because club and association meetings often were held in private homes, a practice that in turn severely blurred the line between public and private. In contrast, during ensuing decades the turmoil of school desegregation split education between public and private realms, which in turn catalyzed and advanced the hardening of public/private and class boundaries that have persisted into the following century. In the Philadelphia Main Line community of Ardmore, as Trecia Pottinger shows in chapter 2, African American residents during the 1960s and 1970s undertook a far more proactive strategy to contend with growing disparities between the availability of affordable housing and their aspirations toward discrete housing units that could afford the opportunity for suburban family domesticity. By working collectively to shape an official community plan and a design for a new condominium project, they successfully shaped the material fabric of their suburb in terms that enabled them to realize their aspirations. Focusing on another register of suburban political activism, in chapter 3 Stacie Taranto documents the success of white Catholic housewives in a New York suburb in spearheading the 1975 defeat of a statewide Equal Rights Amendment. These efforts were nominally counter to the participants' social and political interests as women, but they had deeper roots in the women's investment in a certain realization of the American Dream, a single-family suburban home with a male breadwinner and a female homemaker. It was that status, as homemaker, as well as a much larger vision of suburbia, domesticity, and family life, that they valued having achieved, and that the New York State ERA threatened to erode. By 1976, one year later, gay organizers working out of their houses in the Detroit suburbs had formed the Association of Suburban People, whose members began, as Tim Retzloff shows in chapter 4, to queer their living rooms, backyards, and, occasionally, nearby hotels as sites for gay get-togethers, revues, Tupperware parties, and dances. Pushing from the beginning for political change, the association did so from lived and performed gay spaces in suburbia: the material fabric of suburbia literally became the very medium of change. Turning to a broader scale, Christopher Sellers addresses the rise of environmentalism in suburban Atlanta in chapter 5, demonstrating the exceedingly complex nature of the struggle when the stakes become the articulation of the very terms in which suburban land and space will be defined and used. Sellers documents the roles played by a diverse array of interests—garden clubbers, conservationists, outdoor recreationists, suburban property owners, developers, politicians, and others, actors who were thoroughly engaged in matters of race, religion, class, heritage, and politics—in seeking to determine the extent, accessibility, purpose, and perpetuity of portions of the natural landscape to be reserved for conservation.

The essays in Part II, "Representing," bring together accounts of suburban lives that are conducted and experienced in multiple, intersecting registers, ranging from fiction and festivals to gardening and marketing, the coherence and continuity of which are maintained in narrative terms. In chapter 6, Martin Dines details how writers Pam Conrad and John Barth employ fiction as a medium for exploring the ways in which suburbs, houses, and daily routines become fluctuating, palimpsestic registers of broader regional and global currents such as politics, work, race, and ecology, and how, to make sense of all this, residents continually produce and rewrite their own narratives, weaving these rich and evolving particulars of place into their lives. In chapter 7, Paul J. P. Sandul focuses on a considerably more overt instance of narrative construction and inscription on the community: the techniques by which the leaders and citizens of Orangevale, California, have drawn strategically and selectively from the town's and region's history in fashioning the narratives that inform and guide them both in their historic preservation work and in their articulation of the themes that are celebrated in their festival days and parade, in the process defining their suburb and broadcasting their suburban identities. In contrast, Heather Bailey shows in chapter 8 what happens when there is no widespread consensus on the role that history should play in a community's narrative: debates and discord ensue, in this case centered on whether the constraints that historic preservation might impose on the apparatus of daily life would be welcomed as an asset to the community or spurned as an infringement on opportunities for personal satisfaction. At the level of individual families and individual yards there are small-scale opportunities to diversify ways in which the landscape is fashioned, where individuals and families may construct narratives of belonging and participation. As Ursula Lang shows in chapter 9, the fabric of the garden, embodied in the gardener's work, becomes instrumental in constituting a diversity of everyday lives.

Of course, numerous interests originating well outside any given community frequently introduce other narratives; typically the visions proffered by planners and developers have their own narratives embedded, as David Smiley shows in chapter 10. In his account of the discourse on shopping center design from the 1930s through the 1950s, Smiley details how shopping malls constructed during this period could be overwritten with expectations that the design itself would function as a visual narrative that could resolve tensions between the pedestrian and the automobile and enhance the casual pedestrian experience—with pedestrians and shoppers left, in turn, to respond to that discourse in their own terms, whether consonant or otherwise. Holley Wlodarczyk continues the discussion along parallel lines in chapter 11, examining the central role that discourses of design and marketing play in the production of suburban houses and subdivisions. Bringing together "house of the future" discourses from the 1930s through the 1960s with more recent imperatives to incorporate ecological concerns, Wlodarczyk examines the terms in which corresponding designs are executed, variously touted as technological and ecological progress or clothed in nostalgic archetypes, as components of a broader social contest, an "ideological conflict between faith in the future and longing for the past."

Paralleling several of the essays in Part I that focus on mobilizing change, the essays in Part III, "Gathering," examine instances of residents grappling with and actively shaping the racial, ethnic, and social terms in which their communities will be reproduced. Jodi Rios's study of Pagedale, a suburb of St. Louis, in chapter 12 examines residents' active and public debates over public space and public behavior, with fundamental questions of race and class at stake, and how in the process they invoke stereotypes and ideals of ghetto and suburb in contesting and shaping the community in which they will live. Turning to Northern California's Silicon Valley, in chapter 13 Willow Lung-Amam examines the production of commercial space, specifically shopping malls, in terms that explicitly and deliberately afford

Asian and Asian American customers and visitors spaces of acceptance, identity, culture, and community—resulting in the production of a landscape recognized by local residents as more equitable and livable. Gretchen Buggeln's examination of postwar suburban Protestant churches in chapter 14 chronicles an evolution in the design of church spaces to accommodate a rapidly changing ethos of youth, as churches sought to reincorporate a teen youth cohort that progressively had become more socially alienated in the 1950s and 1960s. While the creation of "youth lounges" and other specifically teen spaces and programs addressed this growing separation of age strata occurring nationwide, it also served as a material response by each individual congregation to the need to retain youth within the fold if the congregation hoped to survive over the long term. With the rise of suburban mega-churches in more recent decades, institutions housing considerably larger congregations with changing and often more diverse values, the challenge for churches has become one of defining who, collectively, their congregations are, and what beliefs bind their members together. As Charity R. Carney shows in chapter 15, the result is an active dialectic between religion and suburbanity, with pastors striving to select and reconcile aspects of each as cornerstones of community to which their congregants are encouraged and willing to aspire.

The essays in Part IV, "Building," examine the physical fabric of suburbia as a medium for suburbanites to use in reshaping their world in terms more conducive to their own needs, interests, and aspirations. Andrew Friedman presents a striking case in point in chapter 16, the story of Cold War double agents who adopted the clichéd apparatus of suburban privacy and anonymity as the perfect cover for their clandestine identities as agents of the Soviet Union (akin to the couple at the center of the recent television series *The Americans*). But while modernist suburban design provided cover for some Soviet agents, it also served as a marketing platform for midwestern home builder Marshall Erdman. In chapter 17, Anna Vemer Andrzejewski chronicles Erdman's success in building his business by melding modernist design inspired by Frank Lloyd Wright with a construction process based on prefabrication, both of which at the start were unfamiliar and even alien to his midwestern clientele. He did so by marketing his designs as efficient and as viable components of the American Dream, terms that potential client families in suburbia would recognize as instrumental to their own interests. Taking us inside the postwar suburban living room, in chapter 18 Dianne Harris details the rise of high-fidelity stereo home sound systems in the 1950s and 1960s. Examining residents' painstaking pursuit of perfect audio fidelity amid aesthetic purity, Harris describes how the private suburban home was transformed into a site of sonic connoisseurship, a site for dancing, singing, listening, and, above all, the performance of privilege and the accumulation of class status and cultural capital. The generation of children growing up in homes of this era remained engaged with music, but as Steve Waksman shows in chapter 19, they deployed domestic space in an entirely different fashion, to a very different end. Eschewing the living room and other formal household spaces, teenagers of the 1960s and 1970s repurposed bedrooms, recreation rooms, and garages to facilitate the playing of rock music, often live, thereby turning the performance of rock music into a basic component of daily suburban life. Yet while the preceding narratives are all anchored in the single-family house, different narratives are performed in other suburban housing types. As Matthew Gordon Lasner shows in chapter 20, suburban multiunit housing complexes have evolved in ways that notably afford the recognition and reproduction of considerable dimensions of difference in suburbia, in structures catering variously to young unattached singles, single seniors, multigenerational households, and gay and lesbian households, and including diverse housing types such as leisure communities, assisted living facilities, and structures with shared facilities serving multiple households. In recent decades, many suburban homeowners have begun to develop a new part of the home by installing outdoor kitchens. As Beverly K. Grindstaff shows in chapter 21, these spaces are fabricated as the quintessential instrument for the performance of cuisine as theater, with the homeowner playing the leading role and thus garnering the cachet and distinction of masculinity (in most cases), prestige, family status, and cultural capital.

In assembling these essays and bringing them into conversation with one another, it is our goal in this volume to broaden the discussion of suburbia by focusing on particular localities and narratives, on the making and doing of everyday lives. Just as there is no viable single definition of suburbia, no single narrative can account for the history or present extent of suburbia. Rather, it is the intersections and conversations among multiple narratives—sometimes consonant, sometimes divergent, often discordant, but ultimately vital—that continually produce what suburbia is and what it will become.

## Notes

1. Google image search results are quite similar for "suburb" and "American suburb." A search using "suburban," however, brings up an array of Chevrolet Suburban sport utility vehicles.

2. When the houses in Daly City's Westlake development were first constructed, the plans and exterior designs were actually highly varied, as were the people who moved into the neighborhood and have since taken pride in the durability their ostensibly "ticky-tacky" houses. Even when tract houses are identical at the start, once residents move in they are never again the same. See Rob Keil, *Little Boxes: The Architecture of a Classic Midcentury Suburb* (Daly City, Calif.: Advection Media, 2006); and Eric J. Pido, "The Performance of Property: Suburban Homeownership as a Claim to Citizenship for Filipinos in Daly City," *Journal of Asian American Studies* 15, no. 1 (2012): 69–104.

3. Leading examples of scholarship and artistic work directly contesting prevailing stereo-types of suburbia include Herbert J. Gans, *The Levittowners: Ways of Life and Politics in a New Suburban Community* (New York: Columbia University Press, 1967); Bill Owens, *Suburbia* (San Francisco: Straight Arrow Books, 1973); D. J. Waldie, *Holy Land: A Suburban Memoir* (New York: W. W. Norton, 1996); and Richard Harris and Robert Lewis, "Constructing a Fault(y) Zone: Misrepresentations of American Cities and Suburbs, 1900–1950," *Annals of the Association of American Geographers* 88, no. 4 (1998): 622–39.

4. For a comprehensive survey of historical and critical writing on suburbia, see Becky M. Nicolaides and Andrew Wiese, eds., *The Suburb Reader* (New York: Routledge, 2006). For histories of suburbia, see John Archer, *Architecture and Suburbia: From English Villa to American Dream House, 1690–2000* (Minneapolis: University of Minnesota Press, 2005); and Dolores Hayden, *Building Suburbia: Green Fields and Urban Growth, 1820–2000* (New York: Pantheon, 2003). Two essays by Mary Corbin Sies address the interrelations of design and domesticity: "The City Transformed: Nature, Technology, and the Suburban Ideal, 1877–1917," *Journal of Urban History* 14, no. 1 (November 1987): 98; and "'God's Very Kingdom on the Earth': The Design Program for the American Suburban Home, 1877–1917," in *Modern Architecture in America*, ed. Richard Guy Wilson and Sidney K. Robinson (Ames: Iowa State University Press, 1991), 16–22. More recently on race see Dianne Harris, *Little White Houses: How the Postwar Home Constructed Race in America* (Minneapolis: University of Minnesota Press, 2013). By focusing on working-class industrial suburbs, Robert Lewis's edited volume *Manufacturing Suburbs: Building Work and Home on the Metropolitan Fringe* (Philadelphia: Temple University Press, 2004) foregrounds the importance of regional economic and geographic circumstances in shaping suburbs in locally and demographically distinct ways. For discussion of the new suburban history and related concerns, see Kevin M. Kruse and Thomas J. Sugrue, "Introduction: The New Suburban History," in *The New Suburban History*, ed. Kevin M. Kruse and Thomas J. Sugrue (Chicago: University of Chicago Press, 2006), 1–10; Matthew D. Lassiter, "The New Suburban History II: Political Culture and Metropolitan Space," *Journal of Planning History* 4, no. 1 (February 2005): 75–88; Margaret Pugh O' Mara, "Suburbia Reconsidered: Race, Politics, and Prosperity in the Twentieth Century," *Journal of Social History* 39, no. 1 (Fall 2005): 229–44; Becky M. Nicolaides and Andrew Wiese, "Introduction," in Nicolaides and Wiese, *Suburb Reader*, 5–9; Amanda I. Seligman, "The New Suburban History," *Journal of Planning History* 3, no. 4 (November 2004): 312–33; and Mary Corbin Sies, "North American Urban History: The Everyday Politics and Spatial Logics of Metropolitan Life," *Urban History Review/Revue d'histoire* 32, no. 1 (Fall 2003): 28–42.

5. See, for example, Lisa McGirr, *Suburban Warriors: The Origins of the New American Right* (Princeton, N.J.: Princeton University Press, 2001); Setha Low, *Behind the Gates: Life, Security, and the Pursuit of Happiness in Fortress America* (New York: Routledge, 2003); Evan McKenzie, *Privatopia: Homeowner Associations and the Rise of Residential Private Government* (New Haven, Conn.: Yale University Press, 1994); Myron Orfield, *Metropolitics: A Regional Agenda for Community and Stability* (Washington, D.C.: Brookings Institution Press, 1997); Myron Orfield, *American Metropolitics: The New Suburban Reality* (Washington, D.C.: Brookings Institution Press, 2002); William H. Frey, *Melting Pot Suburbs: A Census 2000 Study of Suburban Diversity* (Washington, D.C.: Brookings Institution, Center on Urban and Metropolitan Policy, 2001); Bruce Katz and Robert E. Lang, *Redefining Urban and Suburban America: Evidence from Census 2000* (Washington, D.C.: Brookings Institution Press, 2003); Robert E. Lang and

Jennifer B. LeFurgy, *Boomburbs: The Rise of America's Accidental Cities* (Washington, D.C.: Brookings Institution Press, 2007); Dolores Hayden, *A Field Guide to Sprawl* (New York: W. W. Norton, 2004); Robert Bruegmann, *Sprawl: A Compact History* (Chicago: University of Chicago Press, 2005); Andres Duany, Elizabeth Plater-Zyberk, and Jeff Speck, *Suburban Nation: The Rise of Sprawl and the Decline of the American Dream* (New York: North Point Press, 2000); Joel Kotkin, *The New Suburbanism: A Realist's Guide to the American Future* (Costa Mesa, Calif.: Planning Center, 2005); Catherine Jurca, *White Diaspora: The Suburb and the Twentieth-Century American Novel* (Princeton, N.J.: Princeton University Press, 2001); Roger Silverstone, ed., *Visions of Suburbia* (London: Routledge, 1997); Robert Beuka, *SuburbiaNation: Reading Suburban Landscape in Twentieth-Century American Fiction and Film* (New York: Palgrave Macmillan, 2004); Amy Maria Kenyon, *Dreaming Suburbia: Detroit and the Production of Postwar Space and Culture* (Detroit: Wayne State University Press, 2004); Ann M. Wolfe, *Suburban Escape: The Art of California Sprawl* (Santa Fe, N.M.: Center for American Places, 2006); Andrew Blauvelt, ed., *Worlds Away: New Suburban Landscapes* (Minneapolis: Walker Art Center, 2008); Lizabeth Cohen, *A Consumer's Republic: The Politics of Mass Consumption in Postwar America* (New York: Alfred A. Knopf, 2003); James Howard Kunstler, *The Geography of Nowhere: The Rise and Decline of America's Man-Made Landscape* (New York: Simon & Schuster, 1993); David Brooks, *On Paradise Drive: How We Live Now (and Always Have) in the Future Tense* (New York: Simon & Schuster, 2004); Witold Rybczynski, *Last Harvest: How a Cornfield Became New Daleville* (New York: Scribner, 2007); Wendy Cheng, *The Changs Next Door to the Díazes: Remapping Race in Suburban California* (Minneapolis: University of Minnesota Press, 2013); Robert M. Fogelson, *Bourgeois Nightmares: Suburbia, 1870–1930* (New Haven, Conn.: Yale University Press, 2005); Cynthia L. Girling and Kenneth I. Helphand, *Yard, Street, Park: The Design of Suburban Open Space* (New York: John Wiley, 1994); Renee Y. Chow, *Suburban Space: The Fabric of Dwelling* (Berkeley: University of California Press, 2002); Avi Friedman, *Planning the New Suburbia: Flexibility by Design* (Vancouver: UBC Press, 2002); Nicholas Low, Brendan Gleeson, Ray Green, and Darko Radović, *The Green City: Sustainable Homes, Sustainable Suburbs* (New York: Routledge, 2005); and Karen Tongson, *Relocations: Queer Suburban Imaginaries* (New York: New York University Press, 2011).

6. On marketing categories, see the pioneering work of Michael J. Weiss in *The Clustering of America* (New York: Harper & Row, 1988) and *The Clustered World: How We Live, What We Buy, and What It All Means about Who We Are* (Boston: Little, Brown, 2000); for more recent discussion see Nielsen PRIZM, offering research into market, consumer, and customer segmentation, accessed November 18, 2014, http://www.claritas.com/MyBestSegments/Default.jsp. In film, see, for example, *The Wood* (directed by Rick Famuyiwa, 1999), which delves into the stories of a suburban African American couple and their friends on the couple's wedding day. See also the unconventional characters and situations in the television series *Modern Family* (2009–); the quirky pairings of people and their cars with houses in the Progressive insurance television commercial "Matching Cars," accessed November 18, 2014, http://www.ispot.tv/ad/7f0Z/progressive-matching-cars; or P. Diddy's stereotype-subverting music video "Bad Boys for Life" (2002), filmed on the same Universal Studios "Colonial Street" back-lot set where *Leave It to Beaver* and *Desperate Housewives* were produced, accessed November 18, 2014, http://www.youtube.com/watch?v=3Yd4GG3bed0.

7. The recursive nature of social production is fundamental to much social theory. For an early and influential statement, see Anthony Giddens's discussion of structuration in *The*

*Constitution of Society: Outline of a Theory of Structuration* (Berkeley: University of California Press, 1984).

8. Lefebvre writes of space, "Though a *product* to be used, to be consumed, it is also a *means of production*." Henri Lefebvre, *The Production of Space,* trans. Donald Nicholson-Smith (Oxford: Blackwell, 1991).

9. Michel de Certeau, *The Practice of Everyday Life,* trans. Steven Rendall (Berkeley: University of California Press, 1984), 85, 93, 98, 102.

10. Ibid., xii.

11. Peter Kellett, "Constructing Informal Places," in *Constructing Place: Mind and Matter,* ed. Sarah Menin (London: Routledge, 2003), 90, 89.

12. Kathleen Stewart, *Ordinary Affects* (Durham, N.C.: Duke University Press, 2007), 56.

13. Colson Whitehead, *John Henry Days* (New York: Anchor, 2002), 129. On objects as dynamic signifiers and on the fabrication of homeplace through everyday experience of daily practices, objects, and spaces, see Michael Ann Williams, *Homeplace: The Social Use and Meaning of the Folk Dwelling in Southwestern North Carolina* (Charlottesville: University of Virginia Press, 1991); Grey Gundaker, ed., *Keep Your Head to the Sky: Interpreting African American Home Ground* (Charlottesville: University of Virginia Press, 1998); Grey Gundaker and Judith McWillie, *The Spirit of African American Yard Work* (Knoxville: University of Tennessee Press, 2005); Christopher Grampp, *From Yard to Garden: The Domestication of America's Home Grounds* (Chicago: Center for American Places, 2008); Peter Menzel, *Material World: A Global Family Portrait* (San Francisco: Sierra Club Books, 1994). See also Susan Saegert, "The Role of Housing in the Experience of Dwelling," in *Home Environments,* ed. Irwin Altman and Carol M. Werner (New York: Plenum, 1985), 287–309.

14. Max Horkheimer and Theodor W. Adorno, *Dialectic of Enlightenment,* trans. John Cumming (New York: Continuum, 1997), 139.

15. Émile Durkheim, *The Elementary Forms of Religious Life,* trans. Karen E. Fields (1915; repr., New York: Free Press, 1992); Marcel Mauss, *The Gift: Forms and Functions of Exchange in Archaic Societies,* trans. Ian Cunnison (New York: W. W. Norton, 1925). See also Mary Douglas and Baron Isherwood, *The World of Goods* (New York: Basic, 1979), 65, 72; Rolland Munro, "The Consumption View of Self: Extension, Exchange and Identity," in *Consumption Matters,* ed. Stephen Edgell, Kevin Hetherington, and Alan Warde (Oxford: Blackwell, 1996), 255–256; and Pierre Bourdieu, *Distinction,* trans. Richard Nice (1979; repr., Cambridge, Mass.: Harvard University Press, 1984).

16. Dick Hebdige, *Subculture: The Meaning of Style* (London: Methuen, 1979), 104.

17. "The relation between [a given] object and others provid[es] a dimension through which the particular social position of the intended individual is experienced." Daniel Miller, *Material Culture and Mass Consumption* (Oxford: Basil Blackwell, 1987), 147, 175, 190.

18. Allen Feldman, *Formations of Violence: The Narrative of the Body and Political Terror in Northern Ireland* (Chicago: University of Chicago Press, 1991).

19. Margaret Crawford, "Introduction" and "Blurring the Boundaries: Public Space and Private Life," in *Everyday Urbanism,* ed. John Chase, Margaret Crawford, and John Kaliski (New York: Monacelli Press, 1999); Nancy Fraser, "Rethinking the Public Sphere: A Contribution to the Critique of Actually Existing Democracy," in *The Phantom Public Sphere,* ed. Bruce Robbins (Minneapolis: University of Minnesota Press, 1993), 13–18.

20. See, for example, de Certeau, *Practice of Everyday Life*, chaps. 3, 7; bell hooks, *Yearning: Race, Gender, and Cultural Politics* (Boston: South End Press, 1990), chaps. 5, 15; James C. Scott, *Domination and the Arts of Resistance: Hidden Transcripts* (New Haven, Conn.: Yale University Press, 1990).

21. Doreen Massey, *Space, Place, and Gender* (Minneapolis: University of Minnesota Press, 1994), 2.

22. hooks, *Yearning*, 42, 148.

23. Bruno Latour, *Reassembling the Social: An Introduction to Actor-Network-Theory* (Oxford: Oxford University Press, 2005), 12.

24. Arjun Appadurai, *Modernity at Large: Cultural Dimensions of Globalization* (Minneapolis: University of Minnesota Press, 1996), 178, 179, 185, 189.

# PART I
# Mobilizing

# The Social Fallout of Racial Politics

## Civic Engagement in Suburban Pasadena, 1950–2000

BECKY M. NICOLAIDES

When William Whyte's *The Organization Man* came out in 1956, a powerful image of suburban life was seared into the public imagination. Through his observations of everyday life in Park Forest, Illinois, Whyte crafted a portrait of suburban community life marked by intense engagement and interaction. Park Forest was an archetypal "sitcom suburb," built in the late 1940s by large-scale builders, dotted with mass-produced homes occupied by residents with a common age, race, and income profile. In Park Forest, Whyte found neighbors who were connected intimately in the rhythms of everyday life—in the minutiae of child rearing and running homes, in concerns about local civic issues, and even in intellectual and spiritual life. He called it a "hotbed of participation."[1] Although Whyte went on to critique this way of life, symptomatic in his eyes of the troubling postwar trend of groupthink, what he described despite himself was vibrant community engagement in suburbia.

Flash forward to the late 1970s. By this time, just one generation removed, suburbia was perceived as a place of deep social disconnection. M. P. Baumgartner expressed this vividly in her book *The Moral Order of a Suburb,* based on sociological fieldwork in a suburb outside New York City. What she found was a local culture of tolerance and avoidance. The suburb lacked social integration and instead was defined by a sense of indifference among neighbors. What contributed to this lack of community? Some of the very attributes that Baumgartner believed characterized suburban living: the privatism of families, the high mobility of homeowners, and the compartmentalization of social life—all things also present in Park Forest.[2]

This swing from open doors to closed doors captures two powerful images of suburban life in the years since 1950, with the 1970s as an ominous turning point. This broad shift characterizes much of the literature generated in these periods by sociologists, anthropologists, and writers observing suburbia around them. What

3

Women in 1950s Park Forest, Illinois, gathered in homes to share coffee, cigarettes, and conversation—one of many ways that suburbanites socialized and connected regularly. Photograph by Dan Weiner from William H. Whyte Jr., "The Outgoing Life," *Fortune,* July 1953, 88. Copyright John Broderick.

is fascinating about this swing is that the suburban built environment was often implicated in these radically different social outcomes. In the 1950s, for example, Whyte went so far as to diagram how the placement of driveways shaped social networks.[3] By the late 1970s, suburbia was blamed for deep social alienation, marked by the rise of gated communities, built environments of fear and security, and the triumph of privatism. This was the time, of course, when racial barriers began to break down.[4]

The idea of the shift from community engagement to decline culminated in Robert Putnam's influential book *Bowling Alone* (2000). Though his study was a national portrayal, suburbia played a key part in his story. Putnam used Whyte's portrayal of Park Forest as a vivid illustration of postwar engagement. From there, things went downhill. He documented the multiple ways that Americans have withdrawn and disconnected since 1970, signifying an alarming decline in social capital. When he turned to explain the trend, the suburbs emerged as one of several causal forces. Because people spent more time commuting alone in their cars, they had less time "for friends and neighbors, for meetings, for community projects, and so on." Moreover, Putnam argued, social homogeneity common in suburbia tended to

Participation is round the clock at Park Forest. Here, in the United Protestant Sunday School Building, is a fraction of what goes on in one evening. Top floor, from left to right: church choir, the Explorer Scouts (waiting for a quorum to plan next week's hike), World Politics discussion group (to discuss what causes war; a second discussion group meets on a different evening to take up American foreign policy). Bottom floor: high-school board meeting (to talk over interior decoration of the new high school), an organizing committee to organize a new organization (the Protestant Men's Club), Husanwif Club (to watch slides on safety rules for children). This sort of thing goes on all the time.

William Whyte's depiction of vibrant social life in Park Forest was captured brilliantly in this image of a community building on a typical evening. The caption for this photograph describes the many groups tending to their business. The bright lights illuminating the suburban night suggest the life and energy these groups contributed to the community. Photograph by Dan Weiner from William H. Whyte Jr., "The Future, c/o Park Forest," *Fortune*, June 1953. Copyright John Broderick.

dampen civic participation, while suburban sprawl blurred a sense of community boundedness—that is, a sense that people belong to a clearly recognizable neighborhood. Without this feeling, he contended, civic and social engagement diminishes.[5]

While Putnam's work has been critiqued on several fronts, his essential narrative mirrors a broader, accepted portrayal of suburban life since the 1950s—the move from community vitality to withdrawal.[6] This purported shift is the conceptual springboard of this chapter, which is part of a larger project that seeks to interrogate this narrative on two basic levels: first, to ask if it accurately represents suburban life since 1950, and second, to explore the forces that have shaped patterns of suburban community engagement in the years since 1950. It is, at heart, a social history of suburbia.[7] I focus on Los Angeles, homing in on certain communities as case studies to explore critical themes. Two key assumptions inform my approach. First, suburbia is a diverse and dynamic place. There are many kinds of suburbs, and most tend to change over time. I deploy the concept of "historic suburban landscapes" as a means of identifying and analyzing different suburban areas.[8] Second, in order to understand life on the ground, it is imperative that we give attention to the forces that have shaped suburban and metropolitan areas—the essential structural context. Beyond this, we must consider the constitutive elements of social life and identity, such as class, race, ethnicity/immigration, gender, and the life cycle, in seeking to understand processes of community change. I believe the built environment plays a role, but it operates in tandem with a host of other forces.

This essay draws on a case study of Pasadena to explore how race and class have shaped social and civic engagement. Located nine miles northeast of downtown Los Angeles, Pasadena reflects multiple strands of suburban history, including the elemental role of race. The critical role of race has been well established in the suburban historiography. Across broad swaths of space and time, white racial purity came to constitute a fundamental feature of the suburban ideal—to many, a defini- tional element of what "suburbia" means—ensuring the social, economic, and civic health of neighborhoods. The project of maintaining racial separatism thus figures prominently in our understanding of how suburban places have evolved.[9] In the 1960s and 1970s, the color line began to break, opening the door to profound changes in the experience of many suburbanites. In Pasadena, as residents struggled to come to terms with a new civic commitment to racial equality, they realigned their civic and social energies in ways that replicated past inequality but also opened up new, small arenas for the expression of a reimagined, inclusive suburban ideal.

If Los Angeles represents a mosaic of historic suburban landscapes, Pasadena rep- resents a microcosm of that panorama. As one of the older towns in the greater Los Angeles area, it contains nearly every type of historic suburban landscape within its orbit—wealthy picturesque enclaves, old automobile bungalow suburbs, multiethnic working-class suburbs, all-white sitcom suburbs of the postwar years, and post-1980 corporate suburbia. As well, Pasadena emerged as a key regional hub by the 1980s, with a diverse jobs base, universities, cultural centers, and robust retail and service sectors, prompting Joel Garreau to count it among L.A.'s key "Edge Cities," an outlying center of commercial and job growth.[10]

Pasadena's early roots as a wealthy picturesque enclave created the area's social diversity—its wealthy Anglo residents were hopelessly dependent on a workforce of domestics to keep their estates and mansions functioning. Like Evanston, Illinois, or New Rochelle, New York, this was the classic yin and yang of elite suburbia— a picturesque enclave abutted by domestic service suburbia.[11] These laborers were initially African American, then Asian by the 1920s. Latinos, meanwhile, labored in local orchards and railway yards. These historic roots gave people of color a foothold to settle the area permanently—a pattern not always present in high-end, restricted white suburbs. Pasadena instead became a place that embodied the extremes of class and race, a town of extraordinary diversity where rich, poor, white, black, and brown coexisted within common political borders. Yet within this diverse whole, residential, social, and civic life was highly segregated before 1950. Spatially, a core

The yin and yang of elite suburbia is evident in this pair of photographs of early Pasadena. The upper photograph shows the residence of H. C. Durand, Orange Grove Avenue, circa 1898; such opulent estates dotted Pasadena's broad boulevards. The lower photograph shows Beatrice Jolla in front of oranges she picked from the Meeker property in Pasadena, 1918. Above: *Illustrated Souvenir Book: Showing a Few Pasadena homes, with Short Descriptive Data,* issued by direction of the Board of Trade, Pasadena, California, 1897. Below: Courtesy of the Archives, Pasadena Museum of History, Ethel Houston photo album, Black History Collection, BH-D-111-2.

of modest suburban neighborhoods filled out the middle sections, surrounded by wealthy white enclaves along the scenic edges of town.[12]

By the 1950s and early 1960s, crystalline racial boundaries allowed for a vibrant public life to flourish in Pasadena. Most middle- and working-class residents lived fully in the public sphere. (By 1960, Pasadena's population reached 116,000.) Like their counterparts in suburbs nationally, they were joiners. They belonged to clubs, associations, churches, political groups, and parent–teacher associations (PTAs). By quantitative measures, this era represented the peak of associational participation. This impulse to participate flowed out of two streams: the older tradition of social, civic, and philanthropic activism that characterized early Pasadena and the wave of home-front activism that crested during World War II and carried forward. Pasadena had an immense array of civic and social groups, ranging from hobby groups and cultural organizations to service groups seeking to tackle local problems to fraternal orders and ethnic mutual aid organizations to patriotic groups celebrating Anglo pedigrees. Remarkably, in the 1950s and 1960s, forty-six groups met on a weekly basis, suggesting their social importance in the everyday lives of members. Other groups typically met twice or once a month. Most were highly segregated, excluding all nonwhites.[13]

A similar outpouring of participatory energy was present among African Americans, who made up the largest nonwhite population in Pasadena. Interestingly, there were more black fraternal/philanthropic groups than civil rights organizations, reflecting the suburban zeitgeist of the times. Blacks also continued to sustain racial justice organizations, including the National Association for the Advancement of Colored People and the National Council of Negro Women. Scattered sources suggest that there were high levels of participation among African Americans. In the 1950s, the NAACP had about nine hundred members (both black and white); many blacks were also highly involved in churches and PTA work. One source claims that 23 percent of all blacks participated in PTAs, a high rate given that one-third of black adults had school-age children.[14]

Civic and political life was equally robust in the postwar years, animating partisans across the political spectrum. In the 1950s and 1960s, local community was not simply a happenstance setting for political activism. People believed that the local public sphere mattered, that it was the linchpin of democracy. This elevated concern with community and its well-being—heightened by Cold War fears— stimulated civic and political engagement. The locality represented a compelling, needy recipient of participatory energies, a space demanding vigilance and protection, and one where residents felt they could make a difference.[15] This sensibility was expressed in the surging political club movement of both the Republican and Democratic Parties, in the proliferation of local political and patriotic groups, and

Clubs and organizations in Pasadena in relation to the adult population, 1950–2011

| | 1950 | 1960 | 1970 | 1980 | 1990 | 2005–11 |
|---|---|---|---|---|---|---|
| Total adult population (20 years and older) | 80,543 | 83,615 | 80,611 | 87,261 | 99,046 | 110,533 |
| Total clubs and organizations (excluding youth groups) | 316 | 328 | 217 | 254 | 207 | 188 |
| Ratio of clubs per adults | 1/255 | 1/255 | 1/371 | 1/344 | 1/478 | 1/588 |

Sources: *Thurston's Pasadena City Directory, 1947* (Los Angeles: Los Angeles Directory Company, 1947); *Sixteenth Annual Register of the Organizations of Pasadena and Vicinity, 1950*, comp. Bertha K. Shaw (Pasadena: Turner and Stevens Company, 1950); *Thurston's Pasadena City Directory, 1951* (Los Angeles: Los Angeles Directory Company, 1951); *Twenty-First Annual Register of the Organizations of Pasadena and Vicinity, 1955*, comp. Bertha K. Shaw (Pasadena: Turner and Stevens Company, 1955); *Polk's Pasadena City Directory, 1961* (Los Angeles: R. L. Polk and Company, 1961); *Thirty-Second Annual Register of the Organizations of Pasadena and Vicinity, 1966*, comp. Mrs. Stanley H. Stevens (Pasadena: Bank of Pasadena, 1966); *Polk's Pasadena City Directory, 1971* (Monterey Park, Calif.: R. L. Polk and Company, 1971); *Pasadena Community Organizations Directory, 1979–1980*, ed. Frederick Olsen (Pasadena: Pasadena Public Library, 1979); Pacific Telephone, *Bell System Yellow Pages, Pasadena, 1980* (Pacific Telephone, 1980); Pasadena Chamber of Commerce and Civic Association, *1991 Business Directory and Community Guide* (San Diego: Marcoa Publishing, 1991); *Pacific Bell Smart Yellow Pages, Pasadena, 1989–90* (Pacific Bell, 1990); for 2011, Pasadena Public Library Community Directory, http://204.89.9.203/ipac20/ipac.jsp?profile=; William H. Whyte Jr., *The Organization Man* (New York: Simon & Schuster, 1956), 287; U.S. Census of Population, 1950, 1960.

Note: In 1955 Park Forest, Illinois, had about 1 group per 157 adults, compared to 1 per 255 in Pasadena.

in local high-profile battles over the future of public education—traditional versus progressive. In Pasadena, public education was considered a community institution to be protected and fought for—not run away from.[16]

Pasadena's elite, by contrast, straddled public and private worlds. They inhabited a rarified world of private clubs and schools, debutante balls, and secluded neighborhoods, creating for themselves a comfortable cushion of social distance demanded by a town as diverse as Pasadena. This was bonding social capital at its lucrative best, and it was tightly segregated by race. The elite created protected, class-defined social spaces within the city, and in so doing established a structure of private life that would become a model for a broader class stratum in later years. Alongside this private social world, many also participated in the more public associational life of Pasadena—the clubs and service groups that consumed the energies and passions of many local residents.[17]

The geography of engagement in postwar Pasadena reflected a kind of city/ suburb split. People participated in clubs that met in central Pasadena and along its commercial corridors, making the five- or ten-minute drive from their suburban homes. Just as frequently, associational life happened in suburban neighborhoods, whether in members' homes or in meeting rooms at the public schools. The immediate postwar period was, in fact, the heyday of home-based associational life. In 1950, for example, groups meeting regularly in suburban homes included the Garden Club, the Epsilon Sigma Alpha Business Sorority, the Foothill Camera Club, and New Century Club, among many others. A similar trend was apparent among political clubs, both Republican and Democratic. As Michelle Nickerson writes of local conservative women's groups, suburban homes "provided a warm and non-intimidating atmosphere meant to promote the overlapping goals of political discussion and sociability."[18] The Tuesday Morning Study Club is a good example. This conservative women's group held monthly meetings in the San Rafael home of its founder, Marjorie Jensen, where members gathered in the backyard to hear a guest speaker and then engage in discussion. In the late 1950s, at the peak of the group's popularity, about fifty women attended regularly.[19] The suburban home was not simply a privatized domestic space—it was also a place of communal interaction and open doors, a site where public life literally entered in.

By the 1960s significant challenges to racial segregation emerged, driven by the civil rights movement. As legal barriers to segregation fell, Pasadena's deeply embedded racial geography began to shake loose. A series of three major events accelerated that process: busing aimed at school desegregation (the result of both national and local politics), urban renewal, and freeway construction. These actions—highly racialized and politically charged—reshaped the racial geography of the city. They decimated historic neighborhoods of blacks, Latinos, and Asians while spatially confining poor blacks to northwest Pasadena, which had once been a socioeconomically mixed area. The poor also concentrated more heavily in central Pasadena and along the freeway corridors. Meanwhile, middle-class blacks scattered into formerly all-white suburban neighborhoods in western Pasadena and neighboring Altadena, while the picturesque enclaves retained their predominantly white, high-end status. Racial realignment thus precipitated new patterns of class segregation.[20]

The ascendance of racial politics in the 1960s, in fact, signified a high point of political engagement among suburbanites in Pasadena, from all points on the political spectrum. School desegregation represented the climactic issue. For some, the impetus for engagement—steeped in the politics of resistance—created bonding social capital of the shakiest sort, based on defensive claims of white homeowner rights but shadowed always by the option of departure at any moment, an easy alternative in the context of fragmented Los Angeles. For many others, civil rights became the touchstone of robust interracial political activism. A broad-based coalition of progressives—much stronger organizationally than their anti-integration counterparts—worked to ensure a peaceful transition to desegregation. The connections they forged became a source of bridging social capital with a longer future. The political culture of Pasadena, in turn, evolved from conservative to liberal, and the public sphere—in local education, municipal politics, public-sector jobs, and public spaces—grew racially diverse.[21]

A coalition of progressive groups worked to ease the transition to busing in Pasadena, signifying a moment of interracial success during a period of profound racial transition. This photograph depicts early busing in Pasadena, when a multiracial group of parents offered cheerful assistance to black and white schoolchildren. The bridging capital they forged boded well for the future of Pasadena, but social allegiances increasingly realigned around class in later years. Audubon Busing, September 1970. Courtesy of the Archives, Pasadena Museum of History, Pasadena City Schools Negative Collection, 6731F.

At the same time, for a great many, withdrawal into separate spaces—whether divided by race, class, or zip code—became an ever more common pattern. Pasadena thus emerged as a town that was more racially diverse and more liberal but also more segregated than ever by class. The social fallout of racial politics in Pasadena was mixed. These changes occurred against a backdrop of profound demographic and housing transformations after 1970: the white population declined (while still dominating numerically), the Latino population rose significantly, and the black population rose and then fell. This period also saw a greater schism between rich and poor and the shrinking of Pasadena's middle class. Multifamily housing proliferated, clustering especially toward the center of town, alongside the persistence of stable suburban neighborhoods.[22]

Two realms of local life illustrate the ways that racial change reoriented patterns of social and civic engagement in Pasadena: associations and the schools. In the area of associational life, where quantitative evidence is richest, it is clear that there was an overall decline in the number of local groups, suggesting that, by this simple measure, fewer people were joining. But the qualitative side of that story reveals a more complex dynamic beyond simple declension, showing reasons for the downturn as well as areas of nuanced change.

Several key trends are evident. First, the nature of ethnicity- and race-based groups transformed, largely in response to local demographic change. White flight heralded an overall decline in European ethnic and white lineage groups, which had been quite numerous. Latino groups, serving that fast-growing population, remained proportionately small in number. This pattern in a tremendously important demographic group goes a long way toward explaining the overall per capita decline in associations. What it obscures, however, are the ways in which Latinos were likely

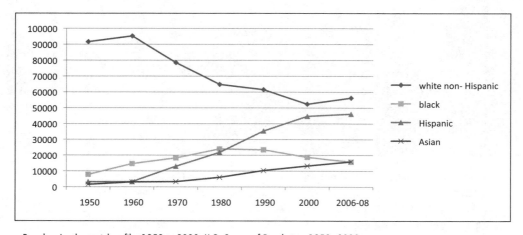

Pasadena's ethnoracial profile, 1950 to 2008. U.S. Census of Population, 1950–2008.

connecting outside the realm of formal organizations. Black and interracial groups maintained respectable numbers, reflecting new demographic realities. Second, the participatory charity work that animated many older service groups in Pasadena gave way to the institutionalization of social services. The professionalization of social services did not signal an end to philanthropic work in Pasadena. To the contrary, it represented a new "end goal" of local charitable groups. They began to embrace a different strategic model—one that would create permanent institutional structures for the ongoing delivery of social assistance. Many of these groups were racially and ethnically diverse. Third, the women's groups that succeeded were the ones willing to embrace the social changes around them. The Shakespeare Club and Junior League represented two opposite extremes. The former continued to restrict its membership, which ultimately stymied its growth; the latter adopted a more flexible, inclusive membership policy, including an embrace of racial diversity, and it grew to its highest levels in the 1990s—the same decade it elected its first African American president.[23] Fourth, political party clubs saw a decline by 1970 due to a combination of internal and external factors having little to do with suburban contexts. On the conservative side, anticommunist groups that had found ripe outlets for grassroots politics, such as the Tuesday Morning Club and Pro America, gradually faded as the Right shifted ideological focus. On the liberal side, the club movement was weakened by a move in the Democratic Party's campaign culture toward professionalization and splintering within the party itself, leading black militants and the radical youth movement to reject the "white establishment" character of the clubs. The numbers were staggering. In California, membership in Democratic clubs fell from 100,000 to 10,000 between 1960 and 1970.[24]

The final trend was that the suburban home receded as a locus of associational life. The spatial experience of belonging shifted to more institutional, impersonal locales. This related partly to the nature of new groups that emerged after 1970; for example, there was a surge in sports-oriented groups that met at their chosen sporting venues. The end result was a diminished role of the home and neighborhood in everyday group life.

In its broadest outlines, the history of associational life in Pasadena comports with the idea that diversity strains the process of community cohesion and engagement.[25] On the simplest level, it appears the town diversified and overall participation declined. Yet, on closer examination, evidence suggests that an inclusive strategy could prove successful with diligent, persistent effort. Groups like the Junior League, Altadena Baptist Church, and the Interracial Women's Club showed how a conscientious commitment to diversity could generate robust engagement and social capital in a transformed postwar world.[26] These groups represented organizational expressions of a more inclusive suburban ideal. In the process, residents kept their distance. The suburban home was increasingly closed off from gatherings. A more clearly defined division was drawn between public and private worlds.

The schools, by contrast, revealed the emergence of stark class segregation in the wake of racial integration, which had selective effects on participation patterns. School desegregation had an ironic—if familiar—denouement. After the initial politically self-conscious period of integration, during which the children of busing made it through and graduated, often celebrating lessons learned in the process, the schools experienced a rapid process of resegregation. The public schools were largely abandoned by Pasadena's white middle- and upper-class suburban families. The principle of education as a public good, which had animated suburban parents for years, was abandoned. In turn, education was bifurcated into public and private worlds. Private schools became retreats for middle- and upper-class whites, and the public schools the province of people of color and the working class, mirroring national patterns. As Kevin Kruse has written of Atlanta, whites' desertion of public education signified a key element of the "privatization of segregation"—one pillar of a broad distressing trend of white flight away from multiple realms of public life.[27]

The public schools as anchors of community engagement were shaken in two ways by this process: first, by disconnecting education from local neighborhoods, and second, by depleting the participatory energies of middle-class families from public school communities. For years, the PTAs had been important points of parental community involvement. In Pasadena, desegregation dealt a harsh blow to local PTAs—from 1970 to 1976, when busing was in full swing, membership dropped from 14,000 to 8,248; by 1997, it fell to 3,370. Withdrawal from these groups was a phenomenon tied closely to class. As school district families descended the socioeconomic ladder and grew ethnically diverse, participation declined. It became harder for PTAs to attract working-class parents with little spare time or familiarity with the school system. By contrast, more affluent Southern California suburban school districts, such as those in La Cañada and San Marino, dodged many of these problems and were able to maintain higher levels of parental participation. In Pasadena, the malaise of parental withdrawal was most pronounced in the world of public education.

In the private schools, it was another story. In the wake of busing, private schools in Pasadena not only surged in number but also evolved in social meaning and cultural orientation. Once the province of the society set, after 1970 they became more diffuse, middle-class, politically diverse institutions. In this privatized sector of the education market, parents could shop for the educational styles that most suited their tastes, avoiding the perennial rancor in the Pasadena Unified School District, where parents seemed to be refighting the same battles over progressive versus fundamental education. For all of the controversy that progressive education generated

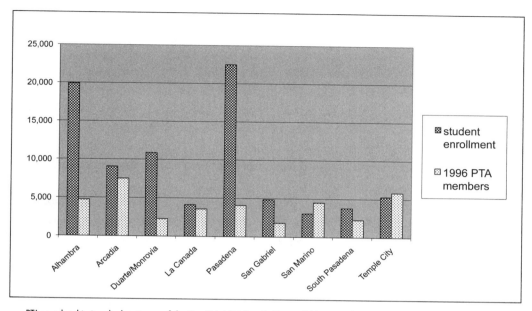

PTA membership in suburban towns of the San Gabriel Valley, California, 1996. Based on data in "Wanted: More Parents," *Pasadena Star News,* March 15, 1998, 1.

in Pasadena, it ultimately found a comfortable home in the world of private schools, attracting liberal/progressive parents especially. Many private schools worked to foster communities of involvement among parents, some institutionalizing it by setting a fixed number of required parent volunteer hours. Within the private realm, schools remained sites of active participation.[28]

At the same time private schools were codifying participation, they continued to represent spaces of racial division. While private schooling became a typical experience for the majority of Pasadena's white suburban kids by 2000, it was increasingly unusual for children of color, despite the best efforts of some schools to diversify their student bodies.[29] Moreover, the geographic disconnect between neighborhoods and schools that began with busing grew by an order of magnitude with the expansion of private schooling. Education was becoming thoroughly unhinged from suburban home neighborhoods, making commuting a daily fact for children and their parents. Like Pasadena's civic groups, schools continued to draw participatory energy, but they did so divorced from the immediate context of suburban neighborhoods.

The post-1970 period did represent a turning point in suburban social and civic engagement, but not simply because of suburban design. Suburban neighborhoods were experiencing stressful processes of social change. Racial diversification, an increasingly common trend in suburbs after 1970, recast the ways suburbanites participated in community life. The case of Pasadena suggests the complex nature of these patterns. While the overall number of social and political groups declined, partly reflecting the disappearance of older Anglo hubs of identity, new groups found vitality in diversity, swinging forward with the times. Other centers of community engagement—particularly the schools—resegregated in ways that etched class divisions more deeply than ever. Participation patterns realigned accordingly. Just as Herbert Gans found in postwar Levittown, class continued to influence participation, with middle- and upper-class families the most active joiners and working-class families less so.[30]

Suburbia evolved as a community locus. Once the busy center of everyday social life, it receded as such through these changes—a likely result of changing perceptions of public trust and profound shifts in schooling. The ways that families used their suburban homes transformed in this context. If racial segregation created social predictability and allowed a vibrant social life to flourish, integration pushed suburbanites into uncharted social waters. A good number of middle- and upper-class suburbanites retreated from these changes, segregating themselves into insular social realms where engagement remained robust. But there were examples here and there of people breaching the stubborn divides of class and race. In settings like the Junior League, diversity became a driver of engagement, not its spoiler. These sites of participation suggested nascent expressions of a new, multiracial suburban ideal.

## Notes

This work received generous support from the John Randolph Haynes and Dora Haynes Foundation. The author thanks Michelle Nickerson and Peter Dreier for helpful suggestions.

1. William H. Whyte Jr., *The Organization Man* (New York: Simon & Schuster, 1956), 357. "Sitcom suburb" is from Dolores Hayden, *Building Suburbia: Green Fields and Urban Growth, 1820–2000* (New York: Pantheon, 2003), chap. 7.

2. M. P. Baumgartner, *The Moral Order of a Suburb* (New York: Oxford University Press, 1988), 11, 13. Baumgartner was concerned foremost with understanding how suburbanites handled conflict in their community, so her ultimate conclusions about the local culture she found were mixed.

3. Whyte, *Organization Man*, 345. Even some writers who argued against spatial determinism—Herbert Gans prime among them—ultimately reached similar conclusions about the vibrancy of suburban community life in the earlier period. Works documenting strong community in suburbia in the 1950–60s include Herbert J. Gans, *The Levittowners: Ways of Life and Politics in a New Suburban Community* (New York: Columbia University Press, 1967); John R. Seeley, R. Alexander Sim, and Elizabeth W. Loosley, *Crestwood Heights: A Study of the Culture of Suburban Life* (New York: Basic Books, 1956); Sylvia Fleis Fava, "Contrasts in Neighboring," in *The Suburban Community*, ed. William M. Dobriner (New York: G. P. Putnam's Sons, 1958);

S. F. Fava, "Suburbanism as a Way of Life," *American Sociological Review* 21 (February 1956): 34–38; Claude S. Fischer and Robert Max Jackson, "Suburbanism and Localism," in *Networks and Places: Social Relations in the Urban Setting,* ed. Claude S. Fischer (New York: Free Press, 1977). Also see Herbert J. Gans, "Urbanism and Suburbanism as Ways of Life," in *Human Behavior and Social Processes,* ed. Arnold Rose (Boston: Houghton Mifflin, 1962).

4. The literature that emphasizes social disconnection, fear, and privacy in suburbia after 1970 is large. Some important examples are Kenneth T. Jackson, *Crabgrass Frontier: The Suburbanization of the United States* (New York: Oxford University Press, 1985), chap. 15; Setha Low, *Behind the Gates: Life, Security, and the Pursuit of Happiness in Fortress America* (New York: Routledge, 2003); Evan McKenzie, *Privatopia: Homeowner Associations and the Rise of Residential Private Government* (New Haven, Conn.: Yale University Press, 1994); Mike Davis, *City of Quartz: Excavating the Future in Los Angeles* (London: Verso, 1990); James Howard Kunstler, *The Geography of Nowhere: The Rise and Decline of America's Man-Made Landscape* (New York: Simon & Schuster, 1993); Christopher Caldwell, "Levittown to Littleton," *National Review,* May 31, 1999; Andres Duany, Elizabeth Plater-Zyberk, and Jeff Speck, *Suburban Nation: The Rise of Sprawl and the Decline of the American Dream* (New York: North Point Press, 2000), esp. chap. 7.

5. Robert D. Putnam, *Bowling Alone: The Collapse and Revival of American Community* (New York: Simon & Schuster, 2000), 214.

6. Recent important critiques of Putnam's work include Robyn Muncy, "Disconnecting: Social and Civic Life in America since 1965," *Review in American History* 29 (2001): 141–49; James Jennings, ed., *Race, Neighborhoods, and the Misuse of Social Capital* (New York: Palgrave Macmillan, 2007); Barbara Arneil, *Diverse Communities: The Problem with Social Capital* (New York: Cambridge University Press, 2006).

7. This chapter draws from Becky M. Nicolaides, "On the Ground in Suburbia: A Chronicle of Social and Civic Transformation in Los Angeles since 1945" (working manuscript, 2014), chap. 3.

8. Making sense of different suburban areas—or typologies—is challenging, particularly for historians seeking to trace out change over time. My analytical framework draws on Dolores Hayden's conceptualization of historic suburban landscapes in *Building Suburbia.* I describe this in Nicolaides, "On the Ground in Suburbia," chap. 1.

9. The literature on race, class, and suburbia is vast. Important works include Carl H. Nightingale, *Segregation: A Global History of Divided Cities* (Chicago: University of Chicago Press, 2012); John Archer, "Colonial Suburbs in South Asia, 1700–1850, and the Spaces of Modernity," in *Visions of Suburbia,* ed. Roger Silverstone (London: Routledge, 1997); Robert Fishman, *Bourgeois Utopias: The Rise and Fall of Suburbia* (New York: Basic Books, 1987); Jackson, *Crabgrass Frontier;* Matthew D. Lassiter, *The Silent Majority: Suburban Politics in the Sunbelt South* (Princeton, N.J.: Princeton University Press, 2006); Kevin M. Kruse, *White Flight: Atlanta and the Making of Modern Conservatism* (Princeton, N.J.: Princeton University Press, 2005); Robert O. Self, *American Babylon: Race and the Struggle for Postwar Oakland* (Princeton, N.J.: Princeton University Press, 2005); David M. P. Freund, *Colored Property: State Policy and White Racial Politics in Suburban America* (Chicago: University of Chicago Press, 2007); Becky M. Nicolaides, *My Blue Heaven: Life and Politics in the Working-Class Suburbs of Los Angeles, 1920–1965* (Chicago: University of Chicago Press, 2002); Andrew Wiese, *Places of Their Own*: African American Suburbanization in the Twentieth Century (Chicago: University of Chicago Press, 2004);

Becky M. Nicolaides and Andrew Wiese, eds., *The Suburb Reader* (New York: Routledge, 2006), esp. chaps. 8, 15.

10. Joel Garreau, *Edge City: Life on the New Frontier* (New York: Doubleday, 1991), 113.

11. Wiese, *Places of Their Own*, 25.

12. Michael E. James, *The Conspiracy of the Good: Civil Rights and the Struggle for Community in Two American Cities, 1875–2000* (New York: Peter Lang, 2005); Laura Voisin George, "Cultivating an Ideal: The Agrarian Aspirations of Pasadena, California, 1873–1895" (master's thesis, University of Virginia, 2010); Ann Scheid, *Pasadena: Crown of the Valley* (Northridge, Calif.: Windsor, 1986); Wiese, *Places of Their Own*; Robin D. G. Kelley, "Black History Project," notes, Pasadena Museum of History; Earl F. Cartland, "A Study of the Negroes Living in Pasadena" (master's thesis, Whittier College, 1948); James E. Crimi, "The Social Status of the Negro in Pasadena, California" (master's thesis, University of Southern California, 1941); Manuel Pineda and F. Caswell Perry, *Pasadena Area History* (Pasadena: James W. Anderson, 1972); Carson Anderson, "Ethnic History Research Project, Pasadena, California" (report of survey findings prepared for the city of Pasadena, March 1995); Home Owners Loan Corporation, "Security Map and Area Descriptions, Metropolitan Los Angeles, California," and City Survey Files, Record Group 195, National Archives, Washington, D.C. For sources on the various sections of Pasadena, see Nicolaides, "On the Ground in Suburbia," chap. 3.

13. See table source note; James, *Conspiracy of the Good*; vertical files of a number of individual organizations, Centennial Room, Pasadena Public Library (hereafter cited as PPL).

14. See table source note; Saundra Knox oral history, in *Advocates for Change: Oral History Interviews on the Desegregation of the Pasadena Unified School District* (Pasadena: Pasadena Heritage, 2007), 74–75; Elbie Hickambottom oral history, in *Advocates for Change*, 190; Kelley, "Black History Project."

15. The importance of the "local" as a site of civic activism is well described in Michelle M. Nickerson, *Mothers of Conservatism: Women and the Postwar Right* (Princeton, N.J.: Princeton University Press, 2011).

16. The best treatment of these educational conflicts is in Nickerson, *Mothers of Conservatism*; also see James, *Conspiracy of the Good*; David Hulburd, *This Happened in Pasadena* (New York: Macmillan, 1951).

17. Ann Scheid, *The Valley Hunt Club: One Hundred Years, 1888–1988* (Pasadena: Valley Hunt Club, 1988); Scheid, *Pasadena*; "Clubs: Can Everyone Join in the Hunt?," *Pasadena Weekly,* January 2, 1986; *Los Angeles Times,* December 31, 1908, June 10, 1910, December 2, 8, 9, 1926, November 1, 1927, December 11, 1928, February 1, 1929, February 18, 1931, November 27, 1932, March 28, May 7, October 8, 1933, September 14, 1947, April 27, 1960, June 10, 25, 1962, June 22, 1963, April 21, 1966, June 26, 1967, June 28, 1972, G4, November 24, 1988, 1; *Pasadena Star News,* December 19, 1947, April 4, 11, 1948, January 30, 1963, July 27, 1967, October 28, 1987, April 19, May 27, 1988, September 13, 2008; *Pasadena Weekly,* March 15, 2001; Barbara Slattery, "Our League: Post War Years" (1952?), 27–29, and "Annual Report of the President, 1960–1961," November 28, 1961, Junior League vertical file, Centennial Room, PPL. On private schools, see sources for table "Clubs and Organizations in Pasadena" and Ave Maria DeVanon Bortz, *Mayfield: The Early Years, 1931–1950* (Pasadena: Mayfield Senior School, 2000). Information on the racial makeup of private schools comes from a survey of yearbooks of LaSalle, Mayfield Senior, Polytechnic, and Westridge, conducted by Jennifer Vanore. There was ample, regular press coverage of debutantes in Pasadena from the 1930s

forward, including many articles in the *Los Angeles Times,* October 28, December 2, 1934, B2, October 18, November 13, December 24, 1949, A7, December 17, 1950, C9, November 15, 1953, December 20, 1955, B1, July 11, 1971, C5.

18. Nickerson, *Mothers of Conservatism,* 40.

19. Ibid., chap. 2. For data on home-based organizations, see sources for table "Clubs and Organizations in Pasadena."

20. These developments are explored in detail in Nicolaides, "On the Ground in Suburbia," chap. 3.

21. For a full listing of sources, see ibid. I drew extensively on coverage by the *Los Angeles Times* and *Pasadena Star News; Advocates for Change;* Kelley, "Black History Project"; Julie Salley Gray, "'To Fight the Good Fight': The Battle over Control of the Pasadena City Schools, 1969–1979," *Essays in History* (Corcoran Department of History, University of Virginia), 1995.

22. U.S. Census of population and housing, 1950–2000, by municipality and census tract; Peter Dreier, "Separate and Unequal: Nowhere in California Is the Gap between Rich and Poor Greater than in Pasadena," *Pasadena Weekly,* September 13, 2007.

23. Material on individual groups drawn from vertical files, Centennial Room, PPL; sources for table "Clubs and Organizations in Pasadena." On the Shakespeare Club, see *Los Angeles Times,* November 24, 1988; *Pasadena Star News,* April 19, 1988, December 5, 1991, June 25, 2004; *Pasadena Weekly,* March 13, 2001. On the Junior League, see *Pasadena Star News,* August 9, 1970, January 20, 1984, February 28, 1987, November 9, 1988, April 13, 1989, October 25, 1991, February 6, 9, May 9, 1992, March 13, 1993, August 5, 2001, March 17, 2002, April 23, 2004, April 10, 2005, March 30, 2009; *Los Angeles Times,* June 9, 1991; *Pasadena Weekly,* October 7, 1994, August 29, 1997; Nicole Weaver-Goller, telephone interview by author, December 17, 2010; Pasadena Junior League, "Annual Report of the President, 1960–1961."

24. Sources for table "Clubs and Organizations in Pasadena." On the Republican clubs, see Nickerson, *Mothers of Conservatism;* Lisa McGirr, *Suburban Warriors: The Origins of the New American Right* (Princeton, N.J.: Princeton University Press, 2001), 262–73; Catherine E. Rymph, *Republican Women: Feminism and Conservatism from Suffrage through the Rise of the New Right* (Chapel Hill: University of North Carolina Press, 2006); Jo Freeman, *A Room at a Time: How Women Entered Party Politics* (New York: Rowman & Littlefield, 2000), 160–61. Information on the Democratic clubs comes from Marvin Schachter, interview by author, December 28, 2010, Pasadena, Calif.; Esther Schachter and Marvin Schachter, interview by author, April 7, 2011, Pasadena, Calif.; Francis Carney, "The Palsy of the CDC," *The Nation,* May 4, 1970, 526–30; McGirr, *Suburban Warriors,* 199, 207; meeting minutes, 1966 to 1980, San Gabriel Valley Democratic Women's Club collection, Huntington Library, San Marino, Calif.

25. J. Eric Oliver, *The Paradoxes of Integration: Race, Neighborhood, and Civic Life in Multiethnic America* (Chicago: University of Chicago Press, 2010); Robert D. Putnam and Lewis M. Feldstein, *Better Together: Restoring American Community* (New York: Simon & Schuster, 2003).

26. These groups are explored in detail in Nicolaides, "On the Ground in Suburbia," chap. 3.

27. Kruse, *White Flight,* 178.

28. A full list of sources on Pasadena schools post-1970 is in Nicolaides, "On the Ground in Suburbia," chap. 3. Key sources include vertical files, Centennial Room, PPL; *Los Angeles Times; Pasadena Star News; Pasadena Weekly; Advocates for Change;* Amy Stuart Wells, Jennifer Jellison Holme, Anita Tijerina Revilla, and Awo Korantemaa Atanda, *Both Sides Now: The Story of School Desegregation's Graduates* (Berkeley: University of California Press, 2009); Harold Kurtz,

"The Educational and Demographic Consequences of Four Years of School Desegregation in the Pasadena Unified School District" (Pasadena Unified School District, 1975); Stephen Mulherin and Monique N. Hernandez, "Pasadena Unified School District: The Abandonment of a Public Institution," *California Politics and Policy,* June 2006, 93, 99, 107–8; Richard D. Kahlenberg, "One Pasadena: Tapping the Community's Resources to Strengthen the Public Schools" (report to the Pasadena Educational Foundation, May 24, 2006); Laura Mulfinger, "Public versus Private: Factors That Influence Middle and Upper Income Families' School Choice Decisions in the Pasadena Unified School District" (paper for Claremont Graduate University, July 1, 2002).

29. Data drawn from U.S. Census and Pasadena Unified School District statistics.

30. Gans, *Levittowners,* 24–31.

## 2

# Race, Planning, and Activism on Philadelphia's Main Line

### TRECIA POTTINGER

Writing in 1972 as president of the Ardmore Community Development Corporation, a nonprofit organization composed of community leaders, Nolan Atkinson asserted, "We are confident and certain that with your help in the centennial year of Ardmore's birth, we will build sixteen new homes of which you can be proud, and about which historians will one day write."[1] Two years later, in the spring of 1974, a crowd of more than fifty people gathered on a lawn at the intersection of Ardmore Avenue and West Spring Avenue to break ground on what would be called the ArdSpring Condominiums, an affordable housing development. A sign at the construction site would declare the project "A Community Effort." The ArdSpring Condominiums exemplified the ways African American residents of Philadelphia's Main Line mobilized to take control over the planning of their suburb in the 1960s and 1970s.

African American civic leaders and organizations working in Ardmore in the 1960s had clear aspirations for South Ardmore. They envisioned Ardmore as a place with well-maintained residential properties, affordable housing, an intergenerational population, and a decidedly residential character. The realities of Ardmore in the 1960s and 1970s diverged from these ideals as commercial interests competed with residential needs, some households struggled to find and maintain affordable housing, and younger generations departed. Beginning in the late 1950s, residents set about reconciling the differences between their aspirations and their realities through individual and collective actions in the areas of zoning, planning, and affordable housing.

The issues with which African Americans grappled and the means they utilized to address these paralleled processes unfolding in urban centers like nearby Philadelphia. In cities across the United States, shortages of affordable housing were widespread, urban renewal spawned debates about control over land use in African American neighborhoods, and community-based organizations emerged to advocate for citizens' interests. Similarly, African Americans in Ardmore contended with a scarcity of affordable housing and an increase in commercial activity, and they formed organizations to address these concerns. This case study demonstrates how African Americans in Ardmore enlisted and adapted strategies used in cities to resist displacement and to shape Ardmore proactively into a suburb that addressed their needs.

These residents, like some of the Pagedale residents Jodi Rios examines in her contribution to this volume (chapter 12), acted when they perceived threats to the suburb in which they lived. For African Americans in Ardmore, the threat came from outside their community and stemmed from conflicts with businesses and local government over land use. In Pagedale, however, black residents across class engaged in policing the social behavior of largely working-class black residents, "disciplin[ing] behavior construed as black" and therefore out of place in a suburban setting.

In this chapter, I explore how African Americans in South Ardmore responded politically to white commercial encroachment into their neighborhoods and to the diminishing availability of affordable housing. After offering a brief history of Ardmore, I examine the organizations African American residents formed to address these concerns and two main projects they commissioned in their efforts to meet the needs of black residents.

## Ardmore's History

Ardmore is a nonpolitical designation for a village that lies within the municipal boundaries of Lower Merion Township. Ardmore is also part of Philadelphia's Main Line, a collection of railroad suburbs that first emerged in the mid-nineteenth century. Main Line developers propagated the vision of idyllic, countryside houses as antidotes to the urban ills distressing the white elite. Nineteenth-century marketing produced a narrative that foregrounded extravagant wealth, grand estates, and whiteness in the railroad suburb, and this narrative persisted through the twentieth century. This dominant narrative masks the continuous physical and human diversity evident in places like Ardmore.

Since Ardmore's earliest period of significant suburban growth in the late 1870s, three distinct sections have constituted Ardmore: an area of larger residential properties to the north, a section of smaller residential properties to the south, and, finally, a commercial and industrial corridor centered on the railroad that divides North and South Ardmore. These zones define both social and physical differences.

Since the beginning of the twentieth century, South Ardmore has been home to a heterogeneous group of working-class residents, a large number of them African

Americans. Many African Americans first came to Ardmore from the South to seek service employment opportunities in the homes and institutions of wealthy white Main Line residents.[2] As the Main Line developed and the African American population grew, the areas in which African Americans worked broadened.

South Ardmore's diversity extended from its population to its built environment. Most of the area began as a collection of larger properties that developers subdivided over time and at a pace faster than subdivision in other parts of the Main Line. From the late 1870s (when subdivision began) through the mid-1920s (when a house stood on nearly every subdivided lot), a patchwork of developments emerged in South Ardmore. South Ardmore's proximity to industry and commerce, its gridlike streets and narrow lots, and its varied housing types set it apart from popular images of the Main Line. Some houses reflected uniform setbacks, designs, and materials, while the characteristics of houses in other subdivided plans varied. Housing types included single-family and twin houses as well as row houses and a handful of multiunit dwellings, all of which were home to South Ardmore's diverse population, including African Americans. Because Ardmore was inconsistent with popular images of the Main Line, it drew criticism from planners and housing reformers who cited such issues as the presence of row houses. Idealized visions of

Several developments of row houses existed in Ardmore, which housing reformers regarded as unnecessarily urban in the suburban Main Line context. Marion Bosworth, *Housing Conditions in Main Line Towns* (investigation made under the direction of the Committee on Investigation, Main Line Housing Association), circa 1912.

the Main Line persisted into the postwar era, masking existing heterogeneity and working to prevent the incursion of yet greater diversity.

## Competing Visions of Ardmore

Across generations, African Americans struggled to find affordable housing in South Ardmore. In the post–World War II era, the expansion of commercial properties into South Ardmore exacerbated concerns about affordable housing. White business and property owners advocated for the conversion of residentially zoned land to commercially zoned land and demolished existing housing to create additional parking spaces.[3] Their aim was to maintain and strengthen Ardmore's longtime status as a commercial hub of the Main Line.

The priorities of these expanding commercial interests often ran counter to those of African American residents, many of whom perceived the expansion of certain types of businesses and parking as threats to the fabric of their neighborhood and to affordable housing. Residents were concerned about increased traffic, reduced housing supply, and diminished parking for residents. While retail, industry, and housing had always existed in close proximity in Ardmore, the advance of commercial enterprises onto previously residential properties toppled this balance. In response, African Americans articulated an alternative, residentially centered vision of South Ardmore in local politics throughout the 1960s and 1970s, signaling an increased sense of agency to shape the built environment to meet their needs.

Early efforts to maintain the residential character of South Ardmore would focus on zoning. In an effort to limit commercialization and maintain housing stock, African American leaders and organizations spoke against proposals to expand commercial zoning, both before township boards and in the pages of local newspapers. In the late 1960s South Ardmore residents began utilizing the terms *commercial creep* and *creeping commercialism* to draw attention to the cumulative effects of case-by-case land-use changes.[4] Over time, African Americans also adopted more proactive approaches to maintaining residential zoning in Ardmore. In 1969, for instance, the Ardmore Progressive Civic Association, a nonpartisan group of African Americans, offered a proposal for what it called "upzoning"—rezoning parcels of land from a commercial designation to a residential one as part of an effort to preserve the residential nature of South Ardmore and to limit the intrusion of commercial establishments that the association viewed as detrimental to the neighborhood.[5]

## The Plan for South Ardmore

Building on earlier efforts to address zoning issues, African Americans eventually presented a holistic vision for Ardmore's future as part of a 1970 master plan.[6] While it addressed a wide range of issues under the title *Plan for Housing and Community*

*Improvements in the South Ardmore Community,* including zoning, education, and economic development, it made housing needs the top priority. Spurred by African American frustration with a perceived lack of responsiveness from the township as well as frustration with discriminatory housing practices, the plan signaled a push on the part of African Americans to work collectively and proactively to meet their housing and planning needs and to shape Ardmore's built environment in a manner that accorded with their vision for Ardmore's future. A number of the ideas raised within the plan had been circulating in South Ardmore, and civic leaders and organizations had been working to address many of the concerns the plan identified. However, the *Plan for South Ardmore* crystallized these ideas, along with those that emerged through the planning process, in a comprehensive assessment and action plan. While African Americans contracted professional planners with new forms of expertise to develop the plan, the plan was driven by the desires of African Americans. The plan exemplified the ways African Americans thought broadly about shaping Ardmore's built environment to meet their needs.

The *Plan for South Ardmore* grew out of an effort by the Main Line branch of the National Association for the Advancement of Colored People to develop a plan that would outline the needs of African American residents living in the southern sections of Bryn Mawr and Haverford. When funding for the project ran short, an entity known as the Ardmore Coalition continued the project and shifted the plan's emphasis to Ardmore. The coalition included individuals drawn from the NAACP who lived in Ardmore as well as students and staff from nearby Haverford College. Among the members were individuals such as the Reverend Leonard Jones, longtime pastor of Ardmore's oldest black church; Nolan Atkinson, who would become the first African American township commissioner in 1974; and Lewis Hazzard, president of the African American civic association and longtime business owner. The group's wide-ranging goals included expanding affordable housing opportunities and addressing housing discrimination, as well as "the funding of a Master Plan for the long and short range development of the Community."[7] To finance the plan's $12,000 cost, the coalition raised funds from local institutions, organizations, and individuals.[8]

The *Plan for South Ardmore* reflected a broader shift in planning practices toward increased citizen participation. The plan's introduction stated this commitment explicitly: "The plan for South Ardmore is one of a new breed of planning efforts where the local citizenry analyzes its own problems and charts its own destiny."[9] Ardmore had been the subject of urban renewal plans in 1964 and 1965.[10] Strong resident participation in the creation of the *Plan for South Ardmore* served as a rebuttal to what the authors characterized as the top-down, technocratic planning practices of the past. The NAACP and later the Ardmore Coalition engaged the services of planning practitioners committed to community involvement in planning. Planners were charged with helping African Americans develop a master plan that articulated their needs rather than dictating a plan from a position of professional superiority.

The emerging movement of advocacy planning also informed the *Plan for South Ardmore*. Advocacy planning emphasized the creation of plans centered on particular populations, especially those that had been underserved and had experienced inequality.[11] Early on in the text, the *Plan for South Ardmore* proclaimed, "The plan for the South Ardmore community is a plan by and for the black community."[12] This approach differed radically from past planning efforts in Lower Merion Township.

While Ardmore had been the subject of many comprehensive planning efforts, none had focused on the needs of African Americans. The Frederick Law Olmsted firm produced the earliest planning effort in Lower Merion Township, and the Main Line Citizens Association funded this effort privately. The township authored its first comprehensive plan in 1928, and new plans followed in 1937, 1954, and 1962. The plans addressed issues such as roads, street lighting, housing, and infrastructure; however, each of these plans assumed perspectives that were ostensibly race neutral.[13] The *Plan for South Ardmore* addressed many of the topics found in the Lower Merion Township's comprehensive planning documents, but it centered the racial identities of African Americans in South Ardmore. This community-driven plan privileged the concerns and participation of black residents and sought to respond to the unique needs of a long-standing suburban enclave that historically had limited say in shaping the built environment at larger scales.

Residents contributed directly to the planning process, and the planners translated the ideals of citizen participation into their methods. Early on, the planners reached out to residents through meetings and surveys to gather qualitative and quantitative data. A series of eleven block meetings provided residents opportunities to identify planning concerns. The planners hoped that through such meetings they could gain insight into "families in the community, the quality of housing seen from the viewpoint of the residents, [and] their attitudes toward housing the community."[14] Information gathered through a house-to-house survey of five hundred black households complemented these meetings.

Residents also had opportunities to review and make recommendations on a draft of the plan. At a meeting at Zion Baptist Church (one of Ardmore's predominantly African American churches) in the fall of 1969, approximately two hundred interested residents viewed a draft of the plan and raised questions and comments. A review period followed, with copies of the draft plan available for viewing at two black churches, an African American–owned dry cleaning shop, and South Ardmore's Afrocentric library.[15]

The completed seventy-six-page plan highlighted the needs identified by South Ardmore's African American residents and outlined proposals to respond to those needs. The scope of the plan was holistic, and it addressed a range of issues under the broad categories of housing, zoning, community facilities and services, and economic development. Housing, however, emerged as the leading topic of interest, with residents expressing their concerns about limited housing supply, high costs, and the intrusion of commerce into residential areas.

One of the study's central findings about housing was a strong interrelationship between housing needs and the ages of residents. The *Plan for South Ardmore* argued that available housing stock did not match the needs of Ardmore's residents as they aged. Lacking alternatives, older residents continued to live in houses that were larger than they needed. This in turn limited the availability of affordable housing for young families, who either lived in dwellings too small for their needs or moved away from Ardmore. The result was a community that lacked balance between older and younger residents.

Contrary to these realities, residents envisioned Ardmore as a place that was home to residents across generations. This included young people who desired to remain in the place where they were raised as they began their own households and seniors who wanted to continue living in Ardmore as they aged. To achieve an intergenerational community, the *Plan for South Ardmore* called for the rehabilitation of existing housing and the construction of new housing units for low- and moderate-income families and for the elderly; such housing would respond to the spatial needs of households at different stages of life. Beginning in the late 1960s, African Americans worked to realize their goal of constructing new housing.

## Ardmore Community Development Corporation and the ArdSpring Condominium Project

In 1969, African American civic and religious leaders in South Ardmore, many of whom had been involved with creating the *Plan for South Ardmore,* helped to establish an organization called the Ardmore Community Development Corporation (ACDC). In addition to Leonard Jones, Nolan Atkinson, and Lewis Hazzard, the ACDC included people like Cleopatra Nelson, a civically engaged Ardmore resident and Democratic Party committeewoman, and Daniel Jones Jr., a lifelong Ardmore resident. The ACDC's purpose was "to combat community deterioration and to secure adequate housing facilities and other related services and conditions for the community of Ardmore, Pennsylvania."[16] By focusing specifically on housing rehabilitation and new construction, the ACDC worked to actualize the vision outlined in the *Plan for South Ardmore.*

The ACDC was a local example of a national movement that was under way. The community development corporation model emerged in the late 1960s as part of broader efforts to alleviate poverty in urban and rural areas. Community development corporations focused on geographically defined areas and prioritized community control in the development process. Drawing on private and public funds, community development corporations engaged in activities spanning housing development, job training, community services, and economic development; however, most directed their efforts primarily toward housing.[17] The ACDC applied a model utilized more often in urban and rural contexts to a suburban area.

In 1971, the ACDC began work on the ArdSpring Condominiums, Ardmore's first affordable housing project. The ACDC mobilized public and private resources to plan and carry out the project and maintained the community involvement that had been a hallmark of the comprehensive planning process. In order to respond effectively to community needs within economic constraints, the ACDC developed a plan for condominiums. The ACDC's willingness to think expansively about the suburban home as something other than a detached, single-family house sometimes brought the project into conflict with long-standing ideas about the types of development that did and did not belong on Philadelphia's storied Main Line.

The ACDC drew on both public and private financing to support the ArdSpring Condominiums project. Under a federal program, the Federal Housing Administration insured the mortgage and subsidized the cost of the project by paying a portion of the interest.[18] Private funding to support the purchase of the land came from sources like a breakfast for area businessmen as well as from less conventional approaches, like bake sales.[19] The different ways the ACDC raised money allowed people of varied income levels to contribute to the project.

The property the ACDC purchased lay at the intersection of Spring Avenue and Ardmore Avenue (one of South Ardmore's busiest roads). The site allowed the ACDC a rare opportunity to construct new housing on one of Ardmore's few vacant parcels of land. The location positioned the condominiums amid a variety of building types and land uses that exemplified the type of physical diversity found in South Ardmore, especially in comparison to wealthier sections of the Main Line. In the areas surrounding the site, one could find a handful of stores and a church as well as detached and twin houses. In spite of the great physical variety already present in Ardmore, nothing like the proposed condominiums existed in the immediate vicinity or in South Ardmore. The ArdSpring Condominiums introduced yet another housing type into this environment and thus represented a difference within a difference.

The ACDC, made up primarily of people who lived or worked in Ardmore, sought the participation of other Ardmore residents both in acquiring the building site and in the condominiums' design process. The ACDC contracted the architectural firm of Ueland and Junker, which had worked on other community-initiated affordable housing developments in the Philadelphia area and also had participated in the development of the *Plan for South Ardmore.* While Ueland and Junker presented initial plans, these proposals were subjected to community input in the form of meetings.[20] From the perspective of the ACDC, community buy-in was essential to the project's success, and opening its planning process allowed the ACDC to build community support. Though the project would house only sixteen families, it clearly had larger significance for African Americans in South Ardmore. In the words of the ACDC's 1972 annual report, "A successful conclusion to this Project will provide additional units of housing where most needed, stimulate new growth and vitality and improve the quality of life in the entire Township of Lower Merion."[21]

In the early stages of planning the project, the ACDC encountered resistance from the township concerning the type of housing that it wanted to construct. Initially, the ACDC intended to build a series of row houses. However, the township refused to approve these plans because of a township ordinance prohibiting row houses; the township also rejected a request to grant an exception for the project.[22] The township's prohibition of row houses reflected a long-standing sentiment that such building types were unbecoming to the suburban context because of their strong urban associations. The Main Line had a long history of placing

Row houses like these in Philadelphia were common in the city, but Lower Merion Township ordinances in place in the early 1970s prohibited them. Photograph by the author.

The Centennial Village Condominiums, located in North Ardmore, were among the earliest condominiums in Lower Merion Township. Photograph by the author.

restrictions on building types and land uses, whether by developers or by townships. In addition, the acceleration of housing development in the years following World War II had created a vocal majority citizenry intent on excluding building types (and implicitly populations) they felt did not accord with their vision of the Main Line as a site of spacious, detached, single-family homes.[23]

The members of the leadership team working on the project came together to consider how they might respond to this obstacle, and from their discussions the idea emerged to construct the project as condominiums. Condominiums were a new form of homeownership at the time and had been permitted in the township only since 1970. As a new type of homeownership, the condominium did not carry the historical baggage of the row house.[24] In order to obtain the designation of condominiums, the team had to adapt the initial plans in two key ways. First, the entire building had to have a common roof, rather than separate roofs for each unit as was planned previously. Second, while units would be owned individually, the exterior land would be owned collectively by the condominium association.

## The Completed Project

The finished project, completed in 1975, consisted of sixteen three-story units. Eight adjoining units faced the front, street side of the property and shared a rear wall with eight adjoining units that faced the rear of the property. The project's inclusion of an off-street parking lot also responded to a need outlined in the *Plan for South Ardmore*, as residents felt significant frustration competing with local businesses for parking.[25]

Architect C. Anthony Junker, who had received community input on the plans, expressed a desire to de-emphasize the project's multiunit status and to integrate elements that recalled single-family houses. In Junker's words, he wanted the design to suggest "houses rather than apartments."[26] Similarly, a *Main Line Times* article published in the early stages of planning quoted Junker as saying, "We are working on a very handsome, domestic exterior using the materials we associate with individual homes such as siding and perhaps masonry."[27] The completed project stayed true to this early vision articulated by Junker, and the building's exterior integrated a mix of materials, including brick, aluminum siding, and shingles. The building's first and second floors were composed of red brick, and the third story utilized aluminum siding. In the context of South Ardmore, where most houses were originally built with brick, the use of brick for the majority of the building's exterior also provided a visual linkage between the ArdSpring Condominiums and their neighborhood context.

Even before the specific plans for the ArdSpring Condominiums were set in motion, the *Plan for South Ardmore* had identified the provision of outdoor space

This view of the ArdSpring Condominiums shows the eight units facing West Spring Avenue. Photograph by the author.

The significant setback of the ArdSpring Condominiums gave the property a suburban-style front yard. Photograph by the author.

in new construction as a high priority, noting, "Private outdoor space is desirable for families with children."[28] The condominiums responded to this call, which echoed claims made elsewhere about the benefits of post–World War II suburban housing for children.[29] The front and side of the property were set back thirty feet from the property line, and the parking lot was positioned on the western edge of the property, all of which left a significant amount of open, green space surrounding the building.

At the scale of individual units, the plans accorded with conventional notions of social and private space in the home. The units, each of which had either three or four bedrooms, were generous in size, ranging from 1,100 to 1,300 square feet at a time when the average house constructed in the United States was 1,500 square feet.[30] The design of the units also responded to housing needs that had been laid out in the *Plan for South Ardmore,* which called for the addition of housing units with more bedrooms to meet the needs of families with children.[31] This was an especially pressing issue given concerns about the out-migration of young families unable to find housing. The decision to develop the condominiums as three- and four-bedroom units helped alleviate a shortage of housing for families with children in South Ardmore and also allowed families to accommodate extended family members.

The ArdSpring Condominiums garnered positive responses. The project received a special planning award from the Montgomery County Planning Commission for "outstanding land development,"[32] and the project also received praise from area residents and on the editorial pages of the local *Main Line Times.*[33] More than twenty-five years later, original homeowners still composed half of all residents, and more than three-quarters had lived at ArdSpring for more than ten years.[34]

## Conclusion

Popular representations of post–World War II suburbs cast residents as passive inhabitants in houses and neighborhoods designed by others. The endeavors of African Americans in South Ardmore during the 1960s and 1970s suggested new ways that residents could collectively shape the built environment of the suburbs in which they lived to satisfy their needs. In the years since the development of the ArdSpring Condominiums, affordable housing projects in South Ardmore have taken on varied forms, in many ways reflecting the legacies of the *Plan for South Ardmore* and the ArdSpring Condominiums. Among more recent affordable housing options have been two apartment complexes for senior citizens, intended to allow residents to stay in the area as they age and can no longer maintain larger homes, as well as ten twin homes for first-time home buyers. In all of these efforts, churches, civic associations, nonprofits, and federal financing have continued to play important roles.

## Notes

1. Nolan Atkinson to Ardmore Community Development Corporation supporters, 1972, Ardmore History (1) to 1980, 43, Lower Merion Historical Society, Bala Cynwyd, Pa.

2. See, for instance, Marvin Porch, "The Philadelphia Main Line Negro: A Social, Economic, and Educational Survey" (doctoral dissertation, Temple University, 1938).

3. See, for instance, "Residents Protest Proposal to Rezone Ardmore Block," *Evening Bulletin*, June 19, 1958, Ardmore—Penna—Zoning, *Evening Bulletin* Collection, Temple University Urban Archives, Philadelphia; Jim Myrtetus, "Ardmore Civic Group Attacks Move to Tear Down Homes for Parking," *Evening Bulletin*, March 29, 1970, Ardmore—Penna—Housing and Apartments, *Evening Bulletin* Collection, Temple University Urban Archives, Philadelphia.

4. Jim Myrtetus, "Atkinson Campaigns to Hold Line in Commercial Creep," *Evening Bulletin*, October 26, 1969, Ardmore—Penna—Elections and Politics, *Evening Bulletin* Collection, Temple University Urban Archives, Philadelphia; Michelle Osborn, "'Creeping Commercialism' Fought in South Ardmore," *Evening Bulletin*, May 5, 1970, Ardmore—Penna—Housing and Apartments, *Evening Bulletin* Collection, Temple University Urban Archives, Philadelphia.

5. James Myrtetus, "L. Merion to Study Plea for Ardmore Upzoning," *Evening Bulletin*, September 19, 1969. The Ardmore Progressive Civic Association presented another petition for upzoning in 1973. Ardmore—Penna—Ardmore Progressive Civic Association, *Evening Bulletin* Collection, Temple University Urban Archives, Philadelphia.

6. Ardmore Coalition, *Plan for Housing and Community Improvements in the South Ardmore Community* (Ardmore, Pa.: Ardmore Coalition, 1970); hereafter cited as *Plan for South Ardmore*.

7. Ibid., 2.

8. Ibid.

9. Ibid., 4.

10. While the urban renewal plans themselves are no longer available, an article published in 1962 provides a broader context for urban renewal in Pennsylvania suburbs. See Nick S. Fisfis and Harold Greenberg, "Suburban Renewal in Pennsylvania," *University of Pennsylvania Law Review* 111, no. 1 (November 1962): 61–110.

11. For a discussion of advocacy planning, see Paul Davidoff, "Advocacy and Pluralism in Planning," *Journal of the American Institute of Planners* 31, no. 4 (1965): 331–37.

12. Ardmore Coalition, *Plan for South Ardmore*, 4.

13. Frederick Law Olmsted and Arthur Coleman Comey, "Advance Draft: Main Line District City Planning Report to the Main Line Citizens' Association," December 31, 1919, Lower Merion Historical Society, Bala Cynwyd, Pa.; Lower Merion Township, *A Plan for Lower Merion Township* (Ardmore, Pa.: Lower Merion Township, 1937); Lower Merion Township, *A Plan for the Growth of Lower Merion Township* (Ardmore, Pa.: Lower Merion Township, 1954); Lower Merion Township, *General Comprehensive Plan* (Ardmore, Pa.: Lower Merion Township, 1962).

14. Ardmore Coalition, *Plan for South Ardmore*, 5.

15. Ibid., 6.

16. Ardmore Community Development Corporation, Annual Report, 1971, Ardmore History (1) to 1980, 42A, Lower Merion Historical Society, Bala Cynwyd, Pa.

17. On the growth of community development corporations, see, for instance, Robert Halpern, *Rebuilding the Inner City: A History of Neighborhood Initiatives to Address Poverty in the United States* (New York: Columbia University Press, 1995); Patricia Watkins Murphy and

James V. Cunningham, "Community Development Corporations and the Emergence of Organizing," in *Organizing for Community Controlled Development: Renewing Civil Society* (Thousand Oaks, Calif.: Sage, 2003), 38–52; and Kimberly Johnson, "Community Development Corporations, Participation, and Accountability: The Harlem Urban Development Corporation and the Bedford-Stuyvesant Restoration Corporation," *Annals of the American Academy of Political and Social Science* 594 (July 2004): 109–24.

18. Ardmore Community Development Corporation, Annual Report, 1971.

19. Ardmore Community Development Corporation, Annual Report, 1972, Ardmore History (1) to 1980, 43, Lower Merion Historical Society, Bala Cynwyd, Pa.; Joan Perkolup, "S. Ardmore Group Halfway to Goal in Fund for Low-Cost Housing," *Evening Bulletin,* November 9, 1972, Ardmore Community Development Corporation, *Evening Bulletin* Collection, Temple University Urban Archives, Philadelphia.

20. Joan Filvaroff, "A Condominium for S. Ardmore?," *Main Line Times,* December 9, 1971.

21. Ardmore Community Development Corporation, Annual Report, 1972.

22. Information on how the ACDC team navigated township restrictions is drawn from author interviews conducted in September 2008 with individuals active in the ACDC.

23. For an example of majority residents' responses to postwar suburban development on the Main Line, see Main Line Times, *This Is the Main Line* (Ardmore, Pa.: Main Line Times, 1955).

24. John Dubois, "Low-Income 'Condo' Lauded in Lower Merion," *Evening Bulletin,* December 23, 1977, Ardmore Condominium Houses, *Evening Bulletin* Collection, Temple University Urban Archives, Philadelphia.

25. Ardmore Coalition, *Plan for South Ardmore,* 13.

26. Dubois, "Low Income 'Condo' Lauded."

27. Filvaroff, "A Condominium for S. Ardmore?"

28. Ardmore Coalition, *Plan for South Ardmore,* 41.

29. Gwendolyn Wright, *Building the Dream: A Social History of Housing in America* (Cambridge, Mass.: MIT Press, 1981), 254.

30. National Association of Home Builders, "From Modest to McMansion: The Average Square Footage of a New Single-Family Home," *Housing Facts, Figures and Trends,* March 2006.

31. Ardmore Coalition, *Plan for South Ardmore,* 13.

32. Dubois, "Low-Income 'Condo' Lauded."

33. "Housing for South Ardmore," *Main Line Times,* December 16, 1971.

34. Property records, Montgomery County Board of Assessors, http://propertyrecords .montcopa.org.

# 3

# Defending "Women Who Stand by the Sink"

## Suburban Homemakers and Anti-ERA Activism in New York State

STACIE TARANTO

By 1974, the feminist-backed Equal Rights Amendment (ERA) to the U.S. Constitution was at a standstill after Phyllis Schlafly and other conservative "family values" activists had organized against it. The ERA contained a single sentence: "Equality of rights under the law shall not be denied or abridged . . . on account of sex."[1] The amendment was first advocated by a small faction of feminists in 1923, but it did not win broad support until the mid- to late 1960s, when the Presidential Commission on the Status of Women, labor unions, and the broader modern women's movement began promoting it. Proponents were buoyed by the fact that in recent years, sweeping new federal and state laws had passed granting expanded legal rights to African Americans and women. Instead of continuing to go through the legal code issue by issue—seeking equal rights for women in areas such as employment, housing, and education—ERA proponents hoped to cover women in all areas of the law with a single amendment to the U.S. Constitution. With little organized opposition yet in place, Congress easily passed the ERA in 1972; the amendment then had to be approved by at least thirty-eight states before the Constitution could be amended. Thirty states, including New York, ratified the ERA in its first year, at which point opponents—led by Phyllis Schlafly and her growing national Stop ERA organization—mobilized against the amendment.[2]

Opponents feared that the ERA would muddy clearly delineated roles and responsibilities for each sex, and, as a result, society and its basic building block—the traditional nuclear family—would be upended. They claimed that homemakers would be compelled to enter the workforce while their children languished in state-run day care, that women would have to serve in military combat, and that public restrooms would no longer be sex segregated. In essence, they worried that by offering women the same legal rights as men, the state would be mandating the same expectations for women and men. Female homemakers would be forced to work outside the home to become "equal" with men, and so on.[3]

Proponents of the ERA tried to counter these charges, sometimes with very dense legal explanations. They noted, for example, that homemakers would not be forced to work outside of the home because the Thirteenth Amendment to the U.S. Constitution, which had abolished slavery, made it illegal to compel someone to work against his or her will—just as the privacy clause in the Constitution would maintain the status of restrooms and other sex-segregated public facilities. Support for the ERA was hurt by the constant defensive posture of proponents, which made it harder for them to articulate what specific benefits the amendment would provide for women.[4]

When the federal ERA's progress came to a grinding halt around 1974, women's rights groups in New York began pushing for a state-level ERA. As one pamphlet argued, "We have no idea when, if ever, the necessary number of states will ratify the U.S. ERA," but "the people of New York State should . . . be guaranteed the right of equal treatment under the law."[5] Supporters assumed that the amendment to the state constitution would pass easily in Albany and reinvigorate the federal campaign. New York, after all, was the epicenter of the feminist movement. Even leading opponent Phyllis Schlafly believed that the amendment would pass in the home state of feminist luminaries such as Betty Friedan and Congresswoman Bella Abzug, and she decided against shifting her group's resources to New York. The state ERA contained the same language as its federal corollary, and more than one hundred organizations endorsed it, including feminist groups and the New York State Democratic and Republican Parties. After all, many figured, who could quibble with equal rights? But despite its perceived inevitability, the state ERA failed by four hundred thousand votes—largely owing to its defeat in the suburbs of New York City, which had grown rapidly in size and political importance since World War II.[6]

This chapter examines how a grassroots network of mostly Catholic, middle-class, suburban white women in New York organized against the state ERA in order to protect their vision for women and the family. These women, who were previously uninterested in politics, mobilized once politics seemed to overlap with issues related to the family and domesticity. They formed a statewide opposition group called Operation Wakeup, which they hoped would "wake up" New Yorkers to the alleged threats posed by the state ERA. One Long Island homemaker likewise saw herself defending fellow "women who stand by the sink."[7] Several scholars, especially those who study Phyllis Schlafly, have analyzed why some women opposed the ERA, but few have examined the fact that many anti-ERA activists were first-generation suburbanites. In New York State, opponents typically had grown up in the working-class ethnic enclaves of New York City. As new members of the suburban middle class, the women were proud that they, unlike some of their mothers, could be full-time homemakers. Many of their husbands had taken advantage of the GI Bill's government-backed mortgages to move into all-white, redlined suburbs outside New York City. The women felt that their families had attained the American Dream—having a male breadwinner and female homemaker in a single-family, suburban home—and they were determined to protect their lifestyle from the perceived onslaught of the state ERA.

Like their impetus to organize, the women's political tactics also reflected how suburban and domestic their lives had become in recent years. Pro-ERA advocates were headquartered in New York City and waged a far more expensive, top-down campaign with paid media advertising. In contrast, opponents had a shoestring budget that was sustained only by the fund-raising tactics that they had honed in local church and civic groups. The women held neighborhood coffee klatches, collected funds in busy shopping centers, spread the word at Little League games, and turned to sympathetic local groups, especially antiabortion organizations, for additional money and volunteers. These tactics enabled the women to form a strong grassroots network of people who perceived feminism in general and the state ERA in particular as affronts to the family (and, by extension, to the women's newly acquired suburban privilege). This essay therefore helps to shift the focus away from the Goldwater and Reagan forces of Sunbelt conservatism that have disproportionately dominated recent historiography on the New Right. By examining how the politics of place overlapped with gender politics in New York's unsuccessful state ERA campaign, this chapter returns northern suburbanites, many of them first-generation homemakers, to their rightful place in the history of modern conservatism.[8]

## Suburban Growth and the Seeds of Protecting Newly Acquired Privilege

The defeat of New York's ERA hinged on a sizable majority of voters opposing the amendment in the four increasingly powerful and conservative suburban counties right outside New York City. These counties—Nassau and Suffolk to the east on Long Island, and Rockland and Westchester to the north and west—experienced rapid growth in the decades after World War II. By 1980, a quarter of all votes in the state came from those four counties. As the political influence of these counties grew, the state's political culture moved to the right. The suburban women who opposed measures like the state ERA helped facilitate this shift. By opposing feminist-backed issues such as the ERA and legal abortion (the New York State Right to Life Party was founded on Long Island in 1970), self-declared "average housewives" across these four counties invented a new grassroots conservatism that the GOP's right wing seized upon in the years before 1980. In doing so, the previously small and ineffective conservative faction of the state's Republican Party became more powerful in these populous suburban counties. With this additional electoral support in these downstate suburbs, conservatives eventually had enough support to usurp the power of the more moderate "Rockefeller Republican" wing of the party, which was based in New York City and, like Governor Nelson Rockefeller himself, had long supported feminist measures such as the state's abortion reform law in 1970.[9]

To understand this shift to the right, it is instructive to begin by looking at what drew opponents to the suburbs—to get a better sense of what they later believed they were fighting to protect. A decade or more before the contentious state ERA battle, most opponents-to-be harbored a very different concern: finding space to accommodate their expanding families. The women came from backgrounds as varied as the tapestry of New York City's neighborhoods from which they emerged; still, they shared certain common experiences. Most had been born during the early years of the Great Depression and grew up in the city's working-class white ethnic enclaves. Their lives were organized around family activities and, often, around the daily rhythms of a Catholic parish. Some of the women had taken college classes or worked as secretaries before getting married in their early twenties. Their husbands generally had similar family backgrounds, and many had served in noncombat military roles during the 1950s—an affiliation that later helped some people move to the suburbs more easily by qualifying for low-interest GI mortgages. Many of the women had children right after marrying and moved to the outer reaches of Queens, Brooklyn, and the Bronx. Their young families squeezed into small apartments as the men finished college degrees and additional schooling at night. Most of the women stayed at home full-time with their children—an opportunity that they relished, and one that had eluded some of their working-class mothers. As their husbands finished their degrees and settled into stable middle-class employment, the women began pining for better schools and more space for their growing broods in the suburbs.[10]

The women and their families generally moved in the late fifties and early sixties to suburban hamlets across the four counties surrounding New York City. They were not the first generation of migrants to settle in these counties. Cheaper mass-production techniques in the housing industry and government-backed mortgages for veterans had led to housing and population surges in these suburbs right after World War II. Opponents of the state ERA comprised a second wave of younger suburban dwellers—many of their families even bought homes from the original owners who had settled there after the war. The houses that they bought varied: from modest Levitt-style ranches and bungalows built in recent decades to more spacious, older Victorian and colonial homes. But the actual style of the house was not important for these upwardly mobile new entrants into the middle class. Simply owning a home in the suburbs—*any* single-family home—and attending to it and to their young families full-time was how many of these women defined success.[11]

The suburbs that the women moved to in the late fifties and early sixties were teeming with developing neighborhoods and young families. When Annette Stern—who would go on to lead the statewide opposition to the ERA—first moved with her husband and children from the Bronx to the Westchester suburb of Mount Vernon in 1958, she and her family joined others doing the same. In Westchester County by 1960, there were nearly four hundred children under the age of five for every one thousand women of childbearing age. Rapid growth in the numbers of expanding families looking to move to the suburbs led to the construction of new homes. Almost a third of all homes in Westchester County in 1960 had been built in the prior ten years.[12]

Massive population growth also occurred in the other three surrounding suburban counties, largely resulting from the construction of new state highways and infrastructure projects. The 1958 completion of the Long Island Expressway—a six-lane highway that runs eastward through the middle of the island from Manhattan through most of Suffolk County—led Nassau County, home to the iconic Levittown community, to experience a 93 percent population increase from 1950 to 1960. Neighboring Suffolk County underwent even more impressive growth, with a 142 percent population surge in that decade alone.[13] Meanwhile, Rockland County to the northwest of New York City had a 53 percent population increase from 1950 to 1960, with most of that growth occurring after the Tappan Zee Bridge, which connects the area to neighboring Westchester County, opened in 1955. A startling 26 percent of all single-family homes in Rockland County in 1960 had been built in the prior five years, after the bridge and the Palisades Parkway and New York State Thruway began servicing the area.[14]

The suburbs could seem like paradise for some women, but they were a highly racially homogeneous slice of utopia. Many white women left New York City's outer boroughs in the late fifties and early sixties when racial turnover was occurring in their neighborhoods. In 1960, for example, 8.5 percent of residents in Queens were nonwhite. While this percentage was far short of a majority, it represented a startling 142 percent increase over 1950—and the trend continued throughout the sixties, with the proportion of nonwhite residents in Queens increasing another 73 percent by 1970. In Brooklyn, the proportion of nonwhite residents also rose throughout the fifties (an 86 percent increase) and sixties (an 85 percent increase).

As more people of color moved into formerly white working-class neighborhoods across New York City, white families headed to the suburbs. The persistence of racial covenants and Federal Housing Administration redlining in the mortgage industry ensured that most of their growing suburban towns were nearly all white. Long Island's Nassau County was, for instance, 97 percent white in 1960. The proportion of white people in many towns along the county's south shore—which had previously been marshland and was almost entirely devoted to new construction of single-family homes—approached nearly 99 percent in 1960. Undoubtedly, the politicized form of the family that many women later sought to protect from the state ERA was shaped, consciously or not, by the racial and demographic makeup of their new suburban surroundings.[15]

These statistics help to give a sense of the bustling suburbs that the women who would later oppose the state ERA first encountered upon leaving New York City in the late fifties and early sixties. New construction abounded as highways and shopping centers changed formally rural pastures into bustling metropolises. Young white families like theirs were everywhere, populating the housing developments, schools, parks, and civic groups. It was a lifestyle that many first-generation suburbanites and homemakers would later try to defend from the perceived threat of feminism and the state ERA—tapping into the suburban infrastructure that surrounded them as they organized to do so.

## Operation Wakeup and the 1974–1975 Legislative Sessions

The process by which previously apolitical suburban women mobilized against the state ERA began slowly in 1974. Feminist groups in New York, in particular the National Organization for Women (NOW), began lobbying legislators for a state ERA in the late sixties. But as lawmakers seemingly had more pressing issues like budgetary matters to contend with first, the state ERA did not emerge from committee for a vote until the spring of 1974. When it did, proponents were confident that it would pass very easily, if not quickly. First the state assembly and senate would have to pass the amendment in two consecutive years (1974 and 1975), and then the ERA would be placed on the ballot as a referendum in November 1975 for voters in New York to consider. The process was cumbersome, but feminist groups and other proponents were confident that the amendment would pass. Women accounted for roughly 59 percent of the state's population in 1974, and nearly 41 percent of them worked outside the home. Proponents surmised that these statistics would translate into wide support for the state ERA—both from legislators hoping to win votes from the state's large female population and from women themselves, especially those who faced job discrimination or supported themselves independently.[16]

In the spring of 1974, the assembly easily passed the amendment while opponents began to form a spiderweb of dissent that was anchored in the suburbs of
New York City. In Westchester County that spring, for example, the aforementioned
Annette Stern, who became the statewide opposition leader, heard feminist icon
Betty Friedan talk about the ERA on the radio. In Stern's view, Friedan was "making
it sound like the home was a prison and . . . that child care was slavery," and "that it
was okay to work for a boss, but not to do things for your husband."[17] Stern, a married homemaker with three young boys from the affluent town of Harrison, decided
to convene a meeting of like-minded individuals because, as she said, "nobody was
speaking for what I consider[ed] my kind of woman," and "it made me curious
about the ERA." She began to spread the word around her community—at Little
League games, dentists' offices, coffee klatches, and the like—until nearly one hundred people showed up at her home for the first meeting of a group that they named
Women UNited to Defend Existing Rights (WUNDER). A similar group with four
hundred members called Women for Honest Equality in National Women's Groups
(WHEN) was formed on Long Island in November 1974. Individual groups chose
different names, but their motivations were the same: they wanted to stop feminists
in general and the state ERA in particular from destroying the "traditional" family
and the suburban and domestic lifestyles that they had built in recent years.[18]

As opposition groups first formed across New York State in the spring of 1974,
they functioned largely unaware of one another—with Phyllis Schlafly's nationally
circulated anti-ERA newsletter the *Phyllis Schlafly Report* as one of the only links
to bind them. A masterful organizer, Schlafly understood the power of projecting
a uniform national message to oppose the federal and various state ERAs. When
Claire Middleton, a housewife living near Plattsburgh in upstate New York wrote
to Schlafly to tell her about her opposition group, called Happiness of Woman-
hood (HOW), Schlafly replied, "You are on sound ground if you stick to the arguments in my newsletters and do not stray afield."[19] Nearly all the local anti-ERA
leaders in New York subscribed to Schlafly's newsletter upon forming their groups.
Schlafly, who was in New York City at the time, was even able to attend the first
gathering of WUNDER at Annette Stern's home in Westchester. She was invited
by the women planning the inaugural meeting, whose real purpose in writing to
Schlafly was to inquire about receiving the newsletter. The process snowballed
across the state to the point where Pat Yungbluth, president of NOW's upstate
branch in Buffalo, complained about a woman in her area "who looks, sounds, and
argues like Phyllis Schlafly."[20]

Claire Middleton's initial outreach to Schlafly also highlighted how antiabortion
activism fueled the anti-ERA movement. In her first letter to Schlafly, Middleton
later recalled in an interview, "I told her that my husband was chairman of the

[New York State] Right to Life Committee, so she knew I was genuine."[21] Schlafly enthusiastically responded to the letter, commending Middleton's nascent anti-ERA activism and writing, "Since your husband is chairman of New York State Right to Life, I know you are OK!"[22] Middleton's antiabortion credentials had secured Schlafly's trust. The antiabortion and anti-ERA movements were ideologically similar, and both attracted people who believed that feminist-backed goals would undermine traditional family life. Schlafly also led the charge in claiming—without concrete proof—that the ERA would make it impossible to outlaw abortion. She likely understood that contacts from the antiabortion movement would be a valuable source of money and volunteers for the anti-ERA movement. Veterans of the antiabortion movement who previously had opened their pocketbooks, testified before legislative committees, and lobbied politicians in the abortion debates were apt to do so again for a cause that they deemed compatible with theirs.

But without a unified effort from all the anti-ERA groups in the state, the women's nascent political efforts were scattered and ineffective—a situation that prompted the creation of Operation Wakeup, an umbrella group that would connect the individual pockets of resistance that had sprung up across the state. When Claire Middleton's group was in Albany one day, she was interviewed by a syndicated radio host covering the capital. Middleton received a telephone call soon after from Lillian Koegler in Westchester County, who knew of her through the New York State Right to Life Committee (RTLC). Koegler, a founding member of WUNDER, the group that was started at Annette Stern's home, had heard Middleton on the radio; she hoped that her opposition group in Westchester could coordinate efforts with Middleton's group upstate in Plattsburgh. Middleton agreed, and in July 1974 Operation Wakeup held its first meeting. Wakeup continued to grow through personal and RTLC contacts throughout 1974, until it eventually encompassed twenty-four local groups and an estimated one hundred thousand people. Stern became Wakeup's president, and the group was led primarily by first-generation suburban women in the four counties surrounding New York City.[23]

Most members of Wakeup were middle- to upper-middle-class white Catholic homemakers in their thirties and forties who previously had been apolitical. Men made up a small percentage of the group, as did women who worked outside the home and non-Catholics. The group's president, Annette Stern, was Jewish, for example, and some Mormons were represented upstate. Although the New York State Conservative Party endorsed Wakeup's efforts, the party politics of the group's members varied. Wakeup attracted both Democrats and Republicans who objected to their parties' support for the state ERA; most were suburban women who had paid little attention to politics until the state ERA seemingly began to threaten their everyday and family lives.[24]

Wakeup's growing influence was evident, if not entirely convincing, when the assembly reconvened for a successful vote on the state ERA in March 1975. Several assembly members mentioned Wakeup's lobbying efforts in the debate that preceded the vote. Even as the assembly debated that day, the gallery above was packed with backers and opponents of the state ERA. Women's groups such as NOW had followed the amendment for years, but the presence of anti-ERA groups in the gallery was new. In the end, however, the assembly approved the state ERA by a vote of 128 to 15. Many legislators were squeamish about appearing to deny equal rights to women, especially in a state where 59 percent of residents were female. Wakeup also lacked the money and high profile of the groups supporting the state ERA—an assemblage of feminist, civic, and political organizations, including the state's Democratic and Republican Parties.[25]

Wakeup's increased visibility in the 1975 legislative session led proponents to form the New York Coalition for Equal Rights (CER) in May 1975 to push the state senate to pass the ERA. The need for a coalition to compete with opponents was especially evident after Wakeup pressed for and won public hearings that March, which roughly five hundred people on both sides attended to air their views. The CER was an umbrella organization designed to unite various groups in the state supporting the ERA. Their membership eventually encompassed one hundred civic, women's, political, and religious groups across the ideological and geographic spectrum, although many were left-leaning and feminist ones based in and around New York City. The CER was managed by Sandra Turner, a paid organizer with deep political experience. Although she had worked on a statewide political campaign before—helping to elect Democrat Mary Anne Krupsak as lieutenant governor in 1974—Turner's experience was much greater in New York City. This contributed to the coalition's more urban orientation, which failed to appeal to voters, especially homemakers in the surrounding suburbs.[26]

With the CER in place, proponents helped stifle a last-minute procedural tactic designed to defeat the state ERA, and the amendment cleared the senate soon after on May 21, 1975, by a wide margin of forty-four to fourteen votes. Wakeup had moved eleven senators into its camp since 1974, but this was not enough to stymie the state ERA's progress. Proponents were thrilled: the amendment would now be placed on the ballot for what they assumed would be an easy statewide victory. The members of Wakeup were disappointed, but they vowed to keep up their fight in the six months leading up to the referendum. Most had become involved in the campaign because they felt that the state ERA would end life as they knew it. If they could convince enough voters to feel the same way by November 1975, they could defeat one of feminists' biggest goals in the state that was the epicenter of the modern women's liberation movement.[27]

## Toward Victory: Building a "Well-Organized, Well-Oiled Machine"

While the CER struggled to compete in the five months leading up to the election, Wakeup built on the deep statewide organization that it had begun amassing during the legislative debates of 1974 and 1975. As Carol DeSaram, president of NOW in New York State, surmised, "It was incredibly naïve of us to think we were dealing with a bunch of sincere but misguided housewives. This was a well-organized, well-oiled machine."[28] Wakeup had several "area contacts" across the state to coordinate local fund-raising, advertising, and debate and media requests. The group also created a "news release chain" through which relevant events across the state, such as debates, would be reported to the central leadership operating out of Stern's home in Westchester, and the information would then be combined and reissued in the form of press releases. By mid-September 1975, Wakeup was sending weekly press releases—detailing its overall message and recent activities—to four hundred television, radio, and newspaper contacts across the state. The CER also installed volunteer representatives in each of New York's sixty-two counties to arrange events and advertising locally. A press kit and newsletters helped keep everyone connected. But the CER did not spring up organically across the state, and much of its high-level support, money, and political experience was centered in New York City.[29]

Although neither side had a budget on par with the typical amount spent in a statewide campaign, the CER enjoyed a sizable financial advantage over Wakeup. The CER frequently asked affiliate groups like NOW to donate to the cause. It sold T-shirts for five dollars each and tried a variety of gimmicks to raise awareness and funds, such as a bike-a-thon across Brooklyn led by local politicians supporting the state ERA. The CER also saved money by having its television and radio advertisements produced by firms upstate that charged less than those in New York City. Despite these efforts, the CER fell short of its $200,000 fund-raising goal, only bringing in about $80,000 and ending the campaign $8,000 in debt. Wakeup, meanwhile, reported raising a total of about $5,000 throughout the campaign, all coming from grassroots fund-raising events such as coffee klatches, bake sales, canvassing in shopping centers, and cocktail parties.[30]

Wakeup relied on tactics that its members had honed in the past—as suburban homemakers looking to stretch household dollars and as members of local cash-strapped organizations such as church groups and PTAs. Annette Stern's good friend Lucille Bachman was married to a printer who produced Wakeup's literature for pennies a page. Members called in to daytime radio shows to air their views—reaching countless housewives across the state without spending a dime—and advertised their cause for free in church bulletins and circulars that were given away at supermarkets. Sympathetic groups, many religiously oriented, also helped out.

The Knights of Columbus, the Catholic fraternal organization, spent about $1,000 on radio time, while RTLC groups spread the word and the conservative John Birch Society doled out $704 in advertising. Wakeup even filed a lawsuit charging that the CER was being supported by the state government and taxpayer dollars since many government agencies and officials endorsed the amendment. In late October 1975 the New York State Supreme Court ruled in Wakeup's favor, but with the November 4 election less than two weeks away, the group worried that substantial damage had already been done. Polls in the final weeks showed that 60–70 percent of New Yorkers favored the state ERA, and Wakeup continued to worry about the CER's more prolific supporters—including almost all of the state's major newspapers and media outlets.[31]

As the election returns began to trickle in on November 4, however, they confirmed the exact opposite result: the state ERA was defeated by a wide margin—57 percent to 43 percent. The outcome moved Wakeup to draw conclusions far beyond the parameters of state politics. Annette Stern argued that the defeat proved that feminists supporting the ERA were a radical fringe. The "women who purportedly speak for women truly don't," she said.[32] Many like Phyllis Schlafly considered the results in New York and neighboring New Jersey—both states with strong feminist movements that had nevertheless rejected state ERAs in 1975—to be a death knell for the faltering federal ERA, which was then stalled at four states short of ratification. Stern likewise promised to use her 100,000-member organization to convince the New York State Legislature to rescind its approval of the federal ERA, which it had passed in 1972. The defeats in New York and New Jersey allegedly inspired federal ERA rescission movements in fourteen other states as well. While none of these initiatives succeeded, the election results in New York, the epicenter of the feminist movement, were arguably a symbolic rejection of the federal ERA.[33]

A postmortem on the election concluded that Wakeup's victory hinged on the votes of women ages eighteen to fifty-nine in the state—particularly suburban Catholic women energized by issues such as abortion. Exit polling showed that women in that demographic voted in higher numbers than any other group that year. Led by married suburban women, 3 million New Yorkers voted on the state ERA: roughly 1.3 million (43 percent) for it and 1.7 million (57 percent) against it. These numbers were likely skewed in Wakeup's favor because the ballots in New York City, the proponents' stronghold, contained only a series of questions, propositions, and constitutional amendments, mostly about rather dull city charter and bond issues; in the surrounding suburbs and upstate, areas of strength for Wakeup, ballots included local races that drew voters to the polls. Perhaps as a result, while the state ERA won by 59 percent to 41 percent in New York City, it lost by 38 percent to 62 percent when the remaining counties in the state were added together.

In the four counties right outside the city where most of Wakeup's leaders lived, the state ERA was defeated by majorities ranging from 52 percent to 61 percent. Since these were very densely populated counties, the state ERA's defeat in these suburban areas was more impactful than its failure in less populous counties upstate, which were traditionally conservative, and rural areas of the state, where the amendment was defeated by as much as 72 percent in some places.[34]

One of the most important by-products of the state ERA fight in New York was the debate about the intersection of politics and family life. As its popular slogan proclaimed, the modern women's movement had helped to make "the personal political" by pursuing matters related to reproduction, motherhood, and child care. In response, many women such as Annette Stern—who, as she later recalled, previously had been too shy to "even ask a question at a PTA meeting" before the state ERA battle—were compelled to enter the public arena to contest this vision of women and the family.[35] The ERA's vague language led opponents and proponents alike to ascribe what they wanted to it, morphing a single-sentence amendment into a symbol of everything from the promise of more equitable credit laws to the onslaught of a unisex society that would decimate "traditional" family life.

Opposing feminist-backed issues such as the state ERA enabled the previously small and politically insignificant conservative faction of the New York State Republican Party to gain power. Conservative Republicans had traditionally had a foothold only in the more rural counties upstate, with a scattering of support in the four downstate suburban counties. But the population of these suburban counties outside New York City exploded in the fifties and sixties. Suffolk County experienced a whopping 142 percent increase from 1950 to 1960, while Westchester grew by 29 percent and Nassau by 93 percent in that period; Rockland had its biggest surge from 1960 to 1970, with a 67 percent increase. As this happened, many first-generation suburban women—including those who later opposed the state ERA—began to see the modern women's liberation movement as a threat to their suburban privilege. The women mobilized a powerful conservative "family values" swing vote in the state—one that defeated the state ERA in 1975 and that conservative Republicans tapped into soon after to increase their electoral advantage.[36]

By 1980, conservative, antifeminist Republicans with suburban appeal had usurped power from the more liberal, profeminist "Rockefeller Republicans" who were based in New York City and had long dominated the state's GOP. When viewed in this light, the failed New York State ERA campaign in 1975 is significant not only because a feminist-backed amendment was defeated in an intellectual and political center of the modern women's movement. The failure is also noteworthy as a crucial step in the migration of political power toward the right and into the suburbs in the mid- to late 1970s in New York State and elsewhere in the nation.[37]

## Notes

1. Jane J. Mansbridge, *Why We Lost the ERA* (Chicago: University of Chicago Press, 1986), 1.

2. Donald T. Critchlow, *Phyllis Schlafly and Grassroots Conservatism* (Princeton, N.J.: Princeton University Press, 2005), 212–42; Claire Middleton, telephone interview by author, January 21, 2008.

3. "Ambitious Project," *Operation Wakeup Newsletter,* undated, ERA Opposition Arguments US and NYS incl. Schlafly Folder, Box 1, L0101-87 Karen S. Burstein Women's Issues Files (hereafter cited as Burstein Files), New York State Archives, Cultural Education Center, Albany, N.Y. (hereafter cited as NYSA); Judy Klemesrud, "As New York Vote on Equal Rights Nears, Two Sides Speak Out; Pro Con," *New York Times,* September 18, 1975, 46; Jane S. De Hart, "Gender on the Right: Meanings behind the Existential Scream," *Gender & History* 3, no. 3 (Autumn 1991): 254–56.

4. State of New York, Senate, New York State Equal Rights Amendment Debate, Bill No. S. 2824, transcript, microfilm (May 21, 1975), 5290–322, 5414–15, 5475, 5454–55, 5581, Senate Records Office, Capitol Building, Albany, N.Y. (hereafter cited as SRO).

5. League of Women Voters of New York State, *Fable and Facts: The Equal Rights Amendment in New York State,* pamphlet, undated, ERA State Campaign Literature Folder, Box 1, Burstein Files, NYSA.

6. Ibid.; Lawrence Klepner and Lesle Lustgarten to Senator Karen S. Burstein, undated 1975, ERA-NY State Campaign Organiz. Speakers Data Folder, Burstein Files, NYSA.

7. Quoted in "End of an ERA?," *Time,* November 17, 1975, 65.

8. "Housewives, $5,000 Beat ERA," *Newburgh News,* December 3, 1975, personal collection of Virginia Lavan Taylor; Lisa Cronin Wohl, "The ERA: What the Hell Happened in New York?," *Ms.,* March 1976, 92, 96.

9. "Results of Voting in the City and Suburbs: Vote on ERA," *New York Times,* November 6, 1975, 86; Richard M. Scammon and Ben J. Wattenberg, *The Real Majority* (New York: Coward-McCann, 1970), 175–84.

10. Annette Stern, telephone interview by author, July 18, 2011; Theresa Anselmi, interview by author, June 7, 2011, West Nyack, N.Y.; Margaret Fitton, interview by author, June 7, 2011, West Nyack, N.Y.; Jane Gilroy, interview by author, June 4, 2011, Merrick, N.Y.

11. Stern, interview; Anselmi, interview; Fitton, interview; Gilroy, interview; Rosalyn Baxandall and Elizabeth Ewen, *Picture Windows: How the Suburbs Happened* (New York: Basic Books, 2000), 88–105.

12. Westchester County Records Housing Deed for Harold P. and Annette Stern, August 15, 1967, Department of Assessment, City Hall, Mount Vernon, N.Y.; U.S. Bureau of the Census, *1960 Census of Population,* Vol. 1, Pt. 34 (Washington, D.C.: Government Printing Office, 1963), 34–50, http://www.census.gov; U.S. Bureau of the Census, *1960 Census of Housing,* Vol. 1, Pt. 6 (Washington, D.C.: Government Printing Office, 1963), 34–36, http://www.census.gov.

13. Edward J. Smits, *Nassau: Suburbia, U.S.A.* (Garden City, N.Y.: Doubleday, 1974), 199, 241; U.S. Bureau of the Census, *1960 Census of Population,* Vol. 1, Pt. 34, 34–13, 34–19; U.S. Bureau of the Census, *1970 Census of Population,* Vol. 1, Pt. 34, Sec. 1 (Washington, D.C.: Government Printing Office, 1974), 34–4, http://www.census.gov.

14. Jeff Canning, "Westchester County since World War II: A Changing People in a Changing Landscape," in *Westchester County: The Past Hundred Years, 1883–1983,* ed. Marilyn E.

Weigold (Valhalla, N.Y.: Westchester County Historical Society, 1983), 212; Linda Zimmerman, ed., *Rockland County: Century of History, 1900–2000* (New City, N.Y.: Historical Society of Rockland County, 2002), 178–80; U.S. Bureau of the Census, *1960 Census of Housing*, Vol. 1, Pt. 6, 34–36.

15. Jane Gilroy, "Question: Intra-Church Relations Committee," e-mail message to author, July 28, 2011; Kenneth T. Jackson, *Crabgrass Frontier: The Suburbanization of the United States* (New York: Oxford University Press, 1985), 195–211, 244–45; Smits, *Nassau*, 199; U.S. Bureau of the Census, *1960 Census of Population*, Vol. 1, Pt. 34, 34–49; U.S. Bureau of the Census, *1970 Census of Population*, Vol. 1, Pt. 34, Sec. 1, 34–72.

16. "Ginsburg to Rap on ERA," *New Feminist* 2, no. 8 (Fall 1969): 3, Herstory, Microforms, New York Public Library, Astor, Lenox, and Tilden Foundations, New York (hereafter cited as NYPL); "ERA Petitions Sent to Ginsburg," *NOW LI*, March 26, 1970, 6, Herstory, Microforms, NYPL; Pro-ERA Coalition, memorandum, undated 1975, ERA-NY Legislative Campaign Folder, Box 1, Burstein Files, NYSA; Nancy E. Baker, "'Too Much to Lose, Too Little to Gain': The Role of Rescission Movements in the Equal Rights Amendment Battle, 1972–1982" (doctoral dissertation, Harvard University, 2003), 210–15.

17. Annette Stern, telephone interview by author, February 16, 2008; State of New York, Assembly, New York State Equal Rights Amendment Debate, Bill No. A. 9030-A, transcript (April 24, 1974), 5147–69, Box 2, L0016 Transcripts of Assembly Debates 1974–79, NYSA.

18. Quotation from Annette Stern, interview with Phyllis Graham, Part I, undated 1976, *Eagle Forum Presents*, WALK Radio Long Island, digitized MP3 recording, personal collection of Phyllis Graham; Pamela Warrick, "Senate Wavering on Rights Measure," *Newsday*, March 31, 1975, ERA-NY Legislative Campaign Folder, Box 1, Burstein Files, NYSA; Klemesrud, "As New York Vote on Equal Rights Nears," 46; Stern, interview, February 16, 2008; Virginia Lavan Taylor, telephone interview by author, March 3, 2008.

19. Phyllis Schlafly to Claire Middleton, April 10, 1974, personal collection of Claire Middleton; Middleton, interview.

20. Pat Yungbluth to Jan Pittman-Liebman, August 24, 1975, Folder 32, Carton 197, National Organization for Women Collection, Schlesinger Library, Radcliffe Institute for Advanced Study, Harvard University, Cambridge, Mass. (hereafter cited as SL); Stern, interview, February 16, 2008; Taylor, interview.

21. Middleton, interview.

22. Schlafly to Middleton, April 10, 1974.

23. Rudolph P. Blaum, *E.R.A. in an Era of Error* (Forest Hills, N.Y.: John Paul Jones Enterprises, 1977), 23–25, 46; "New Women's Group Claims ERA Dangers," *Daily Item*, June 6, 1974, 25, personal collection of Annette Stern; Operation Wakeup letterhead, undated, personal collection of Annette Stern; Klemesrud, "As New York Vote on Equal Rights Nears," 46; Middleton, interview.

24. Operation Wakeup letterhead; State of New York, Senate, Hearings of the Senate Judiciary Committee on the New York State Equal Rights Amendment, Bill No. S. 2824, transcript, microfilm (March 11, 1975), 197–98, SRO; "ERA Defeat: 'Lies,' or 'Out of Touch'?," *Long Island Press*, November 5, 1975, 1, 3, Microforms, Long Island Division, Queens Borough Public Library, Jamaica, N.Y.; Middleton, interview; Stern, interview, February 16, 2008.

25. State of New York, Assembly, New York State Equal Rights Amendment Debate, Bill No. A. 2543, transcript (February 18, 1975), 725, 737–45, 750, 761, 765, Box 5, L0016 Transcripts

of Assembly Debates 1974–79, NYSA; Warrick, "Senate Wavering on Rights Measure"; Pro-ERA Coalition, memorandum, undated 1975; Klepner and Lustgarten to Burstein, undated 1975.

26. Pro-ERA Coalition, memorandum, undated 1975, 1–14; "Some Hits and Misses at ERA Hearing," *Long Island Press,* March 12, 1975, ERA-NY State Press Con. Non-Camp. Lit. Folder, Burstein Files, NYSA; Paula Berstein, "ERA Debate: Will Passage Help or Hurt?," *New York Daily News,* April 8, 1975, ERA-NY State Press Con. Non-Camp. Lit. Folder, Burstein Files, NYSA; Klemesrud, "As New York Vote on Equal Rights Nears," 46; Phyllis Schlafly, telephone interview by author, January 19, 2007.

27. "Special Edition: ERA Alert," *Woman Lobbyist* 1, no. 4 (May 5, 1975), 1–2, ERA-NY Legislative Campaign Folder, Box 1, Burstein Files, NYSA; Gene Spagnoli, "Fem Rights Gain in the Legislature," *New York Daily News,* May 14, 1975, ERA-NY Legislative Campaign Folder, Box 1, Burstein Files, NYSA; State of New York, Senate, New York State Equal Rights Amendment Debate, Bill No. S. 2824, transcript, microfilm (May 21, 1975), 5475, 5581; Alfonso F. Narvaez, "Women's Rights Faces Snag in Albany," *New York Times,* May 1, 1975, 45.

28. Wohl, "The ERA," 66.

29. Quotation from Blaum, *E.R.A. in an Era of Error,* 50; Klemesrud, "As New York Vote on Equal Rights Nears," 46; "Erie County LWV Asks Why," *New York State Voter,* summer 1976, 2, Humanities and General Research Room, NYPL; Wohl, "The ERA," 66.

30. "State ERA," *New York Coalition for Equal Rights Newsletter,* October 17, 1975, 1, ERA-NY State Campaign Organiz. Speakers Data Folder, Box 1, Burstein Files, NYSA; "Holtzman Leads Bike-A-Thon," *Brooklyn Coalition for Equal Rights Newsletter,* undated 1975, ERA-NY State Press Con. Non-Camp. Lit. Folder, Burstein Files, NYSA; "Housewives, $5,000 Beat ERA"; Wohl, "The ERA," 92, 96; Middleton, interview.

31. Claire Middleton to Members of the Board of the New York State RTLC, September 14, 1975, personal collection of Margaret Fitton; Wohl, "The ERA," 92; Blaum, *E.R.A. in an Era of Error,* 57; Stern, interview, February 16, 2008; *Stern v. Kamarsky,* 84 Misc. 2d 447 (Sup. Ct. New York County 1975): 448–53; Baker, "'Too Much to Lose,'" 273; Patricia Gmerek, telephone interview by author, January 25, 2008.

32. Quoted in "ERA Defeat," 1, 3.

33. Ibid.; Sheridan Lyons, "ERA Supporters: Fear Defeated It," *Democrat and Chronicle,* November 6, 1976, 8B, personal collection of Virginia Lavan Taylor; Phyllis Schlafly, "New York & New Jersey—Hallelujah!," *Eagle Forum,* November 1975, 1, SL; Mansbridge, *Why We Lost the ERA,* 13; Baker, "'Too Much to Lose,'" 327–28, 343–46, 355.

34. "Results of Voting in the City and Suburbs," 86; Linda Greenhouse, "Defeat of Equal Rights Bills Traced to Women's Votes: Rights Bill Loss Laid to Women's Votes: The Unisex Toilets, 'Vote against Family' Complacency Noted," *New York Times,* November 6, 1975, 1, 32; Betsy Ruechner, "ERA Defeat Pinned on Women," *Democrat and Chronicle,* November 6, 1976, 8B, personal collection of Virginia Lavan Taylor; "Erie County LWV Asks Why"; Linda Moscarella to *Ms.,* September 25, 1976, Folder 243, Carton 7, Letters to *Ms.* 1970–98, SL; Wohl, "The ERA," 92.

35. Stern, interview, February 16, 2008.

36. Chris Kristensen, John Levy, and Tamar Savir, *The Suburban Lock-Out Effect* (White Plains, N.Y.: Suburban Action Institute, 1971), 1, Westchester County Historical Society Archive, Elmsford, N.Y.

37. Frank Lynn, "Suburbs' Power Mirrored in Tally of GOP Victors," *New York Times,* November 9, 1980.

$$4$$

# Gay Organizing in the "Desert of Suburbia" of Metropolitan Detroit

TIM RETZLOFF

In March 1978, a group called the Association of Suburban People (ASP) held a dance at American Legion Post 374 in Berkley, Michigan, four miles north of Detroit. Drawing about 150 attendees, the one-night event was significant in part because it was so ordinary. The dance was a gay event sponsored by a gay organization. A writer in the group's newsletter boasted that the organization had "liberated on[e] American Legion Hall." Usually closeted gay suburbanites had claimed public space, temporarily and discreetly, in one of the many middle-class white suburbs of the Republican stronghold of Oakland County. During the 1970s and early 1980s, at a time when American society—and many gay men and lesbians—considered gay public space to be urban, the Association of Suburban People sought to assert a gay presence beyond the Motor City. In doing so, the group's members recast the relationship of gays with suburbia. To borrow the words of scholar Michel de Certeau, "they escaped it without leaving it."[1]

ASP originated with men who risked not leaving, men who dared to meet other men for homosexual socializing and sex on suburban turf. In the fall of 1975, the Wayne County Sheriff's Department staged an undercover sting operation that targeted men engaged in homosexual liaisons in Hines Park, a meandering recreation area located adjacent to the suburb of Plymouth in northwest Wayne County. Months prior to the crackdown, Wes Rogalski, a resident of nearby Northville, discovered that a gay social scene had arisen in the vicinity of one of the park's picnic shelters. "You see guys in the park and you see them all the time, so you sit there and talk, you'd sit there in the evening at the picnic table and talk about what's going on, who's the latest tricks and about the different people and stuff like that," Rogalski recalls.[2]

When law enforcement authorities discovered the congregating, they sought to eliminate it. Several men Rogalski had come to know "started to disappear." Between

November 1975 and February 1976, sheriffs assigned to plainclothes duty arrested seventy-two men for accosting and soliciting in the park, including sixty-one in a single month's time. According to the local suburban weekly, the arrestees ranged in age from eighteen to sixty-three and included an engineer, a salesman, a student, and a minister. Rogalski, at the time a thirty-two-year-old telephone lineman for Western Electric, an army veteran, and a lifelong member of the National Rifle Association, was soon among those apprehended. One afternoon, an undercover deputy approached his car after Rogalski had pulled in next to the shelter. "He asked to sit in. I let him sit in," Rogalski says. "We sat and talked for a long time, and then he said, 'Well, you want to go into the building?' I said, 'Okay' and get out and go in. The minute I walk in he pulled out his badge and said, 'You're under arrest.'" Because he never actually solicited the officer, his misdemeanor charges were dropped, but Rogalski's arrest forced him to reveal his sexuality to his mother.[3]

The wave of arrests, coupled with harsh sentences meted out by Judge Dunbar Davis as cases came to trial, motivated Rogalski and several others to take collective action. Royce Dew, though not arrested, joined the effort:

> We met at Wes Rogalski's, around his kitchen table, and the outcome was—because of the stigma, they couldn't call anyone—to have a person that you could call that could bail you out of jail. So that night there were five of us, we each put in twenty dollars, so there was a hundred-dollar kitty, and that was to be a bail fund. From that group, we decided, we started being a social group.[4]

The small gathering inaugurated the first long-lasting, and quickly the largest, non-religious gay organization in metropolitan Detroit since a wave of gay liberation activism in the early 1970s. One of the perks of belonging would be access to bail in case of arrest. Membership cards included Rogalski's telephone number. Just as other suburbanites organized to pursue suburban racial integration and suburban environmental justice, ASP strove to provide remedies to suburban sexual conformity.[5]

Originally called West Wayne Men, the group attracted members through word of mouth and soon dubbed itself the Association of Suburban People. The name invoked the First Amendment right to free association while avoiding direct reference to either homosexuality or Detroit. "It was politically expedient to pick a name like that that wasn't threatening or make people feel uncomfortable," says Rogalski. After its first few meetings, the group promoted itself on Detroit's *Gayly Speaking* radio program, announcing, "Gay people in Oakland and western Wayne County no longer have to feel isolated in the desert of suburbia." Herbert "Bo" Taylor, the group's first chairman, discussed the new group with the show's host, David Krumroy, also himself an ASP founder. "We saw a need to organize not only for social reasons but for political reasons, for reasons of self-protection," Taylor said. According to Taylor, ASP sparked "a new consciousness" and raised "a new awareness of the numbers of gay people in the suburbs."[6]

Save for Taylor, who was African American and who retreated from involvement after the first year, the group was as nearly all-white in its makeup as Detroit's suburbs. "My gay world was almost exclusively a Caucasian world, a white world," recalls founding member Steven Kalt, who offered his family's Royal Oak travel agency office as a meeting place. "I don't think that I saw any African Americans at ASP." Predominantly male, at least a few members were heterosexually married and led double lives, common in the suburbs. Members sometimes teased each other about the boundaries of their identities. A gossip writer for the group's newsletter wondered if one man had "gone straight" when he was spotted with "someone's real wife" at a company Christmas party. Teasing aside, the group built itself on an ethos of mutual protection and provided a setting for gay socializing and sexual camaraderie the members could not find elsewhere.[7]

Most ASP members were bachelors, however, either never married or divorced, and had nice homes and good jobs. Their occupations tended to be white-collar. They included a corporate librarian, a Mercedes service agent, two literature professors, the personnel director at the General Motors Tech Center, the owner of a medical textbook store, and a prominent rabbi. Some blue-collar factory workers attended as well. While participants differed in the degree to which they were out about their sexuality, ASP provided all a safe haven, a place for gay suburbanites to be themselves. For some it served as a forum through which to become more public. Invested in their suburban lives, ASP members and officers learned when and where to selectively reveal themselves.[8]

The Association of Suburban People began as a strictly suburban undertaking, soon attracted attendees from the city, and then later grew increasingly suburban again in its membership. The earliest available mailing list, from 1976, shows 97 local participants, of whom 83, or 85.6 percent, resided in thirty-six different governmental jurisdictions outside of Detroit; only 14 participants, or 14.4 percent, lived inside Detroit. A directory issued in 1980, after the group had expanded its recruitment to entice urban dwellers, shows 100 of 165 local ASP members, or 60.6 percent, residing in forty-one different suburbs within the three-county metropolitan region, and 64, or 39.4 percent, living in Detroit itself.[9]

The proportion of the group's suburban participation continued to rise during the next five years. The directory for 1983 lists 151 local members. The proportion of those living outside the Motor City had increased to 68.2 percent, and the proportion living within the city had dropped to 31.8 percent. Two years later, when ASP changed its name to the South-Eastern Michigan Gay and Lesbian Association, 145 of 203 local members, or 71.4 percent, lived outside Detroit, spanning east, west, and north of the city across forty-six suburbs. Detroiters numbered only 58, representing 28.6 percent of total membership. These shifting demographics reflected not only the increasing white flight from the city but also a less apparent white gay exodus as well. Even as they became more widely dispersed, ASP's gay and lesbian members tended to concentrate in certain favored suburbs, in particular Dearborn, Royal Oak, Troy, and Westland.[10]

Private homes provided the locations for many of the group's social activities. As Royce Dew, then an interior decorator who lived in Westland, remembers, "I opened my home to functions, and that's what they were called, functions. Friends would laugh, 'Oh he's having a *function.*' I was just more on the social end of it." Such functions included regular postmeeting open houses; holiday dinners; euchre, pinochle, and backgammon nights; pajama parties; and occasional erotic and nonerotic film screenings. In the privatized landscape of Detroit's suburbs, part of the allure of ASP social activities for gay suburbanites was the opportunity to express their sexuality freely in their own backyards, sometimes literally. The Raunchy Western Revue, a frontier-themed extravaganza of cross-dressing and camp that began in one member's secluded backyard, became an annual tradition. ASP members also hosted Tupperware parties, tweaking gender expectations and poking fun at their suburban surroundings. Typically, the host or hosts provided maps so that attendees could navigate local areas unfamiliar to them.[11]

Beyond queering private suburban homes, ASP co-opted dozens of public places for its own ends. When the group planned a benefit for the bail bond fund in June 1976, its first public disco dance, members approached hotel staff at the Hilton Inn in Plymouth with trepidation. "We were petrified. Sitting across from this banquet manager and having to say we're a gay group, we want to have a gay dance in your hotel," remembers Royce Dew. "They were open to it. He might have been gay, I don't know." The organization went on to hold successful dances at the Sokol Cultural Center in Dearborn Heights, at the Holiday Inn in Farmington Hills, at the Al Matta Hall in Dearborn, and, in conjunction with Dignity/Detroit, at the Hayride Lodge in Rochester. As Dew's comment about hotel staff possibly being gay suggests, ASP may have been aided by gays in the hospitality industry. Friendly welcome was hardly assured, however. When the Ramada Inn in Southfield quoted a higher rent than it charged a nongay group, ASP nonetheless carried through with its scheduled dance in order to show that gays were model customers and then took its future business elsewhere.[12]

ASP held its general membership meetings two Sundays a month in a variety of banquet rooms in the three-county region, ostensibly heterosexual spaces that

included those at Hudgen's House in Livonia, Uncle John's Pancake House in Redford, the Botsford Inn in Farmington Hills, the Canton Inn in Roseville, and the
Howard Johnson's in Madison Heights. The names of these meeting sites conveyed
the conventional suburban folkways of "family" dining. As a private organization
holding private events in places that were at once private businesses and public
accommodations, the group shielded itself from the public scrutiny that might have
accompanied having a fixed address.[13]

Sites were selected based on personal familiarity and reflected what Michel de
Certeau calls the "tactics of consumption," whereby subordinated people appropriate the property of others to further their own ends. ASP members knew whether
suburban businesses in their daily orbits might be welcoming. The proprietors of
the various venues may or may not have known that ASP was a gay group before-
hand, but once a meeting was under way, the sexuality of attendees generally became
apparent, either from the topics under discussion or from unabashed displays of
affection. Many proprietors appreciated the business and welcomed ASP back.[14]

Other public events included an ice-skating party at the General Motors Technical Center in Warren; roller-skating at rinks in Livonia, Canton, and Dearborn
Heights; horseback riding in Lake Orion; and a group outing to attend the Teen
and Junior Mr. Michigan contest at the Redford Theater in Redford. In the summer,
the group held weekly volleyball games and Memorial Day and Labor Day picnics
in Hines Park, the very place where Rogalski and others had once been arrested to
protect the sanctity of suburban heterosexuality. The litany of place names suggests
sites of strategic guerrilla forays into enemy territory that were simultaneously overt
and covert, daring and cautious, strategically visible and closeted, but that nonetheless epitomized the gay slogan "We are everywhere."[15]

ASP also sponsored excursions out of the suburbs to gay bars within the city.
Monthly club nights served to attract new members and to cultivate support from
bar owners. Daniel Sivil, a Troy resident and computer analyst for General Motors
who presided over ASP in the late 1970s and early 1980s, felt that working with bar
owners "on a mutually satisfactory basis" was crucial to advancing the gay cause.
Besides directing business to key gay-owned establishments, ASP club nights introduced customers who were nervous about venturing into gay bars on their own to
a vibrant aspect of metropolitan Detroit's gay world. Save for rare, token outings to
lesbian bars such as Lady's Love Five West, ASP held the club nights at men's bars
like the Gold Coast, the Gas Station, the Outlaw, and the R&R. Events such as the
Hottest Hairy Chest Contest at the Interchange and Uniform Night at the Ramp
favored masculine gay self-presentation. The flyer for an ASP Halloween party at
the Interchange stated emphatically, "No drags allowed!!!" Club nights rounded

out a social agenda that aimed to remedy the isolation experienced by so many gay suburbanites while reinforcing a gay cultural style that comported with the implicit suburban edict of passing as straight.[16]

Aside from socializing, the suburban group sought to satisfy educational needs as well, for both members and nonmembers. Regular meetings featured speakers who addressed a range of topics, from a male-to-female transsexual talking about her transition to martial arts instructor Jaye Spiro speaking on gay self-defense to filmmaker Greta Schiller discussing her documentary project *Before Stonewall*. In the early 1980s, ASP's education function took on life-and-death significance. In its January 1982 newsletter, ASP first reported the emergence of a terrifying "gay cancer," and over the next half decade, through guest speakers and newsletters, the organization served as a crucial local vehicle for conveying information about HIV and AIDS to its members and others in metropolitan Detroit at a time when most media outlets remained silent. In addition to fostering early AIDS education, the organization held a benefit at the Detroit Institute of Arts in November 1982 that raised $1,400 for Gay Men's Health Crisis in New York.[17]

In a similar vein, in the early 1980s ASP launched an annual symposium, Developing a Positive Gay–Lesbian Identity, in cooperation with the Los Angeles–based Whitman-Brooks Clinic. Set initially at the University of Michigan–Dearborn, the conference showcased workshops that fostered gay self-help, political skills, and community solidarity. In subsequent years the event featured keynote speakers of national prominence, such as novelist Edmund White and pioneering activists Phyllis Lyon and Del Martin. The annual undertaking educated attendees about various aspects of gay and lesbian life and history and sought to tie them to a broader political movement.[18]

As an organization originally formed in response to the Hines Park arrests, the Association of Suburban People actually pushed for political change from the beginning. "When we start talking about politics, we're not talking about a radical politics," cofounder Bo Taylor explained during his early appearance on *Gayly Speaking*. "We're talking about a conservative method of implementing a liberal cause. In other words, we intend to work through well-established political parties and using tried political methods to achieve these political goals." Unlike gay liberation, and akin to the homophile activism that had come before, ASP's members collectively mobilized for reform rather than revolution to transform the suburban environment of their everyday lives.[19]

Furthermore, the group mixed traditional grassroots and electoral politics with a quest for sexual freedom that was infused with patriotic language and imagery. Its original logo featured the initials *A.S.P.* against a background image of the Statue of Liberty. Its earliest goals emphasized repealing the state's sodomy law and counseling men arrested for homosexual activity in parks and at highway rest areas. In 1979, ASP chartered a bus to the National March on Washington for Lesbian and Gay Rights. Since its membership reflected both major political parties, NRA members and one-time gay liberationists, the group sought to be bipartisan. ASP representatives met with Democratic U.S. Representative William Brodhead of West Bloomfield to press him to cosponsor the federal gay rights bill. The group also hosted a cocktail party for the first openly gay delegates to the Republican National Convention when it was held in Detroit in 1980.[20]

Henry Messer, a Dearborn Heights brain surgeon who in the 1960s had been involved in an earlier homophile organization, the Mattachine Society of New York, before moving to Michigan, became a key proponent for ASP to engage in political lobbying. Eager to demonstrate the size and clout of the gay electorate, Messer devoted himself to compiling an extensive mailing list by having people sign in at meetings. "If they didn't want to, that was okay. But if they'd give their name and address and phone number, it was on the yellow pad, which I eventually then put onto a three-by-five index card," says Messer. "We began to build a database that way." Eventually computerized, the database formed the basis for letter-writing and fund-raising campaigns that epitomized a suburban, rights-focused brand of gay activism.[21]

Many of the group's most fervently political members asserted that the path to gay influence lay not only in achieving a large membership but also in pursuing strategic gay suburban visibility. Daniel Sivil stressed this in a letter to Messer in 1983, in which Sivil justified attending a fund-raiser for a nongay cause. "It would seem to me that this positive gay presence out in conservative Sterling Heights is one of the environments we want to foster," Sivil wrote. "After all, gay rights is going to have to be accomplished on many fronts." Historian Kevin Mumford has noted such behind-the-scenes networking and outreach in Philadelphia in the early 1980s, but Sivil and ASP derived their activist strategies from a distinctly suburban perspective.[22]

As the organization celebrated its fifth anniversary in 1981, then-president Frank Martin attributed ASP's broad support to "the fact that we offer social activity, political action, and personal support on an equal basis." Despite successes, Martin observed rifts already forming. "As ASP continues to grow, I worry that it could become factionalized, due to the presence of pro- and anti-bulk rate people, pro- and anti-Club Night people, pro- and anti- whatever," he wrote. Douglas Haller, during his term as information officer in 1980 and 1981, witnessed multiple fault lines that later fractured the organization. Haller recalls rifts between liberals and conservatives, between younger members and older members, between those who lived in the city and those who lived in the suburbs, and, what would become especially vexing, "a beginning of tension between male and female, between gay male and lesbian."[23]

In the mid-1980s, the various schisms came to the fore in a debate over how open members and the organization itself should be. Newcomers saw visibility to be of utmost importance and viewed the deliberate ambiguity of the group's name as damaging to their cause. Philip O'Jibway, an early Association of Suburban People member who used the pseudonym Phil Greene to protect his teaching job, recalls that much sensitivity about the name stemmed from broader, racially fraught antagonisms between Detroiters and suburbanites in the mid-1970s. After years of simmering as an issue, in 1983 the name was changed, with the Association of Suburban People formally becoming simply ASP, Inc. A year later it promoted itself as "*A Social and Political group*." When the membership rejected a name change to the Gay Lesbian Association of Detroit in an advisory vote, newsletter editor and future president Tom Smith insisted that a name change that reflected gay visibility would give the group "a new degree of credibility." Smith felt it was "time ASP came out of the closet." In the words of another, unidentified newsletter contributor, "We are no longer the Association of Suburban People. We should no longer wish to project that image with its many negative inferences." To some members, the figure of the lily-white closeted or semicloseted gay suburbanite had come to connote an obstacle to gay progress.[24]

The organization turned away from the suburbs in terms of geography as well as nomenclature. It moved its regular meetings to the Back Stage restaurant in Detroit and, assuming the expense and obligation of monthly rent, opened an office on West McNichols in the heart of Detroit's gay Palmer Park neighborhood. The changes alienated longtime suburban participants. Already in the summer of 1983, only ten of the original fifty members were still involved, and seven of these dropped away over the next two years. Wes Rogalski was one who stopped attending. "It got beyond me, it got beyond my interest," he says. For Rogalski and others, the group had shifted away from their suburban environment and suburban-based aspirations.[25]

Nita Firestone, a resident of Palmer Park, was one of the newcomers and the first woman elected to the group's board. "I don't think the guys knew what they were getting into when they recruited me," says Firestone, who was just starting her career at Blue Cross and was a decade younger than most ASP members. For years the lack of lesbian involvement had been an embarrassment to many and had handicapped the group's political efforts. At the time, female friends asked Firestone why she was involved in such a chauvinist group. Despite its flaws, Firestone embraced ASP's social, educational, and political aims. She felt that such an organization was needed in metropolitan Detroit to counter anti-gay animus in society. She also believed that ASP's problems could best be fixed from within. Her vision, however, differed from that of the old guard. "It's great to have a woman on the board because you want to be diverse," says Firestone:

It's another thing to have you raise questions about certain things, like: Why do we have a P.O. Box? Why are we called the Association of *Suburban* People? Why are we doing the Raunchy Western Revue? *Why* are we having a bail bond fund for getting picked up in the park?[26]

The absence of founding members, changing territorial focus and scale, and the emerging generational and gender gulf meant that new leaders further distanced the organization from its original impetus and intention. "I never quite understood the suburban part, other than it sounded respectable," Firestone says. In 1985, the association finally came fully out of the closet. With women now more active and in leadership positions, ASP changed its name to the South-Eastern Michigan Gay and Lesbian Association, or SEMGLA. In name and in action, the group had come to represent all of metropolitan Detroit, not just the suburbs. Despite this—or, really, because of it—participation dwindled. SEMGLA disbanded in 1988.[27]

The history of the Association of Suburban People in metropolitan Detroit provides evidence that past gay life was not entirely urban and demographically concentrated; it was also suburban and decentralized, shaped by the fragmentation that John C. Teaford emphasizes as so characteristic of postwar suburbanization. ASP, rooted in the suburban landscape, was one of many male-dominated, rights-oriented organizations that historian John D'Emilio identifies as a primary strand of the U.S. gay movement that emerged after gay liberation. ASP marked a decisive grassroots shift in gay activism in the greater metropolis. The group flourished at a time when gay bars remained confined to Detroit, during a decade when whites fled to the suburbs and Detroit became the largest black-majority city in the country. Moderate and conservative gay suburbanites in ASP rejected the in-the-streets militant activism of the city in favor of a muted challenge to the not-in-my-backyard culture of suburbs. At the same time, however, ASP asserted a surprising sexual dissidence that defied the heterosexual sanctity of Detroit's suburbs, at least until new leaders came along who disapproved of or disagreed with that stance.[28]

Despite its coy name, the Association of Suburban People provided vital social support to its widely dispersed members and helped nurture a new suburban-oriented gay politics. In some sense, ASP can be seen as a form of kitchen klatch activism, providing an ironic counternarrative to Lisa McGirr's conservative suburban warriors in Southern California and Stacie Taranto's anti-ERA homemakers in New York State. Though it could not transcend its own internal contradictions, ASP ultimately reshaped the gay political terrain of metropolitan Detroit. The leadership of ASP harnessed the ascendant gay residential patterns of the suburbs to create a new gay suburban politics that rivaled, and in some ways supplanted, the urban gay politics of Detroit. While the straight suburbs were never exclusively heterosexual, it took the Association of Suburban People to nudge secret gay lives further into the open.[29]

## Notes

1. *ASP Newsletter,* December 1978; Michel de Certeau, *The Practice of Everyday Life* (Berkeley: University of California Press, 1984), xiii.

2. Wes Rogalski, interview by author, July 15, 2010, St. Ignatius, Mont.

3. Hank Meijer, "Sheriff's Squad Arrests Dozens for Accosting and Soliciting," *Community Crier,* March 3, 1976, 1; Rogalski, interview.

4. Royce Dew, interview by author, July 20, 2011, Greenacres, Fla.

5. Within a year, more than fifty participants were involved. In September 1979, the group welcomed its one hundredth member. In August 1980, its two hundredth member joined. By mid-1983, it reached member number 620, though more than half of earlier memberships had lapsed. At its peak, the group had between 300 and 350 actively on its membership roll, with a mailing list twice that. See "A.S.P. Membership Up," *Metra,* September 15, 1980, 22–23; List of New Members, Folder 7, Box 1, Ernest L. Horne Papers, Archives of Labor and Urban Affairs, Walter P. Reuther Library, Wayne State University. On other collective efforts for suburban reform, see Becky Nicolaides, "The Social Fallout of Racial Politics: Civic Engagement in Suburban Pasadena, 1950–2000," and Christopher Sellers, "Ecological Preservation in Suburban Atlanta," chapters 1 and 5, respectively, in this volume.

6. Rogalski, interview; *Gayly Speaking,* broadcast May 20, 1976, WDET-FM, Reel-to-Reel Recording, Box 9, Michigan Organization for Human Rights Records, Bentley Historical Library, University of Michigan; R. Kalt, "New Wayne Co. Group," *Rapping Paper,* June 1976, 12.

7. Steven Kalt, interview by author, February 25, 2010, Royal Oak, Mich.; *ASP Newsletter,* January 1978.

8. *ASP Newsletter,* April 1983; "Alan Redner," *Cruise,* January 27, 1993, 15; Frank Martin, interview by author, November 10, 2009, Huntington Woods, Mich.; Claude Summers, interview by author, October 17, 2011, New Orleans.

9. Association of Suburban People Mailing List, 1976, personal papers of Wes Rogalski; Association of Suburban People Membership Directory, November 1980, Folder "Membership Directories," Daniel R. Sivil Papers, Bentley Historical Library, University of Michigan. Since some ASP members chose not to be listed in printed directories, these numbers omit those most fearful of exposure.

10. ASP Membership Directory, 1983, Folder "Membership Directories," Daniel R. Sivil Papers, Bentley Historical Library, University of Michigan; SEMGLA Membership Directory, 1985, Folder 2, Box 1, South-Eastern Michigan Gay and Lesbian Association Records, Archives of Labor and Urban Affairs, Walter P. Reuther Library, Wayne State University.

11. Martin, interview; Dew, interview. For a sampling of events hosted in people's homes, see *ASP Newsletter,* October 1978, November 1978, December 1978, June 1979, December 1979/January 1980, April 1980, March 1982, March 1983, and November 1983. See also various maps in Folder "Members' Addresses & Directions," Douglas M. Haller Papers, Bentley Historical Library, University of Michigan.

12. Dew, interview; *Gayly Speaking,* May 20, 1976; *ASP Newsletter,* October 1978. For other dances, see advertisement, *Metro Gay News,* September 1976, 11; "ASP Announces Mar. 12 Winter Disco Party," *Metro Gay News,* March 1977, 3; *ASP Newsletter,* July 1980, June 1985;

Flyer for Hayride Square Dance, Folder "Council 1981–82," Dignity/Detroit Records, Bentley Historical Library, University of Michigan.

13. For meeting sites, see *ASP Newsletter,* April 1977, February 1978, March 1978, August 1979, July 1980, November 1981, and August 1982; see also Douglas Haller, interview by author, October 7, 2009, Detroit.

14. Rogalski, interview; de Certeau, *Practice of Everyday Life,* xvii.

15. Kalt, interview; Rogalski, interview; Dew, interview. See also *ASP Newsletter,* January 1979, June 1979, September 1981, March 1982, April 1982, June 1982, and February 1983.

16. On club nights, see *ASP Newsletter,* May 1979, June 1979, September 1979, April 1981, and March 1982; "ASP Club Night at 'Lady's Love' Fun for Everyone!," *Metra,* February 21, 1981, 17; Daniel R. Sivil to Henry D. Messer, March 3, 1983, Folder "Correspondence— Messer," Daniel R. Sivil Papers, Bentley Historical Library, University of Michigan. See also *ASP Newsletter,* August 1982; "Ramp/A.S.P. Uniform Night," *Cruise,* September 24, 1982, 9; Flyer for Club Night at the Interchange, Folder "ASP Events & Publicity," Douglas M. Haller Papers, Bentley Historical Library, University of Michigan.

17. *ASP Newsletter,* June 1977, February 1979, December 1982. On ASP's early response to the AIDS epidemic, see especially *ASP Newsletter,* January 1982, March 1983, May 1983, July 1983, and September 1983. See also "A.S.P. Benefit a Success," *Cruise,* December 3, 1982, 9.

18. "The Development of a Positive Gay Identity," *Metra,* April 1, 1980, 9; "Developing a Positive Gay/Lesbian Identity Conference at Marygrove," *Metra,* [September 30, 1982], 9–10; "ASP Welcomes Guest Speakers Del Martin and Phyllis Lyon at the Annual Whitman-Brooks Conference at Marygrove College in Detroit," *Metra,* April 17, 1985, 12.

19. *Gayly Speaking,* May 20, 1976. Two members linked ASP directly to the early local homophile movement: Hal Lawson, who had headed the Detroit chapter of the Mattachine Society, and Dickson Steele, who had been active in ONE in Detroit.

20. Cathy Couch, "Suburban Gays: Fighting Oppression," *Leaping Lesbian,* October 1977, 15–16; "ASP Conference Plans Lobbying Strategy," *Metro Gay News,* October 1977, 1; "Judge Puts Thumbs Down to Counseling Plan," *Farmington Observer,* March 29, 1979, 3-A; *ASP Newsletter,* September 1979 and February 1982; Jone Lynch, "A.S.P. Cocktail Party Honoring First Two Openly Gay Delegates a Success!," *Metra,* August 1, 1980, 14.

21. Henry D. Messer, interview by author, November 23, 2009, Dearborn Heights, Mich.

22. Sivil to Messer, March 3, 1983. See also Kevin M. Mumford, "Race and the Politics of Sexual Orientation in Philadelphia, 1969–1982," *Journal of American History* 98, no. 1 (June 2011): 49–72.

23. ASP President Annual Report, April 23, 1981, Folder "ASP Executive Board, 1981," Douglas M. Haller Papers, Bentley Historical Library, University of Michigan; Haller, interview.

24. Philip O'Jibway, interview by author, August 1, 2003, Ann Arbor, Mich.; Proposed Bylaws, Folder 2, Box 1, Ernest L. Horne Papers, Archives of Labor and Urban Affairs, Walter P. Reuther Library, Wayne State University; advertisement, *Cruise,* June 29, 1984, 10; *ASP Newsletter,* December 1984. On metropolitan Detroit's urban/suburban rift, see Tamar Jacoby, *Someone Else's House: America's Unfinished Struggle for Integration* (New York: Basic Books, 1998), 259–321.

25. Membership Files Computer Printout, June 11, 1983, Folder 7, Box 1, Ernest L. Horne Papers, Archives of Labor and Urban Affairs, Walter P. Reuther Library, Wayne State University; Rogalski, interview.

26. Nita Firestone, interview by author, March 28, 2012, Brighton, Mich.

27. "A.S.P. Becomes the South-Eastern Michigan Gay and Lesbian Association," *Metra*, August 7, 1985, 71. When the final officers issued a form letter to announce that SEMGLA would cease operations due to "circumstances beyond our control," it quipped in all caps, "PLEASE FEEL FREE TO COME OUT IN OUR ABSENCE"; see SEMGLA Board to Members and Friends, circa 1988, Folder 10, Box 1, Ernest L. Horne Papers, Archives of Labor and Urban Affairs, Walter P. Reuther Library, Wayne State University.

28. Jon C. Teaford, *The Metropolitan Revolution: The Rise of Post-urban America* (New York: Columbia University Press, 2006), 184–89; John D'Emilio, "After Stonewall," in *Making Trouble: Essays on Gay History, Politics, and the University* (New York: Routledge, 1992), 234–74. For a more extensive, journalistic look at post-Stonewall gay politics, see Dudley Clendinen and Adam Nagourney, *Out for Good: The Struggle to Build a Gay Rights Movement in the United States* (New York: Simon & Schuster, 1999).

29. Lisa McGirr, *Suburban Warriors: The Origins of the New American Right* (Princeton, N.J.: Princeton University Press, 2001); Stacie Taranto, "Defending 'Women Who Stand by the Sink': Suburban Homemakers and Anti-ERA Activism in New York State," chapter 3 in this volume. On suburbia as a straight purview, see Clayton C. Howard, "The Closet and the Cul de Sac: Sex, Politics, and Suburbanization in Postwar California" (doctoral dissertation, University of Michigan, 2010).

# Ecological Preservation in Suburban Atlanta

## CHRISTOPHER SELLERS

On a cool afternoon in January 1967, former congressman James Mackay stepped before sixty-six people expressly invited to discuss "the present state of conservation efforts and activities in Georgia." Though exactly what he said went unrecorded, attendees remember a rousing "come to Jesus" speech, inspiring what turned into, at the group's next meeting a month later, the Georgia Conservancy.[1] The place of this first gathering of the Conservancy—early flagship of that state's nascent environmentalism—Druid Hills, an Atlanta suburb, resembled the places where many such organizations were kicking off this movement in other parts of the nation. The Conservancy's founders convened their first meeting at the Fernbank Forest and Science Center, in the middle of a neighborhood originally designed by the Olmsted firm, one of the Atlanta area's fullest examples of what Dolores Hayden has termed the "picturesque enclave."[2] Many of those gathered, Mackay among them, had grown up or now lived in Atlanta's suburbs, especially the leafiest, most affluent, and whitest among them. Here, as elsewhere in the United States and as in other mobilization efforts described in this volume, from those of gays (Retzloff, chapter 4) to anti-ERA activists (Taranto, chapter 3) to African Americans seeking a voice in city planning (Pottinger, chapter 2) to local alliances and groups forming to resist school integration (Nicolaides, chapter 1), early environmentalism, especially in its more popular guises, was largely a movement of suburbanites. That they so actively and collectively sought to counter perceived threats to their physical surroundings illustrates how, in environmental as in other dimensions of suburban history, the agency that mattered was not just that of builders or planners but also that of suburbanites themselves.

Like this newly created Georgia Conservancy, the first chapters of the Nature Conservancy had begun in the suburbs. They arose near New York City and

Washington, D.C., in the early 1950s, around the same time that Sierra Club chapters, with largely suburban membership in cities along the Pacific coast, began seeking similar preservationist goals for federal land out west.[3] Nevertheless, those initiatives, conceived in the mode of an older movement for "conservation," were not what inspired a newer and more popular activism in other regions by the mid-1960s that began styling itself as "environmentalist." As I have shown in *Crabgrass Crucible: Suburban Nature and the Rise of Environmentalism in Twentieth-Century America,* that move, characterized by Samuel Hays as "from conservation to environment," came, in part, as advocates for preserving natural lands shifted their sights increasingly toward the edges and interiors of the nation's largest cities.[4] The founding of the Georgia Conservancy, which occurred in an inner-ring suburb northeast of the downtown, inaugurated a similar cityward movement around Atlanta—but it was only a start. An eruption of suburban preservationist activism followed, dispersed through many of the city's better-off white suburbs to the north and northwest, bringing a wider and more popular resonance to nature advocacy. Among these was a movement that kicked into gear only around the time of the first Earth Day in 1970: to preserve the suburban banks of the Chattahoochee River.

Both the Conservancy's creation and the movement for Chattahoochee preservation did not happen until the later 1960s, in part because at that time Atlanta's sprawl had only just begun to accelerate at a scale—and with impacts—that approximated those in more affluent and urbanized regions of the United States. Urban-edge construction stirred new awareness of those more natural features of yet-unbuilt Atlanta-area lands, as well as rising recreational demands on these places. These changes, when translated into political mobilizing, began to force public officials to switch their long-standing allegiances to builders and developers.[5] Around this city, another more political ferment was also necessary. Up until the early 1960s, the electoral power of Atlanta's suburban, as well as its downtown, residents has been severely constrained by a "county unit" system for state elections, in which victory hinged on winning in a plurality of counties rather than a majority of the popular vote. A relic of the era of Jim Crow, this system meant that every rural county had as much clout as the much more populous counties of the Atlanta area, such as Fulton and DeKalb.[6] Its demise opened the door to newfound political power not just for Atlanta's blacks, rapidly approaching a downtown majority, but also for white suburbanites, who promptly mobilized new modes of nature advocacy. Around Atlanta, the passage that early members of the Conservancy sought was not so much "from conservation to environment" as it was "from rural dominance to conservation." Nevertheless, partly because the Conservancy's gathering rural emphasis steered it away from more cityward concerns, younger and less well connected suburban leaders then arose to convey the cause of ecological preservation closer in, on behalf of Atlanta's great suburban river.

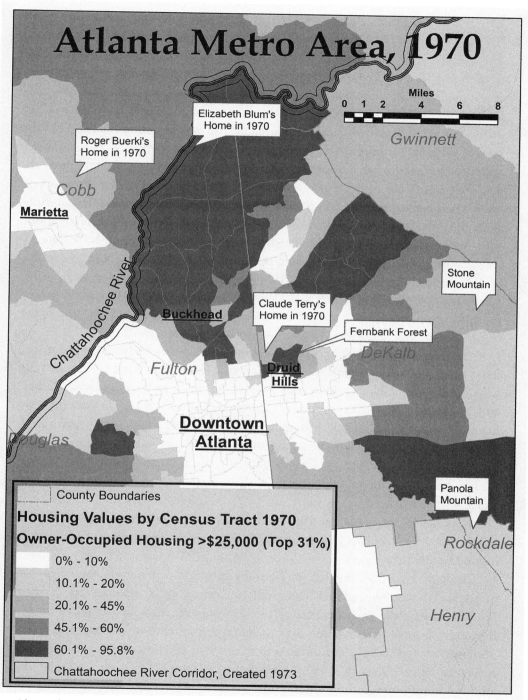

# Atlanta Metro Area, 1970

Miles

0   1   2      4      6      8

*Gwinnett*

Roger Buerki's
Home in 1970

Elizabeth Blum's
Home in 1970

*Cobb*

**Marietta**

Stone
Mountain

Chattahoochee River

Claude Terry's
Home in 1970

**Buckhead**

Fernbank Forest

*DeKalb*

*Fulton*

**Druid
Hills**

**Downtown
Atlanta**

*Douglas*

Panola
Mountain

County Boundaries

**Housing Values by Census Tract 1970**
**Owner-Occupied Housing >$25,000 (Top 31%)**

0% - 10%

10.1% - 20%

20.1% - 45%

45.1% - 60%

60.1% - 95.8%

Chattahoochee River Corridor, Created 1973

*Rockdale*

*Henry*

Atlanta and environs in 1970. Most of the wealthy and less wealthy suburbs to the north and northwest, as well as eastern DeKalb County, were white. Sources: National Historical Geographic Information System and Google Maps.

The Suburban Roots of the Conservancy
in the Era of "Massive Resistance"

The early Georgia Conservancy's membership consisted largely of Atlantans scattered throughout wealthy white suburbs, but no neighborhood of the Atlanta metro area provided more of a hub for the organization's creation than the suburb of Druid Hills. Its garden club, one of Atlanta's earliest, dated back to 1928, and in the 1930s its residents established what was, by some measures, the metropolis's first nature preserve: Fernbank Forest, some eighty acres of woods reputedly never cleared either for farming or for housing, only a mile from downtown Atlanta. For many decades part of a large private estate, since 1939 it had belonged to a private corporation, Fernbank, Inc., owned and run by "interested citizens in the Druid Hills area," to "provide for the children of the area a place where they could learn about the wonders of nature firsthand."[7] James Mackay had worked in Fernbank Forest's small natural history museum while growing up in Druid Hills as the son of the local Methodist minister. Moreover, Druid Hills provided Mackay with an electoral and fund-raising base, as he became DeKalb County's state representative during the 1950s, that allowed him to challenge personally the rural styles and power bases of governance that held sway at both the county and state levels.

A racial moderate, Mackay was also a staunch opponent of the county unit system.[8] Until that was overturned, he and his Druid Hills allies found few opportunities to push park making at the county level or, especially, at the state level. Mackay and other self-professed "modernizers" in growing upper- and middle-class residential communities like Druid Hills applauded the county's widening provision of services, recreational programs among them.[9] Within the state government, the cavalier attitude of Governor Herman Talmadge's administration not just toward the public schools (then under pressure to desegregate) but also toward state parks, which it sought to lease to private venders, offered suburban park supporters a wide political target.[10] Yet by the late 1950s, the closest thing to a new metropolitan-area nature park they were able to achieve was the state's acquisition and development of Stone Mountain.

Rising nearly a thousand feet up from the surrounding plain, sixteen miles east of Atlanta's downtown and past Druid Hills into rural DeKalb, the sheer rock face of Stone Mountain was the world's largest exposed granite monolith, or monadnock. It was also home to rare and unique ecological communities of plants, such as the diminutive *Amphianthus,* an aquatic herb that floated and flowered in pools created by spring rains.[11] Mackay, with support from the Druid Hills Civic Association, among others, introduced the measure in the state legislature for acquiring and developing this mountain as a public park. Nevertheless, the measure made it through the state legislature in 1958 primarily because of how supporters successfully argued the mountain's nostalgic significance for the "lost cause." The mountain harbored an unfinished carving of Confederate military heroes begun in the 1920s by Gutzon Borglum, of Mount Rushmore fame. What made this park project politically viable, in a region shaken to its political foundations over the late 1950s by the civil rights movement and federal court decisions, was the message it promised to deliver about the staying power and supposed prestige of a white racial heritage. Rare species notwithstanding, carving then started up again by the early 1960s on this long-planned sculpture for the monadnock, and the faces of white Southern heroes (i.e., the Confederate trinity of Robert E. Lee, Stonewall Jackson, and Jefferson Davis) were etched into the granite visage of the mountainside.[12]

During the 1950s, as well, no group had emerged around Atlanta that was comparable to those around larger cities in the northeast, such as New York and Washington, where wealthy landowners and garden clubbers had joined together (under the auspices of a group of professional ecologists) to raise money for keeping old estates and farms out of developers' hands. Even at Fernbank, upkeep languished. Although Druid Hills garden clubbers used the site and occasionally pitched in to prune and pick up trash, neither they nor their state association saw fit to create any regional coalitions to acquire the property. Neither the Atlanta Bird Club (a local affiliate of the Audubon Society) nor a local chapter of the Izaak Walton League (a national fishing and hunting advocacy group) nor Georgia's small Ornithological and Botanical Societies stepped in to acquire this or other undeveloped suburban land. Only in the mid-1960s would Fernbank itself find a more permanent home—under the auspices of Emory University and the local school system.[13] As for other local and regional officials, though the Metropolitan Planning Commission had urged that they "do all in their power to preserve" such areas "from developments," for years the commission's recommendations went almost entirely unheeded.[14]

The pathway toward creating the Conservancy opened only with the sea changes that overtook the governments of Georgia as civil rights struggles played out over the early to mid-1960s. Courts finally struck down the county unit system, upholding the principle of "one person, one vote," and suddenly Atlanta's downtown (increasingly black) and also its (ever whiter) suburbs gained new electoral clout.[15] In one of the newly reapportioned congressional districts, now covering DeKalb and other metro-area counties, Druid Hills' James Mackay in 1964 waged a successful campaign to become a U.S. congressman. He directed his staff to set up what they termed "citizens' panels for progress"—made up of "citizens throughout the district who share a common interest and concern"—and one of the panels had an environment-related theme: "water resources." Participating was another Druid Hill resident who helped consolidate the kernel of early Conservancy leadership: Robert Hanie, who taught history to Mackay's son at Druid Hills High School and was a part-time field engineer for the Water Pollution Control Board. Impressed by Hanie's subject-changing presentation on the Western Pennsylvania Conservancy and its work, and also by his suggestion for a Georgia chapter of "the Conservancy," Mackay was around this same time approached by the Nature Conservancy's Washington headquarters about sponsoring a survey of "natural areas" in Georgia. He recommended Hanie to undertake the study.[16] Hanie's work then got an additional boost from the first Georgia governor elected under the new system, the moderate Democrat Carl Sanders. By late 1966 Sanders had successfully pushed for the creation of a state "council on natural areas" to inventory such areas around the state and make recommendations about how to preserve them; Hanie then became head of the council.[17]

Perhaps the biggest impetus to the Conservancy's creation came when Mackay lost that year's reelection campaign, largely thanks to his vote for the Civil Rights Act. He then decided to throw himself full-time into nature-oriented work. Late in 1966, his staff sent out invitations to "Georgia Friends of Conservation" to meet at Fernbank and "participate in a roundtable on the Present State of Conservation Efforts and Activities in Georgia." In January 1967 more than sixty people showed up at the meeting at Druid Hill's Fernbank. Like the 1950s leaders of conservation groups around New York, Philadelphia, and Los Angeles, those running (and most of those attending) the meeting came from the leafiest and best-off urban-edge neighborhoods, mostly near Atlanta.[18]

Over the ensuing months, as the Conservancy acquired a formal shape and agenda, rural land preservation dominated its priorities.[19] The members operated under the assumption—seemingly confirmed by Mackay's electoral defeat—that although the needs to be met were great and urgent, the popular roots for their cause remained limited and shallow. Nor were they committed to making the land they preserved more publicly accessible. The Conservancy's first successful preservation effort, involving Panola Mountain, just outside DeKalb County, offers a case in point. The region's second-biggest monadnock after Stone Mountain, Panola remained "the only major granite exposure in the southeast that man has spared and left unscarred."[20] By early August 1967, the Conservancy had committed to raising $200,000 for this "miniature Stone Mountain." Nevertheless, Panola Mountain, once purchased, would "not [be] available to the public"; it would be available only to "'sympathetic conservation groups' on a tour basis," according to Conservancy spokesperson Robert Hanie.[21]

If Conservancy architects had originally hoped to make the organization into Georgia's leading group for ecological preservationism, their initial top-down structure, their emphasis on preserving land mainly in the state's most rural corners, and their preference for quietly plying upper-level political connections ill fit the concerns of many aspiring activists in Atlanta's suburbs. By 1970, some of these, wishing to engage more local issues, had forced the Conservancy to accept the formation of local chapters—none of which was larger or more active than the one in suburban DeKalb.[22] While the Conservancy did provide an early organizational umbrella for preservationist advocacy of places closer to the city itself, many environmentalists, including those worried about the Chattahoochee River, soon found the need to craft new strategies and tactics of their own.

## Saving the River

One day in March 1970, Roger Buerki parked his car along the highway northwest of Atlanta's downtown, and he and his two daughters got out to wander along the riverbank of a tributary of the Chattahoochee, near where it etches a boundary between Fulton and Cobb Counties. Buerki had moved to the Atlanta area not long before, to work as an engineer at the Lockheed plant in Marietta, but had then been let go. Having time on his hands, he went hiking, as he had done while living in the Pacific Northwest, exploring near his neighborhood on the edge of Marietta, looking for what nature was to be found there. On that day in 1970, he and his young daughters navigated their way down toward the river, searching for garnets as they walked. Along the way they came across a posted sign that, as Buerki realized its significance, took him aback. The very riverbanks he had just begun exploring were being rezoned to enable the building of a public sewer line. Over the next few weeks, as he discovered in his ramblings a series of riverside cliffs—"the Palisades"—that the sewer builders planned to blast away, his shock and anger grew.[23] Buerki had some inkling of what to do, having already been involved with a campaign to preserve parkland during his stay in the Northwest. Quickly finding like-minded others, he, along with his compatriots, started spreading the message about this threat, and a movement to preserve the Chattahoochee was born. Soon it would dramatically bolster the popular as well as institutional supports for land preservation around Atlanta.

While the Georgia Conservancy had its successes, such as Panola Mountain, as the cause of ecological preservation edged closer to the city—to the Chattahoochee as well as to suburban neighborhoods, other groups and networks quickly took over the leadership. It was in these moments as well that the cause of ecological preservation hit a sweet spot of organizing around Atlanta. For one thing, closer-in places were nearer where large numbers of people lived. The residences of three of the most prominent "river rats"—the self-designation of the most committed activists— suggest the range of suburban support: Buerki lived in a middle- to working-class neighborhood out from the industrial suburb of Marietta; Claude Terry, in an ethnically mixed neighborhood just south of Druid Hills; only Elizabeth Blum owned a suburban home more or less along the river itself. Yet all three exemplify how

suburban residents around Atlanta, as elsewhere in the mid-twentieth-century
United States, became increasingly willing to organize and fight to save not just
their own neighborhoods but also wilder lands nearby, which they had also come
to know. Chattahoochee preservation became a popular cause both because of the
river's ease of access for larger numbers of Atlantans and because of the stirring and
exploitation of a growing demand for riverine recreation. Grounding this movement as well was the fondness with which suburban dwellers around Atlanta came
to view the wilder sides of the rural lands that still surrounded them, especially
as these were imminently threatened by development. Around 1970, no corner of
Atlanta was more threatened than the planned intersection of Interstates 77 and
285, Atlanta's new belt highway, very near the Chattahoochee where Buerki and his
daughters had gone wandering.

A story told by Buerki about a developer who sought his approval during the
early stages of the Chattahoochee River preservation campaign captures the clash
of mind-sets that was often involved. Hoping to persuade Buerki that his riverside
apartment complex was going to be nature-friendly, the developer invited the activist to his building site. Where the land for the building had already undergone clearing and the foundation had been poured, he invited Buerki to look around at the
fabulous woods and riverfront upon which residents of the apartments would be
able to feast their eyes. For this developer, as for so many Atlantans as well as other
Georgians, at least up until the later 1960s, the endurance of rural nature was a
given, one that a single development or developer had little chance of threatening.
He did not seem to realize how Buerki's eyes zeroed in on just how many trees had
already been lost to the bulldozer because of his project, how much riverfront
despoiled. For Buerki, as for most other river rats, it had become increasingly difficult to miss what the hands of developers had wrought.[24] Not just the land cleared
by apartment builders but also the horticulture surrounding their own suburban
homes seemed the antitheses of a nature that was more authentically wild, more
compellingly natural. On this last front, Buerki and his allies also broke with many
garden clubbers, supporters of causes like Fernbank's preservation, for whom taking
care of wildlands seemed more of an add-on to their main commitments to cultivating their own neighborhoods and lots.

What was it that led the river rats, and so many others living in the Atlanta area,
to see building sites along the Chattahoochee so differently than this developer still
did? Buerki's own habit of hiking, of exploring wilder lands nearby, played a role; for
him, it went back to his upbringing on the West Coast. Among native Atlantans,
many had been introduced to the pleasures of the outdoors as young people by
organizations like the Scouts and a variety of camps sponsored by churches, the
YMCA and YWCA, and other institutions. Hikes for adults oriented especially

toward viewing of plants, birds, and natural land features became a mainstay, first of the Georgia Conservancy and then of the Sierra Club and other metro-area environmental groups that quickly coalesced over the late 1960s and early 1970s. Slide shows were also important—from those shown at early meetings of the Sierra Club featuring the Grand Canyon and other Western lands to those Buerki presented focusing on the Chattahoochee's wilder stretches. Even the act of naming could have an impact. The designation of the cliffs along the Chattahoochee as "the Palisades" came out of a conversation Buerki had with another early activist, Claude Terry, who compared them favorably to cliffs of that name he had recently visited along the Hudson River, already preserved as parkland.[25]

At the same time, however, what anchored Buerki's and the other river rats' discovery of these remaining wild stretches of the Chattahoochee were their own suburban residences, experiences, and aspirations, as had also been true for those who sought protections for Fernbank. In this sense, the river preservation campaign resembled the campaigns of the Parent–Teacher Associations discussed in Nicolaides's essay (chapter 1) in this volume, or the African American civic associations described in Pottinger's (chapter 2). Yet there was a difference: the geographic focus of Atlanta's newfound environmental activists, the river, did not lie next door to, or even in the neighborhood of, most (but not all) activists' homes. It did, however, constitute part of what might be termed the "informal commons," as yet privately owned, not administered by any government, but still enjoyed by many a resident of Atlanta's northerly stretches because easily accessible via a short drive.

The river's emergence as a center for recreational activities also played a pivotal role in the local support Chattahoochee defenders were able to rouse. Terry's pathway to activism, for instance, came through canoeing. A native Georgian, Terry grew up in rural Forsyth County (just north of Fulton and Gwinnett Counties) and then trained as a microbiologist at the nuclear lab at Oak Ridge; he moved back to the Atlanta area in 1967 to join the faculty at Emory University. He soon struck up a friendship with Mason Kennedy, who had just formed the Georgia Canoeing Association. Terry, a hunter since childhood and long fascinated by Native American weapons, mastered what was, for him, a new sport, driving out from his suburban home to the best place for such in Atlanta's vicinity—the Chattahoochee.[26] If canoeing ushered in Terry's and few others' early familiarity with the river, the more popular, and politically influential, Chattahoochee sport became rafting. In spring of 1970, a local radio DJ, aware of rafting's growing popularity, sponsored the Great Raft Race, which drew a thousand rafters, most of them young, into the Chattahoochee's waves. While many likely drove in from elsewhere, from the counterculture community around Piedmont Park or the scattered local colleges, the suburban proximity of the river course to the city aided the race's early success.

The first Earth Day, on April 22, 1970, also helped stir greater interest in the
Chattahoochee's fate. As part of Earth Day observances, young Atlantans tried on
gas masks in downtown Hurt Park and, at LaGrange College, buried a car. Newspapers and public officials, however, were hesitant in their reactions to these events.
The *Atlanta Constitution* showed pictures of gas masks and "Fight Dirty" signs, and
reported on the many campus talks given on Earth Day, but also noted "overstated
claims of impending doom" and chided the event's dire tenor: "It is important to
observe Earth Day in perspective."[27] At the same time, under the media radar, especially along the Chattahoochee in Atlanta's northerly white suburbs, events were
under way that soon would transform Chattahoochee preservation into one of the
Atlanta area's most popular Earth Day–era crusades.

During the late spring and into the summer, as Terry, Buerki, and an initial
handful of others scrambled for ways to highlight the threat to the river, they targeted not so much developers themselves as the governments of Cobb and Fulton
Counties, which were aiding and abetting riverbank development. Ironically, given
the prominence of the pollution issue at this time, especially in other parts of the
country, the counties were confronting a regional initiative to alleviate water pollution—a cause that had been gathering steam over the previous half decade thanks
to federal financing, new state laws, and more aggressive enforcement. The first
threat to the Chattahoochee that exercised both Buerki and Terry came from trunk
sewer lines that would mar the riverbanks, paid for mostly with grants sponsored
by the U.S. Environmental Protection Agency and intended to divert sewage from
the river's tributaries. Here, in important ways, the emergence of a more popular
environmentalism around Atlanta paralleled that which had grown in other parts of
the country around other, older public health fixes, from DDT spraying against
mosquitoes to the fluoridation of drinking water.[28]

Initially, the river defenders worked through the established vehicles of the
Georgia Conservancy, especially its Inland Waters Committee, which Terry headed.
Yet, even as the Conservancy sought to adjust to Atlanta's upsurge of interest in
things environmental by 1970, its quasi-corporate style and hesitancy to provoke
public controversy clashed with what many river defenders thought necessary to
build support for their cause. They quickly found stronger allies among other recently
created groups more devoted to political engagement: a Sierra Club chapter as well
as SAVE (Save America's Vital Environment). Dramatizing the popularity of recreation on the river, the Great Raft Race became an annual event providing more
than just media attention. Buerki and others hoping to build a movement tallied the
total numbers of rafters to demonstrate the river's recreational value and sought
rafters' support through leafleting and petition drives.[29]

Appeals to this demonstrably "mass" enjoyment of the river marked a clear departure from the Conservancy's preference for inhibiting public access and also for plying influence mainly at top levels, often behind the scenes. The river defenders' tactics also suggested that they had very different ideas about just what and whom preservation was for: it would not just be for scientists and "conservation" education, nor would access suffer strict control, as Conservancy spokespeople had envisioned for Panola. These differences in how the campaign for Chattahoochee preservation unfolded as compared to those for Fernbank and Panola led to mixed responses among existing riverside home and property owners. Some joined the advocacy for preservation, among them Barbara Blum, whose riverside home faced negative effects from Fulton County's sewer building plans.[30] Other homeowners, as they watched this conflict unfold, became more disturbed about the unruly "hippies" who rode the rafts than they were about the sewer builders. These residents worried that a riverine park would just bring more threats to their own investments in peace and quiet. Their skepticism aided the political resistance of developers, who had been accustomed simply to having their way in local governmental decision making but were now learning to play a more defensive political game.

Seeking to counter the ensuing accusations of "radical" "counterculture" imagery, activists stole a page from the Conservancy's playbook and invited key political leaders to join them on tours of the river by canoe or raft. Claude Terry himself served as guide to what was, for many, a new type of sport, in a kind of demonstration river trip by top-level politicians that drew favorable press coverage for the river defenders' cause. Among those who accompanied Terry in his canoe were Sam Massell, then mayor of Atlanta, and Jimmy Carter—though after he had been elected governor.[31]

Over the first year of their activism, from spring of 1970 to mid-1971, the river advocates attained some important breakthroughs, but none that actually reversed the counties' or developers' plans. They then turned to lobbying state legislators, and by early 1971 they had induced a DeKalb legislator to propose a ban on riverside development in the Georgia senate. That bill quickly ran into opposition and died, however, after which the Fulton County commissioners, responding to pressure not just from developers but from residential landowners, decided to rezone riverside land to favor further development.[32]

From that point on, even as the popularity of rafting and the participation in the politics of river defense continued to mount, the activists finally began to achieve lasting change by marshaling their own insider avenues of support, starting with the federal government. Sometime in mid-1971, Secretary of the Interior Robert Morton requested that the EPA ban construction of new sewer lines along the river until an environmental impact statement had been completed—a study that eventually forced sewer builders to bury the lines they laid and abandon their plan to blast the Palisade cliffs. The Bureau of Outdoor Recreation also had a critical impact. In the fall of 1971, after nearly a year of study, in consultation with a group of citizens, its local office published its own plan for turning land along the Chattahoochee into a series of federally run parks—a "string of pearls."[33]

The activists also gained a key ally within Atlanta's social elite when Terry persuaded Kay McKenzie to marshal her own formidable connections on behalf of the river's defense. Wife of the president of Georgia Power Company—which owned long stretches of riverside property—McKenzie was a longtime resident of Buckhead, the wealthiest and most prestigious of Atlanta's northern, inner ring of suburbs. She held a prominent position in Atlanta's Junior League, a women's organization that prided itself on its inclusion of only the best connected and wealthiest of white Atlanta. McKenzie then secured a grant from the Junior Leaguers to pay for the staff and office of a new group: the Friends of the River. The first meeting, announced in June 1971 by the *Atlanta Constitution*, drew some seventy-five people together "to begin a major recruiting program and to announce the opening of a full-time office."[34]

Another change playing to the Friends' advantage was that by early 1971 they had support at the helm of state government in the person of Governor Jimmy Carter. Carter's ascent did not come early enough to save the first attempt to create special state-sanctioned zoning for the Chattahoochee, but his administration did get behind another, foundational initiative later that same year: the empowerment of a new regional vehicle of metropolitan governance. In late 1971, the legislature revamped what had been a strictly part-time and advisory body—the Atlanta Metropolitan Planning Commission—into the Atlanta Regional Commission (ARC). It gained actual state financing as well as some legal decision-making power over local governments across the metro region. Officially, the ARC was supposed to respect local zoning decisions, but it did have the authority to decide on any municipal proposal that might have impacts on neighboring governments. Moreover, since the Chattahoochee riverbanks ran along the boundary between Fulton and Cobb Counties, the new head of the commission, Dan Sweat, took up the question of how to zone the Chattahoochee corridor as his first project for establishing the ARC's authority.[35]

With all these forces rather suddenly aligning to favor the river's protection, a more lasting victory soon followed. In 1973, the state legislature passed, and the governor quickly signed, a bill that sanctioned a degree of land-use control and planning along the Chattahoochee that was unprecedented for Georgia.[36] Of course, building restrictions alone did not yet fulfill the goals of river defenders. They continued their campaign for public acquisition of many of these lands. That cause would not find success until they also struck an alliance with the region's aspiring black politicians, notably Andrew Young, and, indeed, until Jimmy Carter, their erstwhile ally in the governor's office, was actually elected president. Nevertheless, without the prior achievement of that earlier land-use planning bill, by 1978, when Carter finally got to sign the bill creating a National Recreation Area along the Chatta-hoochee, very little riverside land would have remained suitable for federal park making.[37]

## Conclusion

In the early 1970s, the movement to preserve the Chattahoochee was not the only cause to stir widening support and organizing among Atlanta's suburban environ-mentalists. Groups and mobilizations also arose to fight the routes planned for inter-states, against a "Stone Mountain Tollway." In Atlanta's black community as well, suburban residents (similar to those highlighted by Pottinger in chapter 2 of this volume) just moving into what had been white neighborhoods fought downzoning, and those in public housing joined to fight for improving upkeep and fending off the rats. While these mobilizations also achieved victories, and state authority was revamped over a whole range of environmental issues under the Carter governor-ship, the 1972 land-use bill for the Chattahoochee stands out as an early milestone for Atlanta's suburban environmentalists, one that directly responded to their new-found demands and mobilizing. Ironically, this victory itself came not so much at the federal level or the county or other local level, but within the state legislature— precisely that body for which Mackay and other would-be suburban preservation-ists of the 1950s into the mid-1960s had held out the least hope.

Helping usher in this newfound success was the rapid transformation that suburban nature advocacy underwent after the Georgia Conservancy coalesced in 1967. Once a new target for preservation had been discovered closer to home, run-ning right through Atlanta's northerly suburbs themselves, the social bases of this movement (similar to those for gay activism in Retzloff's account in chapter 4 of this volume) broadened, augmenting its clout. The goals of the Friends of the River suggest how, even in the more conservative region of the Southeast, suburban activ-ism was not invariably antigovernmental or conservative, like the PTAs Nicolaides describes. The Friends of the River sought to turn the private public, to achieve federal ownership of the riverbanks. Its success offers a counterexample, as well, to the usual assumptions that the physical environments of America's suburbs reflect primarily the hands and decisions of subdivision builders. In the battles over the Chattahoochee during the early 1970s, private developers were precisely those who lost out, to the collective agency of suburbanites themselves.

Nevertheless, the resistance of many riverside homeowners to what they saw as the questionable, even "unconstitutional" and "radical," initiatives of the river's putative "friends" presaged just how vulnerable this popular politics of nature's defense would prove in the Atlanta suburbs. Once Atlanta's environmental community had hitched its politics to federal interventions, once the expanding sway of the new environmental regime powered by federal agencies, laws, and funding had become clear—and also once an almost entirely white group of environmental activists had cultivated the support of black leaders who were taking over the reins of political power in the Atlanta area—an antienvironmentalist politics gained traction among many of Atlanta's white suburbanites. Not surprisingly, then, Atlanta's suburbs over the later 1970s and 1980s would become birthplaces of a new politics of white property owners' defense, this time not so much against private developers as against the federal government and its environmentalist allies.

## Notes

1. Robert Claxton, *The History of the Georgia Conservancy, 1967–1981* (Atlanta: Georgia Conservancy, 1985), 7; Lucy Smethurst, interview by author, January 20, 2004, North Atlanta, Ga.

2. Robert Hartle, *Atlanta's Druid Hills: A Brief History* (Charleston, S.C.: History Press, 2008); Dolores Hayden, *Building Suburbia: Green Fields and Urban Growth, 1820–2000* (New York: Pantheon, 2003).

3. Bill Birchard, *Nature's Keepers: The Remarkable Story of How the Nature Conservancy Became the Largest Environmental Group in the World* (Hoboken, N.J.: John Wiley, 2005); Stephen Fox, *The American Conservation Movement: John Muir and His Legacy* (Madison: University of Wisconsin Press, 1986).

4. Samuel P. Hays and Barbara D. Hays, *Beauty, Health, and Permanence: Environmental Politics in the United States, 1955–1985* (New York: Cambridge University Press, 1989); Christopher Sellers, *Crabgrass Crucible: Suburban Nature and the Rise of Environmentalism in Twentieth-Century America* (Durham: University of North Carolina Press, 2012).

5. Adam Rome, *The Bulldozer in the Countryside: Suburban Sprawl and the Rise of American Environmentalism* (New York: Cambridge University Press, 2001); Sellers, *Crabgrass Crucible*.

6. Peyton McCrary and Steven F. Lawson, "Race and Reapportionment, 1962: The Case of Georgia Senate Redistricting," *Journal of Policy History* 12, no. 3 (July 2000): 293–320; Calvin Kytle and James A. Mackay, *Who Runs Georgia?* (Athens: University of Georgia Press, 1998).

7. James Mackay, "A Short History of Fernbank (from Its Beginnings to December 1967)," 1967, and Walter McCurdy, "History and Development of Fernbank Science Center," 1967, both in Folder "History of Fernbank Forest," DeKalb County Historical Society, Decatur, Ga.

8. Kytle and Mackay, *Who Runs Georgia?*

9. Dick Hatch, "DeKalb Votes May 18 on Kind of Government," *Atlanta Journal and Constitution*, May 8, 1955. For more on this transformation from rural to suburban styles of government, see Jon C. Teaford, *Post-suburbia: Government and Politics in the Edge Cities* (Baltimore:

Johns Hopkins University Press, 1997); Jon C. Teaford, *The Metropolitan Revolution: The Rise of Post-urban America* (New York: Columbia University Press, 2006).

10. "State's Park Leasing Hit by Mackay," *Atlanta Constitution,* April 20, 1956.

11. Madeline P. Burbanck and Robert B. Platt, "Granite Outcrop Communities of Piedmont Plateau in Georgia," *Ecology* 45, no. 2 (1964): 292–306.

12. Willard Neal, *Georgia's Stone Mountain* (Atlanta: Stone Mountain Memorial Association, 1970); David B. Freeman, *Carved in Stone: The History of Stone Mountain* (Macon: Mercer University Press, 1997).

13. Mackay, "A Short History of Fernbank"; McCurdy, "History and Development of Fernbank Science Center."

14. Metropolitan Planning Commission, "Toward a Metropolitan Park System: Panola Park and Preserve," July 1953.

15. McCrary and Lawson, "Race and Reapportionment, 1962."

16. "Citizens' Panels for Progress, a New Approach to Citizenship," Item 19, and "Looking at Washington, by Rep. James Mackay, October 25, 1965," Item 24, both in Box 7, Mackay Papers, Rare Books and Manuscripts, Emory University, Decatur, Ga.; letter from Hanie to Editor, *Atlanta Constitution,* May 12, 1966, in Georgia Natural Areas Council papers, Rare Books and Manuscripts, Emory University, Decatur, Ga.

17. Legislative Committee on Natural Areas, "Committee Report on Natural Areas (BR 161)," n.d., Folder "Natural Areas Council, Minutes 1966–67," Box RCB-36646, Department of Game and Fish Archives, Commissioners Office, Georgia State Archives, Morrow.

18. Sellers, *Crabgrass Crucible.*

19. Claxton, *History of the Georgia Conservancy.*

20. Jeff Nesmith, "Relic Restoration: Little Group Has Big Ideas," *Atlanta Constitution and Journal,* June 11, 1967, 16-B. Quote on Panola from Georgia Department of Natural Resources, "Panola Mountain State Conservation Park; Brief Historical Background," Folder "Panola Mountain State Conservation Park," DeKalb County Historical Society, Decatur, Ga.

21. Duane Riner, "$200,000 Gets Them a Mountain for Science," *Atlanta Constitution,* August 2, 1967.

22. Claxton, *History of the Georgia Conservancy,* esp. 6–12; "DeKalb Chapter Launches Hard-Hitting Program," *Georgia Conservancy Newsletter,* June 1971.

23. Roger Buerki, interview by author, February 12, 2013, Marietta, Ga.; Keith Coulbourn, "The Chattahoochee Has Friends," *Atlanta Constitution Magazine,* October 10, 1976.

24. Buerki, interview.

25. Claude Terry to Christopher Sellers, "Palisades Naming," April 30, 2013; Buerki, interview.

26. Claude Terry, interview by author, May 21, 2012, Atlanta; Claude Terry, interview by author, November 14, 2012, Atlanta.

27. "Earth Day," *Atlanta Constitution,* April 20, 1970.

28. Sellers, *Crabgrass Crucible.*

29. Buerki, interview; Terry, interview, May 21, 2012.

30. Gregory Jaynes, "Sewer Line Causes Concern," *Atlanta Constitution,* June 18, 1971.

31. John Pennington, "Friends and Enemies of the River," *Atlanta Constitution Magazine,* June 4, 1972.

32. Margaret Hurst, "Rezonings on Chattahoochee Approved," *Atlanta Constitution*, July 17, 1971.

33. Maurice Fliess, "New Song for Chattahoochee," *Atlanta Journal and Constitution*, August 29, 1971.

34. Mike Corbin, "'Friends of River' Organize Here," *Atlanta Constitution*, June 6, 1971.

35. Pennington, "Friends and Enemies of the River."

36. Barbara Casson, "Time's Critical for River Friends," *Atlanta Journal and Constitution*, January 20, 1974.

37. Claudia Townsend, "McDonald Blocks Chattahoochee Bill," *Atlanta Constitution*, September 23, 1976; Craig Hume, "Park Bill Signed by President," *Atlanta Constitution*, August 16, 1978.

PART II

Representing

# 6

# Metaburbia

## *The Evolving Suburb in Contemporary Fiction*

MARTIN DINES

American suburbs are often associated with blankness. This has to do with their perceived demographic and architectural uniformity, and also their emphasis on privacy. There is a venerable tradition of making unfavorable comparisons between the empty spaces between suburban houses—Lewis Mumford's "treeless communal waste"—and the dynamic street life of cities.[1] Above all, however, this blankness relates an absence of history. As Roger Webster remarks, suburbia's "archives are empty. There is no depth from which an archaeology might exhume its objects."[2] Certainly, such apparent depthlessness is accentuated by the ersatz historicity of so much suburban architecture. Additionally, the inhabitants of suburbia are readily depicted as being without roots. Speaking of the denizens of the postwar mass suburbs, William Whyte notes that "the fact that they all left home can be more important in bonding them than the kind of home they left is in separating them."[3] The corollary of this fabricated and tamed modernity is a landscape that is detached from history and devoid of memory.

But the assumption that the suburbs are without history is odd: demonstrably they have undergone change. In the United States, suburban denotes a wide range of habitats developed at different historical moments, from the "romantic" planned communities of the late nineteenth century to the mass-produced tracts of the postwar period and the "technoburbs" of the late twentieth century.[4] Indeed, it is a commonplace within sub/urban historiography that there have been suburbs for as long as there have been cities. Peter Ackroyd employs the conceit in his *London: The Biography*.[5] However, readers have to wait until the seventy-fifth chapter of this seventy-nine chapter volume for the insight. While contributors to Kevin M. Kruse and Thomas J. Sugrue's *The New Suburban History* demand and offer more sophisticated, imbricated accounts of the development of cities and their suburbs,[6] in

81

popular accounts especially, histories of the suburbs are liable to be adjunctive to those of cities. This relegation is in part due to the process of suburban succession: as the suburban frontier advances many localities are understood to become urbanized; in other words, suburbs do not usually stay suburbs for long.[7] The arrival of people not usually associated with suburban settlement—African Americans, say, or lesbians and gay men—is often taken as a marker of a suburb's urbanization.[8] Thus suburbs cannot change; they can only change into something else.

Critical material on the representation of American suburbs in literature and film has contributed to the historical flatness of suburbia. For instance, in her pathbreaking book *White Diaspora,* Catherine Jurca argues that suburban-set fiction has for decades provided a vehicle for expressing the anguish of a white middle class that feels itself to be inauthentic and dispossessed despite its evident affluence and security. Jurca calls this "sentimental dispossession" and asserts that suburban-set novels promulgate a "fantasy of victimization."[9] Certainly, anything that makes clear how class and racial privileges come to be disavowed is enormously useful. What is perhaps less helpful about Jurca's work is the assumption that the suburban story in the late twentieth century remains the "same as it ever was,"[10] recycling the same clichéd imagery and manifesting the same self-pity. To the contrary, a number of American authors have recently sought to demonstrate how suburbs have not only evolved as lived places but also developed their own complex and sometimes contested histories. Thus suburban environments are less places of alienation and dispossession than of attachment.

In so doing, contemporary authors relate many of the earlier observations made by humanistic geographers and scholars of cultural landscapes who are concerned precisely with the phenomenology of habitats undergoing change. For instance, in *What Time Is This Place?* Kevin Lynch defines a "humane environment" as one that "commemorates recent events quickly and allows people to mark out their own growth."[11] This capacity for commemoration is predicated on one for forgetting, or the fading of "these marks as they recede in time or lose connections with present peoples." To be properly habitable, local landscapes must facilitate personal narratives of the lived past; they must enable people to transform their experiences through "dramatic recital."[12] In his work on American vernacular landscapes, John Brinckerhoff Jackson argues that far from being "timeless," as is commonly presumed, vernacular building has not only undergone a long and complicated evolution but has also been inherently responsive to the changing physical, social, and economic needs of its inhabitants.[13] In an essay on the suburban garage, Jackson asserts that "the garage as a family center half outdoors, part work area, part play area, is a family invention, not the invention of designers."[14] It is suburban inhabitants who design and redesign their homes; the home builder merely provides the structure. For Jackson, such adaptation defines the vernacular.

This chapter examines two celebrated but admittedly very different writers: children's author Pam Conrad and avowed postmodernist John Barth. The pairing is less eccentric than it might first seem. Both writers, I will show, employ metafictional techniques to break from the static tradition of suburban writing and to engage with the changing form of America's suburbs. Both conceive of suburban narrative as a kind of "dramatic recital" that articulates personal attachments to place. These narratives coalesce around adaptations of the local environment by its inhabitants, for it is such changes that give sense to their situated lives by providing shape to the stories they tell. But these stories are by no means hermetic: the changes that are registered often index developments taking place within the wider world.

## "Keep in Mind That You Are Making Memories":
## Pam Conrad's *Our House*

Conrad's *Our House* is an account of Levittown, New York, told by six children growing up in its prefabricated environs in consecutive decades following its construction in the late 1940s.[15] Conrad presents each of her child narrators recording significant experiences, acts that always correspond to the creation and habitation of new spaces as Levittown matures. In the first chapter, "Boy Fossil," the young narrator TeeWee Taylor tells of falling through the living room ceiling from the attic where he has been playing. The attic is a space his family hopes to transform: the recently installed full staircase is described by his mother as her "stairway to the stars,"[16] which prefigures it as a place of imagination and possibility. TeeWee memorializes the event in another extension of the family's domestic territory: a cement patio.[17] By inscribing his name in wet cement next to his footprints, TeeWee produces the first of many texts by Levittown children that act as mnemonics for particular experiences of suburban space. As the earliest, TeeWee's is appropriately primitive: a "boy fossil." Subsequently, the children's texts become more sophisticated and indeed literate as Levittown matures as an environment.

The second story, "Night Photograph," pays especial attention to the process of text making and to the spaces involved in and transformed by the production of texts. The bathroom of the young narrator-protagonist Patricia doubles as her father's darkroom for developing photos. Patricia's story is framed by lessons about composition, lighting, and, crucially, perspective. Inspired by the professional photographer Leo Choplin's nighttime images of Levittown, Patricia hopes to record her home environment from the vantage point of the same water tower used by Choplin's crew. That her plans are thwarted (her camera is destroyed when she accidentally drops it from the tower) marks not her failure to create for herself a Levittown text; indeed, it prompts on her part an enactment of text making that promotes memory. Patricia's story ends with her posing in her garden to the flash of fireflies: "Even without pictures, I'll remember every bit of it," she declares.[18] It is striking how the god's-eye view of the official photographer (of the kind described and critiqued in D. J. Waldie's 1996 memoir *Holy Land*)[19] is eschewed for a ground-level experience that unites subject and object. Thus the story suggests that while unusual events do occur in ordinary places, external agents should not be wholly relied upon to give their account.

In the remaining stories, Levittown is shown to be by no means detached from wider historical currents: the effects of war, industrial unrest, de facto segregation, and environmental degradation are felt by the later child narrators—but always in ways that alter the parameters of their environment and daily routines and prompt the creation of narrative. They are also places of trauma. In the book's final story, the young Katie narrates the events surrounding the death of her younger brother, who is killed in a road accident while cycling in Levittown. Her story is really about her quest to produce and locate an appropriate memorial. Once again, it is the Levittown house that provides. As her father prepares the foundations for an extension to accommodate Katie's widowed grandfather, TeeWee's "fossilized" imprint is revealed. Katie leaves her brother's boot prints and name next to those of the unknown child. Like the young Patricia's dancing to firefly flashbulbs in 1951, this is a private, enacted memorialization (for both sets of prints will be covered over with flooring). Yet Conrad's *Our House* encourages the view that such private acts have public consequences, that the suburb holds such memories palimpsestically. Katie concludes: "Maybe that's what neighborhoods are all about. Always changing and growing and sometimes getting worse, but underneath it all, there are invisible footprints pressed into the sidewalks and gardens and wet cement, footprints of all the kids who have ever played there. A kind of remembering that is everywhere."[20]

What is felt to be in evidence here is not so much traces of past lives but textual traces of memorializing acts, acts of remembering that are embedded in the suburban landscape. These traces reify absences, render them tangible. Michel de Certeau argues that such present absences are what make somewhere a place; indeed, "haunted places are the only ones people can live in."[21] In other words, it is the personal stories that give a place its character; they produce ties, making it habitable. These "enigmatic," "inward-turning histories, pasts that others are not allowed to read" also resist totalizing meanings—they "invert the schema of the *Panopticon*," says de Certeau.[22] While its title invites a sense of a shared, public ownership of Levittown, Conrad's book insists that personal attachments to suburban space can be created only through private stories—a spatial practice encouraged, it seems, by an appreciation that other private stories overlay the same place. With the fragmentation of its narrative into six "ground-level" accounts focused on the creation and habitation of new spaces, Conrad's *Our House* achieves three things. First, it refuses external, panoptic accounts of the American suburbs. Second, it breaks apart the conventional bi- or tripartite generational narrative of postwar suburbs— the veteran settlers, the baby boomers, then the Generation Xers—and suggests that a more complex appreciation of generational succession is needed. Third, it rejects suburban literature's traditional insistence on dispossession and demonstrates instead the ways writing can performatively create home attachments. Indeed, in the book's epilogue, the reader is asked to "keep in mind that you are making memories."[23] In view of this instruction, the collection's narrative mode might be described as "present anticipatory," or "preemptive nostalgia." Thus, far from being a site without history, suburbia is shown to be producing history continually.

## "Showing Signs of 'Deferred Maintenance'": John Barth's *The Development*

Superficially, the planned residential development that provides the setting for Barth's collection of nine stories is a very different kind of habitat from Conrad's Levittown. Situated on a toponymically adjusted version of Maryland's upper east coast, the fictional Heron Bay Estates development is hardly the iconic, child-centered American suburb. Rather, it represents the kind of upscale, exurban gated community that has proliferated across the United States since the 1980s. Noticeably, Barth's setting is virtually child-free, being populated in the most part by affluent retired "empty nesters," who seem all too conscious that once-close parents and children have become emotionally and geographically distant. Like Conrad's *Our House*, however, Barth's stories focus on the ways individuals produce texts in order to make sense of the modern residential environments they inhabit. Each of Barth's narrators is a writer: Tim Manning is a retired high school history teacher who has turned "self-appointed chronicler" of Oyster Cove, one of several contiguous but distinct Heron Bay subdivisions; Gerald Frank pens a weekly opinion piece—"Frank Opinions"—for the county newspaper; and George Newett is a self-proclaimed "Failed Old Fart" "fictionist" and professor emeritus following several decades of teaching English literature and creative writing at the local liberal arts college. All of these writer-narrators grapple with the problem of producing what they consider to be appropriate narratives to account for the exigencies of the environment they inhabit and the lives they lead. As a consequence, many of the stories are not organized in the manner of conventional short stories; indeed, often they are preoccupied first and foremost with the troubled process of narration itself.

For instance, Manning insists that he is not a "storyteller" but a "history-teller."[24] Toward the end of the collection's opening story, "Peeping Tom," about a nocturnal interloper to Oyster Cove whose identity, and indeed very existence, is never established, Manning explains to his putative reader: "What You're winding up here . . . is a history, not a Story, and its 'ending' is no duly gratifying Resolution nor even a capital-E Ending, really, just a sort of petering out, like most folks' lives."[25] It would seem that a history of a place and a people does not require, and is likely hindered by, some of the conventional components of a story. Indeed, had it been a story, Manning asserts, he would also not have started it where he did. Instead, the narrative would have opened with the comfortable domestic scene that was disturbed by the first sighting of the Peeping Tom. The several initial expository pages about the Heron Bay Estates would have been lost. But Manning's historical preamble, and other similar passages elsewhere in the collection, crucially gives account of the Heron Bay Estates' maturation, the development's *development*: its being "built out" after the "raw early years of construction";[26] the remodeling of "'colonial' mini-mansions"[27] by their new owners some two decades after being built; more dramatically, the arrival of "Mega McMansions" on keyhole plots and following "teardowns"; and the inescapable signs of "deferred maintenance."[28] Moreover, Manning's narrative expresses the attachment residents feel for their environment precisely because the landscape is undergoing change; such development seems analogous to shifts taking place in their own lives. Many of the collection's stories, indeed, are narratives of decline and loss: their elderly narrators struggle with bereavement, impotence, and dementia. But place attachment does not precipitate simply because human minds and bodies share with bricks-and-mortar structures built-in obsolescence. Their accounts of the Estates' artificially variegated landscape help residents to shape and bring order to their lives. Manning, for instance, speaks of how movements between the different subdivisions represent upward, sideways, downward, or terminal transitions, depending on age, health, and material circumstances,[29] and describes his own progression as his "phased retirement."[30] Also, while conscious that some of it is absurdly euphemistic, Manning and his wife, Margie, employ the jargon of the Estates' developer, Tidewater Communities, Inc., regularly and with some affection. Indeed, sometimes the Estates' official names and expressions prove to be surprisingly apposite, and these felicities generate narrative: few tire of explaining to visitors that Doubler Drive is an appropriate name for a street of "over-and-under" duplexes—a "doubler" is a fisherman's term for a catch of a pair of mating crabs.[31] Settled in TCI's "Assisted Living" development, Manning is prompted to create a more able third-person version of himself to provide him with assistance through his increasingly isolated and difficult life.

By contrast, conventionally told stories are liable to misrepresent the unassuming lives of contemporary exurbia. Subsequently, almost none of the collection's stories involve characters in high-stakes situations or feature startling denouements—even the freak tornado that destroys the entire development in the penultimate story is, like the Peeping Tom, emptied of dramatic potential. Tellingly, one reviewer of *The Development* identified "Toga Party" as the collection's standout story.[32] Of all the stories, this one features proportionally the fewest metafictional interventions and the most "action": it concludes with an attempted suicide (in public, and in fancy dress) of a bereaved elderly resident, followed by a successful suicide pact (behind closed doors) of an apparently contented retired married couple who decide that they have, on balance, little to look forward to. The "satisfying" story elements combine with a depiction of suburban existence as unsatisfying, and a rather familiar account of smug suburban affluence prevails. Clearly, there are certain sorts of stories about suburban life that people still prefer to read.

The collection's numerous metafictional interruptions, which, among other topics, include discussions of counterfactual narrative possibilities and the fabricated nature of the stories' characters, serve as reminders that such familiar, more palatable fare will not be on offer. The collection's fourth story, "The Bard Award," shows an awareness that there exists a tradition of suburban fiction writing in the United States but suggests that merely perpetuating this tradition will be unproductive. The eponymous award is the Stratford College Shakespeare Prize, which is given annually to the creative writing student whose work shows most promise. The prize is associated with failure: none of its previous winners have gone on to make successful careers out of writing; its overgenerous patron, the CEO of Tidewater Communities, Inc., was a budding playwright before lack of success spurred him on to a much more lucrative career in property development; and George Newett admits sanguinely that the Prize Committee, of which he is member, is made up of second-rate writers. The parallels between literary failure and exurban development are not meant to indicate, however, that the former is an inevitable consequence of the latter. Newett, for instance, insists that his muse would have withered regardless of where he ended up living. The problem seems rather to stem from the entrenched conventionality and earnestness of all parties involved. Newett appears to break the cycle of failure with the aid of the most talented student he has ever taught, the freewheeling "*provocateuse*" Cassandra Klause, who has a penchant for all manner of metafictional and performance art–related high jinks. The willful young woman provokes little other than eye rolling from most of her elder instructors; Newett, though, is inspired. Together they conspire to submit a portfolio of Newett's own short stories, edited by Klause, for the Shakespeare Prize. Newett's stories, which hitherto have been serially rejected by publishers, are fictionalized accounts of the people and environment of Heron Bay Estates. For Klause, they are merely "pallid rehashes . . . of 'the 3 Johns' (her dismissive label for Messrs. Cheever, O'Hara, and Updike): the muted epiphanies and petty nuances of upper-middle-class life in a not-all-that-upscale gated community."[33] Thus the numerous frame-breaking moments that occur in *The Development*'s other stories may be presumed to be the work of Klause, or at least a writer reinvigorated by her demands for fresh-ness and self-aware writing. The interventions are improving: far from being just metafictional ticks, they prevent the work from falling into complacent reiteration of earlier suburban narratives. Moreover, by insisting that his characters are as artifi-cial as their habitat, Barth renders absurd the suburbanized middle class's cri de coeur at their own inauthenticity.

The collection's final two stories, which give accounts of Heron Bay Estates' complete destruction by natural disaster, afford an interesting thought experiment. How might a community, given the opportunity, reenvisage its own environment? Would residents have ambitions for the development at large, or solely for their own property? How might they negotiate conflicting visions for redevelopment? For sure, the capacity for rebuilding is a measure of the residents' affluence—references to Hurricane Katrina and the 2004 Southeast Asian tsunami rather acknowledge that the victims of other catastrophic natural events had no such privilege. But here the "teardown," rather than merely indicating the freedoms attendant on wealth, illustrates the residents' attachment to their environment and community. While almost every resident desires to rebuild his or her property, each is aware that this will be meaningful only if more or less everyone else chooses to do the same. Thus place attachment in this habitat extends beyond the perimeters of personal plot. Decisions about how the Heron Bay Estates at large are to be reconstructed are made collectively: as the leader of the Estates' Community Association reminds residents, "It's our baby these days, not its original developer's,"[34] an assertion of design control that echoes Jackson's observations about the suburban home. The only conflict that emerges between residents involves the extent to which the devel-opment should be rebuilt with greater sensitivity to the environment. But even the most radical of the residents acknowledge that a "greener" development must first respect people's place attachments. Thus Barth's collection relates the desire for and possibility of transformation but also more conservative feelings toward space and place.

By stopping short of depicting a singular, determined vision of the future for the Heron Bay Estates, Barth seems rather to confirm Kathy Knapp's thesis that it is "uncertainty that provides a basis for a new suburban literary tradition" in the twenty-first century.[35] The refusal of a number of contemporary writers of suburban fiction to provide determinate endings, Knapp argues, stems from a rejection of the

triumphalist accounts propagated by the American media in the wake of the terror-
ist attacks of September 11, 2001. These media accounts offered comforting but
premature closure; the wounds caused by the attacks, however, have had insuffi-
cient time to heal. The suburbs provide an appropriate setting for examining such
unresolved trauma, for demonstrably they no longer offer a safe retreat from the
world made perilous by the very attitudes that fostered them: the desire for security,
moral minimalism, and compulsive consumption. A consequence of this new meta-
narrative, however, is that the suburbs are reinstalled to explain once again a national
problem, a general malaise. This risks, I would suggest, the obscuration of other
kinds of suburban stories. For sure, Conrad's and Barth's narratives, which were
written either side of 9/11, hardly show the suburbs to be untouched by history or
trauma. Yet neither author presumes to tell a "national" story, and neither employs
a singular "everyman" figure in order to do so. (Their youthful and elderly narrators
are actually unusual voices in suburban narrative, which is dominated by those of
middle-class white men experiencing midlife crisis.) The indeterminacy of Conrad's and Barth's narratives instead stems from the multiple and sometimes conflicting accounts of, and claims made on, suburban environments. These locales are
shown not to be merely symptomatic of economic and social crisis. Rather, they are
environments undergoing change; it is by providing accounts of such changes that
their inhabitants attempt to make sense of their lives and the world around them.

## Notes

1. Lewis Mumford, *The City in History: Its Origins, Its Transformations, and Its Prospects* (New York: Harcourt, Brace & World, 1961), 509. See also Jane Jacobs, *The Death and Life of Great American Cities* (New York: Random House, 1961); Andres Duany, Elizabeth Plater-Zyberk, and Jeff Speck, *Suburban Nation: The Rise of Sprawl and the Decline of the American Dream* (New York: North Point Press, 2000).

2. Roger Webster, "Introduction," in *Expanding Suburbia: Reviewing Suburban Narratives,* ed. Roger Webster (New York: Berghahn Books, 2000), 2.

3. William H. Whyte Jr., *The Organization Man* (New York: Simon & Schuster, 1956), 270.

4. See Kenneth T. Jackson, *Crabgrass Frontier: The Suburbanization of the United States* (New York: Oxford University Press, 1985); Robert Fishman, *Bourgeois Utopias: The Rise and Fall of Suburbia* (New York: Basic Books, 1987); Joel Garreau, *Edge City: Life on the New Frontier* (New York: Doubleday, 1991).

5. Peter Ackroyd, *London: The Biography* (London: Chatto & Windus, 2000).

6. Kevin M. Kruse and Thomas J. Sugrue, eds., *The New Suburban History* (Chicago: University of Chicago Press, 2006).

7. See Yi-Fu Tuan, *Topophilia: A Study of Environmental Perception, Attitudes, and Values* (Englewood Cliffs, N.J.: Prentice Hall, 1974), 225–40.

8. See Andrew Wiese, *Places of their Own: African American Suburbanization in the Twentieth Century* (Chicago: University of Chicago Press, 2004); Martin Dines, *Gay Suburban Narratives*

*in American and British Culture: Homecoming Queens* (Basingstoke, England: Palgrave Macmillan, 2010).

9. Catherine Jurca, *White Diaspora: The Suburb and the Twentieth-Century American Novel* (Princeton, N.J.: Princeton University Press, 2001), 7, 8–9.

10. Ibid., 160.

11. Kevin Lynch, *What Time Is This Place?* (Cambridge, Mass.: MIT Press, 1972), 61–62.

12. Ibid., 62.

13. John Brinckerhoff Jackson, *Discovering the Vernacular Landscape* (New Haven, Conn.: Yale University Press, 1986), 85.

14. John Brinckerhoff Jackson, "The Domestication of the Garage," In *Landscape in Sight: Looking at America,* ed. Helen Lefkowitz Horowitz (New Haven, Conn.: Yale University Press, 1997), 124.

15. Pam Conrad, *Our House,* 10th anniv. ed. (New York: Scholastic, 2005).

16. Ibid., 13.

17. For a detailed study of the design of Levittown and its "rebuilding" by its inhabitants, see Barbara Kelly, *Expanding the American Dream: Building and Rebuilding Levittown* (Albany: State University of New York Press, 1993).

18. Conrad, *Our House,* 40.

19. See D. J. Waldie, *Holy Land: A Suburban Memoir* (New York: W. W. Norton, 1996).

20. Conrad, *Our House,* 114–15.

21. Michel de Certeau, *The Practice of Everyday Life,* trans. Steven Rendall (Berkeley: University of California Press, 1984), 108.

22. Ibid.

23. Conrad, *Our House,* 121.

24. John Barth, *The Development: Nine Stories* (Boston: Houghton Mifflin Harcourt, 2008), 7.

25. Ibid., 22.

26. Ibid., 5.

27. Ibid., 57.

28. Ibid., 5.

29. Ibid., 4.

30. Ibid., 131.

31. Ibid., 58.

32. Sven Birkerts, "Lost in the Rest Home," *New York Times,* October 5, 2008. Students I teach in a course that focuses on the suburbs in American fiction almost unfailingly do the same.

33. Barth, *The Development,* 89.

34. Ibid., 160.

35. Kathy Knapp, "Richard Ford's Frank Bascombe Trilogy and the Post-9/11 Suburban Novel," *American Literary History* 23, no. 3 (2011): 503.

# 7

# Suburban Memory Works

## *Historical Representation and Meaning in Orangevale, California*

PAUL J. P. SANDUL

## Who We Are

In August 2010, *The Onion* (a satiric news publication) featured an article headlined "In This Family We Maintain the Ways of the Old Suburb." In the article, distressed by what he sees as an explosion of consumer goods and shopping locales subverting the familial bonds of those in the Pine Bluffs suburb, the patriarch of the fictional Whitmans, Ben, reminds his suburban offspring that the Whitmans are people of "meager" needs and are satisfied with the consumer choices of yesteryear's suburb; "lo so many years ago in 1987." "Grant us a Domino's pizza and a two-liter of Coke," says Whitman, "and we will make do. We do not ask for more than we require." "Perhaps you don't fully understand the gravity of my words," he says urgently. "You see, if we don't work to preserve these traditions, we lose what makes us who we are. The Whitmans go to the Salty Dog's Miniature Golf Course and Batting Cages. They shop at the Super Wal-Mart on 119, not the one on Eastside Drive, and they are not enticed by the frappucinos at the Starbucks that just opened, because Oreo Blizzards from Dairy Queen are our lifeblood." Wondering how far is too far, Whitman warns his children, "Will this world around us become so convenient that we neglect the very fabric of our souls and DVR *How I Met Your Mother* to watch 'when it's convenient' rather than together, Monday night, over microwaveable . . . pepperoni pizza, as we have since time immemorial?"[1]

While silly, this article underscores several issues concerning suburbanites. Perhaps freshly different for some, the suburban past is the subject of nostalgia for Whitman, who uses it to try to control and make sense of his contemporary life. Yet sarcasm goaded the article's penning. Whitman's suburban memories are a farce and meant for ridicule. The article is comedic precisely because gross consumerism and attachment to a suburban past that many Americans associate with conformity

91

and the loss of individuality, community, and family intimacy color Whitman's suburban memories. Nevertheless, Whitman and his suburban family represent well how practices such as eating habits and television viewership, and even material spaces such as sites of shopping and playing, can facilitate, articulate, and sustain, as Whitman says, "who we are." Whitman's wailing is an attempt to situate his family and their identity in place and through a constructed narrative of familial traditions steeped in shared past practices. *Narrative* in this case refers to Whitman representing a setting, actors, and events of the past. As other scholars have argued, narrative—particularly celebratory stories about the past that evoke ideas of tradition, even the favoring of Oreo Blizzards, and however invented or not—plays a central role in human consciousness and greatly shapes the way we think, speak, and behave.[2] People thus utilize narratives to shape, even manipulate, identity. Identity (a sense of self) is something that is lived in and through activity and so must be conceptualized as it develops in social practices like the suburban ones Whitman describes (including the narrative act itself).[3] Put differently, identity is a means through which people care and think about what is going on, how they come to understand not only themselves but also others. People thus busily narrate their own identities to each other and to themselves. This activity includes engaging stories about the past—that is, historical narratives.

Stories about suburbanites utilizing historical narratives are not just satiric works of fiction. Rather, very real suburban actors care, and often passionately so, about their histories and the places they call home. This passion for the past in suburbs, however, is wholly at odds with the mostly negative impression of suburbia. Critics and popular cultural representations often cast suburbanites as passive pawns negatively shaped by suburbs. Suburbs, the story goes, helped destroy the environment, segregate society, reinforce gender stereotypes and power structures, and flatten out individuality and community. They are bland and boring as well. These criticisms have deep roots, but suffice it to say that studies and insights about what this volume's coeditor John Archer has called "the place we love to hate" reveal a prevailing view of suburbia as a gross outcome and medium of mass society in an industrial-capitalist world.[4] Conformity, uniformity, isolation, standardization, and homogeneity all result and work to subvert individual subjectivity, community, and attempts to forge a democratic society.

Compounding any idea that suburbanites find meaning in their suburban lives and locales and, by implication, utilize historical narratives are critiques by scholars such as Herbert Gans, Edward Hall, Ada Louise Huxtable, and Jane Jacobs, who argue that suburbs deny human needs for historical connectedness. Suburbs, they claim, weaken individual and social identities by pulling people out of history.[5] Another scholar explains the process of young professionals moving into cities in the 1970s by reasoning, "What attracted them ... was a neighborhood's 'historic character.' Perhaps their sensibilities had been shaped by rebellion against the *rootless suburbs* in which they grew up and a desire to live in communities with an *authentic* and aged heritage."[6] Similarly, George Lipsitz reasons that white middle-class teenagers of the 1950s felt no connection to the past in suburbs and sought to find historical experiences elsewhere, locating it eventually in urban enclaves and helping to fuel the rise of rock music.[7] While such critiques have validity, they are not without problems, especially as they risk defining what is or is not "authentic" and characterizing all of suburbia over a longer time span rather than describing just a moment, a singular location, or both. D. J. Waldie, in contrast, in his acclaimed suburban biography of Lakewood, California *(Holy Land),* deplores monotony, uniformity, illusions of peacefulness, and tensions concerning race and class, but he also writes fondly of family and childhood memories, a strong sense of community, and, however odd at times, various commemorative events and local traditions that evoke the past. The problem, according to Waldie, is that while condemning suburbia in the 1950s and 1960s, "the theorists and critics did not look again, forty years later."[8] I am looking again.

A case study of the Sacramento suburb of Orangevale, California, complicates conventional views of suburbs. A focus on historical narrative in suburbia reveals how suburbanites engage in community building and identity formation by utilizing stories about the past. In this context, the practice of utilizing historical narratives falls under the category of what many call cultural memory. While the term *memory* has many connotations, *cultural memory* has come, in part, to signify the sociocultural contexts affecting the remembrance of the past of individuals living in groups (hence it has come to include "social memory"). The idea is that social relationships and phenomena, that culture, ideology, beliefs, and values, all affect the remembrance of the past—something that is *done* in the present. Therefore, memory scholars, in the tradition of social and cultural studies broadly, often look to dissect cultural memory as a way to understand something about the society and culture *producing* said memory.[9] Keep in mind that the story is by no means absent tales of racism, separatism, power, and manipulation. Therefore, while not an apology for suburbia, a review of the various manifestations of cultural memory (memory works) complicates the story. Specifically, I am looking to analyze memory works both by identifying their (re)creation and, like David Smiley in chapter 10 of this volume as he looks to representations in advertising, by contextualizing what they represent to reveal a bit about the contours of the cultural memory of Orangevale, its actual historical character, roots, and processes. The proximate goal is to reveal both what that memory is and what it tells us about Orangevale. The ultimate goal, similar to those of Heather Bailey (chapter 8) and Martin Dines

(chapter 6) in this volume as well, is to reveal how suburbanites engage in the processes of (re)production, (re)interpretation, (re)assembling, and (re)negotiation
of historical narratives that are informed by—and articulated through—memory
works and constitute such a thing as cultural memory in suburbs.

## The Genesis of Historical Narrative in Orangevale

Suburban real estate speculation and metropolitan planning in Sacramento led
to the creation of Orangevale at the beginning of the twentieth century. Some of
Sacramento's top business leaders formed a local growth coalition to both spread
their investment costs and better promote the growth of Sacramento generally to
boost their chances at profit. Therefore, while Orangevale began as a speculative real
estate project, it also served as part of a broader packaging of place in Sacramento.
Billed as a rural suburb, Orangevale included all the amenities one would expect
to find in a suburb at the time: good roads, shade trees, parks, houses, churches,
schools, businesses, and social clubs. Promotion of Orangevale also peddled it as
a "citrus colony" whereby a middle-class lifestyle and way to profit depended on
horticulture. Such combinations of suburban lifestyle and form with horticulture
were common in California at the turn of the century, particularly in Southern California, in suburbs such as Ontario.[10] Indeed, in 1891, California booster Charles
Howard Shinn summed up California's rural suburbs by stating, "A California fruit-
grower is in some respects akin to the middle class of suburban dwellers near Boston
and New York, with this very important difference, that he actually and constantly
makes his living from the soil he owns."[11]

The promotion of Orangevale rested mainly on the nineteenth-century romantic movement and its avowal of sublime rural places as safeguards for democracy
and refinement. The boosters also made sure to add a hype of modernity, such as
a railroad, good roads, and local businesses, to shape a dominant narrative for
how these communities have been remembered ever since. The dominant narrative
of Orangevale thus features a celebration of agriculture and the rural ideal along
with a celebration of innovation and modernity, particularly impressive for a rural-
like community at the end of of the nineteenth century. These two themes beget a
third: progressive-minded individualism and the self-made man. In short, smart
and enterprising men, or so the boosters claimed, moved to and populated rural
suburbs. With their families they came, and often they came with little. Nevertheless,
they recognized a good opportunity when they saw one and worked hard to attain
and maintain it as they built homes, families, and communities. As founders defined
by a go-getting spirit, rural suburbanites and their offspring have subsequently been
cast by memory works as the progeny of entrepreneurialism and refinement. These

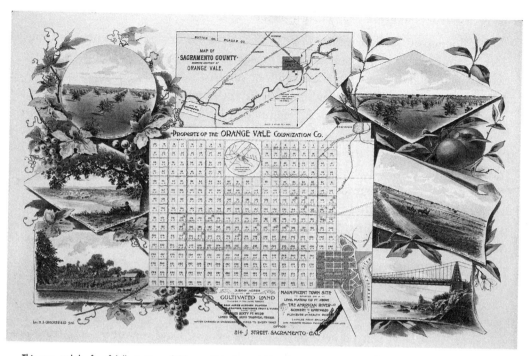

This map and the fanciful illustrations of "Orange Vale," circa 1892, show how boosters originally conceived of the land and how they advertised Orangevale as a thriving community with streets along a grid pattern (urbanity), diligently planned parcels, lush orchards (rurality), and a serviceable bridge across the American River to access the market. The map and illustrations represent the blending of traditional rural idealism and the embrace of modern technology and design. The naming of streets in Orangevale evokes both its rural and modern narrative. As the *Sacramento Union* reported in September 1887, Orangevale's roads "are appropriately designated by names signifying the different varieties of fruit for which the colony expects to become famous." North–south roads, which residents still traverse today, are named for nut trees, and east–west roads are named for shade trees, with exceptions for Main and Central Avenues (named for water lines). Courtesy of the Center for Sacramento History, no. 2002/092/001.

themes, then, constitute a dominant narrative that helps to plot and structure most memory works in contemporary Orangevale. Therefore, as suburbanites in Orangevale attempt to look to the past in constructing meaning in the present, they actively collect from a stock of stories that celebrates agriculture, innovation, and entrepreneurialism. These themes, though originally set forth by Sacramento's boosters, have been continuously repeated or otherwise reassembled in memory works involving Orangevale throughout its existence. In the process, a dominant narrative has gained (and continues to gain) legitimacy through repetition. Put differently, suburbanites in Orangevale have further promulgated, strengthened, and continuously interweave new stories into such a dominant narrative as they search for and help to build community identity and selfhood.[12]

## Memory Works in Present-Day Orangevale

The influence of a dominant narrative in Orangevale is evident in events, community organizations, and recent historic preservation efforts (i.e., specific memory works) and signals the very real existence of suburban cultural memory. For example, Orangevale holds an annual community celebration called Pow Wow Days. The name itself is suggestive, as it references a Native American festivity. As one historian notes, "Playing Indian is a persistent [white American] tradition." Native Americans often serve the same narrative role as the natural landscape, sometimes threatening and sometimes benign, but always subject to domination, and in a postindustrial and postmodern world, white Americans often appropriate Native American customs (including genealogical claims), or at least what they believe are such customs. The argument is that by claiming Native American identity or engaging in (invented) Native American practices, one is making a naturalizing claim to the land and, hence, to history—one is *claiming* authenticity.[13] Even more, such a naturalizing claim to the land begs comparison to romanticized agrarianism, its claim to the land, and how Orangevale's residents have actively woven strands into the dominant narrative.

Pow Wow Days started in 1963 as Chuck Wagon Days—another quintessentially American reference, this time to a romanticized westward movement echoing the theme of Manifest Destiny. Not surprisingly, following World War II, Orangevale experienced its largest period of growth, with an increase in population of about 6.5 percent per year (1,600 to 11,600) from 1950 to 1960, while Sacramento County nearly doubled from 277,140 to 502,778.[14] The population pressures, both within and without, are also suggestive. Internally, the community ties that bind, the security of localized relations and established power structures, seemed threatened, or at least potentially threatened, by the staggering growth of the local population. This also occurred during a patriotic era of Civil War remembrance (centennial), when many Americans looked to the past for meaning in the present. Besides Pow Wow Days, then, a surge in memory works such as local history books resulted in Orangevale to counter, alleviate, or cope with (or some combination of these) an explosion in population that potentially could transform, even dismantle, localized power structures. Orangevale residents thus turned to the construction of memory works to maintain some semblance of the status quo. They seized control of the cultural production process. Likewise, externally, it may be precisely because of the robust growth surrounding Orangevale (and occurring nationally) that the celebration of small-town America, of Orangevale as a semirural community amid an incessantly mounting urban jungle, gained such traction.[15]

During Pow Wow Days, locals gather for several days of games, shows, food, and a parade, including delicious pancake breakfasts, horse shows, and rides. One of the highlights of Pow Wow Days is the parade. Beginning with the inaugural celebration in 1963, the route traversed one of Orangevale's historic "good roads," Central Avenue, also the location of the historic Orangevale Water Company, ending at the Orangevale Youth Center on Hazel Avenue, Orangevale's second-largest thoroughfare. The parade route moved to the main thoroughfare of Greenback Lane by 1965 to accommodate larger crowds, but, ideally, it retained a connection to a so-called good road that figured prominently in the original promotional materials and subsequent historical narratives of Orangevale being a modern community despite its beginnings as a "citrus colony."

Parade participants have included a wide variety of citizens, adults and children representing local clubs, emergency services, schools, and sports clubs. The parade features many notable older clubs, organizations, and services, from the Orangevale Woman's Club to the Grange and Fire Department. While the parade is an event that takes place at any given present moment, it remains the product of historical narrative as it both results from memory and sustains it, hence helping to carry it forward. So past, present, and future collide as the parade is itself a cultural performance and as such must be seen as a site of social action in which individuals and groups of individuals narrate and possibly even reconfigure their identities. The parade, and Pow Wow Days generally, results from a historical narrative of Orangevale as an archetypal American small town that is semirural and values community cohesion (real or imagined), neighborliness, and, seemingly, an aura of "traditional" simplicity. For example, in the photograph here from May 1969, we get a snapshot of what parade participants have looked like over the years and how the parade encompasses representations of scenes from history, particularly through costumes. Notice the picture shows a woman and girl dressed as "pioneers," complete with bonnets and flowing dresses, a wagon train, and participants marching with the American flag, all while they traverse a paved road with palm trees and shrubbery and power lines (modernity). Concerning Orangevale generally, as one observer noted in 1972, "Show me a man with a pickup truck, a gun rack, a cowboy hat and a pair of boots, and I'll show you the spirit of Orangevale." The observer concluded, "If the man doesn't live there, he probably wishes he did."[16] This, in other words, is the power of the small-town image in American life. "It is the small town," said Henry S. Canby, editor of the *Saturday Review of Literature* in the 1930s, "that is our heritage."[17] The small town is synonymous in the American vocabulary with community and invokes deep-seated feelings about highly respectable attributes in American culture. The celebration of the small town in suburban Orangevale, therefore, summons the narrative power of small towns to cast the community as superlative.[18]

Performance is not the only way historical narrative is maintained and further disseminated in Orangevale. Memory works are, by definition, diverse and dynamic.

Pow Wow Days Parade, May 1969. Courtesy of the Center for Sacramento History, Drawer 85, Row 6, Neibaur, May 1969, no. 12/17/1969.

Institutions deeply rooted in a celebratory past in Orangevale help sustain historical narrative as well. Community organizations, some established more than a century ago, remain vibrant in Orangevale and provide the community with a sense
of continuity with the past. Of these organizations, perhaps none (besides several
churches and schools) are more important than the Orangevale Water Company,
the Woman's Club, and the Grange. These organizations dominate historical publications and, as such, deserve attention as the premier institutional and popular
representations offered up by locals and meant to characterize their community to
both themselves and any other potential readers.

The Water Company began in 1896 under the leadership of a member of the
Orange Vale Colonization Company (OVCC), which founded Orangevale in 1887,
and still services the community today. The Woman's Club began in 1913 when
local women met to discuss the formation of a club that would put their talents to
use in building up the community. The Orangevale Grange organized in 1910. In
the language of *The Onion*'s Ben Whitman, the Grange has been an indispensable
actor in weaving together the sociocultural fabric of Orangevale's soul, assisting in
bringing a library to the area, sponsoring local youth groups, helping Orangevale
become part of a local fire district, awarding student scholarships, and supporting
local events. Again, taken together, the Water Company, the Woman's Club, and the
Grange provide community members with a sense of continuity with the past—
anchored to place as well. Still, they represent a particular past.

With the Grange, continuity to the past and narrative are rooted in an agrarian
lifestyle and the adoration of agriculture. With the Woman's Club, continuity and
narrative stem from middle-class values. Moreover, despite being one of the most
clearly and uniquely historically rooted organizations maintained by and for women
in a masculine landscape, the Woman's Club is an organization still largely devoted to
service. With the Orangevale Water Company, continuity and narrative are attached
to the so-called pioneer founders and innovation, with modern technology and
business savvy that seem innovative in an otherwise small, semirural community.
Other institutions such as the Orangevale Library (established in 1912) and churches
such as the Orangevale Methodist Church (established in 1890) convey and project
narrative themes of innovation, refinement, and "traditional" morality.

Another manifestation of historical narrative in Orangevale is found in historic
preservation. Again, cultural memory manifests through a variety of mediums and
in a variety of situations and practices. Moreover, looking at performance and institutional representations of narrative, and now preservation, history books alone
clearly do not embody historical narrative. Certainly many books (or least coverage
within books) exist about Orangevale. Yet deconstructing narratives as they appear
in other types of memory works underscores the depth to which cultural memory

The Orangevale School, built in 1890, is one of the community's oldest schools and operated for more than one hundred years. The old schoolhouse, seen here, was replaced by a larger facility in 1904 as Orangevale's population slowly grew; it remains standing and is a private residence. Photograph courtesy of the Orangevale Open Elementary School and Center for Sacramento History.

exists within this particular suburb. With that said, it would be a gross error to slight the many local and even academic—"outsider"—history books. Rather, especially with preservation in mind, history books help sustain the dominant themes, institutions, and even people covered or accounted for in cultural performances, institutional representations, and preservation. These other manifestations of memory both result from each other and, in turn, contribute to the manifestation of each other. This marks the duality of memory works, certainly, but also the dynamism of cultural memory as that much more powerful. Perhaps obviously, the above also represents moments of transmission when narrative is indeed open to reassembly and some kind of change or alteration. That the dominant narrative by and large does not alter much, if at all, from memory work to memory work thus reveals the emotive staying power of a dominant narrative in Orangevale.

The preservation efforts reviewed below have focused on institutions, individuals, or dominant narrative themes that have also characterized the coverage within history books. The themes, recall, originated with the original booster literature, but they have remained in locally produced narratives as well as in historical works produced by outsiders, most often as parts of larger pieces of scholarship, typically those about metropolitan Sacramento. The point is that preservation concerns, while other impetuses are noted below, follow the lead of previously written history books and other manifestations of memory as such expressions narrow in on what these previous works have marked as historically significant. Moreover, these preservation efforts have been undertaken by proverbial outsiders and point to the influence and success that locally produced narratives have had in affecting the perception of what is historical and thus revered by outsiders concerning Orangevale. So looking to the work of outsiders is really another way of highlighting the real spread of locally constructed narrative, which, again by implication, circles back into maintaining a local narrative meaningful to locals.

The context for preservation efforts in Orangevale follows the suburb's growth from the mid-1970s to 1990, a rise from about 18,000 people in 1975 to 26,266 in 1990. Orangevale also experienced material growth in terms of buildings, houses, businesses, and infrastructure, such as road expansions. As a result, and in connection with national laws (Section 106 of the National Historic Preservation Act) and state laws (Section 15065 of the California Environmental Quality Act), proposals for such projects required historic surveys to determine whether any historic connections would be adversely affected if the projects went forward. Of the proposals that are on file, three places merited such surveys. On one hand, precisely because historical narratives, especially within history books, incessantly highlight these areas, they merit attention for review. On the other hand, they receive attention from preservationists simply because growth projects potentially threatened them and not any of the other places highlighted in the history books.

In 1990, the Sacramento-based firm Historic Environmental Consultants surveyed the Warhaftig House, the Villa, and the Serve Our Seniors Complex. The Orange Vale Colonization Company had the Warhaftig House, which included a packing shed nearby, built in 1888. In fact, according to the survey's author, "it was one of the first four constructed by the company in its initial development and promotional activities." Additionally, the house may have served as a local headquarters for the OVCC. By the late 1890s, Sol (Peter) Warhaftig assumed ownership of the house and his family remained there, including using it as an office for their own fruit-packing endeavors, until 1960. The house's importance, according to the survey as well as most history books, lay in its connection to the OVCC and, for the survey at least, the Warhaftig family. The family stood "prominent in the development and growth of the Orange Vale Colony and its surrounding area," particularly as they ran a fruit-packing business, which employed local women and girls in addition to family members, and because of Peter's service to the Orangevale

Water Company. The survey concludes that the Warhaftig House merits listing on the National Register of Historic Places because it "is an important remnant of its [the colonization company's] existence and influence, and represents a principal aspect of the area's settlement. . . . and [it] represents the theme of settlement." The house's connection to Peter Warhaftig, "an influential and important figure in the growth and development era of the community," also contributed to its significance. Warhaftig's chief importance came thanks to his association with the Orangevale Water Company, which "allowed" for Orangevale's "extensive agricultural development." Finally, the survey's author deems the deteriorating packing shed nearby as significant for its association with early agricultural activity.[19] The house's importance, then, lay in its connection to specific themes characteristic of a dominant narrative that had and continues to have importance in the constitution of the town's historically recited and even performed collective identity, such as the celebrated and revered real estate company and founders, early pioneers, agriculture, and innovation.

The Villa, circa 1894. This photograph is from a booster publication about the Sacramento region, *Sacramento County and Its Resources*, published by the *Sacramento Bee* in 1894, underscoring that rural suburbs like Orangevale are crucial elements in selling a metropolis. Source: James McClatchy and Company, *Sacramento County and Its Resources: A Souvenir of the Bee, 1894, Our Capital, Past and Present* (1894), 70.

The Villa, a stick-style structure built around 1888, originally stood along the bluffs overlooking the American River. The OVCC used it for entertaining clients before it was moved to Greenback Lane in 1916 and became a private residence. The Villa was subsequently moved again, and currently it rests on Oak Avenue (privately owned). While the survey's author concludes that the Villa is important for its association with the OVCC and "settlement" of the area, it does not merit being listed on the National Register for such (because it was moved). Yet, because the Villa represents "a particularly fine example" of a stick-style structure rarely found in the Sacramento area, let alone a "rural" area, it receives demarcation as historically significant. Indeed, stick-style architecture grew from the picturesque Gothic ideals of famed landscape designer Andrew Jackson Downing, a key figure in popularizing the romantic suburban ideal. It flourished in house pattern books of the 1860s and 1870s, peaked in construction in the 1880s, and then fell out of fashion by the 1890s with the rise of the Queen Anne movement. A structurally sound balloon-framed house with elaborate stick work and ornamentation that served no structural purpose distinguished the stick style—favorably and unfavorably. Ultimately, stick-style houses were the quintessential favorites of middle-class audiences and tastes at the time that Downing helped fuel the romantic ideal. In Orangevale, then, a stick-style house such as the Villa emerged as unique—innovative and remarkable—in an otherwise rural community, not to mention its connection to the early founders.[20] In fact, on reviewing the Serve Our Seniors Complex, originally a residence, built in the 1910s, preservationists maintained the structure had limited historical significance.[21] Yet, because the property the house stood on had been associated with the early founders and subsequent development of the area, it merited review for potential preservation.

Suburbanites in Orangevale remember the past in the present to help construct meaning, community, and even a sense of self. Certainly, a catalyst for such remembrance has come from population pressures. Often, population changes have spurred the greater production of memory works. Yet the search for a usable past persists regardless of whether any population pressures exist. Suburbanites have repeatedly utilized narratives about the past, and they continue to do so. In Orangevale, suburbanites have inherited a dominant narrative that celebrates agriculture, innovation, and refinement. They continue to reassemble these narrative themes as they construct their own meaningful narratives about the past through various memory works.

In Orangevale, the use of the past in the present reflects the (re)production of a dominant narrative originally crafted at the beginning of the twentieth century. The usefulness of the past manifested in an opportunity to narrate a particular heritage. A narrative theme that celebrates agriculture conjures up powerful images of

The Orange Vale Colonization Company had a steel truss bridge constructed across the American River, now in Folsom, to reach the gold rush town in 1893. To facilitate access to market as the train left Folsom, the Rainbow Bridge, a reinforced-concrete-arch bridge, seen here, replaced it in 1917 to better accommodate car traffic and weight. The bridges figure prominently in the historical narrative of Orangevale, echoing pride in the early accomplishments and foresight of Orangevale's founders as well as demonstrating the small town's supposed innovation and superior services. This photograph shows a young boy jumping into the American River from the bluffs adjacent to the Rainbow Bridge in the summer of 1970. Courtesy of the Center for Sacramento History, *Sac Bee* Photo Morgue, no. 1109.

William Calder built this house in 1907, and it has been a structural landmark in Orangevale ever since. A Shakespearean actor and producer, Calder emigrated from Scotland just prior to the Civil War. He built a home in Orangevale in the 1890s on Greenback Lane and built this home, which was sometimes referred to as the Calder guesthouse, across the street; palm trees lined the property. A fire in the 1950s damaged a round tower and other elements, but the stories of Calder entertaining famous actors such as the Barrymores here remained intact. Restaurants have tried to put the residence to contemporary use, including the White House Inn, L. W. Calder's, the Ambassador, the Elegant Garden and Afternoon Tea (seen here in 2006), and, most recently, Buffalo Wings and Rings. Photograph by the author.

The Orangevale Orbit Gas Station was built in 1963 (across from Calder's guesthouse at the former site of his main residence, the Palms). The aircraft/spaceship design, created when space travel was new, epitomized the promise of modern science and technology. The gas station's compelling and recognizable architectural design garners attention and shades its customers as they fill up. This photograph, taken in 2006, shows the space age mixed with the agrarian romantic, complete with imported palm trees, typifying Orangevale's historically situated sense of place and memory. Photograph by the author.

An aerial view of Orangevale, taken in 1964, emphasizes the contrast between the Orbit Gas Station "spaceship" and surrounding farms and Calder's guesthouse. Courtesy of the Center for Sacramento History, no. 955/103/138.

independent farmers all cultivating the soul as much as the soil. Agriculture, as dramatized by Thomas Jefferson and nineteenth-century romantics, made Americans more American and brought people (usually men) closer to their natural, and thus spiritual, selves. An agricultural narrative in Orangevale has allowed this community to narrate and maintain a contemporaneous semirural identity steeped in beloved images of small-town America as the bedrock of the republic. The ongoing representation of Orangevale as a semirural enclave contrasts with the modern amenities, infrastructure, and organizations developed there. The conception of Orangevale as innovative allows suburbanites to promulgate a narrative story of progress and achievement, which are hallmarks of a white middle-class heritage. Such a conception of the physical and cultural environment in Orangevale also supports a narrative about entrepreneurialism and refinement as well as underscores, again, a white middle-class sensibility. From narratives of pioneers with Pow Wow Days and agrarianism with the Grange to innovative and refined institutions like the Water Company and the Woman's Club to preservation concerns about sites associated with early founders and exceptional architecture, these narratives form both the idea of the suburb and suburban memory in Orangevale. They are the basis for the construction of suburban identity. Finally, whether real or not, inherited or not, or even exclusionary of other historical phenomena or peoples within the community and whatever they may be, cultural memory, however fabricated, exists. So go ahead and call cultural memory in suburban Orangevale inaccurate, limited, exclusionary, whatever. What you cannot call it, though, is nonexistent.

## Notes

1. "In This Family We Maintain the Ways of the Old Suburb," *The Onion*, August 5, 2010, http://www.theonion.com.

2. Jerome Bruner, *Actual Minds, Possible Worlds* (Cambridge, Mass.: Harvard University Press, 1986). See also Hayden White, *The Content of the Form: Narrative Discourse and Historical Representation* (Baltimore: Johns Hopkins University Press, 1987).

3. Dorothy Holland, William Lachicotte Jr., Debra Skinner, and Carole Cain, *Identity and Agency in Cultural Worlds* (Cambridge, Mass.: Harvard University Press, 1998), 5.

4. John Archer, "The Place We Love to Hate: The Critics Confront Suburbia, 1920–1960," in *Constructions of Home: Interdisciplinary Studies in Architecture, Law, and Literature*, ed. Klaus Stierstorfer (New York: AMS Press, 2010), 45–82.

5. See Mike Wallace, *Mickey Mouse History and Other Essays on American Memory* (Philadelphia: Temple University Press, 1996), 20–21.

6. Ibid., 192; emphasis added.

7. George Lipsitz, *Time Passages: Collective Memory and American Popular Culture* (Minneapolis: University of Minnesota Press, 1990), 122–23, 156.

8. D. J. Waldie, *Holy Land: A Suburban Memoir* (New York: W. W. Norton, 1996), 6.

9. A list of works concerning memory is large; nevertheless, among many other summaries and reviews, I have found James Wertsch's discussion of collective memory very helpful, as well as introductions to readers by, first, Jeffrey K. Olick, Vered Vinitzky-Seroussi, and Daniel Levy, and, second, Astrid Erll and Ansgar Nünning. See James Wertsch, *Voices of Collective Remembering* (New York: Cambridge University Press, 2002); Jeffrey K. Olick, Vered Vinitzky-Seroussi, and Daniel Levy, eds., *The Collective Memory Reader* (New York: Oxford University Press, 2011), 3–62; Astrid Erll and Ansgar Nünning, eds., *A Companion to Cultural Memory Studies* (New York: De Gruyter, 2010), 1–15.

10. Paul J. P. Sandul, "The Agriburb: Recalling the Suburban Side of Ontario, California's Agricultural Colonization," *Agricultural History* 84, no. 2 (Spring 2010): 195–223.

11. Charles H. Shinn, "Social Changes in California," *Popular Science Monthly* 38, no. 6 (April 1891): 798.

12. For a few of the prominent historical narratives concerning Orangevale, see John Cook, "Orangevale Named for Citrus Trees," *Sacramento Union*, May 31, 1959, 1, 3; Catherine Heck, *A History of the Orangevale Community* (n.p., 1990), on file at the California History Room, California State Library, Sacramento (hereafter cited as CHR); Sheila LaDuke, *The History of Orangevale* (Vintage Typographics, 1980), on file at the Orangevale Library; Mary E. Laucher, *History of Orangevale* (n.p., 1962), CHR; Selden Menefee, Patricia Fitzgerald, and Geraldine Fitzgerald, eds., *Fair Oaks and San Juan Area Memories* (Fair Oaks, Calif.: San Juan Record Press,

1960); Orange Vale Water Company, *Information Bulletin* (Orangevale: Orange Vale Water Company, 1958); Orange Vale Water Company, *One Hundred Years of Service* (Orangevale: Orange Vale Water Company, 1996); Gary Pitzer, *150 Years of Water: The History of the San Juan Water District* (Sacramento: Water Education Foundation, 2004); Sacramento County Planning Department, *Orangevale Community Plan: Technical Report* (Sacramento: Sacramento County Planning Department, 1976); Carol Anne West, "Northern California's First Successful Colony: The Orange Vale Legacy," 2001, privately printed history of Orangevale, CHR.

13. Philip J. Deloria, *Playing Indian* (New Haven, Conn.: Yale University Press, 1998), 7; Paul Spickard, *Almost All Aliens: Immigration, Race, and Colonialism in American History and Identity* (New York: Routledge, 2007), 7.

14. Sacramento County Planning Department, *Orangevale Community Plan*, 8; for Sacramento County, U.S. Census Bureau, Table 2, "Land Area and Population: 1930 to 1980," in *Characteristics of the Population*, Vol. 1, *Number of Inhabitants*, 1980 Census of Population (Washington, D.C.: Government Printing Office, 1982), chap. A, California, part 6.

15. For more on the Orangevale Pow Wow Days, see Paul J. P. Sandul and Tory D. Swim (Inloes), *Orangevale* (Charleston, S.C.: Arcadia, 2006), 124–26.

16. "Orangevale," *Sacramento Union*, April 29, 1972.

17. Henry S. Canby, *The Age of Confidence* (New York: Farrar & Rinehart, 1934), 1.

18. For more on small towns, see Kathleen Underwood, *Town Building on the Colorado Frontier* (Albuquerque: University of New Mexico Press, 1987), xv–xvii. Underwood also provides a great bibliography on small towns (133n3).

19. Historic Environment Consultants, "Historic Resources Survey: Report for Harvard Place Subdivision, Orangevale, California; Warhaftig Property," prepared for the Department of Environmental Review and Assessment, Sacramento County Environmental Impact Section (Sacramento: Historic Environment Consultants, 1990), CHR, 6, 11, 9–10.

20. Ibid., 9–10. For more on the stick style, see Vincent Scully Jr., *The Shingle Style and the Stick Style* (New Haven, Conn.: Yale University Press, 1971).

21. Historic Environment Consultants, "Historic Resources Survey: Serve Our Seniors Project, Orangevale, California," prepared for the Department of Environmental Review and Assessment, Sacramento County Environmental Impact Section (Sacramento: Historic Environment Consultants, 1990), CHR, 13.

# 8

# Does This Place Really Matter?

## *The Preservation Debate in Denver's Postwar Suburbs*

HEATHER BAILEY

Many communities are beginning to explore the local stories of their shared recent past just as the wider culture is embracing stories of the last half of the twentieth century. The television historical drama *Mad Men,* for example, recently concluded a seven-season run as a media darling, museums are more routinely hosting exhibits about post–World War II topics, and the historic preservation community is struggling to integrate this recent past and the corresponding category of resources into its activities. The intersection of the professional historic preservation community with residents who live in post–World War II places is sometimes fraught with tension, and often there is a great deal of puzzlement on the part of everyone involved. In some cases the suburbanites fulfill the stereotype of being disconnected from the heritage of the places where they live, but in others they are passionate about laying claim to the identities of their home communities. Preservation professionals often make use of formal processes such as nomination to the National Register of Historic Places or local historic zoning to further their cause, but that course of action can be alienating to a general audience. This is the story of how three communities in the greater Denver metropolitan area traversed the path of preserving recent-past heritage in the suburbs.

Those in the first generation of preservation professionals have long seen recent-past resources as the nemesis of "real" historic preservation (i.e., preservation of pre–World War II historic resources). The standard narrative for retaining historic materials in historic buildings often focuses on the inferiority of some of the more recent building materials. Armed with the knowledge that historic wood windows (ever a hot-button issue) have many features that are irreplaceable and should be repaired at any cost, what is a professional preservationist to do when faced with a building that historically always had vinyl windows? Given that the 1966 National

Historic Preservation Act was enacted in part as a reaction to the mass production of cookie-cutter buildings that were proliferating in the second half of the twentieth century, how does the practitioner learn to apply the philosophy behind preservation laws to these resources that have now become historic? The inclusion of the very resources that were seen as a threat to the historic character of the American built landscape has resulted in some interesting discussions. When this segment of the population asks if post–World War II suburbs are worth saving, a reevaluation of the fundamental philosophy of the profession may be in order.

Subdivision residents often share the belief that their neighborhood is not a place with "real history." Real history would involve a big event or some famous person, not the places where everyday people live. The generation who flocked to postwar suburban developments saw them as emblematic of the romantic American Dream and the abundant opportunities available to all.[1] These developments also emphasized the importance of the nuclear family by reorganizing residential space from multigenerational or multifamily to individual family units as far as the eye could see.[2] As the original residents of these 1940s–1960s suburbs pass on, the meanings they attached to those neighborhoods pass with them. Is there something that needs to be preserved in these places? Should this legacy be commemorated? Should the new residents care about the origins of their neighborhoods? When residents and preservation professionals attempt to find common ground on a topic that is already complicated and uncertain, solutions are rarely simple. Each case is unique, and what seems like the best solution at one time may prove problematic later.

Colorado's Front Range communities were heavily affected by post–World War II development. GIs relocated to the area either to get an education at one of the local universities or to accept jobs with one of the many government offices or contractors. With the growth in the government sector came an unprecedented housing boom. According to one local National Register of Historic Places approved context, "The five-county Denver region experienced a 146 percent increase in its population between 1940 and the end of 1965, growing from 407,962 inhabitants to just over a million."[3] Developers created thousands of subdivisions in order to house this increase in population. Today local governments and residents are exploring what to do with the remnants of the built environment that remain from that period of history, sometimes with mixed results. Should they document and preserve these places? Should they support demolition and redevelopment?

"Everyone Seems to Know about Arapahoe Acres"

The most famous post–World War II subdivision in Colorado is Englewood's Arapahoe Acres, near Denver.[4] While it was significant when initially developed, its current name recognition is a result of the activism of residents in the mid-1990s. Because of their grassroots efforts, on November 3, 1998, Arapahoe Acres became the first post–World War II neighborhood listed in the National Register of Historic Places. At the time it was not even fifty years old, the benchmark that the National Park Service prefers to use in establishing the historical significance of most properties. From the Park Service's perspective, when a property has lasted for at least half a century, it has stood the test of time and is therefore likely to continue to survive and to maintain enough documentation to place it within a strong historic context.

The neighborhood is distinctive in many ways. According to the National Register nomination, "Houses were oriented on their lots for privacy, and to take the best advantage of southern and western exposures for solar heating and mountain views. The surrounding street grid was partially abandoned to reduce traffic speed and discourage through traffic."[5] The result is that when people try to get to Arapahoe Acres, they have difficulty finding their way inside, and once they have entered they are easily disoriented. In 1998 the *Rocky Mountain News* described the subdivision

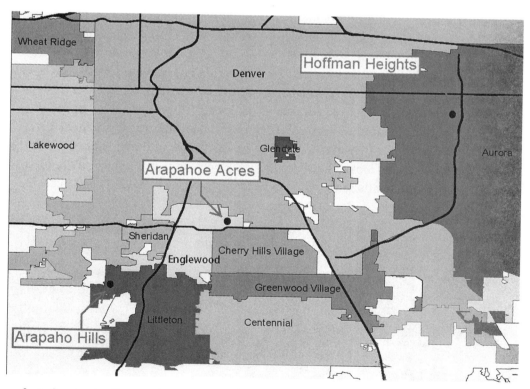

Greater Denver metropolitan area, showing approximate locations of Arapaho Hills, Arapahoe Acres, and Hoffman Heights. Map created with NHGIS, Minnesota Population Center: National Historical Geographic Information System version 2.0, Minneapolis, University of Minnesota, 2011. http://www.nhgis.org.

as "where Englewood goes off the grid and into an oasis of modern design."[6] The purposeful segregation of space allowed for a contained neighborhood and a cohesive aesthetic in tune with most accounts of postwar middle-class suburban design.[7]

Although the homes follow a small set of standardized floor plans, each of the 124 houses in the neighborhood has unique detailing and displays either the International or Usonian style of architecture. Each home was "set at twenty-three to forty-five degree angles to the street behind a twenty-five foot building line."[8] Developer Edward Hawkins collaborated with architect Eugene Sternberg to create the neighborhood.[9] While other neighborhoods of the time were large expanses of monotonous tract housing, these two developers wanted to create a neighborhood with a distinctive character. An architect designed each home, and often a landscape architect designed the yard. Even though the architects designed each small home for a nuclear family, just as the homes in other new neighborhoods were designed, they wanted to use architecture to create a tailored sense of place rather than just focus on a form of house produced as quickly as possible. "They put on flat roofs, with an occasional 'butterfly' shape that fit the feel of Space Age America. Lawns flowed together, relating each property to the next and ripe for expressive landscaping."[10]

The development was a hit and featured several *Better Homes and Gardens* demonstration homes. The magazine even offered a complete set of Arapahoe Acres house plans for twenty-five dollars. While Sternberg had envisioned a diverse neighborhood for social reasons, when he left the partnership in 1950, Hawkins shifted the rest of the construction to more luxurious residences for profit reasons.[11] In part, the community remained largely unchanged because the charismatic Hawkins enlisted homeowners in embracing his vision of how a contemporary neighborhood should look. The members of the predominantly white middle-class community (although there were Jewish residents, which was not always the case in

Arapahoe Acres, street view. Photograph by John Archer, 2003.

the Denver metropolitan area; many neighborhoods excluded nonwhites through their restrictive covenants) joined together through their artistic appreciation for the shared space that they inhabited—an appreciation much like the passion for the past that suburbanites seem to display and engage in, as described by Martin Dines (chapter 6) and Paul J. P. Sandul (chapter 7) in this volume.

The first big shift in neighborhood demographics took place near the end of the twentieth century. According to the *Denver Post*: "For decades, change was not a problem. Most original owners stayed in Arapahoe Acres. . . . Most original owners began to move out in the early '90s, however, swiftly replaced by artists and architects who loved midcentury-modern style."[12] The new owners wanted to celebrate the qualities that they loved about their adopted community, document the history of the neighborhood before more of the original participants passed on, and explore how to preserve the sense of place.

Through the efforts of resident historian Diane Wray-Tomasso, Arapahoe Acres achieved distinction through listing in the National Register of Historic Places. For any property, selection for the National Register involves a rigorous process, requiring a nomination preparer to document the historic resources thoroughly, navigate the document through a state preservation review board, and then ultimately see it through the scrutiny of the keeper of the National Register, an official with the National Park Service (NPS). As the first successful nomination for a post–World War II subdivision, Wray-Tomasso's work underwent extensive scrutiny at both state and federal levels. Concurrent to her preparation of the nomination, the NPS developed its own guidelines for how to list postwar subdivisions, resulting in NPS staff and Wray-Tomasso sharing their findings and collaborating on basic concepts.

In addition to arguing that a post–World War II neighborhood was eligible for listing, Wray-Tomasso had to make a case for exceptional significance because Arapahoe Acres was less than fifty years old in 1998. In some respects, because this development was so unlike typical residential developments of its time, due to its being a uniquely modern enclave and the "practically pristine homes" found there, it could easily pass the test for historical integrity (i.e., how much of the original building fabric is extant), and Wray-Tomasso had ample grounds to make her case.[13] The neighborhood is listed for its significant social history, architecture, landscape architecture, and community planning and development. Wray-Tomasso's comprehensive history served as a rallying point for the newer residents to invest emotionally and intellectually in their neighborhood; in her words, they "honored the vision and sensibility of the older residents."[14] The challenge became what to do next.

As the National Register is largely an honorary program, if residents wanted to preserve the physical environment, then they needed to either update the neighborhood's restrictive covenants (which focused solely on basic construction elements, such as square footage and setbacks, without any mention of architectural style) or adopt local historic zoning. National Register listing does not come with inherent property protections from the federal government (although it does provide an additional level of review for federally funded projects that might affect historic properties). Owners of historic properties must seek out property protections through local government. In a 1998 *Rocky Mountain News* article, the reporter summed up the situation:

> And the people of the neighborhood will have to figure out two things: just how important design and philosophy were to their purchase of a home, and how much control they want over the way the subdivision evolves. The homes are not large, and in an era of mega-square-footage residences, it's a hard reality that some will want to turn the small but perfectly massed homes into more spacious dwellings.[15]

After much contentious discussion, the neighborhood's residents settled on allowing the power of heritage (i.e., an inherent respect for the art and significance of the neighborhood) to be the leading preservation force. They rejected additional restrictive covenants and historic zoning and embraced the "story" of their neighborhood. Arapahoe Acres again became a branding identity, and its popularity spread. Unfortunately, the residents' relatively ephemeral approach to preservation gradually disconnected from their original intentions as the housing market continued to boom. The name Arapahoe Acres became synonymous with the popularity of the neighborhood rather than with its being a preserve for modern architecture enthusiasts. In the words of one resident: "People hear about Arapahoe Acres and say, 'What a cool place,' then move in and start making alterations."[16]

Whereas the surrounding neighborhoods are changing as new property owners demolish existing houses to build massive homes that fill the lots (actions known as "scrapes") or build additional stories on top of what were originally one-story ranches (known as "pop tops"), the homes in Arapahoe Acres are seeing some problematic exterior material changes, and a few have additions that are out of scale and out of character. This seems to highlight the difference between preservation professionals and lay preservation enthusiasts in how they approach honoring the character of historic resources. Preservation professionals would prefer that property owners maintain the historic materials and carry out minimal (if any) alterations to the buildings and landscape. Many homeowners want to adapt their houses to their current needs and also make the houses their own. The two camps often differ in what they see as acceptable changes.

In addition to eroding the historic and original artistic character of the neighborhood, these changes have caused increased tensions among the residents. As property values have continued to soar, newer residents, "attorneys and accountants," have shown that they have different values; they are more interested in the cachet of the neighborhood's name than in the details of its aesthetics.[17] The narrative of Arapahoe Acres is shifting, and that has many stakeholders concerned.

## Arapaho Hills

The mixed success of preservation at Arapahoe Acres inspired the city of Littleton to begin its own efforts to preserve the sense of place of the sister development, Arapaho Hills, in the mid-2000s. The two developments have similar histories. To build Arapaho Hills, Hawkins formed a collaboration with Clyde Mannon, who had served as the contractor and partner for his Arapahoe Acres development. But after designing the sales office with attached carpentry shop (a place to work on detailing on the forthcoming homes) and the first house in the development in 1955, Hawkins exited the partnership and the neighborhood became entirely a product of Clyde Mannon.[18]

Following the model that Sternberg and Hawkins established with Arapahoe Acres, Mannon hired an architect, Bruce Sutherland, to design most of the homes. National firms designed six of the houses for *Better Homes and Gardens* as show homes. One architect designed his own house, but regional architects Sutherland and John Eatwell designed most of the remaining residences. While the development enjoyed early success, by 1960 the region underwent a housing slump, and Mannon scrapped plans for expanding the neighborhood.[19] Although he and Hawkins had envisioned a 160-property development, Mannon developed only 55 of the lots included in the initial 80-lot plat he had filed with the city of Littleton.

Whereas Arapahoe Acres is practically sequestered from the surrounding developments, with its main entrance off of the major thoroughfare, Arapaho Hills has its entrance located along a busy roadway, and the neighborhood's streets easily feed into the surrounding residential developments. Despite exposure on two sides of the subdivision, Arapaho Hills does feature some "off the grid" elements, with the streets winding within the development much as they do in Arapahoe Acres. Further, because a single developer did not tightly control the style of the neighborhood to completion, some of the lots within the neighborhood boundaries (those Mannon did not develop, all located at the western and northern edges) feature houses that are stylistically divergent from the rest of Arapaho Hills' original International and Usonian styles.

In 2007, a few residents approached Littleton city officials to explore preservation possibilities for Arapaho Hills. Specifically, they investigated the possibility of local historic zoning for their neighborhood. By the end of the year, the city granted Arapaho Hills local historic designation. As National Register listing does not come with property restrictions for private property owners, individual property owners can take advantage of preservation easements or covenants. On a larger level, local governments have the capacity to enact local historic ordinances that enable communities to preserve their historic character or the particular sense of time and place that has come to characterize their areas. Arapaho Hills resident Frank Sarcia described living in his 1959 Usonian house by saying, "Every day, it's like living in my dream."[20] Much as in Arapahoe Acres, concerns about property restrictions arose in Arapaho Hills. The local historic designation provides for an additional thirty-day waiting period for property owners wanting to make exterior changes as the historic preservation commission weighs the property's significance. Only when that very limited level of protection was in place did preservationists explore the possibility of further recognition for Arapaho Hills through the National Register. The city hired Wray-Tomasso to prepare the nomination. Moving slowly in an attempt to increase local participation, the city phased the process of preparing a National Register nomination over several years (making use of Certified Local Government grants through the State Historic Preservation Office). This allowed both current and past residents to be part of the discussion about the legacy of the neighborhood.

The grassroots preservation efforts created some tension within the subdivision, which is home to a handful of enthusiastic property owners along with many residents who are much less engaged. On August 28, 2012, Arapaho Hills was listed in the National Register largely due to the efforts of Littleton city staff. Resident Mitch Cowley described his reaction to the listing: "If anything helps a neighborhood, it's pride of ownership. . . . Once others know their homes are significant and important it increases pride."[21] The young families and professionals who are now moving into Arapaho Hills are following a trend similar to the 1990 demographic shift in Arapahoe Acres, in that the new residents are excited about the details of the aesthetics of modern architecture. According to one local journalist, those who are "wanting to move into the neighborhood are those wanting to not only preserve the homes, but strip away any updates made to the homes over the years."[22] Many are furnishing their homes with either original or period pieces. The city has explored the possibility of implementing design guidelines for Arapaho Hills but has not moved forward due to lack of interest on the part of the neighborhood's property owners.

## Hoffman Town

In both Arapahoe Acres and Arapaho Hills, the story has been largely about gentrification and the aesthetic concerns of a predominantly white and upwardly mobile population. Yet, as new suburban historians are apt to remind us, American suburbia is more than just white middle-class residential communities.[23] Not surprisingly, then, the preservation concerns in nearby Aurora about the Hoffman Heights area are markedly different from those two examples, in part because of the neighborhood's physical resources, but also because of its demographics. In 2000, Aurora earned the distinction of being the most integrated city in the United States, and of its neighborhoods the most integrated was Hoffman Heights. By that time, the post–World War II subdivision's population was 69.8 percent white, 23 percent black, 19.4 percent Hispanic, 5.9 percent Asian/Pacific Islander, and 1.3 percent Native American.[24]

While this degree of diversity is a recent trend, the neighborhood, originally branded as Hoffman Town, was always intended for a different demographic. Whereas the neighborhoods in Englewood and Littleton discussed above were designed to be almost exclusively residential, Hoffman Town was designed to be a self-contained community.[25] It was built by Sam Hoffman, who created such communities across the country. Developments such as Arapahoe Acres and Arapaho Hills were nestled within existing urban areas. In contrast, as was typical of community builders, Hoffman tended to purchase large tracts of land outside city limits so that he could organize his communities on his terms without having to worry about local zoning restrictions or having to ask for approval of his plans. The Hoffman Town he organized just outside the city of Aurora featured approximately seventeen hundred homes, "a school, library, fire station and a park. A shopping center was also provided to serve the residents of Hoffman Town, which later became more commonly known as Hoffman Heights in 1952."[26]

Hoffman focused on what he saw as most practical and what would make him the most money. In his words: "Frank Lloyd Wright says he builds houses around the personalities of the people who live in the house. I build houses around the pocketbooks of the people."[27] He marketed to GIs starting families and other young families at the base of the middle-income bracket that American popular culture at the time portrayed as embarking on an upwardly mobile journey to the fabled American Dream.

For the project in Aurora, he purchased Cottonwood Farm in 1946 and "agreed to move forward with the project as long as he had control over the design, construction, and price of the houses as well as the layout of the overall community."[28] To maximize the speed of construction, he offered potential homeowners three basic building designs, which they could customize by choosing from among a standard set of extras. His method of producing neighborhoods quickly led Hoffman to brand himself as the "Henry Ford of the home-building industry."[29]

Completed over the course of 1948 to 1954, the development was a great success. But while Hoffman made his community financially accessible to a broad range of the economic demographic, historic photographs show a homogeneous white population. Such ethnic segregation, a nationwide trend of the time, was actively fostered by the Federal Housing Administration, which refused to provide home loans to integrated areas because it believed that an "influx of blacks made the loans bad risks." The FHA also actively "encouraged the use of restrictive covenants to ensure neighborhood homogeneity and to prevent any future problems of racial violence or declining property values."[30]

Being outside the city limits ensured that Hoffman could reign supreme as he implemented his development, but once the area's population reached a critical mass, residents petitioned the city to annex the neighborhood. Developers within the city resented Hoffman's success and used their political influence to block the residents' petitions each time they came before the city commission. This set the tone for tension, and when Hoffman reached an agreement with the city of Denver in 1952 to provide the necessary infrastructure for a local water and utility district, the city of Aurora, which was physically located between the two communities, refused to allow access. In a marked reversal of attitude, by 1954 the leaders of Aurora determined that the Hoffman community could provide a stable and much-needed tax base and moved to annex it. The previously spurned residents decided to fight the city, resulting in a Colorado Supreme Court decision allowing the city of Aurora to move forward with the annexation.[31]

By that point, however, Hoffman had already begun moving toward relinquishing control of his community. A neighborhood committee that formed in 1952 voted to change the name from Hoffman Town to Hoffman Heights. That same year, Hoffman turned over the local water district to be managed by residents. While his community had a fairly homogeneous look, the residents of Hoffman Heights continued to engage in activism beyond local identity and annexation issues. Much like their counterparts in Arapahoe Acres and Arapaho Hills, the original residents largely remained in the homes over the course of the next several decades. By 1991, a reporter with the *Rocky Mountain News* described the area this way: "The 7,500 residents of this pleasant neighborhood always seem to be working on one project or another—beautifying Del Mar Parkway, getting the city to add lights along the street, fighting to keep the post office in Hoffman Heights Shopping Center."[32] Rather than personifying the stereotype of suburbanites as individuals who felt no sense of ownership over their community, Hoffman Heights residents continued a tradition of local activism throughout the twentieth century.

As perceived blight began to plague nearby areas in the early 1990s, the residents even organized to assist cleanup efforts, including work on businesses along East Colfax Avenue.[33] Despite this activism, the changes in demographics during the 1990s ended up being a tide that longtime Hoffman Heights residents were unable to turn. Rather than an influx of artists and architects, the neighborhood saw an increase in lower-income residents from a wider diversity of ethnic and racial backgrounds. Neighborhood revitalization efforts took on a more militant tone, including an anticrime march in 1994 in which the participants, "after volunteering to be searched for weapons or Mace, . . . walked together from Lansing Elementary School through Highland Park streets, Del Mar Park and the Hoffman Heights Shopping Center."[34]

While city officials continued to try to spin the change in demographics as a sign that their area was welcoming of diversity and could provide opportunities to minorities, there were tensions. In 2005, the *Rocky Mountain News* described one resident's reaction to the demographic shift:

> Doug considers himself an open-minded person, a guy who once enjoyed occasional forays into foreign lands and cultures. Over the past eight years, however, he has slowly moved to a point where he will not patronize businesses that employ non-English speakers. This year, he boycotted the Cinco de Mayo festivities he once anticipated. He finds himself dwelling on newspaper accounts of crimes committed by illegal immigrants.
>
> "I go to the shopping center where we used to get ice cream, and it's now a Mexican restaurant," he says. "Next door is a Puerto Rican restaurant. The movie theater at Hoffman Heights is now Latino. My neighborhood has changed. The schools have changed. The shopping center has changed."[35]

Despite a 2010 report describing the area as "a neighborhood of affordable homes for young couples and 'empty nesters,'" in actuality it has been a draw for a more ethnically diverse and lower-income demographic for the past fifteen years.[36] In addition to the tension between new residents and the old cohort of predominantly white and middle-class residents, the shift has changed the character of the neighborhood in subtle ways. The neighborhood retains many of its original homes through a dynamic of "preservation by neglect." Without the economic pressures that have led developers to demolish midcentury homes in Denver proper so that they can build much larger houses on those lots, Hoffman Heights houses have remained largely unchanged because the residents cannot afford to remodel the homes and investors are not interested in redeveloping the area. While there has been no market-driven push for redevelopment leading to an overhaul of landscape, maintenance issues have resulted in homeowners and landlords (many properties are currently rentals) changing out houses' original building fabric for the most affordable options currently available. As a result, an architectural survey in 2009 found that only 8 percent of homes in Hoffman Heights had enough original building fabric to warrant an intensive survey to prepare for possible National Register listing.

Not all buildings in the neighborhood are decaying away. Some, like the former Big Top Automart turned Thai grocery, have been creatively repurposed. The Big Top stores across the Denver metro area were housed in buildings that looked like circular circus tents, complete with catenary roofs. The more recent owner of the store in the shopping center on Del Mar Circle is both knowledgeable about the history of the chain and fully aware that the pagoda-like appearance is rather apropos to his business.

While some new residents of Hoffman Heights are enthusiastic about the heritage of their adopted community, many just find it an affordable place to live. Whereas residents of other neighborhoods began surveys and National Register nominations as part of grassroots efforts, the historic resources survey undertaken in Hoffman Heights was entirely initiated by the city. Although gentrification has been problematic for other areas, some quarters of Aurora's population would be eager to see a little increase in property values. The Aurora History Museum has hosted exhibits about the midcentury history of the area and even about the genesis of Hoffman Heights, but the city has yet to take the next step of engaging current residents of the neighborhood beyond the initial historic resources survey they completed in 2010.

Do These Places Matter?

While the National Register of Historic Places is not the be-all and end-all for preserving a sense of place, it is a very useful and often-utilized tool for communities

Former Big Top store in Hoffman Heights, now a Thai grocery. Photograph by the author, 2011.

seeking to lay claim to the heritage of their shared built environment. Saving neighborhoods with unique architecture is easier, because their artistic merit is more readily apparent. History is not so clearly evident, and not all post–World War II neighborhoods have documented and distinctive histories.

While neighborhoods with high-art buildings like those in Arapahoe Acres and Arapaho Hills are an easier save, the proliferation of tract housing neighborhoods is a significant part of U.S. history and an important chapter in the evolution of the American residential landscape. As one observer has noted, "Because midcentury modern homes are small by contemporary standards, they are often advertised as great opportunities for expansion or to be scraped off."[37] As more of these buildings disappear, the physical character of the neighborhoods permanently changes. We lose more of this history every day.

On the heritage side of the equation, as increasing numbers of original residents pass on or move out, memories of what particular places have meant either dissipate or become disconnected from the physical places, entombed within museum exhibits. Should new residents seek to continue the narrative? Or is it enough for these evolving neighborhoods to become simply places to live? Is community preservation still primarily a hobby for the affluent and educated?

In 2005, the *Denver Post* summarized the dilemma facing these midcentury Front Range neighborhoods:

> But for every Arapahoe Acres, there are a thousand neighborhoods of three-bedroom brick ranchers with sliding-glass doors leading to a patio, or subdivisions of split-levels with living rooms and kitchens on the ground, bedrooms upstairs, and family rooms downstairs, where windows sit high on a wall and the air feels of a basement. Will these, suburbia's stalwarts, ever experience the loving gushings of fans, historians, city planners and the rest of the architecture-obsessed? . . . Unless you have a distinctive, original ranch, it's going to be tough.[38]

In places where a lack of physical distinctiveness is what is actually distinctive, it is difficult for architecture enthusiasts, historians, and city planners to excite new residents by telling them to embrace the monotony of their neighborhoods as preferable to putting their own stamp on their homes through extensive remodels. Hoffman Heights continues to evolve, and neither the neighborhood nor the city has taken purposeful steps toward place-making. Arapaho Hills is a preservation success story, but being a part of that narrative requires both a particular set of interests (i.e., art and architecture) and a more than moderate income. Arapahoe Acres is in part a victim of its own success, but it does enjoy continued activism that will keep preservation issues at the fore.

The meaning, historical significance, and sense of identity of post–World War II neighborhoods continue to be complicated. Linking historic context to postwar residential spaces is a challenge for urban planners. As has long been the case in historic preservation, grassroots activism is often the most successful course of action. What is the purpose of preservation planning efforts if these places do not matter to those who live there?

## Notes

1. Robert Fishman, *Bourgeois Utopias: The Rise and Fall of Suburbia* (New York: Basic Books, 1987).

2. Ibid.; Kenneth T. Jackson, *Crabgrass Frontier: The Suburbanization of the United States* (New York: Oxford University Press, 1985).

3. Thomas H. Simmons, R. Laurie Simmons, and Dawn Bunyak, *Historic Residential Subdivisions of Metropolitan Denver, 1940–1965,* National Register of Historic Places multiple property documentation form, NRIS 64501105 (Denver: History Colorado, 2011), E3.

4. The quotation that serves as heading for this section is from Sally Stich, "'50s-Style Homes Strike a Chord: 'Midcentury Modern' Coming Back into Its Own among Segment of Buyers," *Denver Post,* October 17, 2004.

5. Diane Wray, *Arapahoe Acres, Englewood, CO,* National Register of Historic Places registration form, February 28, 1998, NRIS 98001249 (Denver: History Colorado, 1998), 49.

6. Mary Voelz Chandler, "Arapahoe Acres Really Built to Last," *Rocky Mountain News,* August 30, 1998.

7. Jackson, *Crabgrass Frontier.*

8. Diane Wray, *Arapahoe Acres: An Architectural History, 1949–1957* (Denver: Wraycroft, 1997), 8.

9. Wray, *Arapahoe Acres, Englewood, CO,* 27.

10. Chandler, "Arapahoe Acres Really Built to Last."

11. Wray, *Arapahoe Acres, Englewood, CO,* 37.

12. Colleen O'Connor, "Arapahoe Acres: Where Old and New Collide," *Denver Post,* March 5, 2012.

13. Betsy Lehndorff, "Back to the Boom—Cutting Edge Still Sharp in '50s Suburban Classic," *Rocky Mountain News,* January 18, 2003.

14. Diane Wray-Tomasso, telephone interview by author, November 11, 2013.

15. Chandler, "Arapahoe Acres Really Built to Last."

16. Quoted in O'Connor, "Arapahoe Acres."

17. Ibid.

18. Diane Wray-Tomasso, *Arapaho Hills Reconnaissance Survey, Littleton, Colorado* (Littleton: Department of Community Development, 2009), 1.

19. Ibid., 2.

20. Quoted in Douglas Brown, "For a Boston Transplant in '59 Ranch House, 'Every Day, It's Like Living in My Dream," *Denver Post,* June 6, 2004.

21. Quoted in Clayton Woullard, "Littleton's Arapaho Hills Named to National Register of Historic Places," *Denver Post,* October 3, 2012.

22. Ibid.

23. Becky M. Nicolaides, *My Blue Heaven: Life and Politics in the Working-Class Suburbs of Los Angeles, 1920–1965* (Chicago: University of Chicago Press, 2002); Andrew Wiese, *Places of Their Own: African American Suburbanization in the Twentieth Century* (Chicago: University of Chicago Press, 2004).

24. Robert Sanchez, "Aurora's Many Faces Suburb Breaks Ground as the Most Integrated City in U.S.," *Rocky Mountain News,* November 26, 2000.

25. For examples of other self-contained, mixed-use suburbs, see Robert Lewis, ed., *Manufacturing Suburbs: Building Work and Home on the Metropolitan Fringe* (Philadelphia: Temple University Press, 2004); Nicolaides, *My Blue Heaven*; Wiese, *Places of Their Own.*

26. Hoehn Architects, *Hoffman Heights, Aurora, Colorado: Reconnaissance Survey* (Aurora: City of Aurora Historic Sites and Preservation Office, 2010), 4.

27. Quoted in "Building Three Places at Once," *BusinessWeek,* July 25, 1953, 356.

28. Hoehn Architects, *Hoffman Heights, Aurora, Colorado,* 20.

29. "Building Three Places at Once," 356.

30. Gwendolyn Wright, *Building the Dream: A Social History of Housing in America* (Cambridge, Mass.: MIT Press, 1981), 247.

31. Hoehn Architects, *Hoffman Heights, Aurora, Colorado,* 20.

32. Guy Kelly, "Hoffman Heights Still Solid as Brick," *Rocky Mountain News,* October 6, 1991.

33. Doug Linkhart, "Aurora Businesses, Neighbors Revitalize East Colfax Avenue," *Rocky Mountain News,* September 14, 1992.

34. Michael Mehle, "Neighborhood Targets Crime: Guardian Angels, Residents March into Highland Park," *Rocky Mountain News,* October 11, 1994.

35. Tina Criego, "Immigration Gap Yawns Wide, Indeed," *Rocky Mountain News,* July 25, 2005.

36. Hoehn Architects, *Hoffman Heights, Aurora, Colorado,* 35.

37. Stich, "'50s-Style Homes Strike a Chord."

38. Douglas Brown, "Midcentury Modern Homes Are Basking in Newfound Respect as Architects and Enthusiasts Realize Their Unique Charm," *Denver Post,* May 1, 2005, L-01.

# 9

# Yards and Everyday Life in Minneapolis

URSULA LANG

I help Sandra add fresh mulch to her boulevard garden. Earlier in the visit, she told me about her relationship to her yard in striking terms, about the ways she interacts through her body with the plants that live there. Sandra has an intensively cultivated yard from front to back—full of plants, seating areas, and art objects. She told me:

> This is where I live. . . . I wake up in the morning thinking to myself, "Ooh! I'm off work today—I can come out and touch my yard." Everybody doesn't feel that way. Others look at it as a chore. . . . What people don't realize is that they think they can put in a plant and that's it. It still has to be *touched.* It's just like a child, they want to feel like they're loved, and they want food and nourishment. I think that you have to really want to do it, the passion has to be within you, to put your hand in the soil. And I love touching the dirt. I like the feel of it. I just can't stand it when I have gloves on. I like the soil. The thing about gardens to me is that they're *living,* and so you want to *touch* them.

Sandra, more than most, articulates her relationship to her yard in terms of an embodied responsiveness between person and plant, including the importance of touch and care over time.

In urban and suburban residential areas, yards are among the sites people can most directly design, shape, and make their own. This essay, based on ethnographic fieldwork with residents in their yards, examines two ways these mundane, familiar spaces may be important lenses into worlds of everyday life: lived experiences of cultivation and inhabitation at the scale of the human body in practice, and the importance of yards in the broader social context of neighborhood life. As people live with yards (often over long periods), these spaces become enmeshed in daily

Sandra mulches her front boulevard garden in North Minneapolis, summer 2012. Photograph by the author.

life. They are sites for a variety of cultivation practices, from the basic maintenance of lawns and existing landscape features to the development of elaborate worlds comprising human and nonhuman elements. As such, they are bound up with—but never completely constrained or explained by—the parameters set by expert designers, real estate developers, formal policies, the extent of private property, or social norms.

## Knowing Yards

Residential front, back, and side yards associated with single-family houses are shaped by a complex mix of organisms, histories of urbanization, climate, governance, social relations, and everyday activities. Access to these spaces remains bound up with fundamentally uneven geographies in American cities and suburbs. Such spaces constitute a kind of connective tissue across multiple boundaries in towns and cities, such as those of property, habitat, and watershed. Yards in the United States have been considered spaces in which hierarchies of care, cultural meanings, and the nature of middle-class property ownership take shape.[1] Yet this rich and variegated nature of yards remains on the margins of scholarly inquiry. Despite their prevalence across urban and suburban residential landscapes throughout the United States, yards have been too often understood as a kind of static aesthetic or cultural product, often reduced to a singular focus on lawns. Scholars have tended to overlook the practices and processes that continually shape and reshape these spaces.[2] In this essay, I examine yards as more dynamic and potentially generative spaces within residential landscapes—as sites of ongoing practices and daily rhythms that constitute a significant part of the sociospatial production of urban and suburban life.

To do this, I follow two recent lines of inquiry about the co-constitution of nature and society. First and most formative has been the broad turn by an array of scholars in the humanities and social sciences toward understanding social and political relationships as embedded within the "vibrant matter" of life itself,[3] often in terms of actor networks, "more-than-human" worlds, new materialisms, relationality, and posthumanism.[4] Here, subjectivity can be pushed beyond correspondence with distinct or individual bodies and instead is understood to be relational. The particular relationships that develop over time among organisms, surroundings, and social formations hold within them political possibilities for how individual and collective life is organized and imagined. Second, this approach to yards is informed by theorizations of everyday life that focus on repetition as sameness and, at the same time, imagine repetition as the possibility for difference and, more broadly, the possibility for sociospatial transformation.[5] This creative power of practice entails not just activities and their effects but also a set of relations of response or interaction—the ways bodies, organisms, and materials affect one another, especially the ways more-than-human worlds make demands, impinge, encroach, interrupt. Taken together, perspectives on more-than-human surroundings in everyday life provide new ways of seeing yards, as well as the broader sociospatial landscapes they constitute.

As part of my fieldwork studying yards, I became acquainted with more than forty-five yards and their inhabitants, focusing on three study areas in Minneapolis, Minnesota.[6] The areas range from a historically white working-class neighborhood organized around railroad lines and related industry, with small single-family homes built in the 1920s and an increasingly diverse population that now includes many Latino immigrants (Northeast Minneapolis), to an area originally developed in the early 1920s with many large four- to six-bedroom homes on spacious lots, which subsequently housed waves of middle-class and upper-middle-class Jewish residents, followed by African American residents (North Minneapolis), to a primarily white upper-middle-class area with large homes built in the 1910s, near several of the iconic lakes in the city (South Minneapolis).

In all of these areas, gridded streetcar lines laid the groundwork for development in the early decades of the twentieth century. Blocks were divided into rectilinear lots on which single-family houses were surrounded by yard spaces. Though originally imagined as suburban, such neighborhoods have become understood by inhabitants as thoroughly urban in relation to more recent postwar and contemporary suburban and exurban development. As with almost all residential neighborhoods, except those in the densest downtown areas, these Minneapolis neighborhoods today are still composed mainly of single-family homes or duplexes with yards. Yards are relatively ubiquitous across contemporary socioeconomic distinctions in the city. The yards also reflect how inhabitants have refashioned, to varying degrees, these once-suburban landscapes in the intervening decades.

The inhabitants who participated in this study differ from one another in terms of class, race, employment, age, and length of time living in their homes.[7] The yards range from bare and self-described "neglected" spaces of primarily grass to intensely cultivated and densely gardened worlds. For the most part, participants did most yard work and gardening themselves. If they did hire or rely on outside help for yard work, it was mainly for basic lawn-mowing services.[8] Each study area comprises five to ten adjacent city blocks, enabling an understanding of the relationships between yards (and their residents) at a relatively fine-grained resolution. This allows for depth in the research. Through yard visits, interviews, photographs, drawings, and participant activities such as keeping a yard journal, a quite surprising array of physical spaces, affective attachments, and understandings has emerged from this project. In addition to semistructured questions and participant observation with people in their yards over several visits, primarily this research was organized around the request to each participant, "Show me your yard." I followed participants' leads in order to see what was important and notable to them about their yards. Situated conversations and interviews then unfolded among raised garden beds and scruffy lawns, amid patio furniture and on back decks. When possible, I returned for additional visits in order to see how yards changed with seasons, time of week, and time of day; in some cases I kept track of developing projects and changes to yard spaces.

## Cultivating Bodies

Cultivation in yards takes shape through gardens and gardening. Cultivation also makes spaces in which to dwell, to inhabit. In both these senses, cultivation becomes an attunement of human bodies with their surroundings and time. In this section I discuss cultivating practices in two main ways. First, and not surprisingly, gardening emerged as a major activity in yards. Here, I examine cultivation as the development of a responsiveness between people and plants, which occurs over long periods. But the cultivation of yards does not focus only on encounters with plant bodies through gardening. Second, I examine how yards are made and maintained as settings people inhabit—backdrops for activities such as sitting, talking, being, and looking. These practices also cultivate connections across time and space, in and through yards. In both cases, the gardening labors and experiences become embodied in the fabric of the yard. The yard, in turn, becomes embodied in these everyday yard practices.

Sandra's perspectives quoted at the beginning of this essay point toward a physical and affective attunement with her yard in terms of immediate physical encounter through touch. She described this more clearly than most study participants. But even less explicitly, touch was important throughout almost all the yard visits—people leaned toward plants, brushed their hands over them as they talked, ran leaves between their fingers, pointed at foliage and pulled it aside. They cradled blooms in their hands and pulled weeds from their footings. Touch was implicit in the ways people described many tasks and activities around yards. Touch is part of a multisensory and embodied inhabitation of yards, along with smell, taste, sound, and sight. These embodied practices of cultivation involve not just the moment of touch between person and plant (an important dimension) but also temporal registers that span seasons and years and suggest that people and their yards respond to, and develop, their respective capacities over long time frames. Sandra explained how touch, care, and cultivation demand a certain degree of responsiveness to plants over time. As she continued, the rhythms of this care came through as a rewarding engagement:

> I don't understand people who just install, and don't want to nurture these little things, and make sure that they're okay. That's the part about gardening that is so rewarding, is that it's a living thing and it gives back to you. I don't care if it's vegetables or plants, but you gonna love it, and it's gonna love you back by producing, and I think that's what it is about.

For Sandra, plants are affected by the care people provide, and people are affected by the growth and production of plant bodies.

Differences from year to year, as well as from season to season within one year, inform how people make decisions about gardening. Often participants recounted to me long and detailed narratives about particular plants—their origin stories, when they planted them, if they had moved them around or divided them, whether or not they liked them, where plants had been "happiest." Kevin, an accomplished gardener, told me about his experiences with one particular plant over the course of years. He described this as an ongoing responsive encounter between himself and the plant. The plant responds to its surroundings and care; in turn, Kevin responds to the plant. He told me:

> I do have a couple of favorite plants, so I always give them extra water. I protect them. One is my yellow lady slipper. I planted it, and I didn't understand much

about how it flowered. The first year, it flowered. The next year, it flowered. The third year, no flower. Well, then I read that it normally takes five to seven years before it will flower, if it's transplanted. And it went for four years without a flower. Now, it's been flowering the past few years, so I guess it's doing all right. But it comes out for a week, and then it's gone. And then it just looks like a weed. But I am pretty excited about this particular plant. . . . A lot of it is waiting. You experiment, and every year it's like, well, that didn't quite work, so I gotta wait until next year. I'll try something else and try something different. A garden, like a painting, is never really finished. A lot of it is just experience, people planting year after year.

One important dimension of this kind of cultivation emerged again and again: surprisingly mobile plant geographies within and across yards. Especially seasoned gardeners constantly "edit," as one woman told me—which entails moving plants and dividing perennials, replanting parts of them elsewhere. Participants often had their own philosophies about the best times to divide or move plants in response to changing seasons. Some gardeners liked to make these kinds of changes in the

Kevin points out a favorite plant, a lady slipper, protected by a makeshift metal cage, summer 2012. Photograph by the author.

fall, whereas others preferred to make them in the spring, based on their memories of what had happened in earlier years.

People talked about yards beyond these more narrow discussions of gardening, as settings for a variety of practices that make spaces in which to dwell. Cultivating plants certainly contributes to the shaping and reshaping of these spaces. Avid gardeners talked about sitting in their yards and admiring their labors, as well as appreciating the growth of the plants and other organisms. But in a broader way, yards become places to be outdoors. Cultivation becomes a way to inhabit yards. Yards serve as settings through which activities occur, as in the case of Jennifer, a woman who lives in Northeast Minneapolis with her husband and their two large dogs. I invited participants to keep a daily yard diary for two weeks—a place to respond to a few questions about yard activities, time spent outdoors at home, and thoughts about their yards. She wrote:

JENNIFER / YARD DIARY / AUGUST 15, 2012 (WEDNESDAY)

*Did you spend any time outdoors around your home today?*

Yes

*If yes, about roughly how long, in total?*

1½ hours

*If yes, what did you do?*

I trimmed up the overgrowth in my yard and played with my dogs in the yard. I'm slowly preparing for guests on Sunday. Also took my dogs out. The yard is starting to look better. I cleared a lot of overgrowth and weeds.

*How do you feel about your yard today? Write any additional comments or thoughts below.*

I'm worried about my sedum that seems to be falling apart in the middle. My cucumber is dying and I don't know why. I picked three flowers (zinnias) and put them in a small vase of my mother's shaped like a chicken (hen).

JENNIFER / YARD DIARY / AUGUST 25, 2012 (SATURDAY)

*Did you spend any time outdoors around your home today?*

Yes. We tend to just hang outside on the weekend—we chat on the patio/driveway. Let the dogs out. Open the garage to fetch certain items. We planned to go to the fair. Outside—we loaded things out of the car to the patio/driveway to prepare to go to the fair. Later in the evening after the fair we got in the hot tub for about thirty minutes.

*How do you feel about your yard today? Write any additional comments or thoughts below.*

I love my yard on the weekends—it's there to add a backdrop to the events (however normal) of my summer.

As Jennifer's remark about her yard as "a backdrop to the events of . . . summer" shows, yards can provide important settings and contexts, beyond the role of gardens and gardening.

These dwelling practices often include individual activities, such as sitting. Many people told me they spend time contemplating their yards from favorite vantage points; often they talked about drinking morning coffee in proximity to their yards and using this time to figure out their day. Bea, who had lived in her home for forty-two years at the time of this research, described this when I asked what she enjoys most about her yard:

Bea's view from her favorite place to sit in her backyard in North Minneapolis, summer 2012. Photograph by the author.

Sitting. I most enjoy sitting. I sit right here. This is my place. I love sitting in my
yard. Especially early in the morning. I have my coffee out here. I read the paper.
And I just look around. It gives me a lot of pleasure, because I feel like older gardens
and older homes deserve a kind of love and attention. So I feel like, this is good.
Whoever comes behind me will get this really nice garden and they will have a nice
place to sit.

For Bea, an accomplished gardener, the cultivation of her yard provides immediate pleasures in just sitting and being in the space. Bea relates this to care over
successive lifetimes of residents of a single house. The cultivation of her own yard
gives her a way to provide future inhabitants with what she considers a meaningful setting—cultivating this yard as a future timespace through her own everyday
practices.

## Yards for Whom?

This question of for whom yards are cultivated opens up a way of thinking through
the social meanings of yards. Cultivating yards entails the confluence of embodied
practices with broader social contexts along city blocks and neighborhoods. In one
front yard in North Minneapolis, Sandra characterized her intensive engagement
with her yard through gardening in very individual terms. Yet when I spent time
with her in her yard, it became clear that this is also a space for gathering key social
relations in place. Large ceramic frogs perch on the low retaining wall, frog figurines nestle between hostas on the boulevard garden, a frog sitting in a miniature
Adirondack chair atop a boulder echoes the full-size Adirondack chairs just behind
it. This is Sandra's yard, and frogs are just one element of her orderly front, side,
and back yards, which also include an array of salvaged objects, sculptures, plants,
and seating areas. She told me:

See, I'm ah—I'm a junker. I'm an artist, I like *stuff.* And so my yard would, to some-
body who is a minimalist, be a nightmare! Because they would say, "Oh my God!
This is just too much!" But that's what I like. That's why I say, it reflects *me.* It doesn't
matter what anybody else says, I just like stuff. . . . I think my yard speaks to people
who like plants and things. And I like that. It's really me. My yard speaks solely
about *me.* I love lots of textures, I love motion, and I love things that—it's that artistic side of me. It's my muse. That's what it is. It's my *muse.*

Beyond this individual motivation to create her yard spaces, Sandra's yard serves
important functions for her immediate neighbors and on her city block. It is a gathering space for a group of men Sandra jokingly calls the "Alley Cats," kids are drawn

to the many frogs, and people who know Sandra even just a little bit feel comfortable walking up into her yard in search of her. While she does not frame her yard practices in terms of these responsibilities or contributions to others' everyday lives, Sandra relishes sharing her space and her artistic eye with others. Through her gardening labors, Sandra's yard becomes part of neighborhood everyday life.

Across the city from Sandra's yard, in the more affluent South Minneapolis study area, an intricately sculpted front yard is populated by small fairy figurines among circuitous water channels and pools made from rocks, with ornate decorative plants perched alongside, as well as benches and sculptures. When I first stopped by to leave a research flyer, homeowner Julia directed me to follow the path

Sandra's side yard includes sculpture, salvaged objects, and plants. Photograph by the author.

as a loop. Using stepping-stones, I crossed a small stream of water flowing into a fountain and followed a stone path through a side yard with benches. I emerged into the backyard, where water gurgled in two large ponds filled with koi and lily pads. Back decks at two levels looked down on the space from above. Finally, the northern side yard was decorated as an outdoor room—"bistro style," shaded and cool. At our first formal yard visit, Julia, Roger, her husband of twenty-six years, and Kate, their teenage daughter, took me on the same route through the yard. They stopped along the way to point out different things. For Roger, an innovative fabric material lining the many pools and water channels was the main feature of interest. Julia showed me views and told the story of the evolution of a yard with few points of interest into this full-blown quasi-public space. For their daughter, particular plants and the tree where she climbs were most important. Passers-by are often invited to walk through these spaces on their own. Julia described some of the ways people interact with the yard:

> I think it's so surprising, and so enjoyable, that we can make one small change and there are people that are so familiar with it, they'll say, "Oh! I love what you've done!" Or sometimes we can hear them talking, they might not see us here, and they comment on things. Sometimes people are very uncomfortable until they are invited up, but then they enjoy it and are very respectful.

Kate added:

> Sometimes, at first, it was a little weird. We were more aware people might be there. And now we're just—we just kind of live our normal life, and we've gotten used to having people go around the house and look around. If we see people are there longer than a few minutes, we'll come out and say, "Oh, do you want to see the backyard, too?" Or we'll just show them around more.

Neighbors routinely asked if I had visited the Fairy Garden yard and more often than not expressed admiration for and complimented the efforts of Julia and her family. Ellen, a retired minister who enjoys gardening but is struggling with challenges from arthritis, told me she walks down the block to sit by the cool water on hot days on the bench built into the front retaining wall or across the sidewalk on the boulevard.

Very few neighbors weighed in with reservations. Barb, who lives two blocks away, told me, "Too many fairy houses, too many fountains, they should have stopped with the waterfall. Excess." Barb linked the intensive cultivation in Julia's front yard with a broader shift in how she has observed people gardening in the city:

Roger, Julia, and Kate in their elaborate front yard in South Minneapolis, summer 2012. Photograph by the author.

Julia's side yard, "bistro style." Photograph by the author.

I think it's interesting that people in the city have gotten so garden conscious and see value in it. On some level, whether it's just personal beauty or satisfaction. Because when I grew up, on the other side of the way, we didn't plant anything. My stepfather kind of forced the issue and planted a few things, but there was no such thing as—*gardening*. But it's a nice phenomenon.

Here Barb was alluding to class differences. She grew up in government-subsidized housing—what she described as "the other side of the way." Class distinctions often take shape in regard to particular plants and gardening practices. For example, although participants engaged in informal perennial plant exchange across all study areas, in the two areas that are more working-class (Northeast and North Minneapolis) these networks were more prominently discussed and elaborated.

As Barb continued to describe the growing interest in gardening, she returned to the physical labors and pleasures of gardening itself:

I think it's probably as much you see other people doing it, but then it does turn into something that's rewarding just for the doing. And I don't know—there certainly seems to be a lot of popular support, the newspapers, and maybe things are more successful for nurseries.

At the same time that Julia and her family enjoy the notoriety of their yard in the neighborhood, it is clear the yard also provides them with their own embodied sense of experience. In the brief time I spent with them in their yard, Julia told me about the importance of having a variety of spaces so that there are places above the fray, just to *be*. We stood on the landing of the two-story deck at the back of the house, watching her husband and daughter fix the back gate. Julia talked with me about how their view has changed over the decades they have lived in the house and described how much she enjoys sitting on the deck:

We had this almost right away when we moved in. Roger built it. So we've spent a lot of time here, and at times over the years there's been a real neighborhood feeling back here. Now with our front yard more interesting, we end up spending more time there. But I still really love to sit here and just look out.

These two intensively cultivated yards in the study provide different inflections about how people articulate their own motivations and skills and how yards are understood and experienced by neighbors. Sandra focused on her own embodied experiences cultivating her yard, though it is clear in spending time with her there that the yard functions also as a social node on the block for Sandra and for her

Julia looks out from the back deck, South Minneapolis. Photograph by the author.

neighbors. This social aspect of her yard resonates with the narratives Julia and her family provided to explain their own quasi-public yard. But in spending time with them in the spaces they have cultivated, it is clear that each member of the family feels the yard spaces through his or her own embodied encounters that happen there. In both cases, the yards are sites for everyday embodied practices and incremental changes over long periods. These yards contribute to life at the scale of the city block and adjacent blocks in ways that exceed the intentions and explanations of the individual inhabitants.

## Conclusion

Yards are spaces of diverse practices, aesthetics, and meanings. What can be seen in these case studies is an attunement between the ways people cultivate and inhabit their yards and the places yards become. I have shown how yards are sites of embodied practices, whether through immediate moments of touch, understandings of the motivations for what people do in yards, or the effects of those cultivating practices in the broader landscape. Yards can be understood as places of encounter—

between different organisms and between human intentions and design visions, particular neighborhood socialities, and the material limits and possibilities of embodied labors involving skill, experience, and experimentation. When inhabitants engage in yard and gardening labors such as weeding, mowing, trimming, and maintenance, everyday patterns become embodied in and through yards.

Cultivating yards entails more than gardening; it is also caught up with cultivating attunements, skills, and relations. These experiences point toward the importance of a need and desire for pause points in daily life—times to notice things, to be in and of the landscape, to think about plant bodies, to watch and wait and be attuned to surroundings, and to simply be outdoors. Yards become places of and for everyday inhabitation. This raises questions about who has access to these kinds of temporalities, spaces, and practices. Yards constitute the very nature of the highly uneven racialized and gendered residential landscapes of single-family homes in the United States. As contemporary pressures mount to alter yard aesthetics toward particular environmental goals and outcomes, incorporating dimensions of yards beyond quantifiable metrics or a focus on end results will be essential for our collective environmental futures.

## Notes

1. Paul Groth, "Lot, Yard, and Garden: American Distinctions," *Landscape* 30, no. 3 (1990): 29–35.

2. But see these notable exceptions to the study of yards and gardens: J. B. Jackson, "The Popular Yard," *Places* 4, no. 3 (1987): 26–32; James Rojas, "The Enacted Environment: Examining the Streets and Yards of East Los Angeles," in *Everyday America: Cultural Landscape Studies after J. B. Jackson,* ed. Chris Wilson and Paul Groth (Berkeley: University of California Press, 2003), 275–92; Russell Hitchings, "People, Plants and Performance: On Actor Network Theory and the Material Pleasures of the Private Garden," *Social & Cultural Geography* 4, no. 1 (2003): 99–113; Lesley Head and Pat Muir, *Backyard: Nature and Culture in Suburban Australia* (Wollongong, N.S.W.: University of Wollongong Press, 2007); Christopher Grampp, *From Yard to Garden: The Domestication of America's Home Grounds* (Chicago: Center for American Places, 2008).

3. Jane Bennett, *Vibrant Matter: A Political Ecology of Things* (Durham, N.C.: Duke University Press, 2001).

4. In human geography, this turn has been informed by various philosophical lineages. For a key review, see Bruce Braun, "Environmental Issues: Inventive Life," *Progress in Human Geography* 32, no. 5 (2008): 667–79.

5. Henri Lefebvre, *Rhythmanalysis: Space, Time and Everyday Life,* trans. Stuart Elden and Gerald Moore (New York: Continuum Press, 2004). See also Jon May and Nigel Thrift, *TimeSpace: Geographies of Temporality* (New York: Routledge, 2001).

6. This is part of a larger research project concerning how yards are made and experienced by residents, especially in relation to municipal governance that is increasingly focused on urban environmentalisms such as sustainability and resilience.

7. Despite my efforts to engage renters in the study areas, participants were primarily homeowners.

8. This fits with broader regional cultural expectations about doing one's own yard maintenance and gardening, emerging from dominant perceptions of rural and farming "roots" in this part of the upper midwestern United States. Compare this with, for example, the prevalence of hiring help for yard maintenance and gardening in a city such as Los Angeles. These differences point to the importance of cultural geographies and meanings of place, and especially the uneven geographies of informal labor for those who can afford hired help with yards and gardening.

# Suburban Rhetorics

*Planning and Design for American Shopping, 1930–1960*

DAVID SMILEY

Midcentury suburbs were constructed as much through images as through platform construction. Suburban homes, office buildings, and shopping centers circulated in the American imagination through drawings and photographs and were deeply implicated in shared understandings of place. Because representations confirm, adjust, or even redact particular views of the social conditions through which, in this instance, suburban buildings appear normal and natural, analysis needs to draw out exactly how this happens. In other words, images do not merely execute the task of representing, they are also provisional demonstrations of the processes through which they are produced and valued. Images, as Sigfried Kracauer wrote, are "interested."[1] Read through images and their circulation, the building of the American suburbs was also an active rhetorical project undertaken by and for particular professional audiences.

Images of the suburban shopping center in 1930s architectural journals helped legitimate suburbs as places for serious professional work. Not only did designed shopping places contrast with the "longitudinal rash," as typical roadside commerce was professionally described, but the new shopping centers also provided visual arguments against older urban patterns.[2] With the apparent slapdash quality of existing city shopping districts, a professional (and civic and real estate) focus on the rational planning of new shopping nodes in the seemingly empty suburbs might yield a more palatable, status-worthy urban image. The suburban shopping center came to stand in for a mythic lost organic city and, at the same time, for an equally chimeric new urban social life, based on an unprecedented type of planning and organization.

This essay examines selected mid-twentieth-century architectural representations of suburban shopping depicting the existing city as terminally problematic

and the suburb as a thoroughly new alternative for such essential activity. Images in
professional circulation illustrate the development of the rhetorical "suburbanness"
(for lack of a better word) of the nonurban shopping center and the shopping
center's emergence as a new form of intervention in the built landscape. Further
bolstered by their incorporation into professional discussions of modernism and
modernization, these images contributed in no small way to strategies of metropolitan development—that is, to the growth and normalization of suburbs.

## 1931–34: Order

The storefront pictured on the title page of a 1931 *Architectural Record* article is
empty, containing nothing but its own spatial volume and naked columns. In this
photograph we see through the transparent display window to the scarcely inhabited open space and buildings beyond. The cylindrical masses of roof and canopy
hover over the recessed glass, and the canopy aligns with the sidewalk. The precision, planar abstraction, and smooth surfaces of the building would soon become
the hallmarks of a particular curation of modernism, namely, those featured in the
Museum of Modern Art's "International" modern architecture exhibition and catalog in 1932.[3] This particular image, which was included in the MoMA exhibition,
heralded the new architectural possibilities of European modernism per se and,
more prosaically if also more radically, of new technical strategies and specifications
for retailing.

The neighborhood store in the Hoek van Holland development by J. J. P. Oud
was the centerpiece of "Planning the Retail Store" in the June 1931 "Technical
News and Research" section introduced into *Architectural Record* earlier that year.[4]
Editor (and recent émigré) Knud Lönberg-Holm's use of the word *planning* rather
than *designing* reminds us that among the claims of early European modernists were
professional and polemical claims for rational methods, functional clarity, and un-
adorned problem solving.[5] Lönberg-Holm, perhaps more radical than his peers of
the Congrès Internationaux d'Architecture Moderne (CIAM) group, saw production and utility as the sole features of a properly modernist view of change. Just as
the term *elevation* replaced *facade* in architectural discourse, the word *planning* signaled an optimistic association with pragmatics, objectivity, and science. Presenting Oud's store in a new "technical section" in *Architectural Record* was part of a shift,
or perhaps a testing of the waters, regarding how modernist architecture in Europe
might become disseminated among and transformed by American architects.[6]

Lönberg-Holm found an auspicious editorial perch in 1930 at the rapidly changing *Architectural Record*. He was hired by Lawrence Kocher, also a recent arrival
at the magazine, whose interests spanned from the Colonial Williamsburg restoration to radical housing proposals to residential subdivision regulations. He, in turn,

# PLANNING THE RETAIL STORE

## By K. LÖNBERG-HOLM

NEIGHBORHOOD STORE, HOEK VAN HOLLAND, J. J. P. OUD, ARCHITECT

Title page showing "Neighborhood Store" at Hoek van Holland project by J. J. P. Oud, in K. Lönberg-Holm, "Planning the Retail Store," *Architectural Record* 69 (June 1931): 495.

had been hired by longtime *Record* editor Michael Mikkelsen, who advocated for the profession to more fully embrace the constructional, material, and economic circumstances of architecture, for which modernism, he wrote, might be suited. Mikkelsen wrote a massive real estate history and guide of New York City, a study of publicly owned electric lighting in Chicago, and critiques of new American building, and he was an officer of the F. W. Dodge Corporation (owners of *Sweet's Catalog* as well as *Architectural Record*), all of which signal his strong interest in the technical and design questions facing the profession, but he had a wider horizon as well.[7] In 1928 he editorialized in *Record* that a "new feeling" was evident in the field, and it was incumbent on the magazines to explore such growth. This was not untypical, as architectural discussions of the 1920s were rife with speculation about the new architecture, but the changing *Architectural Record* masthead revealed a sense of mission and soon included modernist advocate Henry-Russell Hitchcock and technical editors Robert L. Davison and C. Theodore Larson, enabling the magazine to claim modernism as a field of research.[8]

Lönberg-Holm described the Oud store as functionally derived; the circular plan and glass line "insure visibility from the street and contact between shopper and merchandise," and this transparency was matched by the seamless flow of goods: "a minimum of friction and a minimum of time." With visual barriers erased and actual walls reduced, the store fulfilled its utilitarian mission: "The retail store is an outlet for the distribution of commodities." The elimination of bourgeois pomp and decoration transformed individuated desire into a social necessity.[9]

After his initial descriptions of store planning in the article, Lönberg-Holm outlined new technical aspects of location choice (the proverbial creator of real estate value) in the context of the horizontally expanding American city, including trade areas, access diagrams, and store types. This portion of the article was accompanied by a photograph of a 1929 shopping center in Washington, D.C., called the Park and Shop Stores, a radical bit of planning at the time, belying its banality today. This development clearly pointed to new patterns of growth away from the older commercial core of the city. The new trade realities, Lönberg-Holm emphasized to his readers, were no longer determined by foot traffic but rather by automobile accessibility. New community facilities at urban peripheries would have to be designed according to the logics of the delivery truck and the consumer's automobile. It was not imagined in 1932 that such places would come to define the American suburban landscape, but Lönberg-Holm and the *Record* editors considered the Park and Shop Stores a breakthrough and a new, progressive, and pragmatic response to growing patterns of urban growth: suburbanization.[10]

The *Record*'s photograph of the Park and Shop frames a wide building frontage to privilege parking spaces, with the storefronts almost entirely blocked by parked

"Park and Shop, Washington, D.C.," in K. Lönberg-Holm, "Planning the Retail Store," *Architectural Record* 69 (June 1931): 499.

cars. There is little context in the image, and while we see the municipal sidewalk in the foreground, the building and lot demonstrate a new conception. Program and site are not based on traditions of lot line construction, as the buildings are built instead back into the depth of the site. The unity of the arcade canopy is a key visual indicator of a new management model, a unified complex, complementing the efficiency of service organization and the logic of parked and moving cars.[11] It is not an urban image; other buildings are barely evident, and the wide sky above and the broad parking pavement in the foreground have the greatest presence in the photograph, sandwiching the thin line of retail fascia, signage, and shadow. This representation of elements, sky and ground, is not quite available to an urban photographer. This new retail arrangement is horizontal, whereas the space of the traditional city is vertical.

The *Record*'s retailing "Technical News and Research" section challenged architects to keep up with new technical data as well as developments in architectural expression. Advising clients on site selection by charting trade areas and tracking movement patterns to determine the spending capacities of particular populations were among the many once-ignored tasks that now had to become the purview of the architect-as-planner. The emerging "sciences" of management and marketing that created a vast retailing ecosystem across the twentieth century were more than sympathetic to the positivistic tendencies of modernism. The *Record* editors also

included studies concerning efficient commerce, diagrams of movement of goods
and customers, and traffic lighting graphs, all of which yoked together rhetorics of
modernism, technocratic metrics of modernization, and the emerging organization
of the suburban landscape. The fact that the Park and Shop was colonial rather than
Corbusian and shared no apparent features with Oud's shop did not prevent it from
also demonstrating "modernity" as a new solution to new conditions. The modern retailing center, and a modernist program in general, appeared to be smoothly
established in the new horizontality of suburban space.

Architectural Record published the Park and Shop Stores photograph again in a
1932 article, "Neighborhood Shopping Centers," in which the project played the
favored half in a "bad model–good model" pair. The caption of the first of the pair
("Shopping District of Main Street Character") led the reader to denigrate the older
fabric as cheap and honky-tonk, a "Coney Island Architecture."[12] The tight cropping
of the photograph communicates more: claustrophobic, the street wall and the cars
press forward; there is neither foreground, background, nor sky; the heterogeneity
of "unrelated" windows, doors, cornices, roof heights, roof lines, signage, and materials produces a visual cacophony without relief. Cars on the street are tightly packed,
and there does not seem to be enough space for pedestrians or for an unobscured
view of the shops. Sign painters (or perhaps repairmen) emphasize the uncomfortable dynamic of the street—another slapdash layer adding to the visual noise. Even
the ornate street lamps, once a sign of the putatively benevolent politics of urban
improvement, now add to the disarray. The image's lack of space for the eye, much
less the ideal shopper, renders the view tense, as the editors no doubt intended.
Whatever historic value might today accrue to "Main Street," the pejorative view in
1932 underscores the broad discomfort with which professionals viewed the older
conditions of the city.

Parenthetically, it is worth mentioning that the center of the image is occupied
by storefronts of the Woolworth Company and the A&P Tea Company. If the overall image is one of individualized and differentiated enterprises, a visual representation of the street as a site for laissez-faire activities, the presence of two national
chain stores does not quite fit. By 1932, the two stores, one for food and the other
for general merchandising, were already known for undercutting local retailer prices
by virtue of their economies of scale. The chain stores introduced an array of standardized practices for pricing, distribution, and packaging and were integral to the
reshaping of American commerce.[13] In the early years, however, these stores remained on Main Street, and Main Street remained the sole spatial referent for the
center of social life and commerce. The eventual suburbanization of such chain
stores still lay in the future, but the modernization of the landscape was already
under way.

# DRAFTING AND DESIGN PROBLEMS

## NEIGHBORHOOD SHOPPING CENTERS

Keystone View

SHOPPING DISTRICT OF MAIN STREET CHARACTER. This unrelated "Coney Island Architecture" suggests the need for cooperative and unified planning by architects.

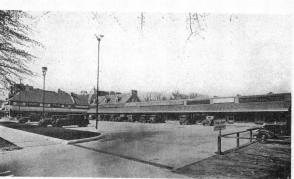

Underwood

A PLANNED GROUPING OF SHOPS with parking space that does not interfere with traffic of main thoroughfare. The design by one architect of buildings for a variety of uses results in uniformity.

"Neighborhood Shopping Centers," in "Drafting and Design Problems," *Architectural Record* 71 (May 1932): 325.

The remedy for the cacophonous "Coney Island Architecture" was the Park and Shop design model, based on "cooperative and unified planning by architects." Coming from the architectural press and aimed at architects, this was no surprise, but the emphasis on shared planning action joined modernism's emerging discourse about collective work to the discourse of the associational state before the New Deal. No longer should each store fend for itself, or be allowed to stand out too much; the unity of the whole "planned grouping" was the key to success. Unity and clarity of the ensemble were provided by the uniformity of individual parts, such as the signage and roof line. In visual terms, the competing details of the Main Street photograph push up against the picture plane while the Park and Shop image offers calm, wide, and deep space. Adding to the problematic rendering, the parking of cars on Main Street, the nosing in and backing out, impeded the active and efficient flow of traffic on the street. In contrast, the Park and Shop's removal of shoppers' cars from the public thoroughfare, such that parking "does not interfere" with flow, created a sense of fluidity and mobility. Ease of motion became a normative and moneymaking desideratum, and only one of the two images could possibly qualify.

The photograph of the Park and Shop Stores made a final appearance in a 1934 *Architectural Record* article on stores by Regional Plan Association of America (RPAA) planners Clarence Stein and Catherine Bauer. This time the paired image is almost solely concerned with a "Main Street" choked with automobiles. The town of Huntington, New York, had taken the desperate measure of allocating the middle lane of its Main Street for parking, in addition to the usual curbside parking. Stein and Bauer were outraged that Main Street had literally become a parking lot, a site of fragmented and even restricted mobility and decreased visibility, overfull in every way. The now-famous Washington, D.C., Park and Shop arrangement offered cooperative and unified planning, spaciousness, ease of movement, a casual yet controlled atmosphere, and convenience—all of which offered a double reading. On one hand, Park and Shop could be understood as progressive and rational, presenting planning as improvement. Yet the easy mobility, the ever-beckoning parking lot, and the scale and use of the building increasingly coalesced into a "suburban" imaginary: a new kind of open and improved nonspecific place with urban-like amenities.

## 1943: No Longer Urban

In the 1930s, cars and trucks became discursive catalysts for reconception of the metropolis, just as they were the literal force for technical questions about the movement of goods and people. Discussions about various mobilities also generated conflicting questions about use and experience of the city, often through the figure of the pedestrian. The person walking, undaunted and unencumbered, emerged in professional and theoretical literature as useful metric and even more

Galloway

Main Street, Huntington, Long Island. Principal shops border this street which is a main arterial highway. Parking is permitted in center of street and along curbs. This has resulted in excessive congestion.

purchasing power, and the modifying factors—income, general character, buying habits, location in relation to larger centers, etc.—are quite capable of analysis and forecast.

There are four principal questions for which the planner must find answers before laying out a new local shopping center. They are:

1. How much local business in dollars may we reasonably expect? (How much lost to and how much attracted from other centers?)

2. How will the local retail dollar be divided by kinds of business?

3. What is the approximate sales volume and size of a successful store in each classification?

4. How much rent can these different types of stores afford to pay?.

Obviously, none of these questions can be answered with complete accuracy. And none of them can ever be answered once and for all. Every community has certain conditions which differentiate it from every other community. Some of these conditions will only be discovered by trial and error.

But there is sufficient scientific data available with which to make a very close approximation to the correct answer to the four basic questions. This should be tested and developed through actual experience and realistic reasoning on the part of active planners and city builders.

The scientific as well as the common sense method of planning retail facilities must begin with an analysis of the number and kind of stores that will be required in a given community. To illustrate this approach to a scientific method of community store planning. we have selected as a demonstration . problem the northern section of Radburn, New Jersey, which will ultimately have a population of about 10,000.

## II. NUMBER AND KIND OF STORES

### Planning Retail Facilities for the Northern Section of Radburn, N. J., 10,000 Population: An Example of Method

**Elements of the Problem**

*Not* front footage; *not* existing ratios between number of stores and population, but:

Underwood and Underwood

Drive-In Market, Washington, D. C. There is convenient and well-lighted parking space for customers.

1. Total sum likely to be spent within the community for different kinds of goods.

2. Most efficient volume of business needed for success in each category.

**Method of Approach**

There are roughly two different methods of getting at the total sales volume, two methods which provide a good common sense check on conclusions. One is based on an analysis of retail expenditures in existing towns of comparable size, location and general character, with due allowance for special features of the case in hand. The other is based on an estimate of the purchasing power of the community, the incomes and probable budgets of the residents. As available material for the first method happens to be much more scientific and complete than that for the second, due largely to the exhaustive Census of Distribution made in connection with the last Federal Census, our estimate of expenditure is based on a co survey of sales in eleven comparable sr.

Huntington, Long Island, in Clarence Stein and Catherine Bauer, "Store Buildings and Neighborhood Shopping Centers," *Architectural Record* 75 (February 1934): 176.

powerful synecdoche. In particular, since shopping in the city was increasingly hamstrung by the problem of congestion, designing and planning around the pedestrian offered professionals the possibility of putting the technologies of commodities out of view and only the commodities on display. With the emergence of city regulations and business practices to mitigate store servicing, urban work began to accommodate the pedestrian—the shopper—but the new suburban shopping center more successfully created "friendly," "clean," and "safely collective" places to serve an expanding white middle-class audience.[14]

This transfer of focus from an automotive to a pedestrian imagery was tested in incremental bits and pieces in the early decades of the twentieth century, with a variety of strategies reorganizing the relations among street, curb, vehicle, sidewalk, and shopper. One small pair of drawings from 1943 indicates the full extent of this shift toward what might be called the suburban episteme. While a student at the Harvard Graduate School of Design, the young German émigré Willo von Moltke illustrated several articles for Dean Joseph Hudnut.[15] A regular contributor to the architectural journals, Hudnut often made pointed suggestions about the implementation of modernist architecture in the United States. In a 1943 *Record* article addressing what he saw as the poor examples of modernist housing then being built, Hudnut urged a reconsideration of many of the tenets of CIAM modernism.[16] Von Moltke's illustrations demonstrated an opposition between the ideational suburban and its rhetorical partner, the necessarily devalued urban.

In his sketch, the state of the city is made clear by a busy commercial district whose four-cornered intersection is made of traditional sidewalks and street-facing stores, cars, people, signage, and unassuming mechanical devices like parking meters and traffic lights. The empty corner lot in the foreground is fenced off and, perhaps, promises development: we see the back of a sign that might illustrate the gleaming building soon to come. Just as likely, the sign might advertise the site is for sale; an abandoned baby carriage and bicycle wheel indicate the lot is already an informal dump. Finally, since the Hudnut article is about housing, the scene might be the view from the window of an already built modern apartment building, a view from someone's living room, showing a slice of "garden" between the city and the new housing. In any scenario, the visualized city is made of small, individually owned lots, and this particular intersection is an example of the "highest and best use" version of capitalist urban life, in which not every property is ripe for investment (or disinvestment) at the same time. That cities typically grow unevenly and take their form from the whims of speculators was unacceptable to Hudnut and his progressive cohort.

The rendering indicates a laissez-faire city not quite under state control. The streets are slightly overfilled with cars, unity is absent, and the varied signage and

Shopping district sketches by Willo von Moltke, in Joseph Hudnut, "The Art in Housing," *Architectural Record* 93 (January 1943): 62. Courtesy of the Frances Loeb Library, Harvard Graduate School of Design.

many billboards bring to mind the earlier "Coney Island" critiques as well as the disdain for commerce maintained by Whiggish elites of the period. In the opinion of modernist urban theorists like Louis Mumford and Sigfried Giedion (as well as "realists" like Robert Moses), such rampant commercialism was a carbuncle on the urban face, simultaneously responsible for and symptomatic of an unsatisfactory civic life.

The scene, however, also indicates change. At the literal center of von Moltke's city sketch is a traffic signal. This humble-looking mechanical device, widely used in American cities since the mid-1920s, was a glowing icon of urban management, not merely a traffic flow regulator. The traffic signal was an integral part of the struggle to bring a new order—social, economic, technical—to the unruly nineteenth-century industrial city.[17] The entire sketch seems to rotate around the signal post, almost unnoticed yet anchoring the image, revealing the unfolding production of regulations, policies, and innumerable professional specializations. In the giving way of older perceptions of streets and speed to newer models of efficiency and flow, the image carries the tensions of modernization.

Despite the changes afoot, there is an ambivalence in the sketch, as if there might be a pleasant, if irregular, rhythm to the place, a hybrid of understandings and uses. Hudnut was relatively agnostic about modernism and the city, and his comments often show a thinly veiled impatience with what he, among others, saw as a totalizing and "dogmatic" approach. Instead, he praised the "colored letterings, bright windows, neon lights and the murmur of crowds" one typically finds in markets and main streets. While he might be accused of nostalgia, Hudnut was no romantic, and he saw the problems of the contemporary city as clearly as any: "I need no expert to show me what havoc automobile traffic plays with [an urban] shopping center."[18] He had little trouble concluding there was no alternative: the car had to be removed if pedestrian calm—the ideological, social, as well as technical goal—was to be achieved. This leads to a startling possibility: Might the representation of the modern urban housing precinct, or any modern project, overlap with the representation of the suburban shopping center?

Von Moltke's image paired with his sketch of the city shows a modest, almost banal, line of shops lightly rendered as a more intimately scaled scene. The absence of cars is quickly apparent, as is the presence of grass where one expects cars, namely, at the now-absent curb. The generous width of the walkway (no longer a side-walk) and its adjacent wide, grassy lawn (grass and paving are flush) puts in doubt any association of an urban image. In fact, the essential elements of this design would soon become ubiquitous *as* suburban: a single story of shops facing a land-scaped walkway lined with benches and planters—with cars removed from view. The stores are uniform and unified; the signage system allows for just a hint of variation, as do the two types of store frontage, enclosed and open (thanks to "new and improved" retractable aluminum systems). Women are comfortable here, bringing their children to scamper on the grass, and the grocer's open storefront is a casual site for small talk and idle conversation. From this, we infer sunny calm, birdsong, and the murmur of domesticity—always signifiers of safety and control. The image conjures a sense of ease and, simultaneously, the reassuring authority of a spatial archetype. In fact, many shopping center architects at the time claimed affiliation with the medieval market or, more ambitiously, the Greek agora, where *civitas* and commerce (they argued) coexisted. Yet these were urban referents, real or imagined, the paradox being that the twentieth century appeared incapable of creating such places anew. Instead, purged of the aggravation of traffic, intersections, and cars, the traditional city as well as the vehicular "park and shop" center were transformed into the leisurely "shops in the park" pastoral so simply rendered by von Moltke.

The "shops in the park" model seemed to offer the social texture and community life that had long been a concern of Hudnut and other progressive observers of urban change. But at what price? Did the suburban shopping center share an "antiseptic calm" with modern housing projects, about which Hudnut also fretted? Is von Moltke's "shops in the park" image one of soulless peace, controlled and neat? Is control the Achilles' heel of a particular moment in the history of design and planning, revealed in an image of unnerving tranquility that has come to be labeled "suburban"? Or, more emphatically, does the image, inhabited by women, children, and shops, reveal the blinkered gaze of a bourgeois taste culture?

Finally, the perspectival construction of von Moltke's two sketches is significant. The urban intersection has a center point that confers an enclosing visual logic, almost as if it were an interior space. More pointedly, the bird's-eye point of view from which we look down on the street approximates a removed and analytic, even maplike, attitude toward the scene. For the bucolic shopping block, von Moltke delineates a strongly raked one-point perspective, with the horizon line at the scale of everyday perception: we are "in" the scene and slightly taller than the woman to our left. The paved and planted surface below and the vast sky above are infinite. Schematic as it is, the little sketch suggests a pleasantly open, suburban continuity: a suspended moment untethered to the frictions of any particular place. It is also modern.

## 1952: Pastoral

The slow transformation of autocentric to pedestrian logic is central to a pair of drawings produced by the office of Victor Gruen for Northland, his first large-scale shopping center. "Tomorrow's Landscape," published in *Progressive Architecture* and

"Tomorrow's Landscape," Northland Shopping Center, Victor Gruen Associates, *Shopping Centers of Tomorrow* (1952), 29. Courtesy Gruen Associates.

in Gruen's own publicity materials (circa 1952), offers the dramatically horizontal and expansive point of view of a driver approaching the complex.[19] The sky above is infinite and clear, the busy-yet-open parking areas offer generous spatial depth, and, lest one be overwhelmed by the scale, the signage in the foreground gives a reassuring (if also mechanistic) sense of location, place, and direction—and four parking lots to choose from!

The drawing title carries multiple readings: "tomorrow" is, simply, a glorious new day, when planning has improved—indeed, solved—the irritating metropolitan problems that today hold us back. This is an achievable, pragmatic tomorrow, not the endlessly deferred future of the "long-haired planners" despised by action takers like Robert Moses and Victor Gruen. This new "landscape" is highly constructed and has become normative, or natural, through the masking of the monumental infrastructural, planning, and topographic work Gruen proposes. The view to our left shows a lower-level entrance indicating (but not quite revealing) a vast service, mechanical, and trucking level around which the complex is organized. With its operational needs out of sight, the depicted landscape is more machine, or even megastructure, than landscape. The systemization implicit in the drawing, the driver's broad point of view, and the scope of the undertaking take us beyond the small-scale planning of Park and Shop or the casual ease of von Moltke's pedestrian market. Here we see how the suburban shopping center, called a "planned regional shopping center" in the magazines after 1950, will transform the messy realities urban shoppers have been instructed to consider onerous and will make such problems magically, and ideologically, disappear.

"Tomorrow's Landscape" spread far beyond the former boundaries of the city and implied the city was no longer the primary or privileged figure. Gruen and Northland's owners, the Hudson Company, proposed three new shopping centers ringing Detroit. Regionalism had been a topic of urbanist discourse since Ebenezer Howard, Patrick Geddes, and many others looked to the larger milieu in which the city functioned, but in the mid-twentieth century the term took on new meaning. Architect, planner, and educator G. Holmes Perkins—who would shortly guide the University of Pennsylvania's architecture school toward broader environmental research—wrote that the balanced, "regional city" would necessarily be the locus of policy, planning, and design; the older city could no longer operate without concern for industrial and residential dispersal as well as the spread of transport and infrastructure. A new landscape would be made of a "galaxy of towns" in a hierarchy of related scales and uses, ranging from new "pedestrian islands" in the city to well-sited "local civic and business centers" surrounded by green space.[20] These terms would soon become the lingua franca of urban planning and design on the American scene, and for Gruen, the new centers would be remade from the useful hearts of older cities and "recentralized" on the periphery.[21] It is not coincidental that Gruen's urban manifesto of 1964, *The Heart of Our Cities,* was a reprisal, albeit transformed, of CIAM's 1952 *Heart of the City.* In the latter, the famed modernist advocacy group turned its attentions to older cities with barely a nod to the significance of the periphery, while for Gruen (and a growing list of supporters at the architecture magazines as well as in the real estate community), new suburban shopping centers would function as relocated urban cores.[22]

From the smooth arrival at the shopping center–machine, the car having been parked, we enter the pedestrian realm. Gruen's other sketch, an early study, fills out the narrative of the constructed landscape. We are within the complex between a parallel pair of arcaded buildings. On the left is a single story of small stores, on the right is the opaque mass of a department store. The one-point perspective creates a powerful visual order, especially because its proportions are typical of a street view, of the sidewalk-and-automotive space on Main Street. Yet a slightly overscaled tree jarringly occupies the center of the drawing. A receding line of trees (and planters) has taken the place of the car in the space, and the centrality of the trees challenges the urban referent of the drawing. In addition, Northland's outdoor spaces were given names like Market Lane, Peacock Terrace, and Great Lakes Court to conjure up vaguely countrified or bucolic associations. But the pivot point of the drawing, the awkward bit of nature shown in this early design for what later became North-land's North Mall, has a another visual role. The isolated tree desultorily placed in its square planter, accompanied by a wan square of brick paving and bench, is set into the project's vast and continuous grid; "nature," in other words, is enveloped in

Shade trees and rest benches will help create a pleasant, relaxed atmosphere in mall areas.

Design sketch, Northland, in "Huge Regional Shopping Center Started near Detroit," *Architectural Record* 111 (June 1952): 26.

a rigid order. In fact, this view demonstrates a socially constructed "second nature," a new landscape, for which the suburban shopping center is context and producer. The "pleasant, relaxed atmosphere" promised by Gruen is predicated on the serene coexistence of nature and machine: the hallmark, according to the classic essay by Leo Marx, of a simplified pastoralism. The garden is in the machine, which, in turn, unproblematically inhabits the larger "garden" of suburban representations.[23]

Finally, the symmetry and unity of the quasi-allée composition, a single space built at once, is a visual complement of the total management that is the core of the shopping center's conception, design, and operation.[24] Shopping center owners and investors were proud of the control that could be achieved in the new arrangement—commerce would be more predictable—but the drawing also signifies the larger system of organized capital newly deployed for post–World War II development. The regime of suburbanization is mediated, partly masked and partly legitimated, through a simplified pastoral imagery.

## 1956: Commercial Picturesque

As early as 1951 (but likely earlier), Marshall Field's store executives looked hungrily to the expanding suburbs beyond their famed Chicago store. A widely circulated image of the result (the Old Orchard Shopping Center, built in 1956) shows a long, irregularly shaped pond with a gently curved planted border, benches, low lights, and occasional trees. Pedestrian bridges gently arch over the pond at two points along its length. This free-flowing, "scenic" landscape element is located in the "North Mall" of the center and is framed by the arcades of the surrounding stores and building masses.[25] This almost-exotic pond feature was designed by landscape architect Lawrence Halprin along with the center's lead architect, Richard Bennett, both of whom advocated design based on what they described as experience over abstraction. Bennett wrote that the suburban shopping center was a unique opportunity to design for the pedestrian, for "everyday rituals," and for "human scale," all elements apparently missing from life in and representations of the city.[26]

The contrast at Old Orchard between the "serpentine" landscape feature and its gridded architectural setting is a simple yet telling statement about the "suburbanness" of the shopping center. Halprin, only a few years into independent practice, was beginning to test experiential possibilities of landscape design as opposed to what he and other West Coast contemporaries described as a history of overly visual approaches to landscape.[27] Complementing Halprin, Bennett had a strong interest in the aesthetic theories of the picturesque. His design for Park Forest Shopping Center (1948–50) demonstrated an explicit interest in broken views, curved routes, and nonaxial spatial sequence. Later, he discussed the pleasures of site planning for short views, local foci, and the meandering stroll, citing the "townscape" ideas of British architect Thomas Sharp and the complex urban propositions of Viennese architect Camillo Sitte. From their ideas about urban space and perception, Bennett advocated a "looking-around-the-corner" design ideal, enriching movement through a site: walking through a succession of images and individual sensations, that is, the picturesque.[28]

The pond at Old Orchard was central to a landscape to be looked *at* as well as *from*. Unlike a singular monumental object or fountain, the pond was a complex element with many features to contemplate and from which varied and unique views were afforded. Its shape and siting were described as informal and casual—hallmarks of the "easy living" of the "new suburban lifestyle," a suburbanness represented as a rejection of the industrial city's gridiron order, its social regulation, and its prescribed behaviors.[29] Through the picturesque, Bennett and Halprin transformed sites and strategies of consumption into a quasi-natural experience, an unproblematized second nature. The design of the suburban shopping center, in these terms, was antiurban but still collective, a perception that continues to guide experience and policy across the American landscape. But a more accurate rendering of the attitude might be a para- or peri-urban ideal, a selective shaping of social life in which urbanity could somehow be attained without the city. Old Orchard achieved this curated social realm and even attained a wee bit of urban tension.

Pond and bridge, Old Orchard Shopping Center, Lawrence Halprin, landscape architect, and Loebl, Schlossman, and Bennett, architects, in "Shopping Centers," *Architectural Record* 122 (September 1957): 224. Photograph by Hedrich-Blessing (HB-20852-Q); courtesy of the Chicago History Museum.

Old Orchard Shopping Center

Postcard of Old Orchard Shopping Center, circa 1960. Author's collection.

At the center of the plan of Old Orchard was a tall office building. Several early suburban shopping centers contained such buildings, although the practice did not last. Cross County Center in Yonkers, New York (Lathrop Douglass, 1955), was anchored by a tall building (one hesitates to say skyscraper), and earlier proposals for Old Orchard by Skidmore, Owings & Merrill LLP, among others, included an office building. These buildings, typically no more than eight or ten stories in height, indicated that the suburban location of the shopping center, and its function as a shopping center, could also serve as a setting for urbanity or, more precisely, a representation of urbanity, for which the tall office building was the chief signifier. As seen in one postcard, the building is carefully woven into the gridded paving of the complex, with the pond, planters, and open space as a gentle foreground, all in a controlled yet intricate composition of elements. Even the Old Orchard logo (in a modern, italicized, sans serif typeface) is offset from the center of the building, giving a dynamic, "up-to-date" reading of the building, the space, and the image. The building is more of a symbol or an abstraction of "the City" than a sponsor of messy urban life. If Old Orchard's pond was the anchor of the second nature defined by consumption, the tall building, the sign of the city, completed a picture in which the social and physical complexities of the existing city were selectively included or elided.

What, then, was the urbanity that could not be associated with the city? In the 1950s, one might say, as did Gruen and many others, the suburban shopping center was a selective replacement of the elements of collective and conflicted life of the midcentury city. Old Orchard's office building, in tandem with the many professional and community spaces, theaters, recreational spaces, and day-care centers in the era's shopping center projects—and in their widespread publicity—shaped a broad, ideological expectation for a new "building type" that would replace an outmoded urbanity with a new, suburbanized urbanity.[30] A controlled, measured, fully composed, no-accidental-building-experiences-please form of spatial agglomeration, complemented by highly studied and carefully calculated real estate and finance operations, the shopping center in the suburb embodied the deep tensions of change in the American landscape. Despite images and tropes of casualness that pervaded American postwar culture, the suburban shopping center was exponentially instrumental, and this tension was the work of representation.

## Notes

1. Siegfried Kracauer, "Photography" [1927], trans. T. Y. Levin, *Critical Inquiry* 19 (Spring 1993): 421–36.

2. Malcolm Cowley, "Continental Highway," *New Republic*, February 25, 1931, 35. See also Benton Mackaye and Lewis Mumford, "Townless Highways for the Motorist," *Harper's Monthly*, August 1931, 347–56; Karl Raitz, "American Roads, Roadside America," *Geographical Review* 88, no. 3 (July 1998): 363–87.

3. The show, *Modern Architecture: International Exhibition,* opened in February 1932. The catalog: Henry-Russell Hitchcock Jr. and Philip Johnson, *The International Style: Architecture since 1922* (New York: W. W. Norton, 1932).

4. The Hoek van Holland project was built in 1924; first English publication was in J. J. P. Oud, "Architecture and the Future," *The Studio* 96 (July–December 1928). See K. Lönberg-Holm, "Planning the Retail Store," *Architectural Record* 69 (June 1931): 495–513.

5. Planning, not form, was the central premise (or conceit) of the architecture championed by the German avant-garde (*Neue Bauen* or *Neue Sachlichkeit*), and the roles therefore of organization, movement systems, constructional systems, and materials were presumed to be the demonstration and outcome of measured need. Some architects with overzealous attitudes toward technology and function, however, were chided by Hitchcock and Johnson; see *The International Style,* 50–54.

6. On Lönberg-Holm, see Marc Dessauce, "Control lo Stile Internazionale: Shelter e la stampa architettonica americana," *Casabella* 57 (September 1993): 46–53.

7. Michael A. Mikkelsen, "Electric Street Lighting in Chicago," *Annals of the American Academy of Political and Social Science* 2, no. 5 (March 1892): 139–44; Mikkelsen, *A History of Real Estate, Building, Architecture in New York City, 1868–1893* (New York, 1898). Particularly notable was a 1917 piece bemoaning American eclecticism and hypothesizing that a study of rural homes would generate a rational theory and practice of design. See Mikkelsen, "A New Influence in American Architecture," *Architectural Record* 42 (August 1917): 146–48.

8. Within a year or two, Mikkelsen hired Henry-Russell Hitchcock, Douglass Haskell, Fiske Kimball, Howard T. Fisher, Theodore Larson, and Robert Davison. Michael A. Mikkelsen, "Two Problems of Architecture," *Architectural Record* 65 (January 1929): 65–66; Mikkelsen, "Expansion of the *Architectural Record* for 1930," *Architectural Record* 66 (December 1929): 501–2; Mikkelsen, "A Word about the New Format," *Architectural Record* 63 (January 1928): 1–2; Michael Tomlan, "Architectural Press, U.S.," in *Encyclopedia of Architecture: Design, Engineering, and Construction,* ed. Joseph A. Wilkes (New York: John Wiley, 1988), 1:281–83; Suzanne Ralston Lichtenstein, "Editing Architecture: *Architectural Record* and the Growth of Modern Architecture, 1928–1938" (doctoral dissertation, Cornell University, 1990), 53; Hyungmin Pai, *The Portfolio and the Diagram: Architecture, Discourse, and Modernity in America* (Cambridge, Mass.: MIT Press, 2002); David Smiley, *Pedestrian Modern: Shopping and American Architecture, 1925–1956* (Minneapolis: University of Minnesota Press, 2013), 31–39.

9. Lönberg-Holm, "Planning the Retail Store," 496, 497.

10. Richard Longstreth has discussed this project as specifically sited along the commuting route into and out of the core of Washington, D.C. Richard Longstreth, "The Neighborhood Shopping Center in Washington, D.C., 1930–1941," *Journal of the Society of Architectural Historians* 51 (1992): 5–34.

11. Longstreth has explored at great length the processes by which the automobile increasingly claimed design and planning attention in commercial work. Richard Longstreth, *City Center to Regional Mall: Architecture, the Automobile, and Retailing in Los Angeles, 1920–1950* (Cambridge, Mass.: MIT Press, 1997).

12. The quotation marks are in the original, as if the term was not the journal's and was somehow a unique qualification. Coney Island had long acted as the whipping post for so-called progressive critiques of deleterious forms of collective life. Robert Moses famously hated the unruly pleasures of the Boardwalk.

13. See, for instance, Godfrey M. Lebhar, *Chain Stores in America: 1859–1950* (New York: Chain Store Publishing, 1952).

14. Carl Feiss, "Shopping Centers," *House & Garden*, December 1939, 48–49, 66.

15. Von Moltke was an adept draftsman and did similar work for others over the years. See, for instance, his work with Edmund Bacon: Willo von Moltke and Edmund N. Bacon, "In Pursuit of Urbanity," *Annals of the American Academy of Political and Social Science* 314 (1957): 101–13.

16. Joseph Hudnut, "The Art in Housing," *Architectural Record* 93 (January 1943): 57–62. See also Jill Pearlman, *Inventing American Modernism: Joseph Hudnut, Walter Gropius, and the Bauhaus Legacy at Harvard* (Charlottesville: University of Virginia Press, 2007).

17. See Peter D. Norton, *Fighting Traffic: The Dawn of the Motor Age in the American City* (Cambridge, Mass.: MIT Press, 2011); Robert M. Fogelson, *Downtown: Its Rise and Fall, 1880–1950* (New Haven, Conn.: Yale University Press, 2001).

18. Hudnut, "Art in Housing," 62.

19. See the remarkable drawing for Bayfair Shopping Center, which puts the viewer in the backseat of the car peering over "Mom's" shoulder, in Smiley, *Pedestrian Modern*, 4.

20. G. Holmes Perkins, "The Regional City," in *The Future of Cities and Urban Redevelopment*, ed. Coleman Woodbury (Chicago: University of Chicago Press, 1953), 26–43. The essays in this volume were almost entirely taken up with planning and design questions raised by regionalization and dispersal. On Perkins's role in expanding Penn's programs toward landscape and planning, see Peter L. Laurence, "The Death and Life of Urban Design: Jane Jacobs, the Rockefeller Foundation and the New Research in Urbanism, 1955–1965," *Journal of Urban Design* 11, no. 2 (June 2006): 145–72.

21. Terms such as *recentralization* were common among those considering the redistribution of formerly urban functions such as commerce (and were evoked as early as the *Regional Plan of New York City and Its Environs,* circa 1930). See, for instance, Kenneth C. Welch, "Convenience vs. Shopping Goods," *Women's Wear Daily*, December 26, 1946, 82.

22. Victor Gruen, *The Heart of Our Cities: The Urban Crisis—Diagnosis and Cure* (New York: Simon & Schuster, 1964). Sigfried Giedion and José Luis Sert were aware of suburban centers in the United States. See Smiley, *Pedestrian Modern*, 232–34.

23. Leo Marx, *The Machine in the Garden: Technology and the Pastoral Ideal in America* (New York: Oxford University Press, 1964). For Marx, the simple pastoral revealed none of the tensions of its construction, unlike the complex version of the pastoral.

24. For an insightful look at the control embodied in the infrastructure of the shopping center, see Timothy Mennel, "Victor Gruen and the Construction of Cold War Utopias," *Journal of Planning History* 3 (May 2004): 116–50.

25. In 1956, shopping centers were not called malls; instead, they housed malls, referring to a more traditional landscape vocabulary.

26. Richard M. Bennett, "Random Observations on Shopping Centers and Planning for Pedestrians," *Architectural Record* 122 (September 1957): 216–18.

27. Marc Treib, "From the Garden: Lawrence Halprin and the Modern Landscape," *Landscape Journal* 31, no. 1 (2012): 5–28.

28. Bennett, "Random Observations." See also "Oral History of Richard Marsh Bennett, Interviewed by Betty J. Blum," Chicago Architects Oral History Project (Chicago: Art Institute of Chicago, 1991), 44–47, 60–71. In this interview, Bennett said he was impressed by the complex use of topography at the Lord and Taylor store on Long Island by Starrett and Van

Vleck with Raymond Loewy (opened 1941). Somehow, Bennett managed not to discuss the American picturesque in the design of parks and, of course, early suburbs.

29. On "the casual," for instance, see Harry Henderson, "The Mass-Produced Suburbs," *Harper's Magazine,* November 1953. William H. Whyte's studies of suburbs also delved into associational vocabulary in a series of articles that became an infamous book; William H. Whyte Jr., *The Organization Man* (New York: Simon & Shuster, 1956).

30. The shopping center was, until the 1960s, considered a new building type. In 1949, Bruno Funaro and Geoffrey Baker observed that "as a building type the shopping center is still in the experimental stage." Bruno Funaro and Geoffrey Baker, "Shopping Centers," *Architectural Record* 149 (August 1949): 110.

# 11

# This Old House of the Future

## Remixing Progress and Nostalgia in Suburban Domestic Design

### HOLLEY WLODARCZYK

Two very different "houses of the future" were recently on the market in the Los Angeles neighborhood of Pacific Palisades. One, originally a General Electric Show-case house built in 1956 and gifted by GE the following year to Ronald Reagan, host of television's *General Electric Theater,* stood out even among its all-electric postwar competition because its overly abundant gadgetry was designed to save energy as well as use it. A 2012 listing of this GE house of the future proclaimed that the large midcentury modern ranch-style home was therefore "environmentally friendly" long before such a designation was fashionable.[1] The other dwelling for sale was the brand new Green Builder Media–sponsored VISION House Los Angeles, first open to the public for tours in 2012. The website introducing this demonstration home asked visitors to "imagine the home of the future: a smart house that takes advantage of integrated design elements, advanced technologies, and intelligent systems to enhance the home's performance." It further boasted of "nurturing and comfortable" living spaces inside the house and out and "durable green products" to "keep the home healthy and safe," all while "returning energy to the grid, adding value to its neighborhood, and replenishing its surrounding natural environment."[2] Separated by half a century, these multimillion-dollar homes sited in established residential areas exemplify broader themes in imagining and goals in constructing a greener suburban future for us all. Whether the focus is limited to installment of energy-efficient technologies or expanded to include integrated building systems and conservation of natural resources, the promotion of these homes in national media advances the idea that a high-tech and ecologically sound house of the future is a realizable dream today. Looking back, however, is often as much a part of this evolving vision of better living as looking ahead, as discourses of progress are increasingly intermixed with elements of nostalgia in the promotion of this greener idealization of tomorrow's home, setting the terms for what is now and yet to be built in suburbia. Together these design and marketing discourses constitute a complex and at times rhetorically conflicted paradigm that nonetheless shapes how individuals conceive of fashioning their own everyday environments.

Conceptualization of the house of the future has long been a vital component in the making of suburbia, discursively and materially. A variety of disparate models of domestic progress on display for the better part of a century have illustrated the great promise of technology for altering everyday spaces and lifestyles, each offering current and prospective suburban residents of its time a new and improved template for living the good life in years or decades to come. Like their iconic predecessors on display at numerous World's Fairs, theme parks, and trade shows, more recent iterations of futuristic exhibits and model homes, along with related media representations and marketing campaigns, have continued to present visions of the possible, often projecting cultural as well as technological trajectories based on past and present circumstances. From the most far-fetched fantastic house designs to the most immediately realizable home applications, each example can be seen as an articulation of domestic desires not yet met, as well as a form of critique addressing extant consumer products, domestic architectures, and suburban experiences.

The historical moment in which any one house of the future is conceived, constructed, and circulated shapes popular understanding of the needs and desires to be fulfilled by the design concept. Discourses prevalent during hard times invest even greater hope in a better future, distant though it may seem. In his essay "'Miracle House Hoop-La': Corporate Rhetoric and the Construction of the Postwar American House," Timothy Mennel demonstrates how "miracle house rhetoric of the 1930s and 1940s was directed explicitly at futuristic solutions, not at ones anchored in the past, and relied far more on assertion, given the absence of actual production, than on memory."[3] In the transitional postwar period, businesses in the increasingly large-scale, standardized housing industry attempted to "deflect consumers' overblown expectations" emanating from prior "miracle house" discourses and "declare victory over the future by focusing instead on what could already be done" with current technologies, materials, and production capabilities.[4] Expectations were adjusted, and even modest mass-produced tract houses with novel conveniences like all-electric kitchens or built-in televisions came to represent reasonable postwar achievement of tomorrow's home. Meanwhile, a variety of experimental dwellings—such as the 1933 Keck and Keck steel-and-glass House of Tomorrow, Buckminster Fuller's 1946 aluminum Dymaxion prototype, and Monsanto's 1957 elevated plastic bubble House of the Future—showcased another vision, one less constrained by traditional forms and materials. These shiny round concept houses may have appeared revolutionary compared to the boxy stick-built ranch and Cape

Cod homes dotting mid-twentieth-century suburban landscapes, but such visual oddities were in line with the mainstream corporate cultural practice of selling technologies of today as integral to the home of tomorrow. Whether promising that Americans could "live better electrically" or enjoy "better living through chemistry,"[5] corporate rhetoric framed a "better" future for consumers as taking place in the detached suburban single-family home.

Hopeful Great Depression–era and wartime "miracle houses" promised a vastly different and qualitatively better dwelling for the average American family in a more prosperous and peaceful future. Bright postwar novelties extrapolated suburban affluence, leisure, and technological innovation based on expectations of even more to come. By comparison, an underlying fearfulness about future living conditions animates house of the future rhetoric in more current examples, including the green intentionality of VISION House Los Angeles as well as the retrospective green lens employed in the reselling of the 1956 GE Showcase home. Idealism is now tempered with a certain level of prescribed pragmatism, an acceptance of dismal forecasts of resource scarcity and environmental decline. A sense of wonder in response to technological progress is moderated by practical calculations about the immediate and accrued costs, both economic and ecological, of implementing and maintaining the latest in home technologies. The ever-increasing complexity of modern life elicits desires for simplicity in contemporary discourse, suggestive of a longing for a comfortable but undemanding life in a future home that, while not turning back completely from the narrative march of progress, works to put technology to better use, such as in further streamlining home production and consumption for greater efficiencies of time, energy, and material, making the suburban dream more sustainable in the process.

Nostalgia is a key factor in framing this trend toward simplicity in contemporary house of the future rhetoric, manifested in aesthetic design choices and the material construction of forward-looking suburban homes today that nonetheless visually recall a mythically simpler past, a time before technology was so thoroughly integrated into the most personal of spaces and activities. Rather than promoting innovative futuristic structures, designers are now packaging progress in rather traditional aesthetic forms and historical house typologies that have previously satisfied popular suburban desires, making the choice of a state-of-the-art eco-friendly dwelling more commercially palatable by embracing rather conventional appearances that fit into well-established residential landscapes. HGTV's 2014 Smart Home is just one high-profile example of a nostalgic house of the future currently in the making, with a facade inspired by Tudor-style cottages that stands in contrast to its high-tech systems and functionality. Instead of featuring a technologically advanced green dream home whose aesthetics match its futuristic rhetoric, this television sweepstakes prize conforms to a much older suburban style, one marking similar new luxury homes in its surrounding posh development outside Nashville, Tennessee.

As Lynn Spigel argues in a chapter titled "Yesterday's Future, Tomorrow's Home," from its earliest manifestations "the home of tomorrow functions most typically as a deeply conservative structure that promises a version of technological progress based on nostalgic longings for privacy, property, and propriety," a paradigm still operational in twenty-first-century suburbia. Citing the popularity of traditional design in otherwise "futuristic homes," Spigel further notes that "the home of tomorrow has historically looked backward." This trend has included Tudor and colonial revivals, and even extended to the postwar mass marketing of modernism as "contemporary," a diluted suburbia-friendly style that "signals something new" yet "is nevertheless modeled on traditional values of comfort and bourgeois display in the well-appointed private home."[6] For all of its technological sophistication and house of the future rhetorical positioning, the "contemporary Californian" style of VISION House Los Angeles continues in this same discursive tradition, one that also influenced the design and marketing of the much earlier GE Showcase home.[7] Remixing elements that simultaneously signify nostalgia and progress is not a new phenomenon, but the particularities of how such marketable blendings of past and future are currently promoted speak to both suburban concerns and aspirations of the moment. While not every model on display always correlates with widely available or affordable consumer choices at the time, each represents opportunities to dream about and plan for what the near future may indeed hold, as well as provides the cultural patterns and materials out of which those dreams may be fashioned and pursued, those plans implemented. Despite current nostalgic design trends and material choices, the modern technological marvel of today's average suburban home was prefigured in the broadest concepts and smallest details of the most innovative past houses of the future. Presented as "model homes," they collectively helped define the terms of the discourse still informing the direction and substance of suburban domestic design.

Precursors to both postwar and millennial examples of house of the future rhetoric and design were a featured part of earlier international expositions attracting significant domestic audiences, especially the 1933 "Century of Progress"–themed World's Fair in Chicago. A dozen full-scale houses constituted the popular Homes of Tomorrow exhibit, showcasing "modern" alternatives to conventional Depression-era housing, including the art deco–styled Good Housekeeping Stran-Steel House. Billed as "the home of the new era" that "you would want to live in," this steel-framed showpiece was meant to demonstrate the affordability, durability, and desirability of prefabricated home construction, while its elegant, magazine-worthy interior furnishings further suggested that technological advancement and stylish, hygienic modern living were compatible with traditional design and comfort. Other homes featured as part of this exhibit more overtly challenged trends toward conventional forms and aesthetics, like George and William Keck's duodecagon House of Tomorrow, which included such 1930s novelties as air-conditioning (which would become a standard feature in later suburban homes) and a built-in airplane hanger (in anticipation of the still-unfulfilled promise of less terrestrial forms of everyday suburban transportation). The unintentional heat gain of the glass curtain wall design is often identified as a factor in sparking the architects' later interest in passive solar design, a relatively low-tech strategy revived in more current green home design. As in the retrospective eco-valuation of the 1956 GE Showcase home, hints of green are increasingly being rediscovered in pre-green-era house of the future models and concepts.

The Good Housekeeping Stran-Steel House, which was on display as part of the Homes of Tomorrow exhibit at the 1933 World's Fair in Chicago, was featured in *Good Housekeeping* that year, including this article describing it as "modern in feeling but retaining the good proportions and nice details of fine tradition in architecture." *Good Housekeeping*, July 1933, 52–53.

While some Homes of Tomorrow on display at the 1933 World's Fair were futuristic in form, others appeared as if they would fit into the suburban landscape of the time. Some fairgoers even built their own personal dream homes modeled on what they saw there, and after the fair's run concluded a few of the actual structures were relocated to anchor a nearby subdivision.[8] Such high-profile national exhibition venues provided conceptual places where the possible future of housing—and of suburbia[9]—could be constructed, contemplated, and debated by average citizens alongside architects, urban planners, and industry leaders. Following the postwar decline in world's fairs held in the United States, year-round tourist destinations such as Walt Disney theme parks provided more permanent though equally sensational venues through which the general public could encounter house of the future exhibits. Much as they did at earlier world's fair pavilions, these newer corporate-sponsored attractions illustrating progress in domestic life functioned simultaneously as commercial marketing and popular entertainment platforms.[10] Several distinct future-themed homes have been featured at Disney parks from the start. Changes over time in their technical focus, material structure, and viewing context illuminate the cultural forces shaping futuristic discourses more broadly, where expectations for "a great big beautiful tomorrow" give way to a creeping nostalgia for "yesterday's future."[11] This trend is further reflected in evolving suburban tastes and consumer options for high-tech houses of the future that look as if they belong comfortably in the past. One of the starkest contrasts between yesterday's vision of the future and more current designs for better living tomorrow can be seen in the prevailing nostalgic aesthetic paradigm that works to conceal visual evidence of technological progress rather than highlight it.

The material out of which each era's house of the future is constructed is also a factor in the physical shape and aesthetic style that vision of the future might take. In addition to meeting expectations, industries related to home building align with the business interests of house-themed entertainment to create and nurture those same expectations, outlining the emerging possibility and desirability of what previously appeared impossible or outlandish. What links the Stran-Steel and Keck houses, as well as a few of their neighbors at the 1933 World's Fair, is a focus on steel as a flexible, economical material medium for building the suburban future. Certain designs, however, have remained a bit too futuristic for mainstream consumer culture, even while dominating the discursive construction of tomorrow's home in popular media and memory. On display at Disneyland from 1957 to 1967, Monsanto's House of the Future was one of the best-known postwar exhibits dedicated to high-tech modernization of domestic structures and lifestyles. A year before it opened at Disneyland, it appeared in the 1956 "Home Show" issue of *Popular Science,* with a headline claiming that this "Plastic House of the future may come in mass-produced, no-upkeep parts that you arrange to suit the whole family."[12] Imagining life in the year 1986, the rhetoric attached to this famous Disney attraction typified the promise of convenient electric appliances with which tomorrow's home would be furnished, like microwave ovens, but also new synthetic materials out of which tomorrow's home would be constructed, like vinyl. Use of molded plastic was expected to be "a trend that will grow . . . as houses emerge from the conventional cube shape and begin to take advantage of the freer forms made possible by modern structural plastics materials."[13]

Though a popular exhibit, this unique vision for the future failed to gain purchase in lived suburban environments. While still enjoying a prolonged cultural afterlife as a curious testament to postwar techno-optimism, retrospectively the Monsanto House of the Future is regarded more as a novelty of its time than as a signpost on the road to the foreseeable future.[14] Plastics would indeed be widely utilized as integral components in the material as well as cultural life of suburbia, exemplified by the introduction of iconic products like Tupperware in 1948, but also in home applications designed to mimic natural materials rather than openly

The unique design and promise of Monsanto's all-plastic House of the Future was featured in the April 1956 "Home Show" issue of *Popular Science,* a year before it opened as an exhibit at Disneyland.

advertising their human-made characteristics. Such versatility allowed these space-age materials to be easily fashioned into either modern- or traditional-looking furnishings and surfaces, but their prevalent use soon came to symbolize cheap or tacky simulation of the real thing rather than evidence of progress in democratizing middle-class domesticity through technology. The future may be largely made of plastic (including more recently introduced biodegradable plant-based and recycled "green" plastics), but within the cultural context of aspirational suburban housing, it remains taboo for it to look as though it is. Following the ten-year run of Monsanto's popular exhibit, form and function were increasingly divorced in suburban home design and rhetoric, respectively looking backward (signifying nostalgia) and forward (signifying progress).

In the Disneyland theater building that once housed General Electric's Carousel of Progress,[15] a quite different vision of the house of the future opened to visitors in 2008. Sponsored by Microsoft and Hewlett-Packard, among other home tech interests, the Innoventions Dream Home was, in many accounts, compared rather unfavorably to Disney predecessors such as the Monsanto House of the Future. Despite the integration of "smart" technologies throughout the updated Tomorrowland home exhibit, it seemed "the future now looked like the past."[16] One preview described how the exhibit was meant to resemble a conventional "suburban tract home outside," while its traditional interior decor softened the appearance of "hardware, software and touch-screen systems that could simplify everyday living." Aesthetically, the "designers decided to stray from the Jetsons-style House of the Future" and tried to create an unintimidating vision of the future "made of wood and steel and finished in muted browns and beiges," a dream house that would ideally be more "accessible to our guests."[17] P. J. O'Rourke, who fondly remembered his childhood visit to the more fantastic Monsanto attraction, quipped that now, "according to Disney, the shape of things to come can be found at Pottery Barn, with a quick stop at Restoration Hardware for 'classic future' touches."[18] A few rooms with fun and novel technologies dominated media coverage at the exhibit's opening, such as a round "Kitchen of Your Dreams" that knows what groceries you have and suggests recipes you can make with them and a "Magic Mirror" that projects items in a teenage daughter's closet onto her reflection for a virtual fashion show.[19] Even with its multiple energy-intensive screens, computer-monitored comforts, and RFID-chipped wonders, as a theme park attraction the Innoventions Dream Home proved not quite futuristic enough in outward appearance to wow critics, while the display did manage to confirm and reinforce backward-looking, forward-functioning consumer home choices already available in twenty-first-century suburbia.

On Earth Day 2012, an eco-friendlier house of the future opened at Epcot in its Innoventions building, set amid other colorful interactive exhibits inviting children

On the website for the Innoventions Dream Home, which opened at Disneyland in 2008, the "Family Room" view includes a caption explaining that this high-tech house of the future is "a mix of Art Nouveau and Craftsman" styles.

and adults to tour, touch, play, and imagine. VISION House, one of several model home exhibits sponsored across the country by Green Builder Media and a consortium of home product manufacturers, was Disney's first overtly "green" demonstration of a better-built and lived-in suburban future, complete with an imaginary eco-conscious nuclear family.[20] More like the 2008 Disneyland Innoventions Dream Home than the 1957 Monsanto House of the Future, the VISION House at Epcot is a house in name only. Its pale brick, mildly contemporary rectilinear facade surrounds a collection of standard-purpose unenclosed rooms complete with the newest in home technologies, including more efficient versions of customary kitchen and laundry appliances, stylish fixtures and furnishings, surface coverings made from reengineered and recycled materials, and centrally monitored security, climate-control, energy, and water-use systems. The combination and coordination of these high-tech, often high-priced products promise an environmentally conscious yet comfortably middle-class lifestyle, conserving natural resources while saving money in the long term. The associated green story is conveyed through interactive digital games embedded in fake solar panels, as well as in every visible aspect of the home's projected construction, furnishing, and operation. Energy-efficient innovations in framing and insulation are revealed in display wall cutaways. A tour guide explains the ecological benefits of having smart systems manage the resources consumed in the course of daily suburban life. And an electric car sits parked in front of a wooden Craftsman-style garage door near the tour's exit point. Such stylistically incongruent juxtapositions of sleek modern technologies and old-fashioned design elements are continued throughout each of the domestic spaces, especially obvious in the bathroom tableau featuring an ultramodern square automated toilet set next to a curvy reproduction Victorian claw-foot bathtub.

Again, the Disney vision of the future looks a lot like the past, or a hodge-podge of pasts, but this time within the context of representing connections with and continuation of past suburban style and function that, in this eco-iteration, will not endanger that future. Rather than exhibiting high-tech homes for tomorrow as complete, unified packages conveying a more singular futuristic theme that encompasses building materials, processes, and living standards, like the 1933 Stran-Steel House or Monsanto's 1956 all-plastic structure, more recent models present a relatively piecemeal approach to both designing and attaining a house of the future, one that could be made incrementally greener through thousands of individual consumer options available now or coming soon. Those who can afford to build a new, technologically sophisticated green dream home from the ground up will find plenty of ideas and resources for doing so while touring VISION House at Epcot, but the exhibit also offers those in the market for a more ecologically and economically efficient dishwasher a chance to see the next-generation product up close without immediate sales floor pressures. Green houses of the future entail novel design and construction methods, but also à la carte shopping opportunities for the many unique products that fill them and optimize home functions. One growing trend in this area of consumer home technologies is wider availability of objects and appliances that fit within the context of currently popular nostalgic suburban home typologies and interiors referencing various historical eras in which the given technologies would be anachronous.

Manufacturers of green home technologies support physical displays like VISION House but also independently promote their smart, eco-friendly product lines in media campaigns that draw on the long history of house of the future rhetoric and the consumer desires elicited by it. General Electric had long sponsored futuristic exhibits at world's fairs and Disney theme park attractions, in addition to the various real-world GE Showcase homes filled with electric conveniences that, over time, redefined domestic space and life. Following earlier forward-looking corporate slogans like "Live better electrically," "Progress is our most important product," and "We bring good things to life," in 2008 GE's most recent theme, "Imagination at work," was given a much more present-tense green rationale with the rollout of "ecomagination" as the organizing principle across General Electric's many businesses, including those related to home appliances and even construction. The eco-inspired future now evoked is one that we need to work harder to prepare for, rethinking past priorities and mitigating the negative effects of past practices, rather than one that we can simply, optimistically, look forward to.

As part of a product line envisioned more as *for* the house of the future than exemplary *of* it, in 2013 General Electric unveiled "Home 2025," a look at what can be reasonably expected in homes just twelve years into the future. Lou Lenzi, head of GE Appliances' Industrial Design Operation, manages expectations from the start on the program's Web page: "This isn't about the Jetsons or pie in the sky ideas," but rather "about reality-based innovation that will be possible over the next decade." Reference to *The Jetsons,* an early 1960s animated prime-time sitcom, is here used to draw contrast between the possible or probable character of a technologically enhanced suburban future and this culturally durable TV image of "suburbia in the sky." Promoting a view of the domestic future based less on fantastic, science fictional innovation than on practical, marketable extensions of current products, Lenzi further positions the GE media campaign as "a high level look at where we think society, culture, and technology is taking us . . . intersected . . . with the ways in which we could make our lives less complex and more enjoyable."[21] The rhetoric of simplification is again deployed to articulate one of the primary benefits of future technologies and the advanced homes we will ideally use them in. Less labor equates to more leisure, a familiar, even somewhat nostalgic, suburban marketing narrative going back to (and beyond) postwar promotion of the all-electric kitchen such as that imagined in *Design for Dreaming,* a short musical fantasy film produced for the 1956 General Motors Motorama featuring the Frigidaire "Kitchen of the Future." New value-added discourses of energy efficiency and environmental sustainability, however, now invoke some level of planet savings through technologically managed home consumption in addition to more free time for "housewives." In the greened discursive construction of the house of our dream future, we can ideally live better, but we can also feel better about where and how we live, countering mainstreamed reflexive critiques of suburbia as an always inherently environmentally unfriendly lifestyle choice.

Other options for dreaming up eco-houses of the future designed to mitigate suburbia's bad reputation of conspicuous consumption and wastefulness look back to discussions within home industry sectors focused more pointedly on construction of the house itself. Whereas examples like VISION House at Epcot inadvertently represent dematerialization of the house-as-structure, highlighting a narrowed range of consumer choices within department store–like staged room displays, others, including the freestanding VISION House Los Angeles, offer more comprehensive views of the future of housing, including how quickly and efficiently houses can be built with as little disturbance to surrounding landscapes and ecosystems as possible. For all of the future-friendly rhetoric employed in promoting them, the materials, methods, and building systems used in many green house of the future models suggest that, in terms of dream homes, what was old is now new again. Smart Home: Green + Wired, a popular exhibit at Chicago's Museum of Science and Industry, was promoted with the tagline "Past meets future in a very now house." Factory built and assembled in the museum's courtyard, the modern green prefab designed by Michelle Kaufmann opened in 2008 and reopened annually through 2013 with refreshed furnishings and updated technologies, yet consistently drawing connections to the natural world as well as a domestically and architecturally nostalgic past. In the 2011–12 brochure for the exhibit, museum president and CEO David R. Moseno acknowledged the Homes of Tomorrow exhibit at the 1933 Century of Progress World's Fair in Chicago as the inspiration for Smart Home: Green + Wired. This Depression-era attraction "unveiled visionary building methods and technologies like prefabricated homes and solar-powered heating." The intention of the newer Chicago exhibit was to promote Smart Home: Green + Wired as a twenty-first-century inheritor to that tradition, where "green" would be seen as the appropriate unifying paradigm for showcasing today's "scientific and industrial innovations, new materials and technologies shaping the homes of our future." Yet the novelty of yesterday was prominently featured in one of Smart Home's displays, "Innovations . . . Then and Now," where obsolete home technologies like typewriters, phonographs, and even video game consoles were juxtaposed with current digital and integrated iterations. Perhaps even more than VISION House at Epcot, the discursive packaging of this house, of the past and present as much as of the future, encouraged visitors to contemplate not just the momentary process in which a home is built but also the full span of time in which it will be lived in, as well as the many unforeseeable changes in *how* it will be lived in.

The shape and character of future domestic dreams have previously been established through the selling of such holistic visions of home as much as of individual products for the home. Rhetoric proclaiming the coming house of the future aside, widespread transformation in the way homes are designed and constructed *for the future* in the built landscape of suburbia has not yet materialized. Though memorable, most houses of the future promising newer, better ways to design or build single-family houses have failed to effect change in home-building industries over the last century. Their discursive power to shape fantastic dreams of home is tempered by the more mundane expectations of everyday experience and limited opportunity, a market condition conducive to the nostalgic over the progressive. As suggested by the House_n architectural research group at the Massachusetts Institute of Technology, "Change is accelerating, but the places we create are largely static and unresponsive." The group's stated mission is to explore "how new technologies, materials, and strategies for design can make possible dynamic, evolving

"Past meets future in a very now house" was the promotional description of the prefab Smart Home: Green + Wired exhibit at Chicago's Museum of Science and Industry, on display from 2008 to 2013.

places that respond to the complexities of life."²² Simplification is again regarded as a virtuous goal for housing, reasserting long-held notions that at least part of a home's function is to provide its residents with a refuge from the demands and stresses of modernity, even as "dynamic" modern technology is recruited to help build it better.

One of the primary challenges to realizing the dream of sustainable suburban housing that respects the past even as it anticipates the future is the rigidity of conventional home design. There is a perceived need to reimagine how houses can be more comfortably inhabited long term in rapidly changing cultural, material, economic, and environmental contexts. Open_1, a 3,500-square-foot MIT prototype finished in July 2006, is a prefab structure "intended to demonstrate how a house can adapt to its occupants' changing needs over time." Offering flexibility and affordability through component and system standardization with the added ability to accessorize further, IKEA-style, its most "revolutionary" aspect is the ease with which residents can add and upgrade new technologies without having to dream of or plan for an entirely new domestic site or structure. Aesthetically, however, this house quite notably "doesn't look like the futuristic stuff of a world's fair."²³ Flexibility thus also encompasses the ability to construct and modify homes that satisfy traditional as well as contemporary tastes, stylistically fitting into existing suburban neighborhoods built in different eras and hopefully lasting well into the future.²⁴ This particularly recent strand of house of the future discourses accommodates the desire of those suburbanites (and urbanites) who may love where they live but dream of making those places as "dynamic" as the proliferation of changing technologies that will continue to alter everyday practices and experiences.

Part of our ongoing nostalgia for the failed futurism of such bold, daring designs showcased at world's fairs, at Disney theme parks, and even on TV shows like *The Jetsons* stems from the sustained wish that we might yet realize their past promises of carefree, comfortable living in suburbia, rendering this broader landscape and lifestyle as durable dreams. A common feature of many of those visions for the future often lost sight of in contemporary discourse is the democratic appeal of that suburban dream, that it would (someday) be possible for *everyone* to achieve it. As Timothy Mennel notes, in the 1940s articulation of Fuller's 1920s concept for the Dymaxion House, "the visionary rhetoric was in abeyance, in part because the selling point of the house was not its futurism but its economy."²⁵ Cynthia Lee Henthorn further acknowledges how this postwar "Wichita" Dymaxion model "offered a presumably rational means by which low-income families could enter the symbolic realm of middle-class identity and even surpass its ideal hygienic standards."²⁶ Modular examples like Smart Home: Green + Wired and House_n are notable among competing recent visions for their promise of more expansive access to the dream of a future that includes suburban homeownership. They further echo sentiments of affordability, flexibility, and simplicity conveyed in the rhetoric surrounding the more modest 1933 Homes of Tomorrow and the 1957 Monsanto House of the Future as well as Fuller's Dymaxion House, though with the additional assurance that they can also be green dream homes.[27] The nostalgia currently permeating suburban domestic design and rhetoric is gradually inclusive of this goal of environmental sustainability, and technology is widely seen as the best way to achieve it. Making that technology less visible or obvious in the home, however, affords greater opportunity to forget how much daily life has changed from "simpler" times characterized by horse-drawn carriages and candle-lit rooms, or even by all-electric kitchens and the novelty of all-plastic homes. High-end concept or tract home model, cutting-edge green design or conventional construction, that try to conceal or camouflage evidence of technological progress through nostalgic aesthetics and natural materials is a signature feature of today's ideal house of the future.

Prognostications about the future of everyday life are always more entertaining (and reassuring) when we are looking back at how much, or how little, has actually come to pass, not least concerning the house of the future. The cultural context of those predictions also shapes the physical context in which the imagined future will be lived. In his *New York Times* review of the Carousel of Progress at the 1964 World's Fair, science fiction writer Isaac Asimov predicted that by 2014 "men will continue to withdraw from nature in order to create an environment that will suit them better." He proposed that suburban houses would be commonly built "underground, with easily controlled temperature, free from the vicissitude of weather, with air cleaned and light controlled."[28] With the exception of "underground," the average new suburban house today largely achieves his vision of yesterday's future. An extension of this dream of control animates current models, extrapolating our reliance on and desire for evolving versions of existing home technologies that were only just emerging in the postwar era. One point of differentiation from Asimov's view, however, is the newfound desire to reconnect with rather than withdraw from nature. Nature and technology are interdependent concepts in current imaginings of a better life in suburbia, one where technology continues to make possible more leisure time in natural environments but also automatically manages and conserves natural resources so that the natural world is itself ideally preserved undiminished into the foreseeable future. This perspective also requires a frame of mind that is partly nostalgic, a tendency to see nature as something that is retreating from everyday life, even in suburbia, and the embrace of certain kinds of suburban design that at least rhetorically suggest a less technologically advanced and therefore more natural lifestyle. Use of house style to soothe perceived uneasiness with technologi-cal progress marks twentieth- and twenty-first-century suburban home trends, from historic Tudor revivals and popular generic Craftsman details to glass walls opening inside to outside spaces in contemporary ranch-style homes. Each nostalgic facade around an increasingly high-tech core exposes an underlying ideological conflict between faith in the future and longing for the past.

When we look back at the variety of optimistically fantastic models of tomor-row's home, the theme of technological progress appears dominant, often at the expense of natural preservation. As we look forward, through the lens of current house of the future exhibits and marketing campaigns, that future seems less cer-tain, less optimistic. Rather than predicting wonders that might become realities half a century from now, relatively timid expectations for what we might experi-ence only ten or twenty years into the future constitute the extent of innovations, in degree rather than in kind, explicit in most commercial addresses to today's dream-ers and tomorrow's consumers. Radical change in the longer view suddenly seems more difficult (and less fun) to imagine. This has consequences for the very real ways in which suburbia could be redesigned and rebuilt as an integral part of a better future. In a 1981 interview, Anne Hewlett Fuller observed that "when you can't see something move, you don't get out of the way. The faster a thing moves, the more chances you have to see what is wrong." The implication is that "in a single-family dwelling there is at least a 50-year lag because of the least visibility of motion."[29] Most single-family houses built in recent years have been designed to remain structurally and visually the same throughout their useful life span, exacerbating the phenome-non of "least visibility of motion" that already limits rapid change and innovation in most sectors of the housing industry. It may indeed become even harder to imagine a wider range of future possibilities while still building and dreaming suburban houses that, no matter how many high-tech gadgets or systems they contain, stylis-tically look back past the last fifty years rather than ahead to the next fifty.

## Notes

1. J. Williams, "Ronald Reagan's General Electric Showcase House," *Curbed LA*, December 16, 2012, http://la.curbed.com.

2. "VISION House Los Angeles," Green Builder Media, accessed November 25, 2014, http://www.greenbuildermedia.com.

3. Timothy Mennel, "'Miracle House Hoop-La': Corporate Rhetoric and the Construction of the Postwar American House," *Journal of the Society of Architectural Historians* 64, no. 3 (Sep-tember 2005): 341.

4. Ibid., 349.

5. "Better living through chemistry" is derivative of DuPont's 1930s slogan "Better things for better living . . . through chemistry." It has occasionally been misattributed to Monsanto in

relation to the all-plastic House of the Future on display at Disneyland from 1957 to 1967; although the message does resonate with the exhibit's optimistic view of synthetic materials as promising a "better" life, Monsanto did not use the slogan.

6. Lynn Spigel, *Welcome to the Dreamhouse: Popular Media and Postwar Suburbs* (Durham, N.C.: Duke University Press, 2001), 385.

7. See, for example, Barbara L. Allen, "The Ranch-Style House in America: A Cultural and Environmental Discourse," *Journal of Architectural Education* 49, no. 3 (February 1996): 156–65.

8. Several of the houses on display as part of the Homes of Tomorrow at the 1933 World's Fair were moved by real estate developer Robert Bartlett to a new subdivision in Beverly Shores, Indiana. Five of them are still standing, preserved by the Indiana Dunes National Lakeshore Park Service, including the Keck and Keck House of Tomorrow. For more information, see "Century of Progress 1933 World's Fair Homes and More," National Park Service, Indiana Dunes, http://www.nps.gov/indu/historyculture/centuryofprogress.htm.

9. Predicting the "World of Tomorrow," the 1939 World's Fair in New York encompassed a wider scope and context for the future of housing than that seen in the 1933 Homes of Tomorrow exhibit. Norman Bel Geddes's Futurama exhibit for General Motors modeled the proliferation of detached suburban homes as part of a built landscape fundamentally reconfigured by new transportation technologies. Even so, it followed an already established pattern of automobile-centric residential development. In the Henry Dreyfuss–designed Democracity diorama, also exhibited at the 1939 World's Fair, the population was imagined as someday soon living in the more verdant, decentralized "Pleasantvilles" surrounding the central city: "Thirty or forty miles from where you are living today—about half an hour by the new safe-speed boulevard—lies the City of Tomorrow." As the exhibit booklet suggests, "You can start to build this city tomorrow morning. . . . There are no trick materials, no imaginary machines." You will "live in a house of your own, in a town nearby . . . a town so agreeable that you call it Pleasantville." Gilbert Seldes, *Your World of Tomorrow* (New York, 1939).

10. Corporate sponsorship abounded at Disneyland, which opened in Anaheim, California, in 1955. A more expansive version of the theme park, Walt Disney World's Magic Kingdom in Orlando, Florida, opened in 1971. Comprising similar themed areas, like Frontierland and Main Street, U.S.A., that invoked strands of American myth, tradition, and nostalgia, both Disney parks also included Tomorrowland, dedicated to themes of technology, progress, and adventurous engagement with the perceived future. By the time the second park opened, however, the original concept for Tomorrowland was appearing somewhat dated in its representation of the future circa 1955. Designed as a more forward-looking "permanent world's fair," Disney's EPCOT (Experimental Prototype Community of Tomorrow) Center (later renamed simply Epcot) opened in 1982 adjacent to the Magic Kingdom, connected to it by a sleek monorail system demonstrating the future of transportation.

11. "There's a Great Big Beautiful Tomorrow" is the song written by Richard and Robert Sherman for the Disney-designed GE Carousel of Progress exhibit. Its optimistic lyrics are repeated at the transitions between scenes of technological progress in a home spanning decades: "There's a great big beautiful tomorrow / Shining at the end of every day / There's a great big beautiful tomorrow / And tomorrow's just a dream away."

12. Ernst Behrendt, "Plastic House," *Popular Science*, April 1956, 144–47, 262.

13. "The Future Won't Wait," *Monsanto Magazine*, 1960, http://www.yesterland.com/futurewontwait.html.

14. A brief 2006 National Public Radio segment featuring Microsoft's prototype smart home of the future began by identifying the Monsanto House of the Future as part of a long history "littered with the detritus of failed utopian homes," since "no one wanted to live in an all-plastic home," and concluding that "those who make technologies often dream bigger than their potential target consumers." Laura Sydell, "Chasing a Habitable 'Home of the Future,'" *Morning Edition,* National Public Radio, May 1, 2006, http://www.npr.org.

15. The GE Carousel of Progress was first seen at the 1964 New York World's Fair, subsequently installed at Disneyland in 1967, then moved to Walt Disney World in 1974. Originally revealing sequential interior scenes of domestic life in a home typical of the late nineteenth century, the 1920s, the 1940s, and "today" as the audience revolved around the circular stage, the exhibit showed improvements in electric infrastructure and home appliances that suggested continuity with the past while setting expectations for an even brighter tomorrow. Once reinstalled at Disneyland and later at Walt Disney World, the final scene, set at Christmastime, encouraged nostalgia for the quaintness of more technologically primitive eras while extending the original family drama of "living better electrically" more firmly into the future. Just as items in the Monsanto House of the Future exhibit were intended to look magical to tourists in 1957, the home appliances and related lifestyle improvements on display in the concluding scenario of the Carousel of Progress were designed to offer a tantalizing glimpse of our future enjoyment of and dependence on them.

16. Werner Weiss, "Monsanto House of the Future," Yesterland, last updated April 27, 2012, http://www.yesterland.com.

17. Gillian Flaccus, "Disney Revives 'House of the Future,'" *USA Today,* February 14, 2008, http://usatoday30.usatoday.com/travel/destinations/2008-02-14-disney-house-of-the-future_N.htm.

18. P. J. O'Rourke, "Future Schlock," *Atlantic,* December 2008, 82.

19. The presentation of these particular features was vaguely reminiscent of the 1956 General Motors *Design for Dreaming* promotional film, in which a housewife dances through the kitchen of tomorrow, which magically does all the work for her at the press of a button, allowing her greater leisure time. This benefit is expressed in a quick-change fashion show of all of the activity-specific outfits the lady of the self-functioning house can wear when she leaves it to "play" outside.

20. As with the Monteverde family imagined to live in Disney's VISION House, the ideal residents of houses of the future are usually presented as stereotypical middle-class nuclear families. P. J. O'Rourke even noted in his piece on the Innoventions Dream Home for the *Atlantic* that the "future family . . . still has one mom and one dad, amazingly enough." Perhaps not surprisingly, midcentury examples like the Monsanto model also assumed this family composition, and it is further imposed with nostalgic kitsch in the display of Fuller's Dymaxion House prototype currently at the Henry Ford Museum, which features black-and-white photographs of a mid-1940s "mom" who "loves" how affordable, stylish, colorful, luxurious, and easy to clean the home's "modern materials" are, while the "dad" is shown admiring how affordable, strong, lightweight, simple to assemble, and easy to maintain they are. This differentiated gendered address is extended to potential suburban buyers and residents of more current iterations, solidifying traditional responsibilities in and for the house of the future. Rather than acknowledging the diversity of family structures and individual relations with the purchase of a home and upkeep of domestic space, the social scripts most often suggested in such exhibits revert to

worn-out postwar clichés that do not always comport with modern suburban experience and identity, if they ever truly did.

21. "Home 2025: GE Envisions Home of the Future," General Electric, 2013, http://www.geappliances.com/home2025. For more details, see the official press release, "GE Targets Net Zero Energy Homes by 2015," July 14, 2009, http://www.genewscenter.com/content/detail.aspx?releaseid=7272&newsareaid=2. In this curiously conservative description of the program's goals, progress is framed in terms of following trends rather than shaping them, reacting to where "society, culture, and technology" are "taking us" instead of leading the way forward.

22. House_n Research Group, Department of Architecture, Massachusetts Institute of Technology, http://web.mit.edu/cron/group/house_n.

23. Dawn Stover, "The House of the Future: Building Blocks," *Popular Science*, November 2006, 84.

24. Jonathan Bell relates how the "house of the future has focused on brief at the expense of site, although it is location that remains perhaps the most complex part of the architectural equation." Suggesting that "architects are increasingly acknowledging the desirability of suburbia, targeting design efforts at new kinds of suburban home," he identifies a handful of proposals that imagine future suburbs "that utilize existing plot sizes, road layouts and patterns of development, and overlay on them a flexible, Modernist aesthetic." Yet, he notes, these "dreams of suburban Modernism are predicated on the continued availability of inexpensive land and the transport and infrastructure that sustain them," conditions assumed by many critics to be in future peril. Jonathan Bell, *21st Century House* (London: Laurence King, 2008), 88.

25. Mennel, "'Miracle House Hoop-La,'" 356.

26. Cynthia Lee Henthorn, *From Submarines to Suburbs: Selling a Better America, 1939–1959* (Athens: Ohio University Press, 2006), 147.

27. As further suggestive of the compatibility of this goal of affordable, aspirational modern suburban housing with more current environmental desires and imperatives, a review of the 2008 retrospective exhibit on Fuller's design work highlights the many ways in which he was actually "green before his time." His belief was that "with the help of knowledge, design, and technology, people can live more while consuming less," even in suburbia. Jessica Leber, "Green before His Time," *Audubon Magazine*, Web exclusive, 2008, http://archive.audubonmagazine.org/webexclusives/buckminsterFuller-webExclusives.html.

28. Isaac Asimov, "Visit to the World's Fair of 2014," *New York Times*, August 16, 1964, http://www.nytimes.com.

29. Interview with Buckminster Fuller and Anne Hewlett Fuller by Jamie Snyder, March 15, 1981, in Stacey Peck, "In Search of a Better World, They Put Their Faith in the Power of the Mind," http://www.salsburg.com. She was here responding to a question on "the lag between invention and acceptance" with regard to her husband's famous yet unrealized domestic designs, like the Dymaxion House.

# PART III
# Gathering

# Everyday Racialization

## Contesting Space and Identity in Suburban St. Louis

JODI RIOS

The Normandy suburbs of St. Louis, Missouri, were conceived of, developed, and marketed as working- and middle-class suburban neighborhoods and shopping districts. Today, however, this area is largely defined as *urban* space in the lexicon of public discourse. The stately homes on curvilinear streets and bungalow houses with picket fences still remain, as do numerous parks, golf courses, country clubs, cemeteries, strip malls, and parking lots.[1] So what has changed to turn suburban space urban?

The recent controversy in the Missouri state legislature and in public debate regarding how to define and deal with underperforming schools in the state clearly reveals that, in the imaginations of citizens, parents, administrators, and policy makers, *urban* stands in for poverty, marginalization, and minority-occupied space, while *suburban* represents economic stability, privilege, and majority-white neighborhoods. What changed in the Normandy suburbs was not the physical environment but the color of the residents and, eventually, the value of their property, as a result of public and private disinvestment.

The discussion that follows was written prior to August 9, 2014, when the shooting of an unarmed black teenager by a white police officer in Ferguson, Missouri, sparked a series of protests in the St. Louis region and across the United States. The Canfield Green Apartments, where the shooting took place, are within the school district now known as the Normandy Schools Collaborative, and the shooting victim, Michael Brown Jr., had recently graduated from Normandy High School. While this essay does not specifically address the Ferguson protests, it does offer insight into the racialized space and sentiments that underlie recent events in this area.

The residents of the Normandy suburbs found themselves in the crosshairs of the urban schools debate when the former Normandy School District, with a student population that is 98 percent African American, lost its accreditation in 2013. Both state and school officials explained the district's demise as stemming from its inability to deal with unfortunate "urban problems"[2]—or, in less polite settings, "the ghetto mentality that plagues the area"[3]—more specifically, a high proportion of female-headed households, violence, and rampant drug problems (although statistics show that rates of violence and drug activity in the area are comparable to those in south St. Louis County).[4] Mobility rates of residents and functional homelessness,[5] which are pointed to as representative of a distinctly urban school district, are two of the biggest challenges faced by the district, and the superintendent has repeatedly called for the use of alternative metrics in evaluating teacher and school performance in "an urban district that has many external challenges."[6] Shortly after the district lost accreditation, the Missouri Supreme Court upheld the state's Student Transfer Program, which requires unaccredited districts to pay transportation and tuition costs (ranging from $9,500 to $21,000 annually per student) for any student requesting to transfer to an accredited district. More than one thousand Normandy students (approximately 25 percent of the district population) transferred to schools in what are apparently the authentic suburbs—based on media representations of the transfer process. Consequently, the district ran out of money in the spring of 2014. A hotly contested emergency funding bill was passed in March 2014 in order to keep the district open through the academic year. The battle over funding was largely framed as a debate about whether Missouri taxpayers should be responsible for bailing out failing urban schools. The district was subsequently restructured by the state board of education, which suspended all contracts, temporarily placed it outside accreditation standards, and renamed it the Normandy Schools Collaborative, prompting a new set of court actions and student transfer debates.

Race—whether the topic is couched in euphemisms or actively invoked—is unequivocally at the center of both formal deliberation and ad hoc discussions regarding the condition and codification of the Normandy school district, including who should be blamed, who should determine the district's fate, who should pay for actions taken, and whose responsibility it is to educate "poor, urban kids."[7] The reactions of parents and other residents in the Normandy suburbs, which are divided between those choosing to leave the district and those choosing to stay, as well as the reactions of residents in the receiving districts, have been highly racialized. After attending a public hearing in the majority-white district that would soon be receiving most of Normandy's transfer students, one Normandy resident commented: "When I saw them screaming and hollering like they were crazy, I thought to myself, 'Oh my God, this is back in Martin Luther King days,' they're going to get the hoses out. They're going to be beating our kids and making sure they don't get off the school bus."[8] The statements by white parents that this resident was responding to included "I now have to worry about my children getting stabbed? Or taking a drug? Or getting robbed? Because that's the issue" and "We don't want [these kids] at Francis Howell."[9] Many people in the receiving districts condemned these sentiments as racist, and when Normandy students showed up in August 2013, some groups of students and parents made efforts to welcome them.

In the Normandy area, the topic of race is also both highly vocalized and played down. It was, however, at the forefront of a recent public hearing at which Normandy school district residents accused the state Department of Elementary and Secondary Education of "putting chains around our ankles," perpetuating separate and unequal education, and intentionally splintering the black community. Several speakers compared putting the fate of the all-black district in the hands of mostly white state officials to slavery, one stating, "All that's missing is the whip," and several residents compared their grandchildren's experience to their own experience growing up in the Jim Crow South.[10] Local and national media have reported on this controversy, including a *New York Times* article and slide show focused on the racial conflict and a PBS Web series that features the debate in a segment asking what has changed since the March on Washington fifty years ago.[11] The ongoing debate over the so-called urban condition of an area developed as suburban neighborhoods reveals the degree to which race, space, and identity are mutually constituted in the everyday imaginations and realities of metropolitan lives. It also illustrates the many contradictions that residents of this area consistently experience relative to outside representations of their community and their own claims regarding themselves and the place in which they live.

The Normandy suburbs challenge the idea that the United States has entered a postracial era.[12] Statistically, race remains a surprisingly accurate predictor of interrelated quality-of-life issues in the United States, including location of residence, quality of education, income, and health.[13] Although legalized segregation and formal obstacles enacted to maintain racial difference in the United States were largely dismantled following the mid-twentieth-century civil rights movement, distinct racialized histories continue to play out at all levels of metropolitan life. Scholars and practitioners concerned with issues of equity must then ask: How are bodies coded by space and space by bodies? How do historical perceptions of space, race, and gender coalesce to affect identity and determine rights in metropolitan areas today? What are the visible and invisible practices that maintain social and spatial disparity in the United States? How do continued distinctions between urban and suburban space in both scholarship and practice reinforce racialized paradigms that support racial projects?

In this chapter, I consider processes of racialization in the context of metropolitan space in the United States today.[14] I argue that racialization, defined as actions and practices that create and maintain systems of domination based on physical and cultural difference, is not only a residue of prior modes of racism but also an active and structuring principle that continues to shape the built environment. While the ideological and political modes of producing racialized people and space are most visible at institutional levels such as municipal code enforcement, lending practices, government funding allocation, and education, *everyday racialization*—the integration of *race thinking* through routine practices—subtly works to produce and reproduce both real and imagined spaces of the city.[15] The ways in which binary distinctions, such as acceptable versus deviant behavior, good versus bad space, and safe versus dangerous places, become associated with people and groups illustrate how everyday racialization takes place. The woman who assumed stabbings, theft, and drugs would become the norm if black students from the Normandy district attended her child's school is an example of this binary thinking. Distinctions between good and bad, however, are ever changing, and associations with things like rap music, the wearing of baggy pants, or what it means to "be ghetto" are mediated by consumer culture and the commodification of racialized practices. The Normandy suburbs, which I will return to later in this chapter, call attention to the extent that space (both real and imagined) is both a player and a product of processes of racialization, and how the continued work of race affects issues of metropolitan equity.

The implications of race are increasingly downplayed in American society, and the popular media have used the election (and reelection) of the first black U.S. president to argue that the nation is achieving a postracial status. Such sentiments are echoed in decisions recently handed down by the U.S. Supreme Court, which wrote in recent majority opinions that race is less significant today than it was during the era of civil rights legislation.[16] Scholars in various disciplines have cited metropolitan examples, such as increased diversity in the suburbs, new forms of cosmopolitanism in central cities, and nonwhite representation in urban government, as evidence that race is less important in American society today.[17] In sub/urban scholarship, it is now typical to find difference cast along lines of ethnicity, class, culture, sexual orientation, and so on, with few acknowledgments regarding how historical modes of racial formation inform differential space. In response to arguments that the effects of race will disappear if one accounts for neighborhood, wealth, education, family history, and so on, John Powell and Caitlin Watt have asked, "What do you think race is?"[18] This is an important question for urban scholars and leads to an even more perplexing question: What explains the paradox between urban policies, laws, and political positions that make no mention of race and metropolitan landscapes where segregation and neighborhood disadvantage stubbornly persist along racial lines?[19]

Urban historians looking at mid-twentieth-century cities have documented the relationship between race and patterns of metropolitan development in the United States.[20] This scholarship has revealed what are today well-known policies enacted to segregate the nonwhite population and deny homeownership to millions of nonwhite citizens across the United States, such as Federal Housing Administration lending guidelines, discriminatory real estate practices, restrictive covenants, and federal urban renewal policy. As Dianne Harris drives home in her recent book on postwar suburbia, the perceived, if not actual, development of post–World War II U.S. suburbs for a specifically white middle class was not only highly orchestrated by institutional policy and real estate markets but also seared into the psyche, imagination, and normative assumptions of the American public through calculated promotion and representation that both produced and maintained normative middle-class ideals as synonymous with white culture.[21] In this way, the suburbs became defined as white space in spite of the fact that U.S. suburbs have always maintained surprising diversity. Margaret Garb, in her book on housing reform in Chicago between 1871 and 1919, shows that the link between race and homeownership began much earlier than the post–World War II era, stating, "Even at the turn of the [twentieth] century, a single-family house set on a tidy yard was fast becoming a mark of household health, respectability, and morality," where perceptions of respectability worked in relationship to whiteness.[22] The American obsession with the single-family house and the importance of property ownership was institutionalized by New Deal–era housing policy and instilled over time in U.S. culture the view of homeownership as a fundamental right tied to white citizenship. The real and imagined boundaries that resulted along racial lines regarding who belongs where in cities were gradually justified through economic, rather than moral, arguments.

Economistic abstractions of social relations, including variations of Marxist theory on one hand and public choice theory and neoliberal theories of development on the other, support economic explanations of power relations that privilege analytics of capital and labor markets and reduce race to an inflection of class or a minimal component of economic determinism. Moreover, recent preoccupations with globalization—the global distribution and flow of information, capital, and surplus labor—inherently disregard and disempower the transformative potential of human agency and localized forms of social reproduction, which are devalued as insignificant compared to new definitions of the geopolitical.[23] Both the economistic and global frameworks explain metropolitan life and space in capitalist terms and flatten our understanding of how race operates (as both cause and consequence) on rights to, and in, the city. Specifically within the design disciplines, scholarship and practice over the past decade have continued to perpetuate spatial binaries (e.g., suburban/urban, stim/dross, vibrant/blighted, productive/unproductive)[24] that reinforce ubiquitous racialized signifiers of white and black space in the American city.[25] The metropolitan landscape of de facto, rather than de jure, segregation is narrated and read today as a postracial site of consumption by developers, designers, nongovernmental organizations, policy makers, grassroots coalitions, and scholars alike, using the language of development and class stratification.

While historians writing in the post–civil rights era convincingly linked race-based policies to patterns of development and spatial disparity,[26] recent sub/urban scholars have rightfully pointed out how this work also obscured rich and complex histories of metropolitan space that did not follow the trope of lily-white, pristine suburbs in contrast to dark and decaying urban cores.[27] In a March 2001 special issue on prewar suburbs and a special section on diverse postwar suburbs in January 2013, contributors to the *Journal of Urban History* successfully refute the urban/suburban binary by calling attention to how the idealized suburbs never existed in the pre- or postwar eras and how deviations from the ideal far exceeded any normative reality of such places.[28] Some recent scholarship, including chapters in this book, go even further to dispel suburban simplifications, foregrounding powerful sub/urban histories and experiences that both complicate and implicate long-held assumptions of what the suburbs are and are not. These authors highlight alternative suburban narratives, such as the nuanced and contingent racial formations of Asian, Latina/o, and African American suburban residents; the contingent history of the suburban apartment complex and suburban row housing in contradistinction to the single-family house as idealized suburban typology; and gay identity and empowerment in relationship to suburban identity.[29] Taken together, this emerging literature also calls attention to complex relationships between race and class distinction and uniquely privileges everyday experience to reveal actual rather than assumed places and phenomena.[30]

Specific to African American experience, a few recent scholars have done much to correct the historical omission of black suburbanization in the United States.[31] For example, historian Andrew Wiese provides an exhaustive account of African Americans' influence on American suburbanization and links this history to the larger black experience in the United States.[32] As part of this work, Wiese identifies typologies of suburbanization in the 1940s previously not recognized as "suburban," in which blacks laid claim to land on the urban periphery of many U.S. cities and reproduced spatial practices from their experience in the rural South. Taking an ethnographic approach from a sociological perspective, Mary Pattillo highlights the Janus-faced nature of the lives of middle-class African Americans and shows how minority solidarity is perpetually troubled by the quest for personal liberation and accumulation.[33] Pattillo reveals how the spatial imagination of the black middle class operates in relationship to whiteness, where it comes into conflict with racial identity when blacks as a group are either forced or choose to live in economically diverse but racially homogeneous metropolitan areas. Farrah D. Gafford's focus on the community scale and importance of identity formation in a middle-class black suburb of New Orleans reveals how place identity pivots around the convergence of race- and class-based determinants and powerfully endures long after the people disappear.[34] All three of these authors, however, privilege the perspective of the black middle class, which carries its own set of assumptions regarding suburban values and suburban lives. As a result, poor and working-class blacks are acknowledged as living in areas beyond the urban core but are distinguished from true black suburbanites and portrayed as a threat to the rights of the black middle class. This is in keeping with the tendency of scholars and the media to qualify suburban locations occupied by poor blacks as something other than true suburbs (e.g., suburban ghettos or suburban slums). As a result, we are left to believe that while suburbs can be defined as something other than white, they are fundamentally dependent on middle-class associations and identity.

Historians such as Steven Gregory and Robert O. Self resist both the urban/suburban binary and the middle-class perspective by focusing on the nuances of African American politics in metropolitan space.[35] Gregory exhaustively traces the interplay of race and class in the African American community of Corona, New York, while Self puts black power and suburbanization in direct conversation with one another throughout his history of Oakland, California, and surrounding suburbs. Both of these scholars' ethnographic studies drill down beyond typical surface readings of white/black dynamics, revealing previously overlooked histories of how the politics of space and struggles for power play out at multiple levels of community and identity formation.

Scholars who have looked specifically at the American ghetto have also traced African American space and experience in the city.[36] Most of this work has been rooted in the field of sociology, where space is treated as a container of behaviors bounded and reinforced through state policy and social pathology.[37] Similar to the trope of the idealized white suburbs, this work often reinforces simplistic representations such that *the ghetto* stands in for racially dependent associations with the urban core and, in some cases, any black space. Several scholars have looked specifically at structural forces of racism and exclusion to explain spatial disparity, although this work runs the risk of oversimplifying complex social processes.[38] Exceptions to such oversimplification come from scholars across disciplines who focus on the generative agency of people *in place* that emerges from marginalized spatial identity. For example, Stuart Hall and his colleagues conceptualize the ghetto as both a real space in which racialized bodies are policed and delimited and as an *imagined geography* of anxiety and danger necessarily conceived in relationship to the politics of racialized space and identity.[39] Michael Keith is concerned with nuanced practices in places identified as the ghetto, such as the generative outcomes of graffiti tagging and street culture, relative to the ways in which the ghetto has been historically represented in the modern city.[40] John L. Jackson Jr. explores notions of racial sincerity and ghetto authenticity while tracing the commodification of ghetto practices and identity by mainstream culture.[41] Mario Luis Small presents the dangers of spatial codification in his descriptively titled essay "Is There Such a Thing as 'the Ghetto'? The Perils of Assuming That the South Side of Chicago Represents Poor Black Neighborhoods."[42]

Recent work that offers alternative readings of metropolitan space—from core to edge—do in fact blur real and imagined boundaries and codifications linked to space and race. However, the fact that this scholarship continues to be bounded by discursive frameworks—designated as suburban, urban, or ghetto literatures— reveals the narrative power of early planning theory such as that of the Chicago school, which defined distinct zones of classification and argued that natural patterns of urban development based on economic drivers *logically* resulted in a white suburban periphery and a nonwhite urban core of ethnic ghettos. Although many have since disputed the natural occurrence of residential segregation and challenged a centrifugal simplification of urban space, the suburban/urban spatial binary continues to haunt metropolitan scholarship.

## Dark Bodies in White Space: The Case of the Normandy Suburbs

The African American families who moved to the Normandy suburbs in the wake of the civil rights movement discovered that the white spatial imaginary dictated their rights to, and in, the suburbs by limiting their options, devaluing their property, and discouraging investment. Later, the same suburban imaginary dictated their own attempts at producing *good suburban subjects* for the purpose of being recognized by the county and securing the resources they had expected to find beyond the city limits. Paradoxically termed a *new suburban ghetto* within urban literature and media,[43] the Normandy suburbs are viewed by many in the region as an unqualified *urban ghetto*, defined by pathologies of poverty, race, and culture. Many of the residents, however, do not accept this representation. Rather, they point to spaces and practices associated with suburbia—detached homes, backyards, public green space, neighborhood policing, political autonomy—and defend the notion that they too are suburban dwellers claiming and defending symbols of privilege and normativity. The intersection of stigmatized black space with the white spatial imaginary in the Normandy suburbs produces unique practices of both liberation and subjugation and provides important insight into what it means to be a racially determined sub/urban citizen.

The racialization of space in the geography of the Normandy suburbs predates suburban development. It was here that many Native American tribes ceded their land to William Clark (of the Lewis and Clark expedition), who represented the U.S. government as the superintendent of Indian affairs. Clark bought nearly half the area's land in the early 1800s for his private residence and as hunting grounds for visiting tribal parties, in the hope of negotiating successful concessions. The area is also the site of the oldest African American commercial cemetery in St. Louis, dating back to the mid-1800s, in which many notable black St. Louisans are buried, including the wife of Dred Scott. By the late 1800s, many summer estates for elite city residents were built in the area. It was further developed as middle- and upper-class railcar suburbs (according to garden suburb typology) in the 1920s and 1930s. Following World War II, the majority of the area was filled in with working-class streetcar suburbs and marketed to first- and second-generation white European immigrants. The neighborhoods were originally unincorporated, but threats of annexation from neighboring municipalities and the ease of incorporation under Missouri state law led to a leapfrogging phenomenon of municipal incorporation between 1945 and 1953. During this time, more than twenty neighborhoods incorporated into semiautonomous fourth-class cities, villages, or hamlets with populations ranging from three hundred to forty-five hundred.[44] Fueling incorporation were residents' desires to maintain neighborhood homogeneity and establish limited home rule governance. Similar to the rhetoric used in other U.S. cities at the time, municipal autonomy and fragmentation were framed as democratic rights of citizenship.[45] Local disputes regarding issues such as elementary school catchment areas, unpopular county ordinances, and proposed mixed-income housing were also catalysts for quick incorporation of small neighborhoods wanting to set up their own, albeit limited, governments. Today the Normandy suburbs constitute a patchwork of twenty-four fragmented municipalities occupying ten square miles of St. Louis County. The area is officially defined by the boundaries of the Normandy school district—roughly Interstate 70 to the north, the inner-belt freeway (I-170) to the west, University City to the south, and the city of St. Louis to the east. Although uneven distribution of services and governance and fierce competition over resources remain common, many local polities recently entered into a joint initiative called Vision24:1 (twenty-four municipalities with one vision), which is intended to build coalitions across the fragmented geography.

As documented by a frenzy of academic research published from 1973 through 1976, the push by African Americans out of the urban core and into the Normandy suburbs at the end of the 1960s attracted much attention from St. Louis County policy makers and local municipal leaders, who attempted to curb white panic and slow what they believed would be an inevitable social and physical decline of

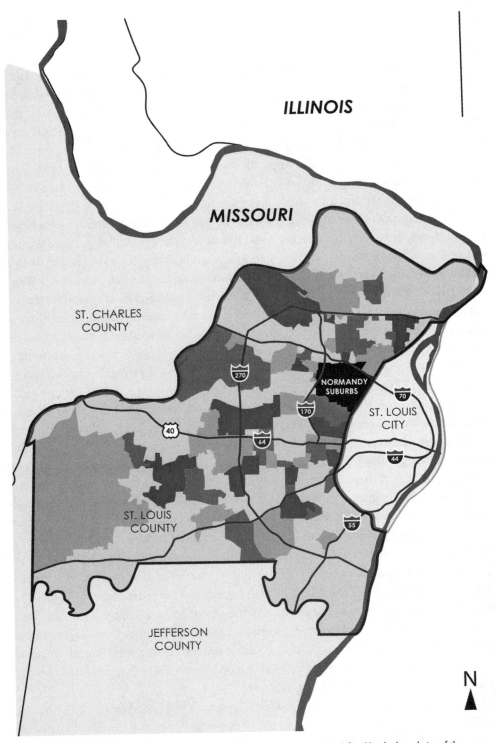

ILLINOIS

MISSOURI

ST. CHARLES
COUNTY

NORMANDY
SUBURBS

ST. LOUIS
CITY

ST. LOUIS
COUNTY

JEFFERSON
COUNTY

N

The area known as the Normandy suburbs includes twenty-four municipalities and is defined by the boundaries of the Normandy school district within St. Louis County. There are ninety municipal governments in St. Louis County, but the city of St. Louis does not reside within any county.

the area.[46] As in many cities across the United States at that time, racial tensions were running high, and today many residents remember practices of violence and property damage aimed at discouraging new black families from buying in the area and white homeowners from selling to black buyers.[47] Blockbusting practices among realtors are well documented, and redlining strategies among lenders became commonplace in St. Louis County throughout the 1970s.[48] Statistics show several areas reaching black populations of 70 percent by 1975 and 89 percent by 1980. Employing a vocabulary of war, studies describe the area as "falling" quickly to "negro invasion." The Federal Housing Administration and the Home Owner's Land Corporation guidelines that established risk ratings for lenders perpetuated the war analogy. With racial homogeneity at the top of the risk assessment list, documents stated that neighborhoods "invaded" or "infiltrated" by African Americans had or would lose all value and "fall" to the "occupation" of blacks.[49] Another study stated: "The ineluctable sequence of *black penetration, to invasion, to succession* becomes predominant under certain circumstances."[50] Recent writings on the St. Louis suburbs continue this narrative regarding the "fall" of communities brought about by "racial tipping"—the ratio of black residents that guarantees an area will eventually become all black.[51]

The prophecy of plummeting home values and declining schools became self-fulfilling as spatial stigmatization followed blacks into the suburbs. One local policy maker remarked, "Ghetto spillover now stretches almost all the way across the county in a northwesterly direction."[52] The spatial imaginary of the ghetto gradually replaced the white spatial imaginary associated with the original suburban spaces and practices, and was based solely on the presence of African American residents. Following this logic, "ghetto" represented any predominantly African American space irrespective of spatial or class specificity. The urban core was no longer the sole container of black space in St. Louis, and this shift distinctly challenged the suburban imaginary of many people. These contradictions of racialized spatial imaginaries heightened the experience and anxiety of race for suburban blacks and whites and raised questions regarding the rights of suburban citizens, the nature and politics of identity in the metropolitan region, and the power of spatial/racial imaginaries to determine experience and practice in space.

## The Case of Pagedale

Developed in the 1940s for working-class Lutherans and Catholics of German and Irish descent, the city of Pagedale is one of the twenty-four Normandy suburbs. The municipality is made up of three neighborhoods that incorporated into one entity in 1950 and is named for Page Avenue, a major thoroughfare running through the city's footprint. The city limits encompass roughly fourteen hundred small homes,

two commercial districts, two large churches, an industrial zone, and a large Lutheran cemetery. In keeping with the suburban imaginary, advertisements for new
homes in Pagedale touted "clean neighborhoods, quiet streets, and a fruit tree in
every yard."[53] The first- and second-generation working-class European immigrants
who moved to Pagedale gained more access to the benefits of citizenship by differentiating themselves from African Americans left behind in the city. Their desire
to live separately from blacks was not merely an issue of racial prejudice—it was a
real and perceived necessity regarding their rights and belonging within American
society. The equation of whiteness with fitness for citizenship and homeownership shaped processes of racialization in the United States and was essential to the
assimilation of European immigrants into "white society."[54] By moving out of neighborhoods identified as ethnic ghettos in the city and into the suburbs, ethnic minorities claimed "whiteness" in contrast to ethnic associations with the "dark" space
of the urban core. As documented in the literature on the American ghetto, by the
second half of the twentieth century, the ethnic ghetto first described in terms of
the Jewish ghetto in Europe no longer held the same meaning in American cities.
The term *ghetto* evolved to represent specifically black space. At the time of incorporation, Pagedale represented a place where immigrant families could leave ethnic
associations of city neighborhoods behind and establish themselves as white citizens participating in the "American Dream."

Twenty years later, the black residents who moved to Pagedale in the 1970s
were motivated by the same desire to claim their rights to the American Dream.
The first wave of black residents joined the ranks of middle-class homeowners and
paid top dollar for the limited number of homes offered to nonwhite buyers. St.
Louis historians and political scientists have noted that the area's proximity to
industry, to racially transitioning areas in the city of St. Louis and neighboring
Wellston, and to the historically black suburb of Kinloch created openings for black
home buyers that did not exist in more insulated and desirable neighborhoods.[55]
As panic set in among white residents and municipal leaders, property values fell,
in keeping with the self-fulfilling prophecy perpetuated by real estate practices.
Many homes were bought as rental properties or sold at depreciated values by the
late 1970s. As a result, many low-income African Americans looking to leave inner-
city housing projects and areas increasingly affected by crowding, drug epidemics,
and limited opportunities were able to move to Pagedale. Social and kinship networks often remained intact when residents from housing projects found suburban
homes near those of family members and old neighbors, creating what some have
described as a mini-diaspora into the suburbs.[56] By 1980, the majority of white residents had left Pagedale, and the community was 79 percent African American. It

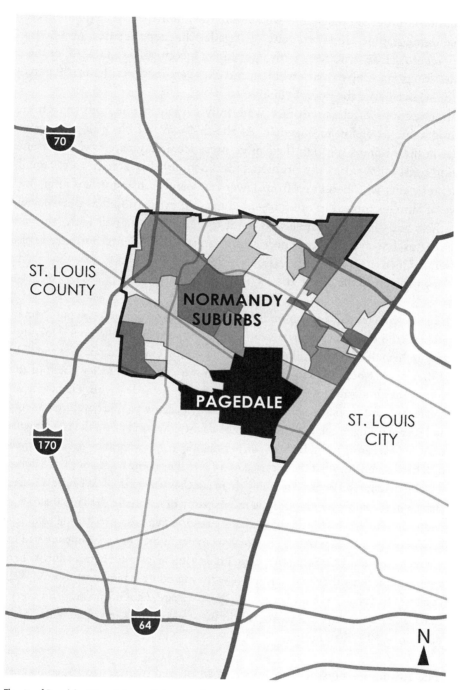

The city of Pagedale, Missouri, is one of the twenty-four municipalities that make up the Normandy suburbs. With an area of 1.1 square miles and a population of 3,300, Pagedale is the second-largest city in the Normandy suburbs and borders six municipalities.

would be another ten years, however, before the municipal leadership reflected the racial demographic. Today the city of Pagedale has a population of 3,304 and is 94 percent African American, with a per capita income of $11,005. All of the city's leadership is made up of black women, and 29.5 percent of residents (39 percent of children) live under the poverty line.[57]

Intersections of class and race were fully evident throughout the process of demographic inversion in Pagedale. As the first wave of black home buyers lost value in their homes through their mere presence, many perceived themselves as having been followed by the problems (and people) they sought to escape. Likewise, residents who benefited from lower rents and housing prices after the first wave of families moved in often resented those they identified as power-wielding "brothers and sisters" and believed them to be closely aligned with "the man."[58] Class status, however, does not necessarily determine residents' outlooks regarding power, subjectivity, or identity. As one resident who moved to Pagedale from the housing projects in the city in the 1970s explains:

> You take families that come from the projects, just like I did, and you put them in a house and they don't know how to act. That's what city living does. Nobody's taught them the difference. It puts them in a position to just run rampant and wild if they haven't been trained to live a certain way. Then when they come to the county they bring all that with them. That's what we gotta deal with. That's why we create laws and ordinances that protect our city because people have investments and we are trying to get our share from the county. We can't prove them right with what they accusing us of. It's *who* you're bringing in and what they're accustomed to. They come with what they're used to. Where they come from, they were doing what they want and nobody teaching them another way to do it. We have a better chance in the county with our little municipality of enforcing the laws that teach people how to live. It's the teachings that we have. When I came to Pagedale I didn't know how to take care of property or how to act in the county. Someone had to tell me—you don't be doing that here. I didn't know it wasn't permissible. When people know what they're doing and why they're doing it they start to say, "Well that's not bad at all, I got my barbecue in the backyard, I got my privacy and everything. I don't have to have all my kids in the street playing and be looking at my neighbor—all in their business.[59]

The attitudes expressed by this citizen are shared by many in Pagedale and cut across class, gender, and generational lines. Current municipal leaders, all of whom are African American, maintain a *moral polity of blackness* defined and deployed paradoxically through the white suburban imaginary and an age-old politics of respectability. The desire to prove authenticity as good suburban citizens in order to claim rights and resources within St. Louis County results in ardent racialization and hypermanagement of bodies in space. Through ordinances intended to discipline behavior construed as black, the suburban imaginary is enforced more stringently than would be considered acceptable in predominantly white neighborhoods, and the city is in the business of subject making—of making good suburban citizens. Several scholars have described the quest for model-citizen status in and through the suburbs by various ethnic minorities, most often Asian Americans. Wendy Cheng describes how Asian and Latina/o Americans "had to either 'pass' as white . . . or evidence a 'proper' relationship to property as conceived as coextensive with a middle-class, white nuclear-family based vision of Americanness" in order to achieve provisional acceptance in the suburbs of Los Angeles.[60] In the case of African Americans however, the specific and long history of racism and differentialized space in the United States produces equally specific suburban practices and outcomes that differ from those associated with other ethnic minorities.

In Pagedale, and in other municipalities of the Normandy suburbs, we find overtly racialized prohibitions: "No sagging pants"; "No loud music or excessive bass"; "No more than two people assembling in public space without a permit"; "No barbequing in front or next to a house"; "No congregating on a porch"; and so on.[61] Pavilions and many park benches have been removed from public spaces in Pagedale, many of which are fenced off and locked. While local ordinances aimed at policing social behavior and space are commonplace in sub/urban living, the formal and informal policing carried out in many municipalities of the Normandy suburbs specifically targets perceptions of so-called ghetto behavior and black male deviance. Pagedale leaders associate efforts to socially and spatially police residents with new development brought about by political alliances with county leadership and the city's strong partnership with a local community support and development agency.[62] While many positive things are happening in Pagedale, including extensive investment, a new bank and grocery store, increased resources in the community, and a low crime rate, the majority of people living outside the area who were interviewed for this study regard Pagedale as similar to, if not the same as, the inner-city ghetto.[63] The public debate around the loss of accreditation by the Normandy school district illustrates similar regional attitudes. Local media coverage that frames public participation as "circus-like" behavior at public hearings and council meetings frustrates municipal leadership and encourages hyperpolicing of so-called black behavior. The ongoing cycle of social policing in relationship to regional perception highlights the contradictions between real and imagined spaces of the city and reveals the power of the suburban imaginary to dictate spatial and political practice.

Not everyone in Pagedale rejects the label of "the ghetto." Many residents claim ghetto identity and refute accusations that Pagedale is not the true hood, or that residents are not "for-real black" and have lost ghetto authenticity—in this case equated with black authenticity.[64] Social media sites reveal music videos, amateur footage of gang fights, and freestyle rap battles intended to establish Pagedale as an authentic ghetto in response to claims by some in the urban core that suburban ghettos are tame, inauthentic versions of the real location of black agency, credibility, and creativity. Pagedale is mentioned in the lyrics of internationally known rap artist Murphy Lee's song "St. Louis Nigga,"[65] to which nationally recognized freestyle rapper Aye Verb has responded with his own music video, "Get to Know a Nigga," filmed in Pagedale.[66] Aye Verb, who hails Pagedale as his turf and uses language rather than violence to do battle (in freestyle rap or smack competitions across the United States), presents Pagedale as representing the authentic "streets of St. Louis," where respect is earned through street cred, although he laments the violence associated with such respect. The local rap group Gangsta Bubs takes the argument one step further in its homage to Pagedale "Luv My Hood," representing Pagedale as a gang-banging hood where violence and drugs dictate the norms of the street, stating "talk bad about the 'Dale, I wish you would, one phone call'll get you put off in the mud."[67] Gangsta Bubs' video is filmed with the intention of claiming the spaces and symbols of Pagedale and begins in front of the mayor's prized "Welcome to Pagedale" sign and the city's signature "Knockout Roses." While these examples are certainly mediated by larger forms of representations and meaning that I do not take into consideration here, many residents proudly embrace the idea of "coming from the hood," which they associate with black culture, and contest claims that Pagedale is not the "real hood."[68] The last example could be dismissed as promoting senseless violence, which I do not intend to celebrate. However, representations like "Luv My Hood" emanate from fierce discrepancies regarding identity and place, as well as specific experiences of race and inequality in the United States, and it is important to acknowledge them as such.

## Conclusion

At first glance, the distinction between those who reject ghetto classification in favor of suburban identity in Pagedale and the other Normandy suburbs and those who view ghetto and black identity as mutually constituted could appear to be broken down to the difference between those who practice a politics of respectability and those who attempt to break free from such politics. Or the distinction could be one of generation, gender, and class differences regarding issues of African American identity. Such distinctions have been described in sociological and urban studies. For instance, Elijah Anderson's distinction between *decent* and *street* culture among African American men, Nikki Jones's description of the inherent tensions between *good* and *ghetto* in the lives of African American girls, and Michael Keith's contrast of the *ethnic entrepreneur* with the *street rebel* in London all highlight the value-oriented conceptual categories regarding conformity and dissonance that determine a so-called moral order within racialized communities.[69] As these authors point out, and as my own experience supports, such clear distinctions do not hold up. Many variations and contradictions regarding situated identities can be found in the attitudes and practices of single individuals across gender and generational lines whereby the degree of "law-abiding citizen" is not necessarily determined by whether a person claims the suburbs, the ghetto, or both. At the center of these phenomena is the notion of authenticity, which pivots around race. In order to claim suburban authenticity, must black residents eschew black (often associated as ghetto) identity, and vice versa? What are the stakes associated with each? And even if they do, will they be granted suburban citizenship? Residents, sub/urban scholars, and certainly those currently embroiled in the fate of the Normandy school district cannot seem to agree regarding whether Pagedale and the rest of the Normandy suburbs are urban or suburban. However, this binary construction of racialized space continues to inform classifications and expectations regarding differentiated metropolitan space across the United States. As a result, the convergence of competing quests for authenticity and struggles over rights to the city play out at every level of practice—including allocations of resources, regional politics, municipal policing, media representation, outside investment, and interactions between neighbors. The significance of black bodies occupying traditional white space in the Normandy suburbs of St. Louis County intersects with multivalent black identities and puts race at the center of perception and action. Race is then the constitutive and operative force determining how political subjectivity, identity, and the physical environment are formed, maintained, and contested.

The case of the Normandy suburbs illustrates the limits and consequences of spatial categorization and suggests that the question "Is it the suburbs or is it the ghetto?" is indeed the wrong one to be asking with regard to such places. Qualifying communities like Pagedale as *suburban ghettos* does not acknowledge the important, if contested, history of metropolitan space that current residents are in the process of making, just as prevailing readings of *the urban* inaccurately describe agentive processes and contingencies currently at work in city cores. As this example shows, race, as signified through both the body and identity, is an active structuring force that informs how urban space is classified, represented, discussed, and ultimately acted upon. Most scholarship and practice focusing on metropolitan areas, however, has not directly confronted how space, like bodies, is inscribed by race. I therefore return to these questions: How do prevailing frameworks of metropolitan analysis

obscure the work of race today? How do continued distinctions between urban and
suburban space in both scholarship and practice reinforce racialized paradigms that
support racial projects?

## Notes

*Note regarding research methodology:* Information on the attitudes and opinions of residents
was collected between 2005 and 2011 through individual interviews, focus groups, and participant observation in conjunction with community engagement courses and design–build
studios, and through my participation as a principal investigator for the Page Avenue Health
Impact Assessment, funded in part by the Robert Wood Johnson Foundation. Over the same
period I established personal relationships with residents as a result of extensive time spent in
the area.

1. The *St. Louis Post-Dispatch* recently produced a video highlighting areas in the Normandy
suburbs, "A Video Portrait of Normandy School District," April 10, 2014, http://www.stltoday
.com.

2. Analysis of transcripts from Missouri Senate Education Committee hearings, public
hearings sponsored by the Missouri Department of Elementary and Secondary Education, and
Normandy School Board meetings held between July 2013 and March 2014 that were focused
on the crisis of the Normandy school district reveals repeated use of the word *urban* in reference
to the problems, challenges, and character of the district.

3. Key-informant interview. This attitude, framed by the rhetoric of personal responsibility, is also repeatedly expressed in letters to the editors of local news publications concerning
this issue. For example, one writer stated: "The citizens of Normandy need to get off their
collective butts and start taking responsibility for educating their children. The reason [other
school districts are successful] is because the parents have worked hard, are involved . . . , and
follow the American tenet of individual responsibility." Letter to the editor, *St. Louis Post-
Dispatch,* February 16, 2014.

4. St. Louis County crime-mapping statistics for 2013, http://maps.stlouisco.com/police.

5. Persons or families may be classified as functionally homeless if they move often between
locations such as the homes of family members or friends, automobiles, or motels. For a discussion of types of housing stability, see Sam Tsemberis, Gregory McHugo, Valerie Williams,
Patricia Hanrahan, and Ana Stefancic, "Measuring Homelessness and Residential Stability:
The Residential Time-Line Follow-Back Inventory," *Journal of Community Psychology* 35, no. 1
(2007): 29–42.

6. Ty McNichol, district superintendent, statement made at a public hearing of the Missouri Department of Elementary and Secondary Education, November 11, 2013.

7. For example, views expressed at the Missouri Senate Education Committee hearing on
bills SB624 and SB516, February 5, 2014.

8. Quoted in John Eligon, "In Missouri, Race Complicates a Transfer to Better Schools,"
*New York Times,* July 31, 2013.

9. Comments made at Francis Howell School District town hall meeting, attended by
author, July 20, 2014.

10. Comments made at a public hearing at the University of Missouri–St. Louis (in Normandy suburbs footprint) at which the Department of Elementary and Secondary Education

introduced its recommendations for how the state of Missouri should deal with underperforming school districts, attended by author, February 25, 2014.

11. Eligon, "In Missouri, Race Complicates"; "Still Segregated," episode 3 in *The March @ 50*, PBS Web series, produced by Shukree Tilghman, September 9, 2013, http://video.pbs.org/video/2365071680.

12. Debates regarding whether or not the United States has achieved a postracial society—one in which race no longer matters in significant ways—have been waged over the past twenty years. For example, see Bill Keller, "Profiling Obama," *New York Times,* July 28, 2013. Scholars such as David Theo Goldberg argue that "postracial" is yet another racist project that obscures racialized systems of power defined by the modern state; see David Theo Goldberg, *The Threat of Race: Reflections on Racial Neoliberalism* (Oxford: Wiley-Blackwell, 2009). For further discussion of postracial questions, see also "Race in the Age of Obama," special issue, *Daedalus* 140, no. 1 (Winter 2011).

13. U.S. Census data, 2010. For examples of data analyses relative to race, see Carmen DeNavas-Walt, Bernadette D. Proctor, and Jessica C. Smith, *Income, Poverty, and Health Insurance Coverage in the United States: 2011,* Current Population Reports, P60-243 (Washington, D.C.: Government Printing Office, 2012); Jeremy Pais, Scott J. South, and Kyle Crowder, "Metropolitan Heterogeneity and Minority Neighborhood Attainment: Spatial Assimilation or Place Stratification?," *Social Problems* 59, no. 2 (May 2012): 258–81; Michael McFarland and Cheryl A. Smith, "Segregation, Race, and Infant Well-Being," *Population Research and Policy Review* 30, no. 3 (June 2011): 467–93.

14. In doing so, I accept John O. Calmore's description of race as "a fluctuating, decentered complex of social meanings that are formed and transformed under constant pressures of political struggle," in "Critical Race Theory, Archie Shepp, and Fire Music: Securing an Authentic Intellectual Life in a Multicultural World," *Southern California Law Review* 65 (July 1992): 2129.

15. Philomena Essed conceptualizes "everyday racism" in "Everyday Racism: A New Approach to the Study of Racism," in *Race Critical Theories,* ed. Philomena Essed and David Theo Goldberg (Malden, Mass.: Blackwell, 2002); John A. Powell and Caitlin Watt distinguish between everyday racialization and racism by decoupling outcome from intent in "Negotiating the New Political and Racial Environment," *Journal of Law in Society* 11 (2010): 31–69.

16. In June 2013, the U.S. Supreme Court struck down key parts of the 1965 Voting Rights Act (VRA), allowing nine states (mostly in the South) to change election laws without answering to federal antidiscrimination guidelines. Critics of the VRA cited the election of Barack Obama as evidence that the law is no longer relevant, and Chief Justice John Roberts agreed that "the country has changed." In the same month the Supreme Court ruled that lower courts must take a skeptical look at affirmative action programs at colleges and universities, stating that institutions must first exhaust all race-neutral processes in order to achieve diversity on campuses.

17. See, for example, Lawrence C. Levy's op-ed "Race and the Suburbs," *New York Times,* October 30, 2008; Elijah Anderson, *The Cosmopolitan Canopy: Race and Civility in Everyday Life* (New York: W. W. Norton, 2009). For a discussion of whether the election of Barack Obama reproblematizes and reracializes black leadership in urban areas, where it had become largely accepted, see Manning Marable, "Racializing Obama: The Enigma of Post-Black Politics and Leadership," *Souls: A Critical Journal of Black Politics, Culture, and Society* 11, no. 1 (2009): 1–15.

18. Powell and Watt, "Negotiating the New Political and Racial Environment," 45.

19. Michelle Wilde Anderson and Victoria C. Plaut discuss this question in their essay "Property Law: Implicit Bias and the Resilience of Spatial Colorlines," in *Implicit Racial Bias across the Law,* ed. Justin D. Levinson and Robert J. Smith (New York: Cambridge University Press, 2012).

20. For examples, see Ronald Bayor, *Race and the Shaping of Twentieth-Century Atlanta* (Chapel Hill: University of North Carolina Press, 1996); David Freund, *Colored Property: State Policy and White Racial Politics in Suburban America* (Chicago: University of Chicago Press, 2007); Colin Gordon, *Mapping Decline: St. Louis and the Fate of the American City* (Philadelphia: University of Pennsylvania Press, 2008); Arnold R. Hirsch, *Making the Second Ghetto: Race and Housing in Chicago, 1940–1960* (Chicago: University of Chicago Press, 1983); Kenneth T. Jackson, *Crabgrass Frontier: The Suburbanization of the United States* (New York: Oxford University Press, 1985); Douglas S. Massey and Nancy A. Denton, *American Apartheid: Segregation and the Making of the Underclass* (Cambridge, Mass.: Harvard University Press, 1993); Raymond A. Mohl, ed., *The Making of Urban America* (Wilmington, Del.: Scholarly Resources, 1988); Amanda I. Seligman, *Block by Block: Neighborhoods and Public Policy on Chicago's West Side* (Chicago: University of Chicago Press, 2005); Thomas J. Sugrue, *The Origins of the Urban Crisis: Race and Inequality in Postwar Detroit* (Princeton, N.J.: Princeton University Press, 1996); Heather Ann Thompson, *Whose Detroit? Politics, Labor, and Race in a Modern American City* (Ithaca, N.Y.: Cornell University Press, 2004).

21. Dianne Harris, *Little White Houses: How the Postwar Home Constructed Race in America* (Minneapolis: University of Minnesota Press, 2013).

22. Margaret Garb, *City of American Dreams: A History of Home Ownership and Housing Reform in Chicago, 1871–1919* (Chicago: University of Chicago Press, 2005), 205.

23. Sallie Marston, John Paul Jones III, and Keith Woodward, "Human Geography without Scale," *Transactions of the Institute of British Geographers* 30, no. 4 (2005): 416–32. See also Eric Sheppard, "The Spaces and Times of Globalization: Place, Scale, Networks, and Positionality," *Economic Geography* 78, no. 3 (July 2002): 307–30.

24. For example, see Alan Berger, *Drosscape: Wasting Land in Urban America* (New York: Princeton Architectural Press, 2006); Lars Lerup, "Stim and Dross: Rethinking the Metropolis," *Assemblage,* no. 25 (1994): 82–100; Deborah E. Popper and Frank J. Popper, "Small Can Be Beautiful: Coming to Terms with Decline," *Planning* 68, no. 7 (2002): 20–23; Justin B. Hollander, *Sunburnt Cities: The Great Recession, Depopulation and Urban Planning in the American Sunbelt* (New York: Routledge, 2011).

25. George Lipsitz developed the concept of the white spatial imaginary in relationship to "the possessive investment in Whiteness" and has more recently linked it to divisions of urban space. See George Lipsitz, *The Possessive Investment in Whiteness: How White People Profit from Identity Politics* (Philadelphia: Temple University Press, 1998); Lipsitz, *How Racism Takes Place* (Philadelphia: Temple University Press, 2011). Michael Keith also uses the conceptual framework of the normative urban imaginary in his analysis of urban space in *After the Cosmopolitan? Multicultural Cities and the Future of Racism* (New York: Routledge, 2005).

26. See Eligon, "In Missouri, Race Complicates"; "Still Segregated."

27. For a comprehensive review and discussion regarding omissions and oversights in the first generation of suburban scholarship, see Matthew D. Lassiter and Christopher Niedt, "Suburban Diversity in Postwar America," *Journal of Urban History* 39, no. 1 (January 2013): 3–14; also see Becky M. Nicolaides and Andrew Wiese, eds., *The Suburb Reader* (New York: Routledge, 2006).

28. *Journal of Urban History* 27, no. 3 (March 2001); *Journal of Urban History* 39, no. 1 (January 2013): 3–100.

29. Willow Lung-Amam, "Beyond Ethnoburbs: Diversity and Immigration in Fremont, California, 1956–2010" (paper presented at the biennial meeting of the Urban History Association, October 25–28, 2012); Wendy Cheng, "The Changs Next Door to the Diazes: Suburban Racial Formation in Los Angeles's San Gabriel Valley," *Journal of Urban History* 39, no. 1 (2013): 15–35; Sarah Potter, "Family Ideals: The Diverse Meanings of Residential Space in Chicago during the Post–World War II Baby Boom," *Journal of Urban History* 39, no. 1 (2013): 59–78. See also the contributions to this book by Willow Lung-Amam (chapter 13), Matthew Gordon Lasner (chapter 20), Trecia Pottinger (chapter 2), and Tim Retzloff (chapter 4).

30. See the contribution to this volume by Becky M. Nicolaides (chapter 1); Margaret Crawford, "Everyday Urbanism," in *Everyday Urbanism: Margaret Crawford vs. Michael Speaks,* ed. Rahul Mehrotra (Ann Arbor: University of Michigan, Taubman College of Architecture, 2005); John Archer, "Everyday Suburbia: Lives and Practices," in "Suburbs: Dwelling in Transition," ed. Steven Logan, Janine Marchessault, and Michael Prokopow, *Public: Art Culture Ideas* 43 (2011): 22–31.

31. For example, see Bruce D. Haynes, *Red Lines, Black Spaces: The Politics of Race and Space in a Black Middle-Class Suburb* (New Haven, Conn.: Yale University Press, 2006); Kevin M. Kruse and Thomas J. Sugrue, eds., *The New Suburban History* (Chicago: University of Chicago Press, 2006); James Rosenbaum, Stefanie DeLuca, and Tammy Tuck, "New Capabilities in New Places: Low-Income Black Families in Suburbia," in *The Geography of Opportunity: Race and Housing Choice in Metropolitan America,* ed. Xavier de Souza Briggs (Washington, D.C.: Brookings Institute Press, 2005); Leonard Rubinowitz and James E. Rosenbaum, *Crossing the Class and Color Lines: From Public Housing to White Suburbia* (Chicago: University of Chicago Press, 2000).

32. Andrew Wiese, *Places of Their Own: African American Suburbanization in the Twentieth Century* (Chicago: University of Chicago Press, 2004).

33. Mary Pattillo, *Black on the Block: The Politics of Race and Class in the City* (Chicago: University of Chicago Press, 2007).

34. Farrah D. Gafford, "'It Was a Real Village': Community Identity Formation among Black Middle-Class Residents in Pontchartrain Park," *Journal of Urban History* 39, no. 1 (2013): 36–58.

35. Steven Gregory, *Black Corona: Race and the Politics of Place in an Urban Community* (Princeton, N.J.: Princeton University Press, 1998); Robert O. Self, *American Babylon: Race and the Struggle for Postwar Oakland* (Princeton, N.J.: Princeton University Press, 2003).

36. The ghetto, as a stigmatized space of separation and exclusion, can be traced to Venice, where it was adopted in 1516 as a mechanism of Jewish containment and gradually came to represent stigmatized urban space across European cities. In American cities, the Jewish ghetto evolved into a space of ethnic marginalization in the late nineteenth century and eventually became synonymous with African American space. See Louis Wirth, *The Ghetto* (Chicago: University of Chicago Press, 1928), including Robert Park's introduction; Franklin E. Frazier, "Negro Harlem: An Ecological Study," *American Journal of Sociology* 43, no. 1 (July 1937): 72–88; St. Clair Drake, "Profiles: Chicago," *Journal of Educational Sociology* 17, no. 5 (January 1944): 261–71; St. Clair Drake and Horace Cayton, *Black Metropolis: A Study of Negro Life in a Northern City* (Chicago: University of Chicago Press, 1945); Robert Weaver (secretary of the

U.S. Department of Housing and Urban Development), *The Negro Ghetto* (New York: Harcourt, Brace, 1948).

37. For discussions linking the culture of poverty to pathologies of the ghetto, see Gilbert Osofsky, *Harlem: The Making of a Ghetto—Negro New York, 1890–1930* (New York: Harper & Row, 1966); Ulf Hannerz, *Soul Side: Inquiries into Ghetto Culture and Community* (Chicago: University of Chicago Press, 1969); Kenneth B. Clark, *Dark Ghetto: Dilemmas of Social Power* (New York: HarperCollins, 1966).

38. For examples of work that shifted the discourse on the ghetto from social pathology toward structural racism, see Hirsch, *Making the Second Ghetto*; Adam Bickford and Douglas S. Massey "Segregation in the Second Ghetto: Racial and Ethnic Segregation in American Public Housing, 1977," *Social Forces* 69, no. 4 (1991): 1011–36; Mohl, *The Making of Urban America.* More recently, Loïc Wacquant has theorized the transformation of the traditional ghetto into a space of advanced marginality and has argued that the contemporary American prison system is the new ghetto. Loïc Wacquant, *Urban Outcasts: A Comparative Sociology of Advanced Marginality* (Cambridge: Polity Press, 2008); Wacquant, "Deadly Symbiosis: When Ghetto and Prison Meet and Mesh," *Punishment & Society* 3, no. 1 (January 2001): 95–133; Wacquant, *Punishing the Poor: The Neoliberal Government of Social Insecurity* (Durham, N.C.: Duke University Press, 2009).

39. Stuart Hall, Chas Critcher, Tony Jefferson, John Clarke, and Brian Roberts, *Policing the Crisis: Mugging, the State, and Law and Order* (London: Macmillan, 1978).

40. Keith, *After the Cosmopolitan?*

41. John L. Jackson Jr., *Real Black: Adventures in Racial Sincerity* (Chicago: University of Chicago Press, 2005).

42. Mario Luis Small, "Is There Such a Thing as 'the Ghetto'? The Perils of Assuming That the South Side of Chicago Represents Poor Black Neighborhoods," *City* 11, no.3 (December 2007): 413–21.

43. The term *suburban ghetto* has been used to refer to poverty and nonwhite ethnicity for at least four decades and has more recently become part of the urban lexicon. For examples, see Richard Koubek, "Wyandanch: A Case Study of Political Impotence in a Black Suburban Ghetto" (master's thesis, Queens College, New York, 1971); Mark Gottdiener, "Politics and Planning: Suburban Case Studies," in *Remaking the City: Social Science Perspectives on Urban Design,* ed. John S. Pipkin, Mark La Gory, and Judith R. Blau (Albany: State University of New York Press, 1983); Alexandra K. Murphy, "The Suburban Ghetto: The Legacy of Herbert Gans in Understanding the Experience of Poverty in Recently Impoverished American Suburbs," *City & Community* 6, no. 1 (March 2007): 21–37; Ronald E. Wilson and Derek J. Paulsen, "Foreclosures and Crime: A Geographical Perspective," *Geography & Public Safety* 1, no. 3 (October 2008): 1–2; Brad Tuttle, "Suburban Ghetto: Poverty Rates Soar in the Suburbs," *Time,* September 26, 2011.

44. For a concise discussion of this history, see Gordon, *Mapping Decline,* chap. 1. See also E. Terrence Jones, *Fragmented by Design: Why St. Louis Has So Many Governments* (St. Louis: Palmerston and Reed, 2000).

45. For an in-depth discussion of the rhetoric of decentralization, see Michan Andrew Connor, "'Public Benefits from Public Choice': Producing Decentralization in Metropolitan Los Angeles, 1954–1973," *Journal of Urban History* 39, no. 1 (2013): 79–100.

46. Bryan Downes, Joan Saunders, and John Collins, "Local Government Intervention in the Face of Mortgage Disinvestment: The Case of Normandy" (report, University of Missouri–

St. Louis study, January 1976); Tom Dyer, "Factors in Suburban Blight: A Study of Housing in Northwoods, Pine Lawn, and Hillsdale" (report, study conducted by Rick Corry and Tom Dyer, University of Missouri–St. Louis, June 1973); Normandy Municipal Council, "Citizens' GOALS Project Report," Don Moschenross, director (November 1973).

47. Key-informant interviews.

48. Gordon, *Mapping Decline.*

49. As cited in ibid., 89.

50. Solomon Sutker and Sara Smith Sutker, *Racial Transition in the Inner Suburb: Studies of the St. Louis Area* (New York: Praeger, 1974), 32; emphasis added.

51. E. Terrence Jones, "The Municipal Market in the St. Louis Region: 1950–2000," in *St. Louis Metromorphosis: Past Trends and Future Directions,* ed. Brady Baybeck and E. Terrence Jones (St. Louis: University of Missouri Press, 2004).

52. Quoted in Gordon, *Mapping Decline,* 25.

53. Developer's advertising pamphlet circa 1948, Missouri History Museum Archives.

54. See James R. Barrett and David Roediger, "Inbetween Peoples: Race, Nationality and the 'New Immigrant' Working Class," *Journal of American Ethnic History* 16, no. 3 (Spring 1997): 3–44; David Roediger, *The Wages of Whiteness: Race and the Making of the American Working Class* (New York: Verso, 1991).

55. See, for example, John A. Wright Sr., *Discovering African American St. Louis: A Guide to Historic Sites* (St Louis: Missouri Historical Society Press, 2002); Scott Cummings, "African American Entrepreneurship in the St. Louis Metropolitan Region: Inner City Economics and Dispersion to the Suburbs," in Baybeck and Jones, *St. Louis Metromorphosis.*

56. Key-informant interviews.

57. U.S. Census data, 2010.

58. Key-informant interviews.

59. Pagedale resident, interview by author, April 11, 2011.

60. Cheng, "The Changs Next Door to the Diazes," 22.

61. As recorded in municipal ordinances (past and present) of the cities of Pagedale, Hillsdale, and Pine Lawn.

62. "St. Louis Stabilization Effort," NeighborWorksAmerica, video, YouTube, December 17, 2009, http://www.youtube.com/watch?v=nHXu8B7yVfA.

63. Key-informant interviews.

64. Key-informant interviews.

65. "St. Louis, You See Me," Murphy Lee, video, YouTube, March 28, 2010, http://www.youtube.com/watch?v=hSvo24UBfpg.

66. "Get to Know a Nigga," Aye Verb, Street Status DVD, video, YouTube, November 5, 2008, http://www.youtube.com/watch?v=2nDHWx3Nwps.

67. "Luv My Hood," Gangsta Bubs, Dub Block Entertainment, video, YouTube, April 20, 2010, http://www.youtube.com/watch?v=Jg0Pu5EtgbU.

68. Key-informant interviews.

69. Elijah Anderson, *Code of the Street: Decency, Violence, and the Moral Life of the Inner City* (New York: W. W. Norton, 1999); Nikki Jones, *Between Good and Ghetto: African American Girls and Inner-City Violence* (New Brunswick, N.J.: Rutgers University Press, 2010); Keith, *After the Cosmopolitan?*

# 13

# The Vibrant Life of
# Asian Malls in Silicon Valley

WILLOW LUNG-AMAM

On a typical Friday afternoon in Fremont, California's Mission Square Shopping Center, known to regulars as "Little Taipei," Chinese grandmothers stake out their turf on parking lot benches while chatting with friends and comparing their grandchildren's latest feats. Outside the 99 Ranch Market, elderly men stand or sit around, smoking cigarettes, playing cards, scratching lottery tickets, and reading newspapers from their hometowns of Beijing, Saigon, and Manila. A few middle-aged women convene at outdoor tables wearing face masks, arm covers, and big-brimmed hats to shade them from the afternoon sun. By three o'clock, many of the parents and the elders have left, while students from nearby Mission San Jose High School are gathering at boba milk tea and frozen yogurt shops, where they listen to the blended beats of American, Taiwanese, and Hong Kong pop blaring over the shops' speakers and browse the magazine racks for gossip on their teen idols from around the world. By evening, older youth replace the teens and fill the cafés until they close at two or even three o'clock in the morning. Families arrive with three generations in tow—grandparents holding their grandchildren's hands while waiting in line outside popular restaurants like the Aberdeen Café. A parking lot dance begins as a swirl of Toyotas, Hondas, and Lexuses with lace-covered seats, Hello Kitty trinkets, Buddha figurines, and Ivy League decals fight for the few remaining spaces.

"Little Taipei" is one of well over one hundred Asian malls in the United States.[1] Asian malls are shopping centers designed to cater to the needs, desires, and tastes of their largely Asian American, and predominantly immigrant, customers. Compared to their more traditional American counterparts, they tend to be more service and food oriented, often with an Asian supermarket anchor, banquet restaurant, and various pan-Asian satellites. They often include hair and nail salons, restaurants, cafés, bakeries, and banks; providers of dental and eye care, massage therapy, acupuncture, and travel services; and book, music, jewelry, clothing, and herbal medicine shops. Some malls are developed as retail condominiums, a form of ownership common in and also unique to Asian malls, which lends to their flexible spatial configurations, management, and uses. For many patrons, Asian malls offer alternatives to urban ethnic enclaves like Chinatowns by providing familiar cultural goods and services in suburban environments they consider to be more convenient, modern, safe, and clean.

Asian malls have grown in tandem with rapid Asian American suburbanization over the past several decades. In 2010, 62 percent of all Asian Americans resided in the suburbs of America's one hundred largest metropolitan areas, making them the most suburban of all racial minority groups.[2] In Silicon Valley, Asian malls have proliferated among the many suburban municipalities to service the needs of newly arrived Asian immigrants who have flocked to the region for high-tech jobs and related service-sector work.[3] Asian malls are important to the suburban landscape in and economy of other centers of Asian American suburban life, such as Monterey Park, California; Arlington, Virginia; Flushing, New York; and Austin, Texas.

The introduction of Asian malls in many North American suburbs has been met by a small number of studies of their unique configurations, ownership mechanisms,

"Little Taipei" in Fremont, California, is one of the many Asian malls in Silicon Valley that have been built in response to the region's rising Asian immigrant population. Photograph by the author.

and politics, particularly in the Canadian cities of Vancouver and Toronto, which have served as popular destinations for Asian immigrants, particularly those from Hong Kong, since the 1980s.[4] Few scholars, however, have considered how Asian malls function in the everyday lives of suburban residents. Particularly in the writings on Asian immigrant suburbanization in the United States, Asian malls often appear only as markers of suburbia's changing demographic, not as meaningful or interesting spaces in their own right.[5]

This essay examines Asian malls as spaces that speak to the social and cultural values, needs, and ideals of their users. Pioneered by scholars such as John Brincker-hoff Jackson, cultural landscape studies have long stressed the need to interrogate everyday spaces for insights about the processes, people, and politics that produce the built environment. In this volume, several authors use this approach to examine mundane and often overlooked suburban places like outdoor kitchens and garages. But, as Martin Dines explains in chapter 6, this has not been the dominant theme in writings about suburbia. From the post–World War II period to the present day, urban scholars have been far more apt to critique suburbanites and suburbia's built form.[6]

The shopping mall has been a particularly popular object of scholarly distain. For many, suburban malls are visible symbols of an overly consumptive, capitalistic, privatized, and increasingly homogenized society. Malls are derided as carceral, securitized zones that limit the diversity and vibrancy of suburban public life and promote mass consumption and the privatization of public space. They are often described as Disneyfied spaces that simulate rather than encapsulate real life. For many, they epitomize the "nonplace" suburban realm, which lacks a sense of place and community. While many critics acknowledge the efforts of early social reformers like James Rouse and Victor Gruen to design shopping malls as centers of social and community life, they view these functions as supplanted by malls' contemporary focus on commercialization, consumption, privacy, and security.

Such critiques of suburbia and its malls, however, often fail to engage with real spaces and residents in substantive, analytical ways.[7] Robert E. Lang and Jennifer B. LeFurgy argue that a deficit of knowledge about suburbia has resulted from the reluctance among scholars and the wider public to regard suburbs as "real places."[8] The bird's-eye vantage point from which many have viewed suburbia has obscured an understanding of it as a lived landscape. In this chapter, I take an approach that seeks to understand how Asian American suburbanites make meaningful and valuable lives through engagement with the built environment and how, in turn, the built environment reflects their social and cultural values and practices. In doing so, I rely on the voices of suburbanites and on-the-ground observations of Asian malls. From 2010 through 2012, I conducted seventy-seven in-depth and semistructured interviews with Asian mall managers, developers, brokers, store owners, employees, and customers as well as observations at ten Asian malls in six Silicon Valley cities.[9]

This view from inside suburbia shows shopping malls in a far different light from that cast on them by various critics. I argue that Asian malls reflect and reinforce many Asian American suburbanites' everyday life practices, their personal and collective identities, sense of community and place, and connection to the Asian diaspora. They are places of vibrant social and cultural life that, for many, embody what it means to be Asian American in suburbia. Their various functions highlight contemporary suburbia as the site of increasing social and spatial diversity that reflects a range of needs, desires, and practices. Extending the work of new suburban historians and others, including several contributors to this volume who have written about the diversity of suburbanites and their lived experiences, this chapter addresses how Asian malls enable insights into how minorities and immigrants have constructed, in the words of historian Andrew Wiese, suburban "places of their own."[10] Asian malls are spaces through which Asian Americans' ideas and ideals about suburban life are expressed, embodied, and embedded and therefore inform their alternative suburban narratives. As urban planners and policy makers scramble to figure out how to make suburbia more sustainable and livable, such perspectives can also inform planning, design, and development policy and practices aimed at better serving the needs and honoring the desires of the increasingly diverse populations who now call suburbia home.

## Places Both Special and Mundane

The Asian mall serves many ritual functions in everyday Asian American suburban life. One of its more important functions is as a source of information—a resource for finding out what is happening in the local community, in the region, and among others in the Asian diaspora around the world. At the various stands outside Asian supermarkets, patrons can pick up the *Chinese New Home Buyers' Guide* or get information on food services, senior living care facilities, recreation, transportation, shopping, entertainment, and professional services in Chinese, English, and several other languages. On the billboards located outside every 99 Ranch Market (also known as Ranch 99 or Tawa), the largest Asian supermarket chain in the United States, with more than thirty-five stores nationwide, patrons can find out about houses for rent, babysitting and tutoring services, and employment opportunities.

Asian malls also typically offer a range of essential services, such as medical, dental, and eye care, with attention to common cultural practices. In Fremont Times Square, the Asian Medical Clinic provides health care that combines understandings of both Eastern and Western medical practices and addresses the common health concerns of Asian Americans. All the clinic's doctors speak Mandarin. Other "essentials" for many Asian Americans are good food and high-quality educational services. Youth are often shuttled to Asian malls to participate in Chinese language classes, test prep, music instruction, and other after-school activities while adults make their ritual trips in and out of grocery stores and restaurants. Milpitas Square sponsors job fairs and career days, among many other events aimed at building the social and economic capital of the Asian American community. In 2010, the federal government stationed census takers in 99 Ranch Markets across the country, an indication that Asian malls are also important sites of political participation for a population infamous for its lack of political engagement.

Malls serve as much as places of special occasion as of daily ritual. Many Asian Americans go to malls to get married and to celebrate holidays, birthdays, graduations, and other significant events. Weddings are such a popular part of the business of many banquet restaurants like ABC in Milpitas's Ulferts Center that customers are encouraged to get married during "off-peak" times of the year. One promotion offered a complimentary one-night stay in a hotel suite and bottles of wine for every

This sign promoting participation in the 2010 U.S. Census was posted at a 99 Ranch Market in Silicon Valley. Photograph by the author.

table for any couple who got married between January and April, in addition to the standard wedding package of a cake, photographer, flowers, karaoke machine, and entertainment by Leung's White Crane Lion Dancers.

## Spaces of Comfort, Acceptance, and Identity

Asian malls are comfortable places for Asian immigrants to gather, speak their native languages, and purchase familiar goods and products from their home countries. Sally, a second-generation Korean American, described the sense of security that her mother derives from shopping at Asian malls as opposed to more mainstream American supermarkets:

> She feels a lot more comfortable [at Asian malls]—in her element. I mean I would too. When she looks at something, she knows exactly what it is. If she needs help, she knows how to ask for help and feels comfortable with that. With English, even though she's pretty good with English, pretty proficient, there's still just that moment of hesitation. If she needs to ask for help, she will probably just ask me to ask.... I think [Asian malls] just give immigrants specifically comfort. Like you've come all this way but this doesn't have to be as foreign as you think it is. You can come into this little enclave that we've made and feel at least at home.

Asian malls are places where immigrants can purchase familiar products from their home countries, especially food. Many Asian supermarkets are stocked with fresh vegetables from all over the world. Photograph by the author.

For Sally, Asian malls serve a function similar to that of urban ethnic enclaves like Chinatowns—they are spaces that help immigrants adapt to life in new places.

For second-generation youth, the Asian mall provides comfort by reminding them not of their homes overseas but of their homes in the American suburbs. The mall connects youth to their families and cultures—it is a place where many go to "feel Asian." Several interviewees confirmed the feeling that one Yelp reviewer recalled as having been "practically raised" in 99 Ranch.[11] They grew up being shuttled to and from Asian malls for art and piano lessons, shopping, and eating out with their families. After they left home, the mall was still a place where many returned with their families during holidays and other special occasions. Ethan, a college student I spoke to at Pacific East Mall in Richmond, said that he spends most of the time during his trips home to Los Angeles being taken out by his parents to their local Asian mall, just as his family had done for out-of-town guests for as long as he could remember. The mall is a place of first jobs, dates, and many childhood memories—an intimately known and familiar space. "They remember the Asian mall," explained John Luk, president of GD Commercial, a brokerage firm in Silicon Valley specializing in Asian malls, in reference to second-generation Asian American youth.

Asian malls also reinforce Asian Americans' everyday cultural practices. At 99 Ranch, those wanting to celebrate Thanksgiving with nontraditional fare can pick up an entire meal consisting of roasted turkey, crispy fried shrimp balls, grilled short ribs, sautéed lotus root with Chinese cured pork, braised rock cod, and chow mein noodles. This alternative to the traditional American holiday normalizes and celebrates Asian cultural practices. "In Ranch 99, I don't feel I am a minority at all," explained one customer.[12]

Asian malls can also help patrons straddle their Asian and American identities by reflecting aspects of both. For example, they can serve as important spaces of identity for transnational youth who spend their lives shuttling back and forth between Taiwan and the United States.[13] Many second-generation youth consider urban ethnic enclaves too "old-fashioned" or "traditional," whereas Asian malls offer more "hip" and "modern" products, like cell phone gadgets and car accessories, that they feel better reflect their lifestyles and preferences. Boba milk tea shops featuring funky modern decor and Taiwanese and American pop music are popular youth hangouts. At Milpitas Square, Quickly, an international chain of boba milk tea shops, features an "In Board" that reports on news of importance to Asian American youth, from the death of Apple founder and CEO Steve Jobs to the latest Chinese pop star drama. Its shelves are lined with Asian American magazines like *East 38,* a Chinese-language publication that reports on Chinese celebrities but is marketed only in Northern and Southern California. Asian malls help to bridge

Many Asian American youth grow up going to Asian malls to attend after-school language, music, and art programs like this one advertised at Newark's Lido Faire. Photograph by the author.

multiple cultural landscapes and blend them into uniquely Asian American suburban spaces.

## Spaces of Culture, Community, and Socialization

Many Asian mall patrons visit often and for long periods of time. At several of the malls I studied, customers would regularly spend several hours there, especially on Friday and Saturday nights, when parking was often hard to find. As marketing scholar Roger Blackwell has quipped, "It appears as if Asians do not go to the mall to shop but rather to take their weekend vacations."[14] At Pacific East, I met several

Asian malls help to normalize the cultural practices of Asian Americans, especially with regard to food. Most Asian supermarkets contain delis that serve a variety of traditional Asian cuisine, like these steamed buns. Photograph by the author.

shoppers who told me they visited the mall every weekend. One Mien teen said that he came to the mall every Sunday after church and several times during the week, mostly to eat and meet up with friends.

The popularity of Asian malls stems in part from their roles as both cultural and community centers. They are places of gathering for everything from celebrations of the Lunar New Year to religious ceremonies. In Silicon Valley, Asian mall events draw crowds that are as large as, if not larger than, those for similar events held in San Francisco or Oakland. In addition to special holidays, malls often host regular cultural events like lantern-making, kite-making, and calligraphy workshops; demonstrations of fine arts; folk dances; puppet shows; and drama and music performances. Los Angeles's Asian Garden Mall holds weekly night markets similar to those in many Asian cities. "The objective of these planned events is to create a social atmosphere to expand the role of an Asian shopping center from purely commercial. By creating a gathering place, it is intended that the center form a social hub that attracts Asians from a wider trade area," concluded a report on Asian malls commissioned by the city of Fremont.[15]

Outside a music store in a Silicon Valley Asian mall, patrons gather around a pianist playing traditional Chinese ballads. Photograph by the author.

Patrons come to the mall to socialize as well as build and renew friendships. They come with friends, and at the mall they commonly run into people they know, sometimes even old acquaintances from Taiwan or China.[16] The mall acts like a suburban main street—a place to see and be seen. On the weekends, mall sidewalks and hallways are overrun with customers dressed in their Sunday best, with the symbols of their success apparent in the cars they drive, the clothes they wear, and the amounts of dishes they order in local restaurants. As H. Y. Nahm notes, "Food is the ostensible attraction [of Asian malls] but the real draw is the chance to renew one's identity by casually rubbing elbows with other Asians."[17] Similarly, Shenglin Chang has observed that 99 Ranch serves as such an important social hub that a trip to the market by a dating couple can serve almost as their official announcement of their relationship to the larger community.[18] Asian malls are places to meet and greet others. Like bowling alleys, movie theaters, cafés, and other "third spaces" that critics suggest have been lost amid contemporary suburban sprawl, Asian malls are places where Asian Americans participate in their local cultural communities.

The role of the Asian mall as a social space is especially important for Asian youth and elderly. A Chinese senior at Northgate Shopping Center in Fremont, who spoke little English and had no family in the area, said that the mall was an important space for him to meet up with old friends and make new ones. He had found his apartment through a posting outside the 99 Ranch Market, and he walked to the mall every day from his home. Recognizing the vital role of these shopping centers for the elderly, several Bay Area groups that serve Asian American seniors, such as Self-Help for the Elderly, provide transportation to and from Asian malls. For many Asian American youth, the malls are also important sites of their social lives and identities. Four Asian American teens whom I met while they were break dancing in the hallways at Pacific East explained that they felt more comfortable and accepted at Asian malls than at other malls in the area, where their presence was more highly scrutinized. All had been coming to Pacific East up to three times a week since they were in middle school, some since elementary school. Two college-age women at Milpitas Square explained that Asian malls are important for suburban youth who have few other places to hang out, especially places with good and cheap food and vibrant nightlife.

Asian malls are also places that strengthen the bonds of family. Blackwell has referred to them as "family places, symbolic of a culture that is able to take commercial and cultural interests and blend them."[19] Mary, who was born in India, told me that her husband will not let her cook on the weekend so that the family can spend time together eating out, often at an Asian mall. "It's a family event on the weekend," explained John Luk, who reported that Asian American families will often reward the grandparents for working hard during the week watching the kids by taking them to the mall. It is not at all uncommon to see three generations of family members streaming in and out of mall restaurants and shops. Asian malls help to bridge the cultural divides between generations. As Nahm observes, they help to show Asian American and non-Asian American youth that "Asian culture offers shiny modern attractions as well as old dusty ones."[20]

Asian malls also attract customers from different social classes and ethnicities and foster their interaction. "There is a sense of the mall integrating different waves of ethnic Chinese immigrants from all over Asia. They may come from different classes, but the mall represents common ground," argues Aiwah Ong. "It's the place where different streams of Asians become Asian-American."[21] Most malls in the Silicon Valley contain a variety of pan-Asian restaurants, customers, and stores selling products that range in quality from high-end jewelry to knockoff pursues and knickknacks. At Milpitas Square, luxury clothing boutiques adjoin gift shops selling cheap imports along their narrow, crowded aisles. At most of the restaurants, even the most popular and seemingly exclusive ones, lunch can be bought for less than ten dollars a plate. Restaurants and supermarkets generally maintain a broad selection of pan-Asian cuisine as well as foods from Latin America, the United

Outside this 99 Ranch Market in Fremont, newspapers are available in twelve languages. The stands are a daily meeting place for people of different ethnicities and social classes. Photograph by the author.

States, and many other regions of the world. Typical of Asian malls' diverse offerings are two of the more popular restaurants in Milpitas Square, Coriya Hot Pot City and Darda Seafood. Coriya describes itself as an all-you-can-eat restaurant "where Japanese shabu shabu meets Korean barbecue to create Taiwanese hot pot." Darda is a popular Chinese halal restaurant where banners with Islamic prayers and pictures of a ritual hajj are displayed alongside Chinese New Year signs. As further evidence of the cross-cultural connections fostered at Asian malls, one Filipina immigrant whom I met at the Northgate Shopping Center explained that although she came to the mall mostly to read up on news about Filipinos in the United States and abroad, because the stands outside 99 Ranch contain so many ethnic newspapers, she also typically picks up other papers to "learn about other cultures." For many patrons, Asian malls are comfortable spaces of new experience that help them to bridge multiple racial, ethnic, and class divides.

## Spaces of Transnational Connection

Asian malls not only connect Asian Americans to their local ethnic communities but also provide them with bridges to loved ones overseas and everyday life in their countries of origin—points of connection to places that are geographically distant but ever present in the minds of many patrons. They do so, in part, by offering a wide selection of Asian brands and products. Popular youth magazines like *éf* and *Body* arrive hot off the Taiwanese presses with the latest in overseas news and fashion. Music from popular Korean bands like Girls' Generation and Super Junior and the latest Japanese anime movies and comics can be found in many mall stores.

Patrons can also virtually link into everyday life in Asia. Televisions in several restaurants broadcast overseas news as well as Korean, Chinese, and Taiwanese dramas and music videos. At i.tv in Fremont Times Square shopping center, customers can sign up for twelve channels of Chinese television, and an employee reported that some of the company's competitors offer as many as eighty-eight channels. Cheap phone cards can be bought for calls to Asia, travel arrangements made for return visits, and money easily sent to relatives at the many Asian bank branches typically found in these malls. East West Bank, which specializes in international banking, bills itself as a "financial bridge." Its patrons can use ATMs anywhere in the world without fees and exchange U.S. dollars for almost any Asian currency. According to Joe C. Fong, Asian banks "provide the missing link between the global hemispheric domains and the Asian diasporic regional field"—they connect the local to the global and the global to the local.[22]

The lived experience of Asian malls also provides a touchstone to distant places. To some, watching the neon lights come up at night, getting stuck in an overcrowded vegetable aisle, or passing a door plastered with flyers and advertisements recalls the

At many Asian malls, patrons can send money home using one of several Asian bank branches or, as this advertisement outside a 99 Ranch Market suggests, Western Union. Photograph by the author.

At night, the neon lights of the Ulferts Center in Milpitas make its shops appear similar to those in many Asian cities. Photograph by the author.

feeling of everyday life in many Asian cities. "It's amazing how much like Singapore or Hong Kong these malls are," observed Ong.[23] Many of the stores are named for popular restaurants in China and Taiwan and carry similar items. During the Lunar New Year, the malls are filled with red banners and signs wishing patrons good luck in the coming year. Fights break out in grocery aisles and parking lots and, just as in China, everyone stops to stare. A violinist and a pianist play classical Chinese ballads outside a music store while an ad hoc group of mall patrons begin ballroom dancing through the hallway. I too sometimes feel as if I am watching a Shanghai street scene.

## Rethinking the Social and Cultural Value of Suburban Space

Contrary to the dominant portraits of suburbia available through the mass media and much scholarly writing, the suburban social and spatial landscape is a diverse, dynamic, and interesting space for the investigation of myriad questions about our urban past, present, and future. Close interrogation of suburbia's lived landscape shows that spaces that may appear to be standardized and sterile in fact reflect and support a diversity of lifestyles, identities, social networks, and everyday practices. While scholarship has shown that minorities, immigrants, the working classes, and other nonwhite middle-class and elite groups have always been a part of the making of suburbia, much work remains to be done if we are to understand these groups' different ways of *being suburban* and how they have shaped and continue to shape the suburban landscape. The Asian mall is but one of many places that serve to reflect suburbanites' increasingly diverse needs, values, practices, and experiences. Scholars need to examine a far greater breadth of everyday places to understand residents' varied suburban narratives and place-making practices as well as suburbia as a lived, dynamic space of diversity and difference.

Grounded analyses generated from within everyday suburban spaces like Asian malls are also useful for rethinking contemporary development norms, standards, and practices. It is painfully clear from the established literature that existing patterns of suburban development and sprawl are environmentally, if not socially, unsustainable. But if urban scholars are, as it seems, wont to condemn suburbia in an effort to achieve more livable places, they also need to take a harder look at what suburbia is and why so many Americans seem to like it. As Edward L. Glaeser argues, "While traditional urbanists may find [suburban American] malls no substitute for the market of the Ponte Vecchio, people do seem to be voting with their feet or at least their tires."[24] The idea that Americans actually like and choose to live in suburbia, as Matthew Gordon Lasner points out in chapter 20 of this volume, has long troubled many urban scholars. But creating better suburban environments requires a willingness to acknowledge this simple truth (in addition to other truths about the sordid race, class, and economic interests that have also made suburbia what it is today). At the very least, it requires that scholars and practitioners, rather than applying formulaic assumptions about what is best for those who live in suburbia, be sensitive to and willing to recognize the diverse needs and desires of those for whom suburbia is an important part of their everyday lives and livelihoods.

Everyday suburban spaces like Asian malls are places through which grounded knowledge of and creative solutions for more sustainable and inclusive suburban planning and design are beginning to emerge. By continuing to look to the built environment as a lived space through and in which residents strategically, creatively, and consistently craft their meanings and identities and create value in everyday places, scholars can continue to push the discourse about places like shopping malls beyond their staid critiques. Asian malls reflect Asian American suburbanites' sense of identity, sense of place, and common cultural practices. Like other shopping centers, Asian malls have emerged as among the more prominent markers in the suburban landscape, not simply because of the desires of greedy developers and corrupt politicians but because they serve the needs of residents for a sense of community, culture, and place. However imperfectly, these suburban main streets continue to serve these vital functions. Critics cannot ignore this reality in their efforts to *reform* suburbia; rather, they must find ways of integrating the best qualities of these places in strategies that *transform* suburbia into a more equitable and livable landscape for all its residents. More productive planning, design, and policy solutions to suburbia's many development challenges will likely come from asking how shopping malls and other banal spaces might better fulfill these roles than from dismissing them.

## Notes

1. In 2008, the website Asia Mall (accessed May 20, 2008, http://www.asiamall.com) estimated that there were approximately 140 Asian malls in the United States.

2. William H. Frey, *Melting Pot Cities and Suburbs: Racial and Ethnic Change in Metro America in the 2000s* (Washington, D.C.: Brookings Institution, Metropolitan Policy Program, 2011), 1.

3. For a history of Asian malls in Silicon Valley, see Willow Lung-Amam, "Malls of Meaning: Building Asian America in Silicon Valley Suburbia," *Journal of American Ethnic History* (forthcoming).

4. On Asian malls' architectural styles, tenant compositions, and other defining characteristics, see Mohammad A. Qadeer, "Ethnic Malls and Plazas: Chinese Commercial Developments in Scarborough, Ontario" (CERIS Working Paper 3, Joint Centre of Excellence for Research on Immigration and Settlement, Toronto, 1998); David Chuenyan Lai, "A Study of Asian-Themed Malls in the Aberdeen District of City of Richmond, British Columbia" (working paper, Vancouver Centre of Excellence for RIIM, 2001); David Chuenyan Lai, "Chinatowns: From Slums to Tourist Destinations" (LEWI Working Paper 89, David C. Lam Institute for East–West Studies, Hong Kong, July 2009); Lucia Lo, "Suburban Housing and Indoor Shopping: The Production of the Contemporary Chinese Landscape in Toronto," in *From Urban Enclave to Ethnic*

*Suburb: New Asian Communities in Pacific Rim Countries,* ed. Wei Li (Honolulu: University of Hawai'i Press, 2006). On Asian malls' "strata-titled" or condo ownership, see Shuguang Wang, "Chinese Commercial Activity in the Toronto CMA: New Development Patterns and Impacts," *Canadian Geographer* 43, no.1 (1999): 19–35; Peter Li, "Ethnic Enterprise in Transition: Chinese Business in Richmond, B.C., 1980–1990," *Canadian Ethnic Studies* 24, no. 1 (1992): 120–38.

5. A useful exception is Joseph Wood's analysis of a Vietnamese shopping mall in Northern Virginia as a site of political refuge, free speech, and cultural community. See Joseph Wood, "Making America at Eden Center," in Li, *From Urban Enclave to Ethnic Suburb,* 23.

6. For a summary of postwar critiques of suburbs, particularly as they relate to the ideal of community, see Becky M. Nicolaides's contribution to this volume (chapter 1) as well as her essay "How Hell Moved from the City to the Suburbs: Urban Scholars and Changing Perceptions of Authentic Community," in *The New Suburban History,* ed. Kevin M. Kruse and Thomas J. Sugrue (Chicago: University of Chicago Press, 2006), 80–98. Contemporary critics include Mike Davis, James Kunstler, Michael Sorkin, and New Urbanists like Peter Calthorpe, Andres Duany, and Elizabeth Plater-Zyberk. Many of the critiques of suburbia and sprawl are summarized in Robert Bruegmann, *Sprawl: A Compact History* (Chicago: University of Chicago Press, 2005).

7. An exception is Margaret Crawford's useful ethnographic look at regional shopping centers in "The World in a Shopping Mall," in *Variations on a Theme Park: The New American City and the End of Public Space,* ed. Michael Sorkin (New York: Hill and Wang, 1992), 3–30. Suburban historians Lizabeth Cohen, Howard Gillette Jr., and Richard Longstreth have also provided balanced analyses of shopping centers. For references, see Lizabeth Cohen, "From Town Center to Shopping Center: The Reconfiguration of Community Marketplaces in Postwar America," *American Historical Review* 101, no. 4 (1996): 1050–81.

8. Robert E. Lang and Jennifer B. LeFurgy, *Boomburbs: The Rise of America's Accidental Cities* (Washington, D.C.: Brookings Institution Press, 2007), 2.

9. Most of the malls observed in this study were built to accommodate predominantly Chinese or Taiwanese American consumers. In Silicon Valley, there are also a number of Asian malls that cater to the needs of Vietnamese and other Southeast Asian populations. I explore the differences among and geographies of Asian malls in Silicon Valley in Lung-Amam, "Malls of Meaning."

10. Andrew Wiese, *Places of Their Own: African American Suburbanization in the Twentieth Century* (Chicago: University of Chicago Press, 2004). For other literature on the new suburban history, see Kevin M. Kruse and Thomas J. Sugrue, eds., *The New Suburban History* (Chicago: University of Chicago Press, 2006); Becky M. Nicolaides and Andrew Wiese, eds., *The Suburb Reader* (New York: Routledge, 2006).

11. Patrick L., "99 Ranch Market Review," Yelp, December 4, 2006, http://www.yelp.com/biz/99-ranch-market-richmond.

12. Quoted in Shenglin Chang, *The Global Silicon Valley Home: Lives and Landscapes within Taiwanese American Trans-Pacific Culture* (Stanford, Calif.: Stanford University Press, 2006), 105.

13. Shenglin E. Chang and Willow Lung-Amam, "Born Glocal: Youth Identity and Suburban Spaces in the U.S. and Taiwan," *Amerasia Journal* 36, no. 3 (2010): 29–52.

14. Quoted in Patricia Leigh Brown, "In California Malls, New Chinatowns Booming; Asian-American Shops Serve as Cultural Centers," *New York Times,* March 25, 2003, 7.

15. Thomas Consultants Development Strategies, "Assessment of Asian-themed Retail: City of Fremont" (report prepared for the City of Fremont, Calif., July 2005), 10.

16. Shenglin Chang found that Taiwanese immigrants in the Silicon Valley often run into former classmates and friends at 99 Ranch. See Chang, *The Global Silicon Valley Home.*

17. H. Y. Nahm, "Great Asian Malls & Supermarkets," Goldsea, accessed February 11, 2013, http://www.goldsea.com/Parenting/Malls/malls.html.

18. Chang, *The Global Silicon Valley Home.*

19. Quoted in Brown, "In California Malls."

20. Nahm, "Great Asian Malls."

21. Quoted in Brown, "In California Malls."

22. Joe C. Fong, "Globalized/Localized Asian American Banks in the Twenty-First Century," *Amerasia Journal* 36, no. 3 (2010): 53.

23. Quoted in Brown, "In California Malls."

24. Edward L. Glaeser, foreword to Lang and LeFurgy, *Boomburbs,* ix.

# 14

## Spaces for Youth in Suburban Protestant Churches

GRETCHEN BUGGELN

In October 1953 the monthly journal *Church Management* reminded its readers, "*Don't forget that this is the children's age.* A generation ago youth controlled the church. Every asset the church had was tuned to youth. That time has passed. This is the children's age."[1] By invoking "the children's age," the author pointed to what Americans now refer to as the baby boom, a rapid rise in the birthrate following World War II. "Youth," or teenagers, who had been at the heart of church programming in the prewar years, faded for a time to the background. The thousands of Protestant church buildings erected in the American suburbs in the immediate postwar years bear this out. These were neighborhood churches, situated among houses and schools and built according to "modern" ideas: low, open, and well-lit buildings spread out on large lots, incorporating lower-cost contemporary materials and construction techniques. Consisting typically of a sanctuary for worship, a small administration area, and a large education wing focused on classroom instruction for the primary grades, the sprawling postwar church plant reflects an emphasis on family worship and the education of young children.[2]

In my field research at suburban Protestant churches, I puzzled over the frequent lack of physical space for teens in the first wave of postwar churches, as well as the increasing designation of "youth rooms" by the late 1950s, features that became standard in the 1960s. Demographically this has an apparently simple answer, but there is more to the story embedded in the details of these evolving spaces. By the late 1950s, the baby boom generation was fast growing into a mass of teenagers, exuberantly flexing the power of a rising youth culture. What model of outreach and inclusion would be effective with this new, sometimes shockingly different generation? This chapter addresses questions about the changing place of teenagers in postwar suburban Protestant churches. Attitudes toward youth and youth programs are revealed in the spaces they came to occupy. The "youth room" was a casual enclave for conversation and small-scale recreation that also served as a launching pad for community service activities. This configuration was rooted in the particular "seven-day-a-week" social practices of the suburban church and middle-class suburban attitudes toward family life. But it also reflected the way in which teen culture challenged the status quo by carving out its own space in the churches. The dynamic evolution of teen spaces indicates a changing understanding of what youth and the church could and would be expected to do for each other.

The idea of adolescence—a particular stage of human development from the onset of puberty to adulthood—gained currency in the late nineteenth century and with it the growth of mandated public high school. At the same time, religious denominations identified the need for a specific ministry to this age group and created nationally centralized youth societies, such as the Walther or Luther Leagues among Lutherans. These societies emphasized the study of Christian scriptures and principles, the pursuit of a Christian lifestyle, and denominational affinity. By the 1930s, a new model of teen ministry was emerging, one that generated influential parachurch (pandenominational) organizations such as Youth for Christ, founded in the early 1940s, a young Billy Graham its first full-time staff worker. The "youth group," a teen fellowship organization centered in the local congregation, also grew in popularity. And, answering a need for ministry specifically directed to youth, congregations increasingly hired "youth pastors," positions that became standard in suburban churches by the 1970s.

Both parachurch organizations and congregational ministry approached teens in a way that was evangelical (emphasizing drawing youth to the church) and relational (modeled on individual discipleship and small-group fellowship). Youth for Christ, for instance, held inspirational stadium rallies for thousands of teenagers, while local church youth groups met regularly for Friday- or Sunday-night fellowship. Historian Jon Pahl describes the nature of youth ministry in the mid-twentieth century as an evolving shift in emphasis from *purity*, efforts to keep youth safe from the negative effects of the secular culture, toward *practices*, opportunities for youth to experiment "with adult roles and responsibilities" within that troubled culture.[3] While Christian purity remained an important concern, according to Pahl, congregations eased up on doctrinal education and increasingly called on youth to practice God-centered living that engaged the wider world and its social and political problems.

Youth ministry addressed the perennial problem of how churches would "keep their older teens in Sunday School after their confirmation into adult membership."[4] This concern heightened with the growth of a separate, often oppositional, youth culture in the postwar years. Historian James Gilbert has documented adults' concern over teenagers' perceived increasing freedom from parental influence, car-culture mobility, and youth-oriented modes of dress and expression.[5] At this critical juncture in their children's lives, parents, teachers, and pastors worried that teens would look to the wrong sources for answers to their important questions.[6] Church leaders rose to the challenge. "In this time of secular unrest," wrote one advocate for youth ministry, "juvenile delinquency has alarmed us beyond comparison. No one has yet found the true cause and blame has been laid at many feet. The one thing we do know is that the church, as it always has, can help."[7] Pastors and church leaders believed the solution lay in creating programs and spaces that recognized the special needs and interests of teens.

Because of the time gap between the first wave of postwar suburban church building and the swelling of the teen population, dedicated rooms for youth were not the foremost concern of early building committees. They had more pressing needs: getting a mob of children into Sunday school and creating spaces that would draw suburban families into the worship and social life of the church. Many building committees faced the classroom problem first, even constructing education facilities before sanctuaries. The aim of congregations, however, was to build as quickly as possible a full complex that included a sanctuary for worship, rooms for education and administration, and comfortable and flexible social spaces.

Attention to the particular needs of teens, not forgotten but deferred, thus fits in with an overall suburban church program that designed educational and fellowship activities to address the unique needs of family members of all ages.[8] In 1953, church building consultant William Leach noted this significant American innovation embodied in the proliferating suburban churches. "What other age has built for family use and general utility as the modern American churches are now doing?" he asked. "I suggest that a congregation plan its building as a family plans its home. There must be facilities for all age groups and many kinds of social activities."[9] Educational and psychological research increasingly identified distinct needs of, and appropriate environments for, specific age groups, from infants to seniors, and congregations organized space accordingly.

The multiplying social functions of suburban churches, as noted by Leach, led critics to attack suburban churches as too-comfortable, insular social organizations that betrayed Christianity's potentially transformative role. The suburban churches themselves, however, stated practical theological motives for this focus. America's postwar secular culture was seductively comfortable and attractive to people of *all* ages, and the churches saw the danger of a Christianity that consisted only of attendance at Sunday worship. A deep integration of faith into all of life's activities seemed all the more urgent because communities of newcomers did not have the generational influences and structures of accountability they had left behind. A social appeal was not intended to be an end in itself; rather, it was a strategy to get people in the door. Persis Smith, writing in 1958, noted, "It is widely accepted that today's churches in the Western World count heavily upon the social side of church life as an appeal to many who need urging to come to church, and as a means of holding them there." Smith argued for a carefully planned social program that constantly and deliberately integrated religious content, "so that in belonging, our beliefs are strengthened."[10] This presumed connection between *belonging* and *belief,* where membership in the church's social world would lead to the development of Christian character, explains a great deal about the development of the suburban congregation's youth programs.

Congregations worked to create safe spaces that teens would find appealing. Desiring to teach that "companionship, recreation, and spiritual development are not unrelated facts of life," experts suggested drawing teens to church "by establishing youth fellowship centers, making areas in the Christian Education Building available for games and roller skating, and by equipping properly for a program of Christian recreation."[11] Architect John Heyl reported in 1959:

> To answer the cry against the problem of juvenile delinquency, many churches are developing youth programs designed to attract youth away from mischief generated by boredom. These programs are usually weekly assemblies or canteens, properly chaperoned, which, with very simple attractions, hold the interest of a hundred or more young people. Sandwiches, confections, and soft drinks are purchasable or, on special occasions, are provided free of charge. . . . These gatherings provide lively fun. Young people can enjoy each other, generate away their abundant high spirits, and come under the influence of the church and its programs.[12]

The Coca-Cola Company seized upon this emphasis, and Coke ads peppered the pages of the church periodicals of the period, emphasizing how the presence of a Coke machine would help make teens "think of the church as the natural center of their social life."[13] Such language reveals concern that the church be able to control the social activities of teens, safely defusing their "abundant high spirits" and potential threats to moral behavior. It also illustrates the welcoming, albeit initially tightly managed, of elements of secular youth culture into the space of the church.

Adults hoped teen programs and spaces would successfully compete with other social attractions and thus keep teens under the influence of the church. Some suburban churches continued what was essentially an urban prewar (that era when "youth controlled the church") pattern of teen programming anchored in extensive athletic facilities. In 1953, for example, the Westwood Lutheran congregation bought twenty acres of land in the prewar Minneapolis suburb of St. Louis Park. The church began its ambitious building program with a $365,000 "education and youth center" and for several years held its worship services in the gymnasium.[14] This booming church of two thousand members opened the youth center one night each week, providing a "hot supper, movies, special speakers, panel discussions, and recreation" for teens in the "youth center with a teen-age lounge" and "club room."[15]

For the majority of financially strapped suburban parishes, this model of outreach was impractical. They did not have the resources or inclination to build such extensive athletic and recreational spaces.[16] Church recreational facilities, it should be noted, were not solely the province of teens; they were shared by the entire congregation. New schools and athletic centers in many suburban communities increasingly provided recreation facilities, and formerly robust church athletic leagues gave way to high school and community-based recreation programs. Structural changes in new suburban communities thus rendered expensive athletic facilities a less persuasive target for churches with limited building funds. An example of a more typical postwar church plant without designated youth facilities is Salem United Church of Christ (1962) in the Chicago suburb of Oak Lawn. The church's new Christian education facilities included a "church school office, crib and toddler rooms, and classrooms for Nursery, Kindergarten, Primary, Lower and Upper Junior and Confirmation."[17] Although some kind of youth fellowship group existed in virtually all congregations, initially many of them held meetings and activities in church fellowship halls or Sunday school rooms, not their own dedicated spaces. As John Scotford advised building committees in 1955, teens "need large rooms, but it does not follow that these should be class rooms. Church parlors and the minister's study can serve them well."[18]

The combination of teen spaces with fellowship halls and lounge areas proved to be an awkward one. Presbyterian minister and drama teacher Dane R. Gordon's

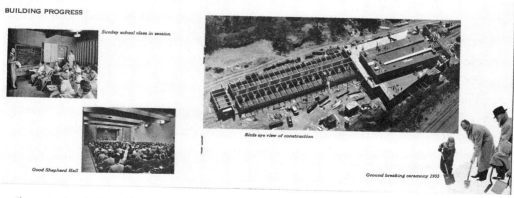

The construction of a large athletic and recreation center and classroom wing, Westwood Lutheran Church, St. Louis Park, Minnesota, 1955. Courtesy of Westwood Lutheran Church.

one-act play *Sorry, This Is a Church,* published by *Your Church* magazine in 1965, begins (and ends) with a group of four loose and straggly teenagers "listening to rock and roll which they have turned up very loud on a record player."[19] Three elderly ladies of the congregation chide the teens for their loud noise and rough behavior, and soon the building committee evicts the teens from their temporary social space in order to hold a meeting. After the adult committee finally vacates the room, the teens shuffle back in, turn their music on, begin dancing, and the curtain falls. Gordon's amusing play delivered the message that adults who tried to control the use of church space and enforce decorum were fighting a losing battle. Teens, inhabiting their own social world, were going to do what they were going to do— listen to music, talk, and dance. An emphasis on adult propriety, Gordon's play suggested, was not inviting for teens.

Most churches capitulated to this reality by giving teens their own small recreation spaces, not much different from suburban basement dens. The most common solution was to designate a youth room, a relatively large space with some recreational accoutrements (shuffleboard or Ping-Pong, radio or record player), comfortable seating, and accommodation for casual sociability. Designers often noted the importance of providing the proper atmosphere by promoting an informal visual and material character. "Religious leaders find that young people will often discuss serious religious problems . . . with the record player or television or radio going full blast."[20] The congregation of First Baptist Church in Bloomington, Indiana, desired an attractive youth space as early as the mid-1950s, rooms for ninth to twelfth graders that would have a "club room informality" centered on a capacious fire pit, kitchenette, and Ping-Pong table.[21] At the time, First Baptist was moving out from the center of Bloomington, and the congregation maintained its sensitivity to youth learned in the Indiana University community as well as its distaste for the old mode of church building. Architect Edward Sovik's midcentury modern building promised spaces as comfortable and inviting as the new houses springing up around the church. One church member, interviewed in 2010, remembered being attracted to the church by a charismatic young pastor and remarked that she had "gotten out of the basement and wasn't going back," a reference to the damp and dark education and fellowship spaces often found in the nether regions of the older Bloomington churches.[22] Youth rooms of this era, modeled on the "club room," could have polish and adult appeal. Charles Stade designed a new youth room for Winnetka Presbyterian Church with a similar warm, suburban aesthetic in mind, a beautiful space centered on a fireplace wall that nonetheless shows little attention to the particular interests of teens.

A hearth was also central to the new modular fellowship space built by Our Saviour Lutheran Church in Croton-on-Hudson, New York, in 1965. This addition,

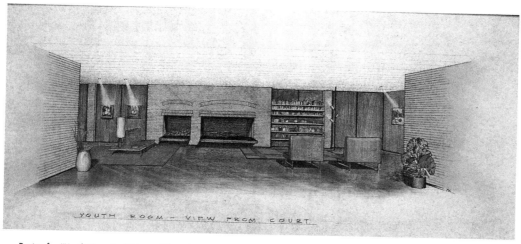

Design for "Youth Room" addition to Winnetka Presbyterian Church, circa 1965. Charles Stade, architect. Courtesy of Winnetka Presbyterian Church.

celebrated by the religious press, consisted of six triangular rooms that opened onto a core space with fireplace, skylight, and food service area. Teenagers used this multipurpose space as well as a basement recreation room with a Ping-Pong table, "offered to the community as a teen canteen."[23] (The architects notably regretted not including a proper niche for the inevitable Coke machine.) A published assessment of Our Saviour's fellowship area stressed how far this shining example stood from the reality of many postwar church buildings. Plentiful windows and warm wood furniture gave the addition a "living room atmosphere" and offered a striking contrast to "the institutional atmosphere prevalent in so many of our church schools in their attempted, and often inadequate, reproduction of public schools. This warmth enables the student to identify the church as something other than a public institution."[24]

This problem of differentiating religious organizations from schools architecturally became more important as 1960s teenagers brought their mistrust of social institutions to bear on their suburban churches. The Reverend Martin Marty claimed in 1963 that, "set upon by the young anti-institutionalist Christians on campus and in youth groups," the "residential parish is in trouble."[25] Business as usual would not be sufficient. Congregations recognized that in order to remain relevant to youth the church needed to "enlarge its concerns beyond the small group of young people who still come to Sunday school, and be willing to minister to youth without demanding either membership or loyalty in return."[26] Many congregations "found that their most successful ministry is simply to provide a place where teenagers can gather in relatively unstructured situations," sometimes even without much overtly religious content.[27] For teenagers in the 1960s, neither the formal classroom nor the formal living room proved to have lasting appeal. They sought a different model of fellowship, one that was youth driven and required informal, flexible spaces.

To retain the teens (and their parents) who were leaving the churches in great numbers, churches gave them more freedom to engage the world in their own way.[28] Jon Pahl argues that the creative response of the churches led to innovative and largely effective programs: "Diversification and focus, rather than decline, accurately describe the way in which youth ministries shifted."[29] Youth, and youth ministries, in Pahl's account, took the lead in areas such as ecumenism, global vision, and social justice programs that allowed and encouraged youth to leave the protective space of the church and to *practice* their faith in the world. Community action, informal conversation about moral issues such as racism and poverty, and ecumenical efforts among youth groups characterized church-based youth programs of the 1960s. The twenty-four-hour hunger fast and the ubiquitous summer mission trip of today's suburban church youth groups are the legacy of this change in emphasis.

Architectural experiments indicated this shift as well. In the 1960s, some congregations adopted another new model of youth fellowship, the coffeehouse. If teens wanted a place to play guitar, dance, and debate contemporary issues, why not create that kind of a space in the church? In 1967, for instance, Community Presbyterian Church in Mount Prospect, Illinois, opened a youth hangout called the Catacombs Coffee House in the parish house basement. The teens themselves operated the coffeehouse, under the supervision of adults, and "the facility offered youth from our church and from the surrounding community a place to gather and relax, enjoy music, conversation, and hold serious dialogue on significant issues of the day."[30] The coffeehouse, decorated and operated by teenagers, denoted openness. It gave them the space to engage and critique inherited truisms and their parents' suburban world. Churches did not hand over their buildings to radical youth, but they did give them more room to breathe, and the youth room, reflecting and shaping this independence, took on a life of its own.

Were the typical youth spaces in suburban churches anything like the examples found in prescriptive literature and architecture journals? In my field research in suburban midwestern churches as well as in many conversations with persons who grew up in these churches, I have found that most church youth spaces established in the mid-twentieth century embodied neither highly developed church youth programs nor sophisticated coffeehouse-type approaches. Experiences naturally varied according to denomination, locale, size of youth program, and congregational resources. But most suburban teens, it seems, generally coped with spaces that were simple and ordinary—makeshift youth hangout rooms, often carved out of existing spaces in the lower levels or distant wings of church plants when space became available. The reality, not surprisingly, was often far from any adult ideal. A woman who grew up in the suburban boomtown of Park Forest, Illinois, sums up the trend succinctly: "Hope Lutheran Youth Group in Park Forest! They had a youth room with a ping pong table, and a stereo and old couches, etc. We'd go there on Sunday evenings."[31] The current youth room in St. Matthew's United Church of Christ in Wheaton, Illinois, is a typical, if later, example of what most youth rooms had become by the 1970s. This dark room, once a portion of the original second-floor sanctuary, is cluttered with electronic equipment and old furniture, its walls plastered with Christian rock posters.

Who or what is responsible for this typically rough, backroom youth space? Did shabbiness become the price of authenticity for teenagers? One current church worker laments such spaces as they exist today: "UGLY youth rooms. Stinky, moldy, trashed up rooms where nothing ever gets put away—much less dusted. And oh the paint colors!!"[32] Yet former youth generally recall these rooms fondly, as places they felt comfortable and at home. These unstructured rooms are the result of the trends described above: giving teens the freedom to define their own spaces in the church, accommodating a youth aesthetic (with minimal investment), and emphasizing a relaxed and informal social way of being. They also reveal that, despite attempts to combine youth space with congregational fellowship space, when possible—perhaps for aesthetic reasons as much as anything—the two functions

Youth room, St. Matthew's United Church of Christ, Wheaton, Illinois, 2014. Photograph by the author.

were and are commonly segregated. As in most suburban homes, teen spaces are *not* the first rooms churches would show their guests.

The "youth room" is indicative of a ministerial structure that treated teens as a social group apart, a status reified by American culture at large during the postwar years. A bulletin circulated by the National Council of Churches of Christ around 1960 showed concern for this trend in offering advice for the builders of "rooms for youth and adults." The writer noted, "The movement towards building specialized youth facilities (i.e. the 'youth wing' or the 'youth building') has been questioned sharply in recent years, because such facilities have been credited with contributing to the spurious idea that youth are not yet churchmen, that they are, somehow, merely 'waiting in the wings' as representatives of the 'Church of tomorrow.'"[33] This critique was perceptive, and the attitude it addressed might have been part of the reason that many suburban churches did not initially create separate youth rooms. Not only do these spaces indicate a kind of liminal status for teens in the churches, but they also often exist, physically, on the margins, leading to less interaction between generations.

These informal social spaces illustrate the postwar development of suburban youth ministry and its compromises. Teens formed part of their church congregations, yet their culture set them apart. Congregations found a way to offer them the safety and oversight of community at the same time they provided comfortable spaces in which teens might think and act for themselves. This spatial pattern remains to this day in many suburban congregations—dedicated spaces offer teens room in which to play out nonconformity without leaving the bounds of the church.

Saddleback, a suburban megachurch in Orange County, California, offers an interesting contemporary coda to this story. Saddleback's new twenty-million-dollar youth ministry center, the Refinery, arguably the most impressive youth ministry facility in the world today, opened in 2008 and now serves thousands of young people, from middle schoolers through young adults, each week. Outside the large building complex are a skate park and a beach volleyball court. Inside the building a café, an arcade, a gymnasium, and a theater with auditorium seating support a wide variety of both structured and informal youth activities. The architecture is rugged, industrial, and alive—fiber-optic cables shoot colored lights up through the concrete floor, and the aesthetic is edgy and unfinished. As geographer Justin G. Wilford notes, the building's "faux-urban pastiche" offers "accessible narratives" for suburban youth today by referencing "desires for . . . subversion and transgression."[34] It is tempting to view this space as yet another example of Southern California's manufactured, hyperreal landscape, institutionalized nonconformity that rings false. Yet the adults who planned this extremely popular space believe, as postwar congregations came to understand, that teens need a space different and apart (and here it is an entirely separate building), although held within the overall structure of the church. According to the church's director of property development, Ryan Keith, Pastor Rick Warren himself "weighed in heavily" on the youth center, emphasizing that the space needed to be attractive and fun in order to be both "a place where Christian students can hang out in a good positive spiritual place" and a place where they can bring their non-Christian friends into the "church family."[35] It will be interesting, over the long run, to see if the Refinery is perceived as an authentic expression of youth culture by the youth themselves, and how the youth will adapt the space for their own unforeseen purposes.

## Notes

1. "Steps towards New Building," *Church Management,* October 1953, 32.

2. See Gretchen Buggeln, "Form, Function, and Failure in Postwar Protestant Christian Education Buildings," in *Religion and Material Culture: The Matter of Belief,* ed. David Morgan (London: Routledge, 2010), 193–213.

3. Jon Pahl, *Youth Ministry in Modern America: 1930 to the Present* (Peabody, Mass.: Hendrickson, 2000), 7.

4. Charles Vincent Rowe, "A Building for Youth Education: Our Saviour Lutheran Church, Croton-on-Hudson, New York," *Your Church,* September–October 1965, 39.

5. James Gilbert, *A Cycle of Outrage: America's Reaction to the Juvenile Delinquent in the 1950s* (New York: Oxford University Press, 1988).

6. Ibid., 202–5.

7. Joyce A. Seitzinger, "Profile of Christian Recreation," *Your Church,* October–December 1958, 47.

8. The graded Sunday school curriculum, which recognized the particular needs of each age group, emerged under the influence of progressive educational reform in the 1920s. A new class of professional religious educators attempted to further this progressive approach in the 1930s. But those were turbulent decades for the church, and not until after World War II, when the divide between liberal and evangelical churches softened, did nearly all the denominations warm to this influence. As in so many areas of postwar American life, faith in a professional class and a professional system grew—in this case encompassing educational reform, psychology, and science. The 1950s were especially innovative and rejuvenating for the American Sunday school, as indicated by the reams of Sunday school curricula, visual aids, and teacher training materials produced. See Robert W. Lynn and Elliot Wright, *The Big Little School: 200 Years of the Sunday School,* 2nd ed. (Nashville: Abingdon Press, 1980), 120–43.

9. William Leach, "The American Church Building," *Church Management,* January 1953, 16. See also "Making the Church Homelike," one of the "Briefs for Church Buildings" published by the National Council of Churches in the late 1950s and early 1960s, undated manuscript, National Council of Churches of Christ in the United States of America, Division of Christian Life and Mission, 1945–73, NCC RG 6, Box 52, Folder 12, Presbyterian Historical Society, Philadelphia. This brief encouraged churches to plan spaces that would feel, to parishioners, like "an extension of their home."

10. Persis Smith, "Adequate Social Planning for the Church," *Your Church*, April–June 1958, 20, 49.

11. Editor's note, *Your Church*, April–June 1958, 49.

12. John Heyl, "Planning the Fellowship Hall," *Your Church*, January–March 1959, 41.

13. Coca-Cola advertisement, *Your Church*, April–June 1958, 21.

14. "A Parson's Dream Come True: Hard Work, Neighborliness Key to Westwood's Success," clipping, *Saint Louis Park Dispatch*, May 6, 1954, Westwood Lutheran Church Records.

15. Ibid.

16. At the National Conference on Religious Architecture held in Los Angeles in 1959, delegates debated the question of the gym, concluding that "(a) It's usually impossible to also use the same space for fellowship and dinners, etc.; (b) poorest use of church's money; (c) ping pong and shuffleboard *are* useable in regular fellowship hall; (d) Question of gymnasium really boils down to basketball. When ten play, what do the others do?; (e) It is hard to create right atmosphere for real fellowship in a gym." See "Summary of Work Groups on Christian Education" in typescript report on the National Conference on Religious Architecture, Los Angeles, 1959, IFRAA, Box 5309, American Institute of Architects records.

17. "Salem United Church Will Dedicate New Facilities," news clipping, May 24, 1962, Salem United Church Records.

18. John Scotford, *When You Build Your Church* (Great Neck, N.Y.: Doniger and Raughley, 1953), 123.

19. Dane R. Gordon, *Sorry, This Is a Church, Your Church*, March–April 1965, 24.

20. John Knox Shear, ed., *Religious Buildings for Today* (New York: F. W. Dodge, 1957), 137.

21. Printed document by Structure Committee, undated, church records, First Baptist Church, Bloomington, Ind.

22. Helen Stout, interview by author, March 11, 2010, First Baptist Church, Bloomington, Ind.

23. Rowe, "Building for Youth Education," 40.

24. Ibid.

25. Martin Marty, "Building for a Christian Parish in a Secular Culture," address delivered at the 1963 National Conference on Church Architecture, Seattle, typescript conference report, 13, IFRAA, Box 5309, American Institute of Architects records.

26. John E. Morse, *To Build a Church* (New York: Rinehart, Winston, 1969), 23.

27. Ibid.

28. Pahl claims, "Fully 80 percent of baby boomers recently reported leaving the church or lessening their participation in it during adolescence, and their children (and grandchildren) have fared no better." Pahl, *Youth Ministry in Modern America*, 119, citing Peter C. Scales et al., *The Attitudes and Needs of Religious Youth Workers: Perspectives from the Field* (Minneapolis: Search Institute, 1995), 13.

29. Pahl, *Youth Ministry in Modern America*, 131.

30. Community Presbyterian Church, *The Upward Trail, 1951–2001: The First Fifty Years at Community Presbyterian Church* (Mount Prospect, Ill.: Community Presbyterian Church, 2006), 19.

31. Elaine A. Patterson, post on "Grew Up in Park Forest" Facebook Group, April 30, 2012, http://www.facebook.com/#!/groups/36085514558.

32. Stephanie Caro, "A Massive Tip for Renovating Your Youth Room," Small Church Ministry blog, April 6, 2011, http://blog.simplyyouthministry.com/small-church/a-massive-tip-for-renovating-your-youth-room. See also the Youth Ministry Room Ideas website at http://youthroomideas.com.

33. "Rooms for Youth and Adults," typescript of *Brief for Church Builders,* circa 1955–65, National Council of Churches of Christ in the United States of America, Division of Christian Life and Mission, 1945–73, NCC RG 6, Box 52, Folder 12, Presbyterian Historical Society, Philadelphia.

34. Justin G. Wilford, *Sacred Subdivisions: The Postsuburban Transformation of American Evangelicalism* (New York: New York University Press, 2012), 78.

35. Ryan Keith, e-mail correspondence with author, August 19, 2013.

# 15

# Sanctifying the SUV

## Megachurches, the Prosperity Gospel, and the Suburban Christian

CHARITY R. CARNEY

Jesus had a favorite suburb. According to pastor Leith Anderson, Jesus's favorite suburb was Bethany, and the Messiah actually commuted to Jerusalem to work. All of his "best friends" lived in Bethany (Mary, Martha, and Lazarus), so it made sense for Jesus to live in a suburb instead of in the urban center.[1] Although Anderson does recognize that Bethany may have been different from the modern extraurban manifestations of sprawling gated communities and planned neighborhoods that have come to represent suburban life, he insists that Jesus was, like so many Americans today, very much the suburbanite. The minister has only one purpose for placing his savior in a suburban environment: to demonstrate that the suburbs can be useful and "authentic" spaces for spiritual activities. He argues, for instance, that Jesus performed his "top miracle" in Bethany by raising Lazarus from the dead. What Anderson attempts to accomplish in this narrative is to combat the notion that suburbs are spiritual vacuums, void of any real religious substance. If Jesus lived and prospered in one, he asserts, then so can many Americans.

Like Anderson, many of today's evangelicals strive to reconcile their suburban lifestyle with their Christian walk. There is a heavy emphasis in modern Christian literature on how believers may be "good stewards" in a consumer-oriented environment—an environment that often conjures a suburban mythos. The growing megachurch movement combines popular religion with suburban culture to offer a possible solution to the divide between faith and consumption. A church qualifies as "mega" when it has an average attendance of at least two thousand per week; some megachurches have more than sixty thousand congregants.[2] These massive churches provide extremely large, contemporary services in state-of-the-art buildings and are generally constructed for the preferences of suburban congregations. The forms of

"Desk, Fort Wayne, Indiana, 2007." Blackhawk Church in Fort Wayne, Indiana, is a nondenominational congregation with an average attendance of more than fifteen thousand people. Like many megachurches, Blackhawk relies on sound and visual equipment to entertain and connect with congregants. Photograph by Joe Johnson.

entertainment and doctrinal foci of these churches differ based on their particular suburbs and local demographics, but one thing that remains constant is megachurch leaders' rhetoric regarding the churches they promote. The suburbs (even the stereotypical and unrealistic image of picket fences and cookie-cutter houses) represent a common motif in evangelical literature and sermons.[3] Megachurches promote and defend an image of prosperity and plastic religion that reflects a self-imposed image of the suburb that they seek to serve.[4] This essay situates the megachurch in a suburban context, exploring architecture, ritual, and rhetoric that connect congregations to their surroundings. It presents the rhetoric of megachurch pastors, proponents, and opponents who identify megachurches as a suburban phenomenon and argues that megachurches have constructed their architecture and services to reflect the self-selected symbols of suburbia, offering their own contributions to the national discourse over the nature of suburbia.

Suburbs provide the physical settings for megachurch growth as well as part of a carefully crafted imagery used by megachurch leaders to promote their messages. The rapid rise of megachurches is in part due to their geographical positioning. They offer convenience to churchgoers—the physical locations of the main structures and smaller satellite churches (buildings constructed for the convenience of congregants who want to avoid commuting) are often in suburban areas and next to major roads and interstate highways.[5] From a spatial perspective, the suburb can be defined as a place that allows a differentiation between work life and family life through the commute; this differentiation of space protects the home from the grind of the city. Historically speaking, suburbs developed around cities as people utilized public transportation or personal automobiles to travel from their homes in decidedly distinct family communities into city centers to work.[6] Today there are various permutations of this theme, with exurbs, inner suburbs, distant suburbs, and cities often blending and shifting their boundaries. Within this ambiguous environment, what the megachurch often provides is the sense of a distinct space for community gathering in an era in which suburbanites are looking for social anchors. Scholars also argue that megachurch planners find suburbia an attractive location because it offers lower land prices and fewer zoning restrictions than do urban centers.[7] Whether megachurches are located in suburban areas or with satellite campuses throughout cities, their pastors and services often cling to a suburban myth of middle-class prosperity and romanticized self-sufficiency, even if these characteristics are not truly representative of the suburbs in which the churches are planted.

While megachurches across the United States tend to share common characteristics (large buildings that are often repurposed, prosperity gospel theology, seeker-sensitive services, and neo-Pentecostal emphases), most of these congregations are situated in the South. In his work on postsuburban religion, Justin Wilford presents evidence from the Hartford Institute that southern states host about 50 percent of the nation's megachurches; the Midwest and West are home to between 20 and 25 percent of these congregations, and the Northeast claims less than 12 percent. Because of the number of megachurches in the Bible Belt, the South has an important impact on megachurch culture. California and Illinois also figure in prominently as states that have high proportions of these massive congregations.[8]

The national appeal of megachurches is multifaceted; it can be attributed to the decidedly bourgeois language their leaders use via the prosperity gospel, the conservative ideology that they affirm, and the architectural grandeur of the structures themselves. Whatever their focus, megachurches are designed as self-contained, self-sustaining environments, offering services intended to attract and keep members. Each church attracts thousands of congregants by constructing spaces that reappropriate and repurpose common and identifiable objects, products, and places that feel familiar. In his study of Lutheran megachurches in California, Stephen Ellingson contends that church leaders remake traditions in an attempt to grow membership. Part of the reasoning for this is the congregations' "embeddedness" in the larger religious world. This change leads Ellingson to describe megachurches as "posttraditional" and preachers as *bricoleurs* in their construction of a new faith.[9] Suburbia is the site of that process of bricolage—a process of cultural construction through which megachurches combine older faith traditions, newer versions of prosperity gospel theology, repurposed and grandiose architecture, and contemporary musical and pop culture references.[10]

Architecture is one of the major components of this process of bricolage. "Suburban megachurches," scholar Eileen Luhr argues, "attracted new members with nonthreatening architecture that mimicked suburban designs, pastors who wore casual clothes and preached about everyday issues, and a contemporary worship style that featured up-to-date music."[11] An example of this reappropriation is Lakewood Church in Houston, Texas. Pastor Joel Osteen's suburban congregation grew so large that the church moved into the former Houston Astros baseball stadium to accommodate their numbers. The structure was transformed into a maze of youth and children's rooms, a bookstore and coffee shop, and a sanctuary adorned with plush purple-velvet pews, state-of-the-art lighting and sound, a giant golden globe, and two waterfalls behind the pulpit.[12] Megachurches, however, do not have to repurpose stadiums to be successful. LifeChurch.tv is one of the largest churches in the United States, but it does not meet at a central location. Instead, branches of the church have been founded in movie theaters and strip malls, where members can attend Sunday services connected via satellite to the organization's senior pastor, Craig Groeschel, or another teaching pastor. Worshippers are also invited to join services on the church's "Internet Campus" at home if they cannot attend a service in person.[13] By repurposing and revising the mode of delivering their messages, megachurches reproduce commercial culture and the mechanisms of capitalist consumption through convenience and competition, with churches offering a variety of services in a manner similar to suburban malls.[14]

Although they are diverse, many megachurches build their identities around capitalism and commercialism—two forces that help shape the landscapes of American suburbs. The moneymaking and hierarchy-driven megachurch relates directly to the business world, with which many members of the suburban middle class are familiar.[15] One *New York Times* contributor traced the relationship between the development of the megachurch and the "corporate-organizational complex" and found that megachurch pastors operate more like CEOs than like traditional preachers.[16] This direct parallel between the suburban megachurch and the corporate world may have contributed to the prevalence of these enormous congregations

"Dove, Monroe, Ohio, 2007." This neon dove rests above the sanctuary of Solid Rock Church in Monroe, Ohio. A Pentecostal congregation of about four thousand, Solid Rock is known for its Jesus statue outside the church building; the sculpture stands fifty-one feet tall and can be seen from the interstate. Photograph by Joe Johnson.

across the United States. Texas serves as a good example of this connection between corporate clout and megachurch religion. The state hosts large companies such as Exxon, ConocoPhillips, AT&T, and Valero Energy. It is also home to a total of 157 megachurches, including 4 of the 10 largest megachurches in the country. Houston's Lakewood Church is easily the largest church body in the United States to date, with more than forty-six thousand worshippers attending service every Sunday.[17] Lakewood is a suburban outcropping of the megachurch, with people driving to the complex as they would to a basketball game to bear witness to the festivities.

The selection of the suburbs for the planting of the majority of megachurches speaks to their leaders' capitalist ingenuity. Since the late 1980s more than 75 percent of megachurches have been built in suburbs, and by the 1990s most of the new megachurches were being constructed in distant suburbs or exurbs because of these areas' lack of zoning restrictions and the advantage of lower taxes. Such areas also have access to "the type of people most attracted to megachurches: consumer-oriented, willing to commute great distances, highly mobile and often displaced, with a traditional nuclear family structure."[18] As Saddleback Church, a megachurch in Lake Forest, California, bragged on its website in 2010, it was "growing to a community near you. We want to make it easy to get to Saddleback and make it enjoyable when you arrive!"[19] This advertisement represents the strategy and philosophy of megareligion in the American suburbs: it strives to entertain and appeal to individuals seeking a church home in a way that speaks to a suburban following.

The business-oriented model is only one way in which megachurches have taken on unique characteristics that draw in droves of converts. Praise music serves as a ready example of the process of megachurch bricolage. Most megachurches rely on contemporary worship practices, including music that uses a variety of rock instruments, peppy tempos, and repetitive refrains.[20] Songs are intended to uplift rather than condemn and focus on the value of the individual rather than the collective. In his work on Lutheran megachurches, Ellingson describes praise music as optimistic and simplistic, arguing that it "present[s] the Christian story and notions of God in . . . reductionistic terms so that the difficult, ambiguous, and negative aspects (e.g., sin, sacrifice, death) of Christianity and Christian theology are avoided."[21] This scholarly observation withholds judgment of the quality of praise music and the emotional experience it produces. Carol Demong, a former mega-church congregant and a critic of megachurch practices, does not use the same re-straint. According to Demong, megachurch worship teams give old hymns a new pop persona. "If an old hymn is given a nod," she observes, "it will be sporting a mini-skirt and spiked hair—louder, speeded up, with difficult phrases reworked."[22] In making worship music easy to sing and choirs and their leaders easier on the eyes, churches use popular culture as a reference point and try to tailor their ser-vices to potential religious consumers (read: members). In their quest to bring in more souls, Demong insists, "planners seem to have decided that Mega needs to look like, feel like, sound like, think like, and act like the culture might look, feel, sound, think, and act after it had been given a good de-lousing."[23] Therefore, mega-music and other trappings of worship represent a coming together of familiar cul-tural forms and an optimistic, uplifting Christian message. Demong's criticism of megachurch music is strikingly similar to jibes made at the suburbs by their critics, who claim that a plastic and sterilized veneer coats suburban communities.[24]

Praise music and entertainment are just some of the reasons behind the success of megachurches in the United States. Some megachurch supporters accuse the "land of plenty" in which these churches are located of having *no* identity and argue that megachurches are important because they create "a small-town community in a placeless suburbia."[25] Megachurch pastors, however, are not working within a space devoid of culture or place. In fact, one of the reasons they are so successful is that they have a firm understanding of the character of their suburbs and a distinct desire to connect to fellow suburbanites in their own corners of the country.[26] Although there are regional variations, megachurches share similar musical styles, architectural features, and messages of prosperity, indicating the predilection of their leaders to present a consistent vision of the new Christian ideal—an ideal that often seeks to entertain, bless, and grow.

The ideal does involve some potential problems that these congregations have had to overcome. Suburban space can be defined in many ways, but megachurches share a unique characteristic that has often been ascribed to suburbia: separation. Scholars have described suburbs as places distinct from urban centers or the rural beyond.[27] In some suburban communities, a sense of separation and distinctiveness drives a feeling of alienation and marginalization. For some churchgoers, this leads to defensiveness and complaints of victimization.[28] But it is that very notion of marginality, combined with a utopian vision and conservative values, that helps to create and define a unique suburban sense of place and self.[29] Charismatic/neo-Pentecostal preachers relate to these emotions and to the suburban lifestyle through sermons that simultaneously point out the unique stresses in suburbanites' lives and give suburban congregants the spiritual power to face these problems. In a 2013 sermon at Lakewood Church in Houston (Osteen's congregation), popular megachurch preacher Joyce Meyer asked the congregation to "stop complaining" about life's inconveniences and listed a litany of problems that she assumed members of her audience might face. She elaborated on reasons she could have complained over the past two months, ranging from spraining her toe when it got caught in her underwear, losing her pants at the spa at a five-star hotel, her staff not being able to find an open Starbucks for her morning coffee, and receiving the wrong bedspread after ordering one through the mail. Meyer's message focused on the problem of the modern Christian constantly complaining, but her larger point was muddled with references to her economic status and consumer culture. Christians should not complain about their houses or cars, she continued, because they asked for them and God gave them those blessings. "If gas prices rise, believe God will give you money to pay for how much you need to get to where you need to go."[30] Meyer used the neo-Pentecostal touchstones of "name it and claim it" (like claiming the gasoline or a house or car) prosperity theology and related it to the middle-class and formulaic suburban consumption. As Meyer's sermon indicates, megachurch pastors consider the special demographics of their audience: megachurchgoers are likely to have more education and more wealth than average churchgoers.[31] Leaders of megachurches base their teachings on issues (materialism, commercialism, social mobility, and affluence) that have relevance to the particular perspective of these congregants.

Writing on the special qualities of evangelical suburban living, Albert Hsu challenges church leaders to craft their messages to appeal to the middle class. According to Hsu, "The suburban life is a spiritual quest," a pilgrimage, and megachurches need to respect this perspective when designing their mission to suburbanites.[32] In an obvious overstatement, he argues that if megachurch pastors could reach suburbanites, they could actually save the world.[33] To accomplish this goal, Hsu suggests, pastors must relate to their audiences and adjust their messages and approaches to better suit their congregants. Consider, for instance, the value of Christian sacrifice. Hsu recommends that instead of asking their congregations to fast or to give up alcohol (conventional evangelical commands), pastors should tell them to drive only one SUV instead of two for one week or to use public transportation. This will remind suburban Christians that some Americans have to deal with these inconveniences on a daily basis. He tells his readers that in heaven there will be no cars whatsoever, and believers need to get used to that fact. "While Revelation's picture of the New Jerusalem is undeniably an urban city environment," he explains, "nobody even speaks of driving there. We always look forward to *walking* on those streets of gold."[34] In his projections, Hsu firmly attaches himself to middle-class attitudes, comforting his readers by reminding them of their relative affluence but also appealing to their desire for upward mobility. One day, he postulates, his stereotypical suburban believers will have to sacrifice their large, expensive cars, but in exchange they will live in the splendor of the most glorious (unpolluted, nonthreatening) city.

David Goetz, a Christian journalist, also sees suburban religion as a special project and, like Hsu, insists that faith can be practiced in the suburbs, just in a slightly adjusted way. "You don't have to hole up in a monastery," he urges, "to experience the fullness of God. Your cul-de-sac and subdivision are as good a place as any."[35] While not all megachurch services may incorporate talk of SUVs or gated communities, the picture that they create of modern religion remains the same: they all maintain a particular perspective on suburban life, Christian sacrifice, and Christian success in order to appeal to the assumed audience in their surrounding communities. In an earlier article that Goetz wrote for *Christianity Today,* he references Kenneth T. Jackson's *Crabgrass Frontier* and argues that "what Jackson observed sociologically [that the space of our physical surroundings shapes our behavior], I've concluded must also be true spiritually." Living in the Chicago suburbs, Goetz addresses the subject of suburban faith as a process that has unfolded in communities throughout the United States. Goetz wryly explains that Christian consumerism is one by-product of suburban religion, with "church migration patterns [that] tend to follow whatever church has the 'buzz'—the 'biblical' preacher, the new

"Screens, Louisville, Kentucky, 2007." One of the fastest-growing megachurches in the United States, Southeast Christian Church in Louisville, boasts an average attendance of more than twenty thousand each weekend. The services are held in the round, and large screens enable all congregants to see the proceedings. Grandiose church buildings also project the idea of prosperity to members and visitors. Photograph by Joe Johnson.

contemporary service, the nuevo liturgical service, the acoustical, postmodern service, the youth ministry with the great weekend retreats and exotic mission trips." "Choice," he concludes, "is a beautiful thing."[36] What many megachurches try to provide is the best of all worlds, a collection of all these amenities so the suburban family need *not* choose.

One of the most influential instances of a megachurch adopting such a culturally driven message occurred at Willow Creek Community Church in South Barrington, Illinois, a suburb of Chicago. As early as 1975, Willow Creek set out to restructure the way that it worshipped, focusing on what its leading pastor, Bill Hybels, termed "seeker-sensitive" services. According to *Christianity Today*, the church used "its Sunday services to reach the unchurched through polished music, multimedia, and sermons referencing popular culture and other familiar themes."[37] The seeker-sensitive model influenced other congregations, like Ed Dobson's Calvary Church in Grand Rapids, Michigan, to make their ministries "consumer oriented" and to "place the gospel in a culturally relevant context."[38] In order to determine what issues were culturally relevant to their communities, these seeker-sensitive churches relied on surveys and statistics, developing business plans for expanding their numbers. In 2007, however, Willow Creek released a new study titled "Reveal: Where Are You?" and admitted that its previous model had been a "mistake" because it directed the church's message toward the needs of the unchurched rather than its members. Despite this admission, Willow Creek continues to depend on "marketing methodology" and a "target audience," and still relies on suburban consumerism to attract people to its sanctuary on Sunday mornings.[39]

In many ways, the seeker-sensitive movement has shaped and been shaped by suburban stereotypes. Past scholars described the suburb as a "bourgeois utopia," defined in part by homogeneity and segregation (from the working class, from other races, from the dirt and pollution of the city). The more the middle class grew, however, the more the suburbs expanded and diversified. Despite these changes, megachurches have not given up on many of the original suburban ideals.[40] They nod to interracial and interclass cooperation—many of these churches serve a broad

"Sanctuary, South Barrington, Illinois, 2008." Willow Creek Community Church pioneered the seeker-sensitive model of service that emphasizes entertaining and appealing to potential congregants with messages of uplift. The sanctuary at Willow Creek is designed to make services accessible for more than twenty-five thousand worshippers. Photograph by Joe Johnson.

demographic—but they also maintain a commitment to exclusivity and homogeneity. Megachurch preachers emphasize the separation between their churches and
the world and encourage congregants to guard themselves against sinful coworkers
or friends. Some pastors go so far as to develop an explicit fear of the world in their
congregants. (This category would especially include John Hagee at Cornerstone
Church in San Antonio, Texas, where he preaches a Zionist, pro-Israel doctrine and
prophesies about the coming Armageddon.)[41]

The content of megachurch sermons does the most to unite believers in a singular understanding of God and God's plan for their lives. Many of these megachurch
messages aimed at middle-class (and aspiring middle-class) suburbanites rely on
some version of the prosperity gospel—a doctrinal device that feeds into suburban
ideals focused on wealth and security. The prosperity gospel preaches (to quote
televangelist and practitioner Joyce Meyer) that "God wants you to have nice things"
and that Christianity does not require poverty but instead should lead to financial
"blessings" from the Lord.[42] It also encourages believers to accept wealth or gifts
of talent and beauty as being from the Lord, relieving perceived suburban guilt in
a society constructed on the foundations of attainment and appearances. Carol
Demong believes that making modern Christianity relevant to acquisitive suburbanites is a dangerous practice. It produces "uncomplicated, pre-digested Mega junk
food" centered on the message "I'm okay, God is okay, and he seems to like me for
some reason."[43] In many megachurch sermons, God likes believers enough to promise them temporal wealth in addition to everlasting life. One scholar defines the
prosperity gospel as a movement derived from the mind-cure theories of the nineteenth century, with the modern doctrine teaching that "verbal confessions of faith
possess the metaphysical power to compel God's blessings."[44] Bruce Wilkinson
popularized the current conception of this doctrine when he released his best-
selling book *The Prayer of Jabez* in 2000. It sold one million copies in February 2001
alone. According to the prosperity gospel, blessings can come in many forms, from
physical healing to financial success because, Wilkinson claims, "your Father longs
to give you so much more than you may have ever thought to ask for."[45]

Perhaps the most renowned prosperity preacher today, Joel Osteen has a particular penchant for reaching a broad audience not only in Houston and its suburbs
but also across the United States and the world. He has found a niche with his
prosperity-soaked message of hope and happiness and convinces his followers that
God wants them to live a comfortable (what he terms "blessed") life without financial hardship. Instead of relying on scriptural parables, Osteen often prefers to use
modern-day anecdotes to reach congregants, a strategy that seems to have contributed immensely to his popularity.[46] In 2010, during the economic crisis, Osteen
continually promised his followers that God would help them out of their despair

and, if trusted, would grant them the financial fruits for which they asked. In an online post, for instance, Osteen insisted that God causes "reversal and restoration" if believers give him praise. "Believe Him for restoration in your retirement and savings," Osteen implored. "Believe God for restoration in that business that you lost. There is nothing too difficult for God to do. Everything that was stolen can be restored in your life. God always gives us double for our trouble and He likes to outdo Himself." God can even restore stock market losses, Osteen insisted, if one truly has the faith that he will.[47]

Osteen's perspective is part of a growing neo-Pentecostal movement that has rooted in many megachurches. Pastors preach prosperity to largely suburban audiences in these churches and tailor the doctrine to local demographic needs. In Dallas, T. D. Jakes stands out as the corporate-minded, charismatic leader of the Potter's House, a mostly African American megachurch founded on the prosperity gospel and nationally recognized for its religious teachings on financial aggrandizement and commercial success. Jakes spells out his thoughts on prosperity in his book *Reposition Yourself.* He says that success means getting good grades if you are a student, "closing a deal" if you are a CEO, owning a home if you now rent, or "owning a Mercedes to park in front of your condo" if that is your desire. In America, he explains, there is too much contempt and disdain for the wealthy. His teachings try to make his followers feel more comfortable with affluence, and he promises to show them how God can help them become even more prosperous.[48]

For middle-class African Americans, this message of prosperity strikes a profound chord. An article published in *Ebony* magazine in 2001 explores the power that Jakes has over the black community in Dallas and calls the African American preacher a "trailblazer." He relates religion to contemporary culture, "binding tradition to modernity," *Ebony* explains, and "encourag[es] his members to buy stock and build wealth" rather than be content with mediocrity.[49] Perhaps because of the segregation of earlier suburban communities and socioeconomic disparities that resulted from racial prejudice and lack of opportunity (both educational and occupational), African Americans are drawn to Jakes's version of prosperity gospel theology. Since the 1980s and 1990s, more black Americans have moved into suburbs like those surrounding Dallas, Texas.[50] Jakes's message of accepting success without shame finds an eager audience among the growing African American middle and upper-middle classes in these suburbs. "Open your arms up to God and receive your blessing," the popular preacher entreats his willing believers as they "plan to be blessed" financially.[51]

Paula White delivers a similar message of abundance to congregants in Tampa, Florida, even when they may have little hope in their financial futures. The young, petite, blond preacher took over as senior pastor of Without Walls ministries in

2009 when her ex-husband, Randy White, resigned because of health problems.[52] Paula White has latched onto the prosperity movement but has made it relevant to many women in a way that Jakes may not. In a sermon that she delivered on May 23, 2010, titled "Increase," White told her congregants to "Bring on the Big." She claims that God often "anoints" his faithful with future gifts that often do not "line up with current conditions." For instance, God may tell a struggling individual to begin a company, even if the person cannot make the mortgage that month. Or he may encourage a woman to buy a wedding dress even if she has not had a date in ten years. The key is to be ready for the blessing, White implores, and to understand that "it's TOO BIG for you, BUT just right for HIM and YOU!"

White shares personal examples to explain her points—examples that resonate with a middle-class, consumer-oriented cohort. White compares God's blessings to the actions of a shipping company, for instance, admitting that "she orders a lot through the mail," items like "cute shoes for a conference." Sometimes "they try to deliver—BUT no one is there to receive it," a situation similar to when God tries to give believers "NOTICE" and they ignore his messages. Often there can be "DELAYS in delivery," White notes, and she compares these delays to Satan's stonewalling God's blessings to prevent a Christian from benefiting from them. "The enemy has been trying to discourage you," she exclaims, "make you disbelieve by DELAY. BUT DELAY doesn't mean denial." In fact, she argues, God actually has his own "tracking system," much like UPS, and he "watches over his WORD to perform it." By comparing God's blessings to modern consumption, White makes the prosperity gospel relevant to middle-class religious consumers.[53]

Joel Osteen may have summarized the megachurch movement's appeal best himself when he said of his ministry: "I shouldn't put it that way, but it's an unusual thing that for some reason people that don't normally go to church, I think I have a way—not just me—but of making things not too—and I don't mean this wrong— but not too religious. You know, make it for the everyday person."[54] But that "everyday person" is not just *any* person. He or she is the individual Matthew Hagee (son of John Hagee and pastor of Cornerstone Church) describes in his work on Christian prosperity. "Who are you?" he asks his reader. "Not the nine-to-five you or the weekend recreational extreme sports you or the *summa cum laude* class of '96 you—but the real you. Too many people find their identity in the wrong place, and I believe there is a good reason why."[55] Even as Matthew Hagee detracts from the stereotypical suburban identity to ask his audience members to reevaluate their souls, he also legitimates and relates to that identity. And *that* approach is one of the major keys to megachurch success.

Megachurches like Cornerstone barter for tithes with promises of prosperity, but they would not be successful in convincing congregants of their utopian visions if they did not interact with their particular suburban surroundings. Megachurches often borrow and create a suburban sense of place and notions of "authenticity" (authentic architecture, authentic music, authentic relationships), and they are also empowered by the wealth of many of these suburban communities to spread their messages to other parts of the nation and, in some cases, the world.[56] The exchange between megareligion and the suburbs has produced a megachurch enterprise that expresses both the fears and the desires of the modern middle class. It has gained enough authority through utopian vision and prosperity theology to shape suburban response to economic, cultural, and political trends.

Evangelicals are not unaware of this expanding influence of the suburban megachurch. Many view it as an opportunity to reach souls previously lost, to demonstrate the power of the gospel through the sheer number of members collected and money tithed. As president of the National Association of Evangelicals, Leith Anderson emphasizes the importance of suburban belief for the future of Christianity: just as Christ ministered from his suburb of Bethany, so, too, can the suburban Christian. "Suburban churches can and do influence America," the preacher declares. "Suburban churches can and should reach millions of people, disciple generations of Christians, steward billions of dollars, parent tens of thousands of new congregations, and advance the gospel of Jesus Christ in the hundreds of nations on our earth."[57] It is the megachurch that allows for this grand vision, and it is a vision shared by a constantly growing number of megadisciples. And because of this deep connection to place, the megachurch is both a product of and a prescriptive for suburban desires, anxieties, and fears in modern America.

## Notes

1. Leith Anderson, foreword to *The Suburban Church: Practical Advice for an Authentic Ministry*, by Arthur D. DeKruyter (Louisville, Ky.: Westminster John Knox Press, 2008), ix. The author of this book, DeKruyter, served as the pastor of a large suburban church on the outskirts of Chicago for thirty-two years, from 1965 to 1997. During these years, he led Christ Church of Oak Brook, a nondenominational congregation with a weekly attendance that averages two thousand and a message that reaches even more listeners through televised broadcasts. The church's building sits on twenty-two acres and houses a student center, library, counseling center, "state-of-the-art" media center, and preschool. "History," Christ Church Oak Brook, accessed July 3, 2010, http://cc-ob.org.

2. Scott Thumma and Warren Bird, "Megachurch Definition," Hartford Institute for Religion Research, accessed October 23, 2013, http://hirr.hartsem.edu/megachurch/definition.html.

3. Dolores Hayden describes these stereotypes as "sitcom suburbs." Even though recent literature has diversified the definition of the suburb, megachurch leaders and writers often draw on the romanticized version as presented by Hayden. Dolores Hayden, *Building Suburbia: Green Fields and Urban Growth, 1820–2000* (New York: Pantheon, 2003).

4. David Chidester, *Authentic Fakes: Religion and American Popular Culture* (Berkeley: University of California Press, 2005), 52–53.

5. Most megachurches are "increasingly located in newer suburban areas." Scott Thumma and Warren Bird, *Changes in American Megachurches: Tracing Eight Years of Growth and Innovation in the Nation's Largest-Attendance Congregations* (Hartford, Conn.: Hartford Institute for Religion Research, September 2008), http://hirr.hartsem.edu/megachurch/megastoday2008_summaryreport.html.

6. Justin G. Wilford, *Sacred Subdivisions: The Postsuburban Transformation of American Evangelicalism* (New York: New York University Press, 2012), 11–12.

7. Scott Thumma and Dave Travis, *Beyond Megachurch Myths: What We Can Learn from America's Largest Churches* (San Francisco: John Wiley, 2007), 11–12.

8. Wilford, *Sacred Subdivisions*, 55.

9. Stephen Ellingson, *The Megachurch and the Mainline: Remaking Religious Tradition in the Twenty-First Century* (Chicago: University of Chicago Press, 2007), 14, 24, 67.

10. For sources on suburban bricolage, see Claude Lévi-Strauss, *The Savage Mind* (Chicago: University of Chicago Press, 1962); Robert Fishman, *Bourgeois Utopias: The Rise and Fall of Suburbia* (New York: Basic Books, 1987). For religious scholars' take on bricolage, see David Lyon, *Jesus in Disneyland: Religion in Postmodern Times* (Malden, Mass.: Polity Press, 2000), 18; Ellingson, *The Megachurch and the Mainline*, 14, 27, 67.

11. Eileen Luhr, *Witnessing Suburbia: Conservatives and Christian Youth Culture* (Berkeley: University of California Press, 2009), 6–7.

12. For more on Lakewood Church's move, see Charity R. Carney, "Lakewood Church and the Roots of the Megachurch Movement in the South," *Southern Quarterly* 50 (Fall 2012): 60–78; Shayne Lee and Phillip Luke Sinitiere, *Holy Mavericks: Evangelical Innovators and the Spiritual Marketplace* (New York: New York University Press, 2009), 25–52.

13. "Who We Are," LifeChurch.tv, accessed July 14, 2010, http://www.lifechurch.tv.

14. For more on suburban church architecture, see Gretchen Buggeln's essay in this volume (chapter 14); for additional insight into suburban mall culture, see Willow Lung-Amam's contribution (chapter 13).

15. For a more complete look at the corporate influence on suburban life, see Becky M. Nicolaides and Andrew Wiese, eds., *The Suburb Reader* (New York: Routledge, 2006); Gary S. Cross, *An All-Consuming Century: Why Commercialism Won in Modern America* (New York: Columbia University Press, 2000), 193–252.

16. Tom Kuntz, "Who Moved My Cathedral?," *New York Times,* Idea of the Day blog, July 6, 2009, http://ideas.blogs.nytimes.com.

17. "Fortune 1000 Custom Ranking," *Fortune,* accessed January 10, 2010, http://www.cgi.money.cnn.com/tools/fortune/custom_ranking_2008.jsp; Jesse Bogan, "America's Biggest Megachurches," *Forbes,* June 26, 2009, http://www.forbes.com; Thumma and Travis, *Beyond Megachurch Myths,* 8.

18. Thumma and Travis, *Beyond Megachurch Myths,* 11.

19. "Home," Saddleback Church, accessed September 9, 2010, http://www.saddleback.com.

20. In their essays in this volume, Dianne Harris (chapter 18) and Steve Waksman (chapter 19) present more on the "sounds" of the suburbs.

21. Ellingson, *The Megachurch and the Mainline,* 120.

22. Carol H. Demong, *The Bleating of the Sheep, and Other Essays: A Voice for People Tired of Mind-Numbing Churchianity* (Longwood, Fla.: Xulon Press, 2008), 32–33.

23. Ibid., 34–35.

24. See Hayden, *Building Suburbia*.

25. Thumma and Travis, *Beyond Megachurch Myths*, 17.

26. For a study that addresses specifically how suburban landscapes are formed and how their cultures are then defined, see Richard H. Schein, "The Place of Landscape: A Conceptual Framework for Interpreting an American Scene," *Annals of the Association of American Geographers* 87 (December 1997): 660–80. Some earlier scholars have found a "symbolic placelessness" in some suburban areas. See David Mark Hummon, *Commonplaces: Community Ideology and Identity in American Culture* (Albany: State University of New York Press, 1990), 158. Hummon also describes how urbanites view suburbs as homogeneous, conservative places that lack any kind of distinction (86–92). This attitude, however, is challenged by the fact that suburbs have developed a very distinct identity (even if others reject it), and that identity provides a foundation for successful megachurch doctrine.

27. Mark Baldassare offers an early definition for the modern suburb (which would not have applied to Jesus's Bethany): Suburbs "are the municipalities and places in metropolitan areas outside of the political boundaries of the large central cities. Suburban communities differ from central cities in the presence of sprawling, low density land use, the absence of a central, downtown district, and the existence of a politically fragmented local government. They differ from rural areas in that the economic activities of suburban residents and businesses are primarily in manufacturing and services, rather than in agriculture." Mark Baldassare, "Suburban Communities," *Annual Review of Sociology* 18 (1992): 476. This definition has come under some scrutiny, however, and conflicts with new developments in suburban studies. In his foreword to Nicolaides and Wiese's edited volume *The Suburb Reader*, Kenneth T. Jackson admits that the suburb is difficult to define and that "the study of suburbs will never be finished because cities and metropolitan regions will continue to evolve in the decades and centuries to come" (xxii). In other words, Baldassare's definition would *not* apply not only to Bethany but to many newly created and growing American suburbs. In their introduction to the same volume, Nicolaides and Wiese argue, "Suburbia is a landscape that is ubiquitous, a backdrop to life so commonplace that few take conscious notice of it" (1). Even though no certain definition may exist for the suburb, the backdrop it has created informs our national understandings of race, gender, class, and political ideologies as well as religion.

28. H. B. Cavalcanti argues that marginality is built into conservative Christians' faith across America and that a mentality of victimization defines mainstream conservative religion. H. B. Cavalcanti, *Gloryland: Christian Suburbia, Christian Nation* (Westport, Conn.: Praeger, 2007), 10–11. Kenneth T. Jackson emphasizes the sense of isolation that suburbs drive (isolation of separate subdivisions and even of neighbors, and isolation of the suburb itself from the city). Kenneth T. Jackson, *Crabgrass Frontier: The Suburbanization of the United States* (New York: Oxford University Press, 1985), 272–73. For a discussion of isolation and fear in gated communities, see Setha M. Low, "The Edge and the Center: Gated Communities and the Discourse of Urban Fear," *American Anthropologist*, n.s., 103 (March 2001): 45–58.

29. In her work on conservatism and youth culture, Eileen Luhr argues that conservative values are incorporated into the contemporary worship services and other forms of entertainment used in modern megachurches. Luhr, *Witnessing Suburbia*, 6–7.

30. Joyce Meyer, "Stop Complaining" (sermon delivered at Lakewood Church, Houston, February 10, 2013).

31. This finding is based on the 2009 research of the Hartford Institute for Religion Research. Scott Thumma and Warren Bird, *Not Who You Think They Are: A Profile of the People Who Attend America's Megachurches* (Hartford, Conn.: Hartford Institute for Religion Research, June 2009), http://hirr.hartsem.edu/megachurch/megachurch_attender_report.htm.

32. Albert Y. Hsu, *The Suburban Christian: Finding Spiritual Vitality in the Land of Plenty* (Downers Grove, Ill.: InterVarsity Press, 2006), 9.

33. Ibid., 27–28.

34. Ibid., 73.

35. David L. Goetz, *Death by Suburb: How to Keep the Suburbs from Killing Your Soul* (New York: HarperCollins, 2006), 20.

36. David Goetz, "Suburban Spirituality," *Christianity Today*, July 1, 2003, http://www.christianitytoday.com.

37. Matt Branaugh, "Willow Creek's 'Huge Shift,'" *Christianity Today*, May 15, 2008, http://www.christianitytoday.com.

38. Ed Dobson, *Starting a Seeker Sensitive Service: How Traditional Churches Can Reach the Unchurched* (Grand Rapids, Mich.: Zondervan, 1993), 13, 16.

39. Branaugh, "Willow Creek's 'Huge Shift'"; Bob Burney, "A Shocking 'Confession' from Willow Creek Community Church," Crosswalk, October 30, 2007, http://www.crosswalk.com/pastors/11558438.

40. Robert Beuka, *SuburbiaNation: Reading Suburban Landscape in Twentieth-Century American Fiction and Film* (New York: Palgrave MacMillan, 2004); Fishman, *Bourgeois Utopias*, x, 3–4.

41. For examples of Hagee's messages to his followers, see John Hagee, *Can America Survive? 10 Prophetic Signs That We Are the Terminal Generation* (New York: Howard Books, 2010); Hagee, *The Beginning of the End: The Assassination of Yitzhak Rabin and the Coming Antichrist* (Nashville: Thomas Nelson, 1996).

42. Quoted in David Van Biema and Jeff Chu, "Does God Want You to Be Rich?" *Time*, September 10, 2006, http://www.time.com.

43. Demong, *Bleating of the Sheep*, 34–35.

44. Loyal Rue, *Religion Is Not about God: How Spiritual Traditions Nurture Our Biological Nature and What to Expect When They Fail* (New Brunswick, N.J.: Rutgers University Press, 2005), 356.

45. Bruce Wilkinson, *The Prayer of Jabez: Breaking through to the Blessed Life* (Sisters, Ore.: Multnomah, 2000), 12.

46. For examples of these parables, see Joel Osteen, *Your Best Life Now: 7 Steps to Living at Your Full Potential* (New York: Time Warner Book Group, 2004); Osteen, *Become a Better You: 7 Keys to Improving Your Life Every Day* (New York: Free Press, 2007); Osteen, *It's Your Time: Activate Your Faith, Achieve Your Dreams, and Increase in God's Favor* (New York: Free Press, 2009).

47. Joel Osteen, "You're Your Song," Joel Osteen Ministries, accessed July 14, 2010, http://www.joelosteen.com/HopeForToday/ThoughtsOn/Finances/KeepYourSong/Pages/KeepYourSong.aspx.

48. T. D. Jakes, *Reposition Yourself: Living Life without Limits* (New York: Atria Books, 2007), 7–8.

49. Kelly Starling, "Why People, Especially Black Women, Are Talking about Bishop T. D. Jakes," *Ebony,* January 2001, 108–14.

50. Andrew Wiese, *Places of Their Own: African American Suburbanization in the Twentieth Century* (Chicago: University of Chicago Press, 2004), 255–92.

51. Lillian Kwon, "T. D. Jakes: 2010 Will Be a Year of Double Portion," *Christian Post,* December 26, 2009, http://www.christianpost.com. See also Becky Nicolaides's and Jodi Rios's essays in this volume (chapters 1 and 12, respectively).

52. Sherri Day, "Without Walls Pastor Randy White Steps Down as Ex-Wife Paula White Steps In," *St. Petersburg Times,* July 11, 2009.

53. Paula White, "Increase: Part 1," Without Walls International Church, May 23, 2010, http://www.withoutwalls.org.

54. Quoted in Jesse Bogan, "A Conversation with Joel Osteen" *Forbes,* June 26, 2009, http://www.forbes.com.

55. Matthew Hagee, *Shaken Not Shattered: Finding the Purpose, Passion, and Power to Stand Firm When Your World Falls Apart* (Lake Mary, Fla.: Charisma House, 2009), 11.

56. In her historiographical essay "How Hell Moved from the City to the Suburbs," Becky Nicolaides examines how scholars have tried to locate the role of authenticity in the modern American suburb. She also connects suburban life to the teleological notions of hell and how heaven and hell have come to define suburban life. This allusion to hell and the suburbs only bolsters the power of the megachurches as they seek to exploit a belief in the sinfulness of the world and the need to insulate oneself from the dangers of society—usually suburban society. Becky M. Nicolaides, "How Hell Moved from the City to the Suburbs: Urban Scholars and Changing Perceptions of Authentic Community," in *The New Suburban History,* ed. Kevin M. Kruse and Thomas J. Sugrue (Chicago: University of Chicago Press, 2006), 80–98.

57. Anderson, foreword, xiv.

# PART IV
# Building

# 16

# The Fabric of Spying
## Double Agents and the Suburban Cold War

ANDREW FRIEDMAN

In the clichéd portrait of the post–World War II era, suburbia was a national choice, materializing the desires of an American family pent up by depression and war. Families bought single-family detached houses in bedroom communities on easy credit. Men commuted to work in the city by car, sometimes on a new national highway, and secured a gendered sphere of homemakers and breadwinners, concerned only with reproducing upright children and stocking the single-family house, lawn, and driveway with the consumer trappings of midcentury abundance. A halo of cultural associations clung to this portrait, some cherished (privacy, family, locality, nature, upward mobility), some damned (conformity, banality, boredom).

For more than a decade, the new suburban history has pivoted on attacking this cliché. Scholars have revealed postwar suburbia as one stage in a long process of urban decentralization;[1] excavated the diverse industrial, working-class, and multiracial communities that also defined suburbs, as well as the self-made ways all suburban residents personalized mass space;[2] and recovered how suburban activism fundamentally altered American politics at the local and national scale in a process often led by women, and how those "domestic" women were engaged all along in the economically crucial labor of social reproduction that made the U.S. economy function, working inside and outside the home.[3] "Choice" was only a set of political economic forces, from federal policy and infrastructure to developer manipulation, that produced suburban space and the racial realignments of the greater metropolis in the long civil rights era.[4]

In this essay, like many scholars of new suburban histories, I turn to an understudied group of suburban actors to reveal a political texture to suburbia heretofore invisible in the field: the spies and double agents who populated the suburbs around the Pentagon in Arlington, Virginia, and the Central Intelligence Agency

261

headquarters at Langley, Virginia, after the Pentagon's opening in 1943. I am not concerned primarily with the singularity and originality with which these actors brought the global Cold War to life locally through the uniqueness of their community and culture; rather, I am interested in the degree to which their politics depended on the post–World War II suburban portrait to function. Doing work designed not to form community but to undermine the U.S. nation-state, double agents in the Northern Virginia suburbs strategically mined the gap between easily accessed and simplistic suburban tropes of privacy, domesticity, family, locality, infidelity, and middle-class convention, the utilitarian realities of this broadly developed and interconnected metropolitan landscape, and their own fraught global labor bound up with loyalty, treason, spying, and geopolitics. Built forms rhetorically invoked for their role in mass-reproducing a gendered, racialized middle-class suburban political and familial identity perfectly fit the geopolitical labor of Cold War treachery in unexpected ways. In this case, to turn away from the clichéd suburban portrait would be to misunderstand how double agents' lives and spying became possible, even as these agents occupied the suburban landscape with a radical, even treasonous, nonconformity.

In examining their life stories, particularly that of the most damaging double agent in U.S. history, the family man and self-identified suburbanite Robert Hanssen, the subject of many true-crime, governmental, and cultural works, I argue in this essay that attention to the ways the suburban cliché is deployed by suburban actors to accomplish nontraditional political and life ends is an important and often overlooked arena of investigation for social historians of suburban space. More broadly, I investigate how clichéd suburban spatial qualities opened up opportunities and ran cover for other kinds of social and political experiences, how the nature of suburban form as an open, individualized platform and framework for the creation of meaning and self suited double agents and allowed them to do their work. Finally, I suggest that the frequent appearance of the "metropolitan" or the "national" scale as the broadened horizon of many new studies of post–World War II suburban America has made it hard to interpret suburbs such as Northern Virginia. Rather than accepting the transnational influences of the global economy or new migrants who reoriented a domestic suburban culture toward the world at a later, more "global" moment, Northern Virginia was from the start a staging ground for a critical global politics for the middle-class suburbanites who were its earliest residents.

## The Twenty-File-Mile Zone

In 1943, the Pentagon opened in the swamplands over the Virginia border from Washington, D.C., in Arlington. It brought with it several of the nation's first freeway-scale cloverleaf intersections and early-model large Federal Housing

Administration–insured suburban housing experiments. Along old turnpikes, ailing train and trolley routes, and, soon, the new Shirley Highway, new tract housing and garden-apartment complexes sprung up, many sheltering federal workers. The CIA opened its headquarters in Fairfax County to the north in 1961. Between these basic institutions, a sociopolitical landscape of spying and subversion took shape. American Cold Warriors fighting Cold War battles from the corridors of Langley or the offices of the Pentagon populated their suburban company towns.[5]

By 1960, there were also more than thirty-five hundred Soviet-born residents of the city of Alexandria and Fairfax and Arlington Counties.[6] Many assumed roles on this suburban Cold War battlefield. Russian and Soviet bloc men and women joined early American intelligence efforts in Europe and migrated home to continue to work for the CIA and the Pentagon, where their language skills and ethnicity sent them rocketing up the ranks. KGB spies and diplomats from the Soviet embassy in D.C., some assigned as case officers managing American moles in the U.S. government, also moved to Northern Virginia, drawn to its suburban amenities and twin conveniences to their places of work and targets of opportunity. They were also guided to the place for logistical reasons. Soviet diplomats and their families were allowed to travel only in a twenty-five-mile zone around D.C. without giving advance notice to the State Department, which limited their choices of residences and their operational sphere.[7] The developing suburbs stretching through Northern Virginia from the D.C. border twenty-five miles out to Dulles Airport at the western edge of Fairfax County—known colloquially as the Dulles Corridor— perfectly suited these requirements. Soon, local residents also included the moles in the Soviet diplomatic service who secretly served the CIA and, in time, a new crop of Soviets who defected to the United States and took up residency and citizenship.

The classic cinematic image of Cold War intrigue is perhaps the wet bridge in Berlin at night, but the speculative suburban U.S. landscape and its associated tropes staged encounters of spies in metropolitan Washington. By early 1950, James Jesus Angleton, who became the CIA's legendary chief of counterintelligence, moved with his wife Cicely to 4814 Thirty-Third Road, a new house on a "quiet, hilly street" in North Arlington, near the future site of the CIA headquarters. Angleton liked Arlington, according to his wife, for the "anonymity" not possible in the city and for the easier parking.[8] At the house, he entertained his close friend, the bon vivant Kim Philby, another protagonist central to CIA history and high-stakes Cold War gamesmanship, the intelligence agent and liaison from the British who spied for the Soviet Union and became perhaps the leading inspiration for all representations of the deep-cover mole in the extensive cultural and literary record of Cold War spying. When Philby's famous Cambridge spy ring began to be exposed in 1951, he felt so tied to the suburban landscape that he went to Virginia for a few days to "relax," and discard his secret cameras, before being recalled to Britain. Another member of Philby's spy ring in D.C., Guy Burgess, sped in his Lincoln convertible through Northern Virginia's narrow country roads with his paramours, eliciting the fury of local police. Philby even joined the Angletons at their Arlington house for Thanksgiving, turning the celebratory American domestic performance designed to link the private with the national into a channel to relink private duplicity with national threat.[9]

Through such relationships, suburban intimate life in Cold War Northern Virginia came to sway between these poles, geopolitical and domestic, public and private. When, in 1961, a Soviet, Anatoly Golitsin, defected to the United States and took up residence in a suburban safe house in leafy Great Falls, the spy reiterated both Angleton's earlier tie with Philby and its suburban setting, as he became Angleton's new confidant and partner in counterintelligence. Working together, Angleton and Golitsin launched the "molehunt" that defined CIA history through the 1960s and 1970s, as the pair, with a roving eye of suspicion, accused American-allied agents worldwide of spying on the United States—including others from the Northern Virginia suburbs.[10]

Angleton's single-family suburban house was one landmark in a broad cultural landscape for geopolitical labor. The KGB directed its spies in the U.S. Army, repatriated to the Pentagon from posts in Berlin and Paris, to buy "modest but nice" houses on tree-lined streets in Alexandria to entertain influential officers. Other double agents from the U.S. Army became local real estate agents so they could provide the Russians personal information on the many U.S. government employees hunting for housing in developing subdivisions.[11] GRU and KGB intelligence agents took apartments in buildings such as Wildwood Towers and Skyline Towers, sometimes leading FBI agents on car chases through the surrounding suburbs. While the FBI preferred to meet its in-place Soviet moles in Arlington safe houses and hotel suites, American spies met their KGB handlers in the suburbs' commercial landscape. Agents did brush passes at Alexandria's Zayre chain department store; used as contact points strip malls with well-placed pay phones, such as the Belle View Shopping Center in Alexandria, the Heritage in Annandale, and the Old Keene Mill Shopping Center in Springfield; traded information by marking phone books at the local McDonald's; and waited monthly in Arlington pizza joints for the Saturday-evening calls that would send them to Austria for their secret rendezvous. By the early 1970s, in apartment complexes such as Idylwood Towers, CIA officers and CIA double agents lived side by side in buildings designed and managed to suit their need for temporary local housing with instant community amenities. At local bus stops, KGB agents arranged meetings between Soviets who had defected to the United States to work for the CIA and their siblings still in Russia in efforts to coax the defectors to spy for the motherland. If Soviet diplomats were separated from their Russian-speaking wives and children in Falls Church department stores, more considerate agents spying on them for the FBI would slip out of the background long enough to reunite the confused family members before resuming their covert tail jobs.[12]

For many Soviet defectors, single-family subdivision safe houses in Vienna, McLean, and Great Falls provided their first glimpses of American soil after they were spirited through the dark suburbs from after-hours flights into Dulles Airport. Northern Virginia provided the ranch-house and Cape Cod dachas promised them in return for their work. The regional mall of Tysons Corner—well-known in urban studies as a model for the dense knots of sprawl in the suburbs known as "Edge Cities"—was often their introduction to American consumer abundance, the place where they outfitted their suburban safe houses, alongside mistresses recruited by the U.S. government, on shopping expeditions at department stores such as Bloomingdale's and Woodward & Lothrop. In their leisure time, KGB agents posted to the area corresponded with American spies in the mall's parking lot, ditched their cars in the mall's lot to throw off surveillance tails, went shopping at Tysons with their wives, and stayed the night at Tysons hotels. Special FBI units operated out of local strip malls as they hunted American double agents, and when they caught their prey, U.S. officials interrogated the turncoats in suites in the same office landscape surrounding Tysons.[13]

Frequent overlap between savvy suburban living and geopolitical deception defined the culture. In one example, commuting from the townhouses springing up near the line for the new D.C. Metro, CIA officer Edward Lee Howard, the only American ever to defect to a dacha in Russia, used his Langley-issued human-size dummy to beat the new high-occupancy vehicle lanes during rush hour on Route 66.[14] By this time, the landscape of reward that Howard found outside Moscow and the one Soviet defectors found in the suburbs of Northern Virginia had become even more strongly mirroring, after the KGB built its own new headquarters in the Moscow suburbs at Yasenevo, a seven-story modernist commuter complex in the woods intentionally designed to echo the CIA headquarters at Langley, known to KGB officers as "the Russian Langley" and seemingly ordered by Andropov as a kind of weird joke on the Americans.[15] By 1985—known in the United States as the "Year of the Spy" after FBI agents arrested eleven Americans in the CIA, the National Security Agency, the U.S. Navy, and the private sector, all for spying against the United States, mostly for the Soviet Union, three in a single week[16]—double agents in Northern Virginia had reached an absurd density. Soviet defectors had been known to bump into each other at barbershops on Maple Avenue in Vienna and make plans to meet up again in local chain hotels.[17] But despite Ronald Reagan's

purges and his Manichaean escalation of Cold War rhetoric, two of the most damaging double agents in U.S. history, the Northern Virginia residents Aldrich Ames and
Robert Hanssen, rather than being intimated by Year of the Spy trials, began spying
in earnest while the cases broke that year, watching coverage of them on TV and
reading news about them in the local papers, convinced they could do better.[18]

## Robert Hanssen's Suburban Cold War

In 2001, the FBI arrested Robert Hanssen, a fifty-six-year-old FBI special agent who
worked in analysis and counterintelligence against the Soviet Union, and charged
him with spying for the Soviet Union and Russia for some two decades. In his surface life, Hanssen was an ideal citizen of Reagan's suburban America. He lived with
his wife and six children in Vienna, an incorporated town located near the Dulles
Corridor's geographic center. A conservative Opus Dei Catholic, he sent his kids
to Opus Dei private schools and attended church every Sunday; his wife, Bonnie,
drove a minivan, he drove a Ford Taurus. He thought Democrats were evil. He practiced shooting at the National Rifle Association range off Route 66 with his best
friend, a U.S. Army lieutenant colonel. He believed in family values and thought
that communists were godless, homosexuality was immoral, and a woman belonged
in the home. His children grew up to be Young Republicans and to intern at the
Heritage Foundation.[19]

Yet Hanssen served the Soviet Union and Russia, taking $1.4 million in cash,
three diamonds, and a Moscow bank account for his work.[20] He told the Soviets
where the U.S. president would hide during a nuclear attack, the names of U.S. spies
in the Soviet Union, and details of all the national intelligence plans and spending for entire years. He told them about a tunnel under the Soviet embassy in D.C.
where spies listened to their meetings and phone calls, how the United States eaves-
dropped on their satellites in space and their compounds in New York, and what
was discussed, word for word, in U.S. counterintelligence meetings.[21] Hanssen's conservative values were not a "cover" for his spying. He believed in them. They were
his life. Yet so was spying.

The suburban town of Vienna had a similar double life in this period. In the
1980s, Vienna's natural atmosphere was drawing an influx of CIA agents who were
being priced out of glitzier McLean yet still looking for space convenient to the
Langley headquarters. With comparatively affordable wooded land and new subdivisions clustered around the recently completed Route 66, Vienna was also sprin-
kled with safe houses for Soviet defectors at that time, bringing the new migration
of CIA officers together with their target sources. Spies shared not only the same
highways and towns but also the same streets, blocks, and parks. Vienna was one of
the Year of the Spy's greatest platforms. Aldrich Ames helped debrief defector Vitaly

Yurchenko, once the number two man directing KGB operations against Americans across the world, in a tan-and-brown brick townhouse with a wet bar, a rec room, and a fireplace on Shawn Leigh Drive, across Nottoway Park from Hanssen's first Northern Virginia house, on Whitecedar Court. Before he fled back to the Soviet Union, claiming the CIA had kidnapped him, Yurchenko went for walks with his guards on the grounds around the local Oakton High School.[22] Colonel Ryszard Kuklinski, the CIA's spy in communist Poland in the 1970s and early 1980s, settled with his wife, Hanka, and his sons in a two-story brick house in Oakton around this time. As Hanssen spied for the Soviets down the street, Kuklinski ate at the homes of local CIA agents and invited them to drink champagne at his Oakton home when he became an American citizen. Eventually Kuklinski had to move when a car with Soviet diplomatic plates was seen parked outside his house. It is little recognized that the car could have been there in the first place to clear one of Hanssen's local dead drops.[23]

Hanssen's persona countered conventional notions of the spy. There was nothing dashing about him. He put vital documents and disks he copied from the FBI's files into packages and handed them over. He gave the Soviets some six thousand confidential pages.[24] Although generally agreed to be the most damaging Soviet spy since Kim Philby, whom Hanssen claimed as a model, Hanssen was the anti-Philby in the eyes of his chroniclers: a close-living, terminally sober husband and religious family man veneered over a creepy egomaniac. Almost disappointed by his surreal mundanity, the numerous true-crime texts on Hanssen resort to insulting him: his problem was not that he was a spy, but that he was a loser, he dressed in black, he was unpopular at work, he was a computer geek, he was an Opus Dei zealot. What none of these cultural texts treating Hanssen broach is perhaps his most centrally accessible cultural identity: Robert Hanssen was a suburbanite. The suburban ethos used to judge what was wrong with him, essentially that he "didn't fit in," confirms his participation in a suburban rhetorical field without acknowledging it.

Hanssen's life in an idyllic suburb that was also a hotbed of Cold War intrigue confounds clichéd notions of those who turned against the United States and the places where they lived. But it also stresses the degree to which the "apparatus" of suburban space, in John Archer's words, its single-family houses, parks, strip malls, culs-de-sac, and byways, became a key international political space, central to the Cold War, even if, on the ground, the suburban landscape remained "illegible" as a geopolitical, internationally permeated place—wrapped in the cover story of its own domesticity, normality, blandness, and repetition.[25]

Hanssen thrived within these paradoxes. He was a commuter on suburban streets, a lover of space and nature who walked his dog, Sunday, in the park near his house, a homeowner who appreciated family and privacy. These were the exact qualities that enabled his life as a Cold War spy. I use this sequence of key suburban

spaces—street, park, house—as a framework to examine Hanssen's work because it
provided the framework for his spying. But Hanssen's work also provides insight
into the complex intersections between individual life and the suburban built environment more broadly. In recent years, scholars have worked to articulate indigenous features of suburban space. Rather than looking at disjointed objects and
familiar features in isolation—the detached house, say, or the private cul-de-sac—
these researchers have instead theorized suburbs as working through interlocking
hierarchical and regional sequences of subtly interconnected spatial forms, examining the ties among "yard, street, and park," the interwoven "fabric of dwelling."[26]
One striking aspect of the Hanssen story is the degree to which he and his KGB
handlers became keen observers of just this sense of the interactions among nature,
built form, and the ecology of the suburban region.

Hanssen's "fabric of spying" depended on this awareness, on a mutually constitutive overlay of two distinct cognitive maps of the suburbs. On one map, his was a
life of clichéd suburban experiences: destination commutes, detached single-family
houses and culs-de-sac, and the gendered, classed tropes and consumer habits that
often came with them. On another map, he made diligent use of the interconnected
reality of the fabric of suburban space. Cold War intelligence agents' global and
incendiary work creatively mined points of opportunity in the gap between these
two suburban visions for their cover. In doing so, double agents like Hanssen fix
attention to the ways lived experience and suburban cliché met in suburbs like those
in Northern Virginia, creating opportunities for counterconventional spatial practices that remain invisible in studies of American suburban real estate development
at the national scale for the very reason that these practices emerged from local,
specific cultures of use, even if ones, in this case, always and immediately oriented
not to the local but to the global.

## Suspicious Commuting on Local Roads

It is striking how much of Hanssen's life, like the lives of many in the crowded
Northern Virginia of the 1980s, was spent in his car. He commuted to work at the
J. Edgar Hoover Building on Pennsylvania Avenue in D.C. in the stream of traffic
that left Vienna every morning. He commuted home to his family at night. He also
dropped information for the Soviets and picked up his payments in the small suburban parks tucked into the interstices between subdivisions in Vienna, McLean,
Arlington, Chantilly, Springfield, and Falls Church. Driving across the region seems,
in fact, a central way he experienced spying. Yet Hanssen traveled local roads that
people use to run short errands, visit friends, go grocery shopping, and go home
to traverse a much wider field of suburban Northern Virginia—at odd times and in
uncertified directions.

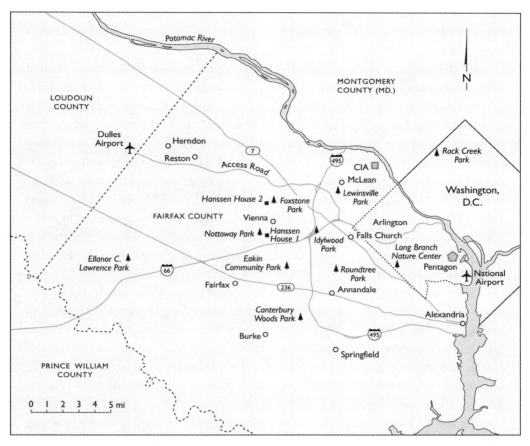

Robert Hanssen's houses and parks in Virginia and Washington, D.C.

Hanssen's handlers arranged his park dead drops in a rough circle extending southeast toward D.C. from Hanssen's home in Vienna and encompassing the Northern Virginia landscape where KGB agents had settled and historically worked most frequently. The circle loosely tracked the Capital Beltway 495, which also appears strategic. The sites seem determined primarily by the fact that each one provided multiple escape routes by car, quick egress along both good local roads, and highway ramps the Soviets could use in a hurry. The transport networks of spying thus depended on roads operating at various scales—local, neighborhood, regional through road, metropolitan highway, interstate—both in their interdependence and in their functions as distinct modes of circulation. This was exactly the understanding of the Northern Virginia road system held by county planners, even if one rarely experienced in its totality by the average suburbanite, bound by the fastest route home.[27] Although they lived in subdivisions and commuted like other residents, spies thought like the planners, more regionally, aggregating similar destinations and environments across regions to increase the utility of the suburban fabric's repetitions.

For the KGB, arranging these itineraries could involve elaborate work that brought Russian agents into their own intimate relation with the suburban landscape's breadth and detail. KGB officers, as a matter of practicality, became not only good consumers at the Tysons Corner mall but also careful observers of the vernacular landscape, as they studied maps of Northern Virginia to identify park sites, countryside, and woods for what one agent called "places that were at once remote, yet at the same time accessible." "On the map, a place might look fine for a drop," recalled Oleg Kalugin, the major general who helped run KGB operations around D.C. "But in reality it might be in the midst of a rural black community, where the presence of white men would be suspicious. Or it might be near a police station. Or a military base. So we put an enormous amount of thought into the location of the drop sites."[28]

Hanssen's unexceptional routes also emphasized pathways defined by their slowness, their inconvenient everyday qualities, to make long-distance commutes in secret. Northern Virginia's major highways—the Beltway, I-66, and the new Dulles Toll Road—exaggerated the separation effect of the little towns and villages of Northern Virginia with their discrete exits. The local routes that had linked Northern Virginia's rural villages since the early days of mass suburbanization and guided their suburban development allowed Hanssen to access the sprawling Northern Virginia suburbs as an integrated, strategic system while simultaneously dispersing his efforts through a variety of isolated "places" that residents commonly see as having little to do with one another. Multiple routes also led to each place, enabling him to vary his itinerary to prevent detection, particularly important for a man who once wrote to his Soviet handlers that "constraints breed patterns. Patterns are noticed."[29] If someone saw Hanssen driving to his prearranged contact points, he would just look like any other suburban commuter navigating a patternless sprawl. Driving against the grain in this fashion had a cloaking effect, one well suited to the spy's global and geopolitical labor.

## Suburban Parks as Mapping Devices

In the suburban portrait, nature gives suburbs their grammar of privacy—trees in front of windows, hedges guarding housefronts, lawns holding back the street. In a landscape permeated by nature, forested parks can have the feeling of an afterthought—an additive to a larger bucolic terrain rather than destinations in their own right. Hanssen benefited from this too. The parks he used for his dead drops were wrapped in a useful isolation not likely in city parks.

Hanssen took advantage of a system that was relatively new, even in the 1980s. Charles C. Robinson, a landscape architect, worked with the Army Corps of Engineers and with Frank Lloyd Wright at Fallingwater before settling in the Vienna area and starting the Fairfax County Park Authority in the 1950s. Often using parcels left over by builders who went bust or undevelopable floodplain land granted by developers who wanted to generate goodwill with local officials, he aimed to redress rapid suburbanization's "little regard for living open space." But not until the 1970s were these open spaces converted into actual parks. Nottoway, Lewinsville, and Idylwood—three parks where Hanssen left intelligence for the KGB and picked up his payoffs—all arrived in this era. Their advertising argued for why Hanssen used them, such as the *Enjoy Nottoway Park* pamphlet from 1985 that lauded the park as "secluded but convenient."[30] In the Year of the Spy, those were not neutral adjectives but functional, operational guidelines—the exact reasons the KGB gave for choosing the sites.

Unlike office buildings, bars, hotels, or train stations, parks blended with the grammar of suburban landscaping. Two Hanssen parks were merely adjuncts to subdivisions where he lived, fusing, in a sense, with his own property. Foxstone, the park where he was arrested, was only a meandering walk down the street from his house at 9414 Talisman Drive, extending his own wooded privacy. He could walk from his backyard to the geopolitical forest where he dropped information for the Soviets, carrying garbage bags that made it look like he was taking out trash or cleaning up after his dog. Nottoway Park bore a similar relationship to 9531 Whitecedar Court, Hanssen's first house, where he lived as he was restarting his double agent work. Small-scale parks defined but blurred the margins of subdivisions. Through their use, spying could become contiguous with quotidian suburban relaxation, extending the lawn's tapestry.

Soviets also enjoyed the parks' charms. For every drop Hanssen cleared or placed under a park bridge, behind him a Soviet agent passed. KGB agents spent hours strolling quiet Nottoway Park. Others drove past the quiet entrance to check for surveillance.[31] At the very moment of their spying, these agents had a collective sensory experience of Vienna that remained wrapped in its natural setting, its woods and its calm central street called Maple, laden with brown strip malls and prefabricated mansard roofs. Interpenetrated with nature, the suburban cultural and visual environment occluded the busy geopolitical activity for any but the most intent observers, even as that same natural environment enabled such activity. The Soviets expressed an awareness of this doubleness of suburban space in Northern Virginia, which coded the geopolitical as the suburban for cover, through Hanssen's parks' code names, alphabetized and added over his twenty-year career as a spy. They did not choose Russian names for the parks, but American ones. Each was blander than the next, as if satirizing the guest list to a Northern Virginia potluck of the time: BOB, CHARLIE, DORIS, ELLIS, FLO, GRACE, HELEN, LEWIS, LINDA. One park was even called DEN, like the restorative suburban room.[32]

Suburban parks were underused open spaces invisible to streets and passersby, amid a wider cultural landscape where privacy and domesticity trained people not to ask too many questions of their neighbors. Still, unlike rural landscapes far into Virginia, they were convenient for Hanssen and his handlers. Landscapes difficult to reach from KGB residences would have necessitated awkward drives, drawing prying eyes in small towns and on lonely rural streets, not to mention ringing alarms for the U.S. surveillance teams that trailed Soviet agents, particularly on trips that broke with routines. In everyday life, only infrequently would someone from Arlington picnic in a McLean park or travel from Falls Church to a Vienna park to play baseball. But Hanssen traveled between these parks. For him, the parks were knowable, small-scale landmarks that could organize trips around the corridor. They were spaces that every place in the Dulles Corridor had, yet ones that lacked connection with the pace of development. In a park, Hanssen would not arrive one day to find that a creek bridge arranged as a drop site with the Soviets by letter months before had suddenly been replaced by a mall. Amid these routine traits of stability, familiarity, and protection, the parks took on a new vernacular meaning for the suburban double agent.

The Home of the Home Front

Yet the place where Hanssen started and returned was perhaps the Dulles Corridor's most resonant geopolitical site, the source and oasis of the suburban commute and its moral center—his suburban home.[33] Tropes attached to the single-family home structured Hanssen's work as a double agent. The labor performed by his wife, with six kids to care for, made his spy work—gallivanting around at all hours—possible. His four-bedroom house, a "California contemporary" split-level built in 1978 and named Manzanita for a western shrub, gave observers "no clue ... its owner may have been collecting cash and diamonds from the Russians" explicitly because the clichéd post–World War II suburban portrait and its linkages to domesticity, gender, race, and respectability had molded cultural perceptions to make the suburban house seem to communicate values opposed to treason and even politics itself. Hanssen's "off-limits" private domain in the basement, where he stored intelligence en route to the Russians, was mirrored by rooms in countless houses where men carved out secluded private spaces as their own retreats and rewards in homes ostensibly defined by "family" and "living" rooms.[34] His investment of payments from the Soviets in his new, extra-large, European-influenced deck and concrete patio in summer 1990 was only a common gesture at a time when many wealthy suburbanites were building additions and retrofitting in classic acts of display and personalization. It also just happened to ensure that KGB money built at least one suburban deck in Vienna's Bennett Kiln subdivision, sealing the Russian political investment into Northern Virginia's everyday suburban forms.[35]

Hanssen's spying and story also paid obvious homage to the second half of the suburban cultural cliché attached to the single-family home—one that contrarily held that "nice" houses like Hanssen's were always the sites of suspicious, even monstrous, practices, only masquerading as suburban normalcy: a mass cultural fear bred from the kinds of extreme privacy and defensive localism that rippled through the wider suburban ecology.[36] But it must also be recognized that in the highly geopoliticized Northern Virginia suburbs, this twin half of the suburban cliché ran cover for another, more material and surprisingly repetitive, feature of the suburban double agent landscape: the fact that geopolitical anxieties arising from spying and extreme secrecy frequently used the heterosexual, separate-spheres gender divisions and ideas about gendered life taken for granted in these American suburbs as the canvas for their self-expression. In the intimate space of the home, repressed

Robert Hanssen's first house in Northern Virginia, on Whitecedar Court. Photograph by the author.

Robert Hanssen's second house in Northern Virginia, on Talisman Drive, where he lived at the time of his exposure and arrest. Photograph by the author.

international relations resurfaced as anxiety and threat in quite material ways. Spy techniques and realities disavowed as they defined the wider professional landscape entered the bedroom, and both were corrupted. The suburban double agent simply carried his work home with him, like all overworked suburbanites.

Chroniclers habitually turn to Hanssen's personal life as an index of his treacherous work as a spy. He was not only a fervent anticommunist and devout conservative who spied for the Soviets but also a loving husband and family man who set up a closed-circuit video camera so an army friend could watch him with his wife without her knowledge. He sent his friend naked photographs of Bonnie, let him peer in the window from their suburban deck while the couple had sex, and posted salacious stories about Bonnie online. He went to strip clubs, where he found a secret girlfriend whom he bought a Mercedes and took on a trip to Hong Kong. Yet another sign of the suburban script at work in the Hanssen story is that many accounts point to these sexual practices uncertified by the purely private, heterosexual, and devotional narratives of the suburbs as indicators of Hanssen's political corruption, rather than focusing on his deception of his wife as its own point of violation. But the frequency with which illicit sex was the bedfellow and intimate theater of spying on all sides of the Cold War is an underresearched area of study in Cold War history and a perpetual feature of double agent life in suburban Northern Virginia. For the double agent, it was doubly useful. The infidelity frame gave Hanssen a kind of psychic structure for his trips away from his house around the corridor, not to mention commonality with other suburban men and women creeping out at night for their own surreptitious assignations.

When the FBI bought the five-bedroom house across the street from Hanssen's (on, one might add, a quite narrow street), installed new wiring on the block, filled the house with spies, drew its window shades, covered its picture window with a mattress, and began searching Hanssen's car, bugging his private spaces, and reading his hard drive, the cycle was complete. Spies were doubly spying on Hanssen's house—the FBI on him, he on his wife. Such experiences of Cold War laborers like Hanssen demonstrate the hectic effects at the level of individual, everyday experience of inhabiting a "private" built form that, from its post–World War II inception, was often heavily freighted as a "public" political symbol and invoked as a geopolitical necessity. At the same time, they display the ways that gendered spatial arrangements and clichéd constructions of the suburban home could be rapidly redeployed to provide the infrastructure for double agent labor, becoming a crucial site not only for its logistics and cover but also for its sublimation and release through the machinations of suburban family life.

These same clichés could also prove the double agent's undoing because of the very generic ways that the cover of suburban domesticity and privacy could be equally manipulated by the neighbors—be they FBI agents or, in many cases, the curious figures the FBI calls "Gs." Gs are members of the Special Surveillance Group, civil servants hired by the FBI, in the words of one researcher, "to look like ordinary citizens" and to avoid the attention of people who would recognize a traditional G-man. "A young mother with a baby in a stroller, joggers, street repair crews in hard hats, an old man with a cane, telephone linemen, white-haired grandmothers with shopping bags, young lovers necking in the park—all may be Gs on the job."[37] Before his arrest, Hanssen was followed by Gs for a long time without his knowledge. They operated often in the suburbs of the Dulles Corridor, in the background of Hanssen's life. They even moved onto his street. The closer a person's image came to a notable suburban cliché, the better a G he or she could be. The Gs were functional only because of suburban expectations. Any of Northern Virginia's subdivision houses could be safe houses or staging grounds for Cold War spying. Any of its friendly neighbors could be Gs. Not all were, of course, but that was the point. In Cold War Northern Virginia, clichéd ideas about banality and normality consistently provided their own form of cover.

## Homeward Boundaries

The development of mass suburbia after World War II is forever bonded with the cultural landscape of the Cold War; these two resonant sites defined the second half of the American twentieth century, a bond solidified by Elaine Tyler May's influential articulation of the suburban home's central role in Americans' working through the anxieties and life patterns of Cold War containment domestically in her 1988 classic *Homeward Bound,* a book that continues to define the study of the post–World War II suburban landscape and Cold War cultural history.[38] But the prominence of those political-cultural connections and the certainty that the effect of foreign policy domestically is primarily representational have also mystified the depth to which the American suburbs, at least in Northern Virginia's case, were not merely a restorative landscape and canvas for Cold War concerns but a key, overlooked Cold War battlefield.

Despite their illegibility within the suburban landscape, KGB agents, CIA agents, FBI counterintelligence agents, double agents, and triple agents shared the cushy consumer spaces of booming Northern Virginia sprawl. They lived in the same high-rises, strolled through the same parks, stood in the same parking lots, patronized the same pizza places, supermarkets, strip malls, even the same beds. As they recruited each other, turned against each other, studied each other, interrogated each other, and whispered each other's names, they made visible an obvious point: these people knew each other. In a profession defined by gaining trust, loyalty, and friendship, they competed for affection and popularity in a suburban world where even Hanssen's KGB handler thought he might be "simply bored."[39]

In one sense, in their language of triumph and countertriumph, exposure and counterexposure, dead drops and brush passes, safe houses and shady rendezvous, intelligence agents on all sides had more in common with one another than they did with the citizens of their own countries. Across the world, including in Northern Virginia, they hunted for ways to turn indigenous built landscapes toward the cynical global necessities of Cold War intrigue. This essay registers some ways this worked in an American suburb. Further research perhaps awaits that would illuminate the manner in which the suburban norms and consumer habits of U.S. and Soviet agents influenced the work of the Cold War writ large. But for the study of the suburban fabric, double agent spatial practices draw attention to a more mundane, yet understudied, feature of suburban space: the suburban cliché itself. Many start their work from the commonsense assumption that this cliché needs correction and replacement. I would suggest that perhaps it ought not be tossed out too hastily. Rather, the cloak of the cliché might be viewed as one key site for the experimentation and creativity through which diverse actors inhabit and recreate suburban space, as, within the cover and layered privacy of expectations, they turn clichéd suburban typologies to their own manifold, unpredictable life ends—ones that transcend the "American suburb," or even the very idea of "locality," as ends in themselves.

## Notes

1. Dolores Hayden, *Building Suburbia: Green Fields and Urban Growth, 1820–2000* (New York: Pantheon, 2003); Richard Harris and Robert Lewis, "The Geography of North American Cities and Suburbs, 1900–1950: A New Synthesis," *Journal of Urban History* 27 (2001): 262–84.

2. Becky M. Nicolaides, *My Blue Heaven: Life and Politics in the Working-Class Suburbs of Los Angeles, 1920–1965* (Chicago: University of Chicago Press, 2002); Andrew Wiese, *Places of Their Own: African American Suburbanization in the Twentieth Century* (Chicago: University of Chicago Press, 2004); Wei Li, ed., *From Urban Enclave to Ethnic Suburb: New Asian Communities in Pacific Rim Countries* (Honolulu: University of Hawai'i Press, 2006); Karen Tongson, *Relocations: Queer Suburban Imaginaries* (New York: New York University Press, 2011); Wendy Cheng, *The Changs Next Door to the Díazes: Remapping Race in Suburban California* (Minneapolis: University of Minnesota Press, 2013).

3. Adam Rome, *The Bulldozer in the Countryside: Suburban Sprawl and the Rise of American Environmentalism* (Cambridge, Mass.: Cambridge University Press, 2001); Lisa McGirr, *Suburban Warriors: The Origins of the New American Right* (Princeton, N.J.: Princeton University Press, 2001); Matthew D. Lassiter, *The Silent Majority: Suburban Politics in the Sunbelt South* (Princeton, N.J.: Princeton University Press, 2006); Dolores Hayden, *Redesigning the American Dream: The Future of Housing, Work, and Family Life*, rev. ed. (New York: W. W. Norton, 2002).

4. Hayden, *Building Suburbia*; Eric Avila, *Popular Culture in the Age of White Flight: Fear and Fantasy in Suburban Los Angeles* (Berkeley: University of California Press, 2004); Robert O. Self, *American Babylon: Race and the Struggle for Postwar Oakland* (Princeton, N.J.: Princeton University Press, 2003); George Lipsitz, *How Racism Takes Place* (Philadelphia: Temple University Press, 2011).

5. Andrew Friedman, *Covert Capital: Landscapes of Denial and the Making of U.S. Empire in the Suburbs of Northern Virginia* (Berkeley: University of California Press, 2013).

6. U.S. Census, *U.S. Censuses of Population and Housing: 1960, Final Report PHC(1)-166. Census Tracts: Washington, D.C., Md., Va., SMSA* (Washington, D.C.: Government Printing Office, 1960).

7. Milt Bearden, *The Main Enemy: The Inside Story of the CIA's Final Showdown with the KGB* (New York: Random House, 2003), 89.

8. Tom Mangold, *Cold Warrior: James Jesus Angleton—The CIA's Master Spy Hunter* (London: Simon & Schuster, 1991), 28, 218.

9. Phillip Knightley, *The Master Spy: The Story of Kim Philby* (New York: Alfred A. Knopf, 1989), 32, 148; Yuri Modin, *My Five Cambridge Friends* (London: Headline Book, 1994), 212; Mangold, *Cold Warrior*, 43; Kim Philby, *My Silent War* (New York: Grove Press, 1968), 191; Anthony Cave Brown, *Treason in the Blood: H. St. John Philby, Kim Philby, and the Spy Case of the Century* (Boston: Houghton Mifflin, 1994), 428–29.

10. David Wise, *Molehunt: The Secret Search for Traitors That Shattered the CIA* (New York: Random House, 1992); Pamela Kessler, *Undercover Washington: Where Famous Spies Lived,*

*Worked, and Loved* (Washington, D.C.: Capitol, 2005), 142; Anatoliy Golitsyn, *New Lies for Old: The Communist Strategy of Deception and Disinformation* (New York: Dodd, Mead, 1984).

11. John Barron, *KGB: The Secret Work of Soviet Secret Agents* (New York: Reader's Digest Press, 1974), 199–229.

12. Victor Cherkashin, *Spy Handler: Memoir of a KGB Officer: The True Story of the Man Who Recruited Robert Hanssen and Aldrich Ames* (New York: Basic Books, 2005), 144; Ronald Kessler, *Spy vs. Spy: Stalking Soviet Spies in America* (New York: Charles Scribner's Sons, 1988), 40, 54, 71, 81, 124, 174–75, 197, 215, 230; Lawrence Schiller, *Into the Mirror: The Life of Master Spy Robert P. Hanssen* (New York: HarperCollins, 2002), 137; Howard Blum, *I Pledge Allegiance . . . : The True Story of the Walkers, an American Spy Family* (New York: Simon & Schuster, 1987), 106; Pete Earley, *Family of Spies: Inside the John Walker Spy Ring* (New York: Bantam, 1988), 65; David Wise, *The Spy Who Got Away: The Inside Story of Edward Lee Howard, the CIA Agent Who Betrayed His Country's Secrets and Escaped to Moscow* (New York: Random House, 1988), 42; Ronald Kessler, *Escape from the CIA: How the CIA Won and Lost the Most Important KGB Spy Ever to Defect to the U.S.* (New York: Pocket Books, 1991), 30, 72, 177; David Wise, *Spy: The Inside Story of How the FBI's Robert Hanssen Betrayed America* (New York: Random House, 2002), 39–40, 200; David Wise and Thomas B. Ross, *The Invisible Government* (New York: Random House, 1964), 201; Kessler, *Undercover Washington*, 122–23; Charles R. Babcock and Michael Getler, "High-Ranking Soviet Expelled Here," *Washington Post*, February 5, 1982.

13. See, for example, Tim Weiner, David Johnston, and Neil A. Lewis, *Betrayal: The Story of Aldrich Ames, an American Spy* (New York: Random House, 1995), 59; Cherkashin, *Spy Handler*, 138, 145, 216–17; Stanislav Levchenko, *On the Wrong Side: My Life in the KGB* (Washington, D.C.: Pergamon Brassey's, 1988), 173–75; Arkady N. Shevchenko, *Breaking with Moscow* (New York: Alfred A. Knopf, 1985), 359, 363; Judy Chavez, *Defector's Mistress: The Judy Chavez Story* (New York: Dell, 1979), 32, 55, 70–72, 164–69; James Adams, *Sellout: Aldrich Ames and the Corruption of the CIA* (New York: Viking Press, 1995), 3, 102, 128, 210; Kessler, *Escape from the CIA*, Kessler, *Spy vs. Spy*.

14. Wise, *Spy Who Got Away*, 43, 63; Edward Lee Howard, *Safe House: The Compelling Memoirs of the Only CIA Spy to Seek Asylum in Russia* (Bethesda, Md.: National Press Books, 1995).

15. Oleg Kalugin, *The First Directorate: My 32 Years in Intelligence and Espionage against the West* (New York: St. Martin's Press, 1994), 125, 235, 287; Christopher Andrew and Oleg Gordievsky, *KGB: The Inside Story* (New York: HarperCollins, 1990), 532, 614, 655.

16. Cherkashin, *Spy Handler*, 224–25; Bob Woodward, *Veil: The Secret Wars of the CIA, 1981–1987* (New York: Pocket, 1987), 552–54; Kessler, *Spy vs. Spy*; Walter Shapiro, "A Fitting End to the 'Year of the Spy,'" *Newsweek*, January 6, 1986; George D. Moffett III, "'Year of the Spy': More Were Caught, but Security Is Still Lax," *Christian Science Monitor*, December 24, 1985; Patrick E. Tyler, "Record Year Puts Spy-Catchers in Spotlight," *Washington Post*, November 30, 1985.

17. Wise, *Molehunt*, 21–22.

18. Cherkashin, *Spy Handler*, 16, 225.

19. Wise, *Spy*; Adrian Havill, *The Spy Who Stayed Out in the Cold: The Secret Life of FBI Double Agent Robert Hanssen* (New York: St. Martin's Press, 2001); Schiller, *Into the Mirror*; David A. Vise, *The Bureau and the Mole: The Unmasking of Robert Philip Hanssen, the Most Dangerous Double Agent in FBI History* (New York: Atlantic Monthly Press, 2002); Elaine Shannon

and Ann Blackman, *The Spy Next Door: The Extraordinary Secret Life of Robert Philip Hanssen, the Most Damaging FBI Agent in U.S. History* (Boston: Little, Brown, 2002); *United States v. Robert Philip Hanssen,* Affidavit in Support of Criminal Complaint, Arrest Warrant and Search Warrants, Federal Bureau of Investigation, February 2001, http://www.fbi.gov; notes in Box 11, Folder ca. 1980–1999 Miscellaneous Notes re Robert Hanssen, Papers of Richard B. O'Keeffe, Special Collections, University of Virginia Library, Charlottesville. Other key Hanssen cultural texts include the film *Breach,* directed by Billy Ray (Double Agent Productions, 2007); Robert Littell's novel *The Company* (New York: Penguin, 2002); and the made-for-television film *Master Spy: The Robert Hanssen Story,* written by Norman Mailer and directed by Lawrence Schiller (20th Century Fox, 2002). Hanssen details in this essay repeat in many of these texts.

20. *United States v. Robert Philip Hanssen,* FBI affidavit.

21. Vise, *Bureau and the Mole,* 239–45; Tim Weiner, *Enemies: A History of the FBI* (New York: Random House, 2012), 347.

22. Kessler, *Escape from the CIA,* 49, 59, 66.

23. Benjamin Weiser, *A Secret Life: The Polish Officer, His Covert Mission, and the Price He Paid to Save His Country* (New York: Public Affairs, 2004), 292–93, 300–301, 304.

24. *United States v. Robert Philip Hanssen,* FBI affidavit, 6.

25. Kevin Lynch, *The Image of the City* (Cambridge: MIT Press, 1960). On the "apparatus" of suburban space, see John Archer, *Architecture and Suburbia: From English Villa to American Dream House, 1690–2000* (Minneapolis: University of Minnesota Press, 2005).

26. Renee Y. Chow, *Suburban Space: The Fabric of Dwelling* (Berkeley: University of California Press, 2002); Cynthia Girling and Kenneth Helphand, *Yard, Street, Park: The Design of Suburban Open Space* (New York: John Wiley, 1994).

27. Brent Stringfellow, "Personal City: Tysons Corner and the Question of Identity," in *Embodied Utopias: Gender, Social Change and the Modern Metropolis,* ed. Amy Bingaman, Lise Sanders, and Rebecca Zorach (New York: Routledge, 2002).

28. Kalugin, *First Directorate,* 86–87.

29. On roads in the area, see Nan Netherton et al., *Fairfax County, Virginia: A History* (Fairfax, Va.: Fairfax County Board of Supervisors, 1978); C. B. Rose Jr., *Arlington County, Virginia: A History* (Arlington, Va.: Arlington Historical Society, 1976), 46, 74–76, 165, 189; Havill, *Spy Who Stayed Out in the Cold,* 22.

30. *Enjoy Nottoway Park,* pamphlet (Fairfax County Park Authority, 1985), Parks Files, Virginia Room, Fairfax County Public Library, Fairfax, Va.; "Charles Robinson, 66, Headed Park Authority," *Washington Post,* February 7, 1972. Also see multiple local news articles and park authority press releases in Parks Files, Virginia Room: *A History of the Fairfax County Park Authority* (Fairfax County Park Authority, 1982); Mona Enquist-Johnston, "The 1960's: Parks Emerge," in *Volunteer Voice* (Fairfax: Fairfax County Park Authority Resource Management Division, Winter 1999); Raymond G. Hay, *Public Parks and Recreation in the Northern Virginia Region* (Fairfax: Northern Virginia Regional Park Authority, June 1962); *Action for Open Space* (Fairfax: Northern Virginia Regional Planning and Economic Development Commission, November 1965); and Fairfax County Park Authority, various maps, 1973, 1974, 1977, 1978, 1989, 1991–92, Map Room, Library of Congress, Washington, D.C.

31. Cherkashin, *Spy Handler,* 235; Havill, *Spy Who Stayed Out in the Cold,* 123–24.

32. Vise, *Bureau and the Mole*, 83; Wise, *Spy*, 77; Kessler, *Spy Vs. Spy*, 54.

33. Dell Upton, *Architecture in the United States* (Oxford: Oxford University Press, 1998); Havill, *Spy Who Stayed Out in the Cold*, 18.

34. Tom Jackman and David A. Vise, "Friends Recall Regular Guy, Secret Room," *Washington Post*, February 21, 2001; Kevin Johnson, "Former Spy Hanssen's House Is on the Market," *USA Today*, April 18, 2011; display ad, *Washington Post*, May 6, 1978; Fairfax County Land Records information for Parcel ID 0381 34 0004, Fairfax County Department of Tax Administration.

35. Permit No. 90192B0770, Bennett Kiln Street File, Zoning Building Permit Review Office, Fairfax, Va.

36. See Lipsitz, *How Racism Takes Place*.

37. Wise, *Spy*, 209.

38. Elaine Tyler May, *Homeward Bound: American Families in the Cold War Era* (New York: Basic Books, 1988).

39. Cherkashin, *Spy Handler*, 236.

# Selling Suburbia

## Marshall Erdman's Marketing Strategies for Prefabricated Buildings in the Postwar United States

ANNA VEMER ANDRZEJEWSKI

In October 1953, *Life* magazine bestowed praise on Marshall Erdman, a thirty-two-year-old builder based in Madison, Wisconsin, for his innovations in prefabricated housing. Noting that Erdman's houses were not the first or the cheapest prefabs, *Life* singled them out for being the "best designed." The magazine praised the "clean lines" and "large windows" of the "efficient" model one-story dwelling featured in the article, which the author claimed extended to the other nine customizable prototypes developed by Erdman. The *Life* article hailed Erdman's "U-form-it" houses as a breakthrough in prefabricated housing. The article also represented a breakthrough for Erdman in bringing his Madison-based firm and its products to the attention of a national audience.[1]

Although profiles of builders were common in postwar American shelter magazines and trade journals, an article in a national weekly newsmagazine such as *Life* was quite a coup. Erdman's prior media exposure had been confined to Madison newspaper articles about his veterans' housing or his role as general contractor on Frank Lloyd Wright's Unitarian Meeting House (1948–51).[2] During this period features about novel ideas in home building appeared in mainstream news outlets with some regularity and prominence, given the acute postwar housing shortage. Such coverage helped people make sense of the vast array of new options in the building industry designed to meet this critical demand, including prefabrication.[3] While the affordability and ease of prefabrication appealed to postwar American consumers, some remained skeptical about the potentially monotonous appearance of prefabricated buildings. For Erdman to be praised as melding prefabrication with "good design" in *Life* meant a potential boon for Erdman's career—and also

# IMMIGRANT
# AND AN IDEA

ERDMAN (LEFT) AND PARTNER PEISS INSPECT BLUEPRINTS FOR KIT HOUSE

CUTAWAY MODEL WAS LEFT UNFINISHED TO SHOW CONSTRUCTION DETAILS AND DEMONSTRATE FURTHER STEPS TOWARD COMPLETING HOMEMADE HOUSE

## Efficient package plan saves $5,000 on a well-designed homemade house

EVERYTHING AMATEUR WILL USE, TWO TRUCKLOADS, IS ARRAYED HERE

Of all the experts who have tackled the big idea that Americans can build their own homes, the most promising is a 32-year-old Lithuanian immigrant named Marshall Erdman. In the U.S. since 1938, he studied architecture at the University of Illinois. Two years ago Erdman joined Woodworker Henry Peiss of Madison, Wis. to produce an ingenious you-build-it house. Based on the formula that the amateur can save at least $1 an hour by doing all carpentry and finishing, the Erdman-Peiss package uses many shortcuts to make the work foolproof. The amateur uses precut, premarked lumber, cabinets of building-block flexibility, a new paper which both seals and finishes inside walls, a simplified heating-duct system. Jobs like plumbing and digging the basement are done by professionals as part of the package. Neither the first nor cheapest "kit" but probably the best designed, this puts up a $14,000 house for $9,000, without lot. Though kits are now available only within 75 miles of Madison, Erdman and Peiss are already planning to expand deliveries to a 400-mile radius.

CONTINUED ON NEXT PAGE

"Immigrant and an Idea," *Life,* October 26, 1953, 139.

represented the beginning of a marketing strategy he would adopt as he expanded his production on a national scale during the later 1950s and the 1960s.

This chapter examines Erdman's marketing efforts for his prefabricated buildings. Erdman began his career advertising his houses in local newspapers, in promotional materials distributed from his sales office, and through model homes (particularly those he built for Madison's annual Parade of Homes). His collaboration with Frank Lloyd Wright on a series of prefabricated housing models during the late 1950s spurred Erdman to use Wright's name to court the national press. As he subsequently expanded his efforts in prefabrication to the medical sector, Erdman promoted his special expertise in medical building design. He published a series of essays in leading medical journals in which he advised doctors on the required components of the model suburban medical office (e.g., convenient parking, individual patient rooms, high windows for privacy) and the benefits of the suburban "doctors park" located proximate to suburban housing developments. He also used testimonials from patrons of successful projects to help him court potential clients who sought to distinguish themselves individually while also taking advantage of the relative affordability of prefabricated construction.

Postwar builders of prefabricated structures faced a skeptical audience as well as steep competition from other merchant builders. Erdman sought to distinguish himself by promoting *customization* and "good design" as distinguishing features of his prefabricated buildings. Whereas Levitt and Sons, Eichler Homes, and large prefabricated house companies such as Lustron and National Homes had several models from which customers could choose, Erdman advertised options *within* prefabrication; one could choose a model prefabricated building and then customize elements of it, ranging from the number of bedrooms (or examination rooms in the case of doctors' offices) to choices of materials to interior features (e.g., furniture or cabinetry). He also emphasized that the core designs for all his buildings came from licensed architects, albeit at an affordable cost. Erdman thus appealed to the heavily consumer-oriented culture of the postwar period by selling efficiency while also appealing to the individuality and modern taste of the middle-class suburban client. This ultimately allowed him to extend his business outside Madison and the region in order to bring his prefabricated buildings to a national audience.

Using records from the Erdman family's private archives of the Erdman Company as well as advertisements in the popular press, in this chapter I discuss Erdman's career in order to show that postwar suburbanization cannot be fully understood without close study of the daily lives of those responsible for building it, including the marketing strategies builders used to sell their buildings to their suburban clients. The discussion situates Erdman's everyday practices—particularly as they relate to advertising and marketing—spatially and materially in postwar suburban culture.

In Erdman's case, we see him operating as part of an interlocking web of local and national discourses on suburbanization, prefabricated housing, and advertising, which he navigated from the founding of his Madison-based business in the late 1940s through the expansion of his firm's reach across the United States by the early 1960s.

Erdman began his career building small, suburban veterans' houses in Madison's rapidly expanding suburbs. After completing his degree at the University of Wisconsin under benefits of the GI Bill, Erdman and his wife, Joyce Mickey, went into business in June 1947. They did so after market demand led them to sell their own self-designed and self-built house in the Sunset Village neighborhood on Madison's (then) rapidly suburbanizing far west side. Erdman had little professional experience in architecture at the time aside from a course he took as a freshman at the University of Illinois.[4] Despite his lack of formal training, Erdman recognized an opportunity for success in the building industry as a result of pent-up demand for housing after World War II. Madison faced an acute housing shortage as the population increased more than 30 percent from 1940 to 1950, growth fueled in part by the expansion of the University of Wisconsin's flagship campus.[5]

From the start, Erdman's ambitions extended beyond simply building houses to meet a need, and he immediately set out to market himself as doing something innovative. During the winter of 1948, Erdman hatched an ambitious endeavor to build eleven small houses in Sunset Village, to be marketed toward veterans like himself for $8,000 each (some of the lowest-cost veterans' housing in Madison at the time). For this project, the husband–wife team designed the houses and negotiated charitable terms with local suppliers and subcontractors. This approach earned Erdman a front-page spread in the *Wisconsin State Journal* newspaper, which praised the "young builder" for convincing subcontractors and suppliers to build the houses at a very low profit. The article was about Erdman as much as about the houses; it included a prominent picture of the husband–wife team at a drafting table.[6] The clients Erdman courted were much like himself—young, recently married, and individualistic—and the article's personalization of Erdman's own story likely worked to appeal to this very clientele. In the end, the project was not terribly successful. Only four of the eleven houses were actually built. Moreover, Erdman had to sell them at nearly $3,000 more than he anticipated to break even; in 1948, the Sunset Village houses were advertised in the *Wisconsin State Journal* as retailing for $10,850.[7]

Despite these setbacks, Erdman spearheaded more initiatives to build veterans' housing, for which he also courted the local press. In September 1948, Erdman headed a team that proposed a "co-op" veterans' home project in response to lackadaisical municipal efforts geared toward providing rental apartments for vets.

Erdman and his team of seven other local contractors—six of whom were veterans themselves—pledged to build 143 veterans' houses at a reduced rate that could best the price of city-funded rental units.[8] Erdman figured prominently in the media coverage surrounding this project. He explained that although his plans for Sunset Village had run amok, the co-op plan would prove more feasible. Erdman positioned himself in the stories surrounding the project as meeting a critical housing demand, particularly for needy veterans. Despite the fact that he was simultaneously trying to sell his speculatively built Sunset Village homes, he asserted that the demand for them far outweighed what he could build, claiming that he had more than twenty-five applicants for his four low-cost houses.[9]

Erdman relied on local media attention of this sort to promote his fledgling business, and he courted the press aggressively when he turned to prefabrication during the early 1950s. Although marketing efforts were very much part of the consumerist culture of the postwar years, Erdman faced particular challenges given the lingering skepticism about prefabrication. As Colin Davies has discussed, modernist architects—among them Le Corbusier, Buckminster Fuller, Walter Gropius, and Frank Lloyd Wright—had explored prefabrication during the first half of the twentieth century with meager results.[10] Prefabrication had been advocated during World War II as a means of housing war workers, and after the war many builders turned to prefab technologies as a way of satisfying the growing demand for low-cost housing. Among the most notorious of these was Levitt, who built seventeen thousand houses near Hempstead, Long Island, beginning in the late 1940s, the development that became the first "Levittown." The ranches and Cape Cods were built using precut timbers and mass-produced components that could be assembled, according to Levitt, in a twenty-six-step process that he compared to an auto assembly line. Levitt may have been the most well-known and perhaps most prolific postwar builder to use prefabricated technologies, but he was not alone; prefabricated kit houses were marketed nationally by firms such as National Homes of Lafayette, Indiana, and the short-lived but much-hyped Lustron Corporation, as well as smaller-scale builders working locally. In Madison, one of these was John Tilton, a builder from Rochelle, Illinois, who built prefabricated houses on Madison's east side during the 1940s in collaboration with the Harnischfeger Company of Milwaukee.[11]

Erdman likely first learned about prefabrication during his time at the University of Illinois during the early 1940s. While there, he studied briefly with James Lendrum, who founded the Small Homes Council in 1944 to advocate for low-cost housing using prefabricated technologies.[12] For Erdman, prefabrication offered advantages by allowing him to increase his output and reduce costs; the challenge was convincing a somewhat skeptical public to accept it. Despite the inroads prefabrication had made in the housing industry nationally (Levittowns being the best example), colossal failures—such as that of the Lustron Corporation—weighed heavily on the public's mind. Further, the public feared the mechanical, monotonous appearance of prefabs. Erdman's local competitors also fought to sell prefabrication to a skeptical public. In an advertisement in the *Wisconsin State Journal*, Madison-based Silverberg and Sinaiko, local dealer for National Homes, touted the progressive nature of its prefabricated homes—which it lauded as having the "charm" of other modern houses for less money. Part of the charm came from local furnishings, which gave a degree of customization to "tomorrow's home . . . today."[13] Ads such as these mitigated consumers' potential concerns about monotony by appealing to avant-garde taste.

It was in this context that Erdman teamed with local lumber supplier Henry Peiss in 1951 to develop a line of low-cost, somewhat customizable prefabricated homes called U-Form-It houses. Drawing the attention of *Life* was a major boon for Erdman; he later claimed the piece was the result of connections a former sales employee (eventual U.S. senator William Proxmire) made for him.[14] The piece, mainly a photo spread, included photos of Erdman with Peiss, a view of a house under construction (presumably in Madison), a view of the supplies on-site ready to be assembled, and various shots of the construction process. The short write-up praised the "ingenious" nature of the house, which allowed the "amateur" home builder the opportunity to use "precut, premarked lumber, cabinets of building-block flexibility," and other amenities to build a "$14,000 house for $9,000."[15] The do-it-yourself nature of the homes (minus site work) was their chief appeal, according to the article. These houses were targeted at middle-class, highly individualistic suburban consumers who sought to achieve their dreams of homeownership by having a stake—in this case, literally—in the building of their own homes.

To be called "ingenious" was high praise for a builder of Erdman's scale, who had by that point built fewer than one hundred houses and had yet to fully implement his vision. As the article noted, up to that point he had built these houses only locally. But he aspired to extend his production geographically, hoping to market the houses eventually within a four-hundred-mile radius of Madison. The generic nature of the photos in the article—which stressed innovative construction materials and techniques—implied that the houses could be built anywhere. Such an appeal to individual consumers' particular desires was a core part of Erdman's marketing strategy.

The article proved a boon to Erdman's prefabrication business. In a locally published biography, one of Erdman's former associates claimed Erdman received ten thousand letters in the wake of the *Life* essay and struggled to keep up with demand for the U-Form-It houses.[16] In an article published in the *Capital Times* in March 1954, Erdman announced a $250,000 expansion of his Madison factory on University Avenue, including construction of a 22,000-square-foot plant to manufacture the panels for the U-Form-It houses, which Erdman anticipated would be completed at the rate of five daily.[17] Although the houses were marketed as potentially "self-built," they were rarely built by the homeowners; Erdman employees acted as contractors initially (commissioned real estate agents and builders outside Madison later served in this role), and certainly site work and utilities were always done professionally. Nevertheless, Erdman's concept caught on quickly, and he used the notoriety gained from the *Life* article to expand construction of the U-Form-It houses to elsewhere in Wisconsin as well as to northern Illinois and eastern Iowa.

The week the *Life* article appeared, Erdman took out a three-quarter-page ad in the *Wisconsin State Journal* in which he boasted of the article and described the features of the "do-it-yourself" house. The advertisement showcased the main strategy Erdman used to market his prefabricated buildings throughout his career: customized prefabrication.[18] In the ad, Erdman touted prefabrication as reducing costs and streamlining the process, thus making the home more affordable. But the ad's photo captions suggested that his homes were hardly "cookie-cutter." Erdman had at that time ten different models available, providing his clients an array of options at differing costs. Moreover, he offered "add-ons" in the form of factory-built furniture as well as his own U-Form Kitchens (advertised as part of the subcontractors section). In keeping with the *Life* article's mention of "good design," Erdman showcased the fact that all his house models were designed by modern architects Weiler and Strang and the furniture by former Taliesin apprentice Herb Fritz—names that were well-known in Madison. What the ad suggested above all was Erdman's belief that good design can work in tandem with prefabrication, providing a degree of customization while at the same time making use of efficient technologies that streamline production.[19]

Customization within prefabrication also defined promotional materials the company distributed in association with the U-Form-It homes as Erdman sought to expand production of his prefabs beyond Madison in the wake of the *Life* essay. These advertisements omitted references to Madison architects, as if to say the homes could be built in any new suburban development. An advertisement for U-Form-It homes in the local Janesville, Wisconsin, newspaper, for example, included an abstract drawing of a U-Form-It rather than a photograph, suggesting the degree of customization possible in the ten existing models, an idea the text supported by claiming the house could be built in "most communities."[20] Thus, as he broadened his practice beyond Madison, Erdman adjusted his strategy such that he appealed to "good design" and the aspiring middle-class modern consumer without relying on the local references that pleased his Madison customers.

# This week's **LIFE** looks at the

(ON YOUR NEWSSTAND NOW)

# Erdman-Peiss Pre-cut "Do-It-Yourself" House

*Open for Your Inspection this Week – Sunday 12 noon to 9 p. m., daily 8 a. m. to 6 p. m.*

10 DIFFERENT MODELS AVAILABLE AS DESIGNED BY WEILER & STRANG, ARCHITECTS

## *Now Available in the Madison Area for $9,000*

News is news! And the big news is Life Magazine's article on the Erdman-Peiss pre-cut "Do-It-Yourself" House which you can build on your lot for only $9000 —with no down payment and only $63.42 per month (including principal, interest, insurance). The "Do-It-Yourself House is a modern, 3-bedroom home with dining "L", full basement, and large windows. The $9000 purchase price includes — all materials and excavation, foundation, plumbing, electrical work and heating done for you by profession foundation, plumbing, electrical work vice and assistance on all the rest of the "do-it-yourself" work.

*Model home at Erdman-Peiss Lumber Co. Yard*
5117 UNIVERSITY AVE.    PHONE 3-5355

Sample room shows interior completed with Herbert Fritz "Do-It-Yourself" furniture.

*These manufacturers and subcontractors will help you build your house.*

| **MAUTZ** Madison, Wis. | **ANDERSEN FLEXIVENT** Windows Distributed by **ROBERTS SASH & DOOR CO.** Chicago, Ill. | **MA-TI-CO MASTIC TILE CORPORATION OF AMERICA** |
|---|---|---|
| **KRAJKO CONCRETE CO.** Concrete Basement Walls & Floors Madison, Wis. | **WELCH PLUMBING CO.** Madison, Wis. | **BRANDES** BASEBOARD HEATING Madison, Wis. |
| **LUNDHOLM ELECTRIC CO.** Madison, Wis. | **U-FORM KITCHENS** MANUFACTURED BY **MARSHALL ERDMAN & ASSOC., INC.** | **HERB FRITZ** DO IT YOURSELF FURNITURE |

Advertisement in *Wisconsin State Journal*, October 25, 1953. Courtesy of the Wisconsin State Journal.

Promotional brochures distributed by Erdman's company contained rhetoric common in house advertisements all over the country during the 1950s, including references to "family living," flexible space, and ease of use, but they also asserted that Erdman homes were distinct in offering "architect design" at a modest price.[21] A 1956 brochure boasted that only "the finest architects designed Erdman homes," offering clients an array of floor plans, material choices, and kitchen configurations. Prefabricated technology lay behind the homes—something the company did not deny—but the choices within the ten different models (with various options within them) meant that each home was, at least to an extent, unique. The brochure noted, "It will be *your* home, reflecting your personality and designed and built to provide a lifetime of comfort, convenience, and satisfaction."[22] It also displayed a sketch of drafting tools as a reminder of the "custom" design in each house. A price catalog for the period October 1, 1956 to January 1, 1957 showcased fifteen different house options (based on seven basic models) ranging in base price from $13,255 to $17,000. Garages were also offered, in detached or attached and one- or two-car options, or, for a lesser cost, a homeowner could purchase a carport. Add-ons came in the form of changes to window placement, higher-quality windows, additional length (at $6.00 per extra square foot), extra partitions (at $2.75 per linear foot; the models were mainly open planned), vestibules, fireplaces, kitchen built-ins and higher-quality appliances, and other features.[23] Millwork and wall panel assembly were done at Erdman's Madison factory, from which the packaged kits were delivered to the building sites. Erdman's team of contractors helped local homeowners with assembly early on, but by the time of the 1956–57 catalog, it appears that the base house cost also included labor for nearly the entire assembly. The U-Form-It "experiment" thus abandoned aspirations for self-building but preserved the idea of customized prefabrication using "good design" principles.

Erdman's strategy made sense in light of dominant discourses of postwar suburban America, which favored individualism and cultivated the idea of individual self-expression. Prefabrication meant that the single-family home was in reach of a broader segment of the population, and yet the fact that it was customizable meant that everyone could achieve their individual desires. Moreover, Erdman's emphasis on affordable, good design also appealed to the postwar middle-class suburban consumer, who aspired to modern taste but did not want to break the bank.

Erdman's commitment to melding fine design and customization with prefabrication was solidified when he commissioned Frank Lloyd Wright to design three prefabricated housing models to add to his already extensive U-Form-It line. This collaboration appears to have come about sometime in 1955, judging from correspondence in the Taliesin archives.[24] A letter Erdman wrote to Wright in late December indicates there was "great deal of interest" in the initial plan for the first model,

THE FINEST ARCHITECTS

*designed Erdman homes for every family need and every budget*

The skill and artistry of leading architects are your special bonus when you build an Erdman home. Some of the most famous names in architecture planned our homes to meet the needs of every family.

Within the framework of a broad variety of floor plans, your Erdman home can be everything you've ever hoped for.

A view you're fond of? Frame it with luxurious Anderson window walls. We'll put them where you want them!

Like a rustic shake roof, or do your tastes run to the flat, modern look? Want redwood siding, or perhaps cedar or brick? Like a

rakish carport, or do you prefer a double garage? All these options are yours in an Erdman home.

How about your kitchen? Formica counter tops, of course, and the finest birch cabinets, but what about built-ins? Do your dreams include a built-in stove and oven . . . dishwasher . . . disposal . . . a built-in freezer and refrigerator in rich, lustrous copper?

Yes, your Erdman home can have all these and more. It will be your home, reflecting your personality, and designed and built to provide a lifetime of comfort, convenience and satisfaction!

*Your Erdman Home . . . the Home Designed for Family Living,* 1956. Courtesy of the Erdman Family Archives.

such that Erdman wished to begin construction of the first prefabricated house early that next year.[25] Erdman's intent, as the correspondence and the promotion of the Erdman–Wright prefabs make clear, was to make Wright's architecture affordable to the masses. Repeatedly he lobbied Wright for simpler, lower-cost plans; in a letter dated February 10, 1956, Erdman wrote to the architect that he was "still very much interested in a somewhat smaller house all on one floor which could be built for about $15,000. There is considerable interest in the house which you have done, but being so large, it naturally would be more limited than a somewhat smaller house."[26]

Despite Erdman's concerns that Wright's plans were beyond the reach of his middle-class suburban client base, the opportunity to work with Wright was too big for Erdman to pass up. Erdman launched an all-out marketing blitz for the Wright-designed prefabricated houses that included national publicity, local media attention, and targeted marketing leaflets intended for possible clients. With plans in hand and construction under way on the first model during the summer of 1956, Erdman scored a major coup: a December cover story in *House and Home*. This represented a tremendous opportunity, and Erdman had to scramble to finish the house in time for the photo shoot; according to Erdman's recollections some thirty years later, it was the interior that had to be completed quickly.[27] The article featured a full-color spread of exteriors and interiors of the first prefabricated house, with plans, sections, and details, and emphasized the revolutionary nature of the project:

> It is big news because it gives prefabrication—once the stepchild of home building—the prestige associated with the greatest name in contemporary architecture. It is amazing news, because the principal advocate of standardization and modular planning had to wait 60 years before he got his chance to put his original theories into practice. Wright had been designing panel construction systems since 1910 using materials like wood, steel and concrete.[28]

The magazine explained how Erdman, the "prefabricator," had fused the formal elements of Wright's architecture with his own prefabricated production model. The result was a prototype that "has every basic design idea in Wright's vocabulary, yet it can be produced within the prefabricator's budget."

Erdman seized on further opportunities stemming from interest generated by the *House and Home* piece. The *New York Times,* which had published a brief notice about the house on October 14, 1956, featured a lengthy illustrated piece on December 21. This *Times* article is particularly interesting for the attention Erdman gave in it to his own work on the design. Erdman explained the house was intended for those "who want Wright but cannot afford him," thus crediting Wright for the design but attributing the "affordability" to himself. Where Wright wanted cypress panels on the exterior, Erdman used less expensive Masonite, the seams of which were held together by redwood battens. Moreover, whereas a typical Wright house would have wood shingles, Erdman used asphalt, but in a ridged layout that echoed the horizontality of the Masonite and redwood panels of the walls. "I'm satisfied with it because it dignifies prefabrication," said Erdman, giving the house the flavor (in the *Times* writer's words) of Wright but on a reduced budget.[29] Erdman also had been courting other high-volume media outlets. A letter of January 11, 1957, addressed to Wright from *Look* inquired as to Wright's interest in having the houses profiled in that magazine on the basis of "several conversations" the editor had had with Marshall Erdman.[30] And with this first model and other prefab houses designed by Wright, Erdman issued press releases that subsequently generated newspaper articles across the country that hailed the Erdman–Wright prefabs as a breakthrough in prefabricated housing.[31]

Despite all this media attention, Erdman still had to earn commissions, which meant marketing to individual clients (unlike the U-Form-Its, the Wright-designed houses were never meant to be self-built and required experienced contractors

ERICA'S BIGGEST INDUSTRY MONTHLY FOR AMERICA'S BIGGEST INDUSTRY

# House & Home

DECEMBER 1956 SIX DOLLARS A YEAR — ONE DOLLAR A COPY

TECTS · APPRAISERS · BUILDERS · CONTRACTORS · DECORATORS · DEALERS · DISTRIBUTORS · FHA-VA · MANUFACTURERS · MORTGAGEES · PREFABRICATORS · REALTORS

**FRANK LLOYD WRIGHT** designs a prefabricated house—page 117

NEWS BEGINS ON PAGE 33   FOR COMPLETE CONTENTS SEE PAGE 115

Cover of *House and Home,* December 1956.

on-site).[32] As with all of his marketing efforts for prefabricated buildings, Erdman relied on selling *customized* prefabrication. The back cover of a brochure produced by the company in 1959 featured a photograph of Wright and Erdman and stressed that each house was "no ordinary house" but "a work of art." It also stated that each prefab dwelling was "personally approved" by Wright, just as the site plans had to be approved by the Frank Lloyd Wright Foundation.[33] A company-produced "prospectus" on the first prefabricated home similarly touted the "custom" nature of the Wright–Erdman prefabs, again promoting Wright's personal involvement. The prospectus also emphasized the options possible for the client considering a Wright–Erdman prefab:

> At present this house is available in both a three bedroom model of approximately 2000 square feet, 85 feet long, and a four bedroom model some 240 square feet larger. The latter house is larger throughout . . . bigger kitchen, living room, dining room, and bedrooms. . . .
> The house can be built without a basement, with a partial or full basement, or with the basement exposed, making it possible to have additional rooms and bath downstairs with doors leading out directly to a patio.

Other customization could occur "with the approval of the architect and Erdman Homes," such as substitution of brick or stone for concrete block, customized floor coverings, and air-conditioning. Wright consulted on the site plan and oversaw any changes, thus giving the homeowner the "stamp" of the architect (for the $750 fee Wright earned per house); prefabrication, meanwhile, reduced the cost, allowing Erdman to reach more clients than he would if he built strictly custom-built Wright designs.[34] The ideal client, then, aspired to an architect-designed home, but within the realm of a middle-class budget.

Erdman also marketed the opportunity to build Wright-designed prefabs to contractors, since he relied on them to build the houses; he was further motivated by the simple fact that he wanted to make a name for himself in the building industry. His chief efforts were devoted to convincing Wright to deliver a speech in conjunction with the 1958 convention of the National Association of Home Builders in January. Erdman conceived of the idea the previous November; in a letter to Wright of November 11, Erdman explained his plan "to have a model built in Chicago" of the prefabs to show prospective builders as well as to have Wright himself give a lecture on the virtues of prefabrication: "You could show them [builders] that they can now build your type of house through fabrication for about the same price as they are paying for the ordinary boxes. This type of lecture by you should have quite an effect on these builders. . . . Needless to say, it would be quite a boost to our company and to the sales of the Frank Lloyd Wright Prefabricated house."[35] Wright resisted initially, writing back to Erdman that he could not possibly plan two months ahead.[36] But Erdman somehow convinced Wright to give the speech on January 22 in the Crystal Ball Room of the Blackstone Hotel. Erdman also hosted a reception in Wright's honor the day preceding the talk; he invited select builders to view a model of the first prefabricated house and drawings of the second, as well as learn more about building them. An invitation to builders boasted that the prefabs were "designed for discriminating people who desire . . . unique design at moderate cost" and urged the builders to "be the FIRST to build the Frank Lloyd Wright

*Frank Lloyd Wright Prefabricated Houses Manufactured by Marshall Erdman Associates, Inc.,* 1959. Courtesy of the Erdman Family Archives.

Prefabricated House in your area."[37] For Wright, the speech allowed him to revisit ideas he had originally argued in 1909 in his famous lecture "Art and Craft of the Machine," in which he advocated for the use of standardized materials to streamline construction.[38] For Erdman, the speech was part of his larger marketing plan to sell "customized prefabrication" to builders, who would erect more of the prefab houses on commission from the Erdman Company.

Erdman also had to sell the prefabricated model houses that he had built speculatively on Madison's west side. His challenge in selling these was cost; the actual cost for the execution of the original two Wright-designed houses far exceeded Erdman's original hopes for a "low-cost" house (that is, one selling for less than $20,000). Costs for both appear to have been close to double the estimate, largely because of extensive site work and "add-ons" (materials, appliances, and furniture).[39] Erdman was unable to sell the second prefabricated model home during its premiere in Madison's 1959 Parade of Homes, despite its being the most talked-about house on parade that year.[40] The eventual purchaser of the house, Mary Ellen Rudin, did not even visit the house with her husband, Walter, during the parade; she went to see it only at Erdman's urging several months later. Rudin later recalled how Erdman

"Wright Prefab Joins 'Parade of Homes,'" *Wisconsin State Journal*, June 14, 1959. Courtesy of the *Wisconsin State Journal*.

offered them "add-ons" during their visit, mainly in the form of Wright-designed furniture. According to Rudin, Erdman stressed to the young faculty couple that this was their chance to have a low-cost house by the "Master." Rudin's statements suggest the consistency of Erdman's marketing program, which extended into his other simultaneous building ventures as well.[41]

The Erdman–Wright prefabs proved largely unsuccessful; only a handful were actually built because of the costs of site work and transportation from factory to site, which resulted in houses that far exceeded the low cost Erdman had anticipated. Erdman's other major initiative in prefabricated building during the late 1950s proved much more lucrative, however.[42] Erdman conceived of prefabricated medical buildings simultaneously with the Wright prefabs, and he relied on the same principle as he sold them: customization within prefabrication.

Erdman's idea for prefabricated medical buildings originated from what he later claimed was a "mistake." He had applied for and received rezoning to erect a two-story L-shaped medical building to accommodate up to sixty doctors in thirty offices, which he hoped would solve an acute shortage of medical office space in Madison. In addition to the offices (with their waiting rooms and examination rooms), the building was to include a gymnasium, a pharmacy, and a day-care center for employees' children. However, after gaining approvals in February 1952, Erdman could not rent space in the building.[43] As he explained several years later: "Although everyone thought the medical arts building a good idea, for various reasons, no one wanted to rent the space in advance. . . . One doctor did not want to rent because he thought he might not like his neighbor. Another wanted changes to meet his particular desire which we could not make. A third thought he wanted to own his own building rather than pay rent."[44] The solution Erdman derived out of this experience was the "doctors park": a collection of small, one-story prefabricated medical buildings, each accommodating space for one to three doctors, surrounded by ample parking. Prefabrication gave doctors a means of buying their own space; customized options within that system allowed them to "plug and play," choosing features that met their particular needs. The doctors park suited the rapidly accelerating practice of suburbanized medicine, which took everyday medical practice out of crowded downtown hospitals and into the rapidly expanding postwar suburbs, where doctors could more easily meet with patients, especially for routine care.[45] Clustering the buildings together in a "park" meant patients could draw on diverse expertise even as individual doctors could customize their own spaces around their particular, often specialized, practices.

Advertisements for the doctors parks stressed the ways that the medical buildings could be customized while also heralding the advantages of prefabrication. An advertisement for the doctors park in Des Moines, Iowa, touted the "efficiency" of prefabricated medical buildings, which meant the doctors did not have to deal with the "hassle" of planning and construction.[46] Like the U-Form-It and Wright–Erdman prefabs, these buildings could be customized around the individual buyers' needs. In a lengthy profile article published in the *Milwaukee Journal* in February 1957, Erdman promoted "efficiency" and "flexibility" as the chief benefits of purchasing a prefabricated medical building. From an efficiency standpoint, the buildings were "no fuss"; Erdman claimed that one could be built in sixty days for $16,000 to $80,000, depending on size—much less than the cost of a "custom" building. More significant was that such buildings allowed doctors a means of "obtaining modern, efficient space to fit their equipment and medical practices." A base building of twenty-four by forty feet was standard; this contained a waiting room, reception area, four exam rooms, a lab area, and other service spaces, with a corner entry vestibule. From here, doctors could add rooms or units in modules. "Flexibility of size is one of the features of the buildings," Erdman emphasized, noting that larger practices could opt for duplex and L-shaped models for additional cost.[47] Both the Des Moines advertisement and the newspaper article also explained Erdman's association with Wright—something that the builder relied on increasingly from the late 1950s on in marketing his buildings.[48] Erdman also asked clients to write testimonials about the buildings and made these available to potential clients.[49]

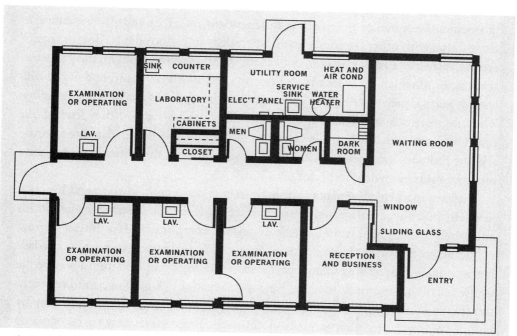

Plan in "Prefab 'Prescription' Offered for Clinics," *Milwaukee Journal*, February 24, 1957. Redrawn by Sarah Fayen Scarlett, April 2014.

A key part of the marketing for the medical buildings was Erdman's promotion of the suburban setting for the offices. To have space to accommodate the buildings—and surround them with ample parking—Erdman had to sell his clients, the doctors, and their patients on essentially suburbanized medicine. He did this repeatedly in advertising brochures put out by the company as well as in press releases and news stories when the parks were erected. A profile piece on the Rockford, Illinois, doctors park in the *Erdman Newsletter* of July–August 1964 boasted of the advantages of the park's suburban setting. After noting the park's advantages for customers, including "solving" the problem of inaccessibility and lack of parking downtown, Erdman listed the benefits the location offered to doctors: "Generally, enough land can be purchased in suburban or outlying areas at a relatively low cost to allow sufficient area for buildings and parking. This type of location takes the practice of medicine to where the patients are, and gives them easier access and suitable parking space."[50] Erdman likened the doctors park concept to suburban development generally: "The growth of shopping centers in outlying areas has shown that people prefer to shop where they can park. We are simply taking the idea one step farther, in believing that people visiting physicians and dentists prefer to visit offices where they can find parking."[51] Moreover, Erdman praised the fact that the parks allowed doctors "individuality" while at the same time allowing them to work in consort with other doctors whose offices were elsewhere in the park: "For a group of doctors interested in maintaining independent practices and yet remaining in close touch with other doctors who are specialists in various fields, 'doctors parks' are the answer."[52] Erdman also insisted that his parks blended in with the suburban landscapes of which they were part; he promoted an office mentioned in the *Milwaukee Journal* piece as "looking as much like a house" as like a doctors' building. The one-story size and landscaping of the doctors parks meant they looked like the suburban ranch and split-level houses in the neighborhoods flanking them—a point Erdman also used to sell the buildings and even their clustering in parks, much like suburban neighborhoods.[53]

Erdman marketed the parks nationally to gain new clients and expand his business. He took out advertisements in papers across the country during the late 1950s and 1960s as the prefabricated medical building component of his business grew, including a small ad in the *Wall Street Journal*.[54] But a key part of his new marketing agenda was advertising in medical journals. On top of representing a new venue for Erdman, this approach suggests how specialization—which occurred throughout the building industry during the postwar years—required builders to employ targeted marketing to reach specialized audiences. Erdman was savvy in recognizing this, and he played it to the hilt with doctors who purchased and occupied the prefab buildings, proclaiming in 1960, "When we begin planning a Doctors Park . . . the doctors become patients and we're the doctors. In most cases we know more what the doctors need than they do."[55] Indeed, Erdman claimed special expertise in the medical industry, arguing that he spent five years surveying doctors, architects, medical equipment experts, and technicians about features as he developed prototypes for the medical buildings.[56] His expertise was noted in a 1956 article on prefabricated offices in *Medical Economics,* which showcased only Erdman examples and, at the end, explained that anyone interested should contact Erdman & Associates, "the only company in the country that specializes in designing and building prefabricated medical offices from start to finish."[57]

Erdman's medical expertise was displayed for the community of doctors above all through a series of articles he wrote for *Physician's Management (The Doctor's Business Journal)* from October 1963 to June 1964. This platform gave Erdman the opportunity to disseminate his ideas on medical facilities, covering factors such as soundproof construction, examination and waiting room layouts, parking arrangements, and site landscaping. Erdman explained how his solutions arose naturally from the functional demands of the medical profession, insights into which he had gleaned from years of extensive research. In an essay published in November 1963, Erdman focused on door placement, explaining how examination room doors should swing inward in the direction of the examining table, rather than toward the adjacent wall, to give the patient privacy from persons in the corridor.[58] Erdman also recommended that examination rooms should be entered from the hallway, not from consultation rooms. A door from the consultation room, Erdman explained, resulted in loss of "a considerable amount of space" and also a loss of "sound protection" (aural privacy being a major concern in medical consultation). Elsewhere in *Physician's Management,* Erdman described in detail the need to address concerns about patients' privacy while they exited the office and during billing; the need for chairs and hooks in offices for garment placement; and options for waiting room arrangements (including placement of furniture and traffic flow).

In Erdman's appeals to the medical community, his program of emphasizing efficiency alongside customization came through as strongly as it did in his other projects. In his article for the December 1963 issue of *Physician's Management,* for example, Erdman stressed the need for individual solutions to shared problems, much as he did when emphasizing the customization possibilities of his prefabricated houses. Erdman's marketing for his medical buildings relied on rhetoric similar to that he used in advertisements for his suburban houses as well as the rhetoric of postwar consumer culture generally, in which the virtues of "individual expression" were sold alongside a collective interest in efficiency. Erdman's marketing of his prefabricated medical buildings formed part of a broader suburban middle-class marketing philosophy prevalent in the postwar decades, then, in which the postwar

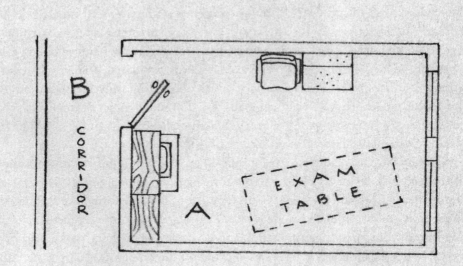

The door to an exam room should swing into the room, concealing the patient (A) from the person entering or from corridor traffic (B).

Marshall Erdman, "Management Blueprint: Door Placement in Exam and Consultation Rooms," draft copy for article in *Physician's Management.* Courtesy of the Erdman Family Archives.

discourse of individualism collided with the postwar discourse of community—something I have discussed elsewhere.[59] We might think of Erdman's customized doctors' buildings—which had individually distinct elements while sharing basic form and features—as we would houses in a postwar middle-class subdivision. Erdman made such a comparison frequently in the literature advertising his medical buildings; these structures shared features that expressed the needs of the overall medical community and its emphasis on efficiency while also meeting the particular concerns of their individual owners/users. This was equally true of Erdman's prefabricated schools and churches, which also formed part of his business during the 1950s and 1960s; that business eventually expanded such that the company established branch offices and factories in New Jersey, Connecticut, California, Georgia, Texas, Virginia, and Colorado.[60] Erdman also expanded into prefabricated modular office furniture, developing and marketing the popular Techline line during the 1970s—itself a combination of prefabrication and customization.[61]

Erdman's marketing efforts for his prefabricated buildings offer telling evidence of how a postwar builder, intent on meeting the rapid demand for expansion in the suburbs, astutely recognized that his clients wanted buildings that were at least partly customized to (and therefore expressive of) their individual needs. In advertising for his prefabricated houses—whether in shelter publications, local publicity, or mainstream news outlets—Erdman capitalized on the possibilities for customization as well as the notion of "good design," suggesting that prefabrication could work hand in hand with modern, up-to-date styling that satisfied the individual desires of the middle-class suburban consumer. This message continued when Erdman began specializing in prefabricated medical buildings. Although he remained wedded to the idea of customized prefabrication to sell these buildings, he also had to promote his medical expertise to another group of suburban consumers, suburban doctors, whose offices in suburban doctors parks formed a new part of the rapidly expanding suburban landscape.

Examining how builders such as Erdman targeted their products to a rapidly growing suburban clientele is vital for telling a revised suburban history. Marketing and advertising were key in the making of the postwar suburbs, as competition was fierce and the client base somewhat skeptical, especially of innovations such as prefabrication. As this chapter has shown, marketing materials offer telling evidence of how builders attempted to sell new innovations as they worked to expand their businesses and, above all, as they began to specialize—a major trend in the later twentieth-century building industry. Moreover, such materials show how builders themselves were grounded in the suburban spaces in which they lived and worked, as well as how they sought to appeal beyond their own communities to a national audience, as Erdman did as his career progressed. As we seek to expand our knowledge of and appreciation for postwar suburban landscapes, attending to these kinds of marketing materials allows us to deepen our knowledge of builders and their everyday suburban lives and recognize that the strategies these builders used were vital in helping millions realize the "American Dream" in postwar America.

## Notes

1. "Immigrant and an Idea," *Life*, October 26, 1953, 139–46.

2. Lucy McDermott, "Break Ground for Unitarian Church," *Capital Times*, August 12, 1949, 6; "Unitarians Hurry Completion of New Meeting House," *Wisconsin State Journal*, August 19, 1951, sec. 2, p. 4; "Young Man with an Idea, Old Success Saga Finds New Hero," *Milwaukee Sentinel*, October 7, 1951. A series of articles also appeared in the *Wisconsin State Journal* in 1948 and 1949 regarding Erdman's efforts in veterans' housing, which are discussed later in this chapter.

3. See, for example, the high-profile piece on William Levitt's Levittown in Joseph F. Kelly, "Up from the Potato Fields," *Time*, July 3, 1950.

4. Erdman's college transcript shows he took a course titled "Architectural Projections" in the fall of 1940 and earned a D. He returned briefly to Illinois in the fall of 1960 for further studies in architecture; he earned an A in design and average grades in his other courses that semester. Transcript, Erdman Family Archives, private collection.

5. Daina Penkiunas, "University Hill Farms: A Project for Modern Living," *Wisconsin Magazine of History* 89 (2007): 19.

6. "Builder Cuts Rates for Vets' Homes," *Wisconsin State Journal,* February 8, 1948.

7. Classified ads, *Wisconsin State Journal,* November 29 and December 1, 1948.

8. John Newhouse, "Private Contractors Plan Co-Op Vet Homes Project," *Wisconsin State Journal,* September 14, 1948.

9. John Newhouse, "Co-Op Housing Plan Backed by Realtors," *Wisconsin State Journal,* September 15, 1948.

10. Colin Davies, *The Prefabricated Home* (London: Reaktion Books, 2005), 11–43.

11. See Anna Vemer Andrzejewski et al., "Eken Park," in *Housing Madison: Where We Live, Where We Work,* ed. Anna Vemer Andrzejewski and Arnold R. Alanen (Madison: Departments of Art History and Landscape Architecture, University of Wisconsin, 2012), 163–65; Jim Draeger, "Prefabulous Madison: Prefabrication in the Capitol City," in Andrzejewski and Alanen, *Housing Madison,* 166–67.

12. Doug Moe and Alice D'Alessio, *Uncommon Sense: The Life of Marshall Erdman* (Black Earth, Wis.: Trails Custom, 2003), 74–75. Erdman claimed in a 1982 interview to have been involved with Lendrum's Small Homes Council, although his time at Illinois predated the council's formation. On this history, see University of Illinois at Urbana-Champaign, Small Homes Council, University of Illinois Archives, accessed December 16, 2014, http://archives.library.illinois.edu.

13. Advertisement, *Wisconsin State Journal,* July 6, 1951.

14. Moe and D'Alessio, *Uncommon Sense,* 76.

15. "Immigrant and an Idea," 139.

16. Moe and D'Alessio, *Uncommon Sense,* 78.

17. "Erdman Firm to Build $250,000 Factory Here," *Capital Times,* March 18, 1954.

18. Advertisement, *Wisconsin State Journal,* October 25, 1953, sec. 2, p. 3.

19. See similar promotional material touting Erdman's connection with the *Life* article in "New Building Group Formed," *Waukesha Daily Freeman,* March 18, 1954, 15; "'Package Plan' House Is Built on Cumberland Drive," *Waukesha Daily Freeman,* March 26, 1954, 2; advertisement, *Janesville Daily Gazette,* May 22, 1954, 5.

20. In advertisements elsewhere in Wisconsin, Erdman did not mention local Madison architects and businesses; this suggests that he employed different marketing strategies based on his clientele. See ad in *Janesville Daily Gazette,* May 22, 1954, 5. Also see advertisement, *Waukesha Daily Freedman,* February 11, 1955, 10.

21. Through the 1950s, Erdman relied on local architects to produce designs for U-Form-It models as well as his medical buildings. U-Form-Its were designed originally by Weiler and Strang, a local firm known for modernist design, according to the *Wisconsin State Journal.* The prototypes for the prefabricated medical buildings were designed by William Kaeser, a modern architect in Madison known best for his houses based on Wright's Usonian scheme.

22. *Your Erdman Home . . . the Home Designed for Family Living,* brochure, 1956, Erdman Family Archives.

23. Price catalog, October 1, 1956–January 1, 1957, Erdman Family Archives.

24. Paul E. Sprague, "The Marshall Erdman Prefabricated Buildings," in *Frank Lloyd Wright and Madison: Eight Decades of Artistic and Social Interaction,* ed. Paul E. Sprague (Madison: Elvehjem Museum of Art, 1990), 151.

25. Marshall Erdman to Frank Lloyd Wright, December 29, 1955, Frank Lloyd Wright Correspondence, 1900–1959, archived by Frank Lloyd Wright Foundation, Scottsdale, Ariz. (hereafter cited as Wright Correspondence).

26. Marshall Erdman to Frank Lloyd Wright, February 10, 1956, Wright Correspondence.

27. Marshall Erdman in *About Wright: An Album of Recollections by Those Who Knew Frank Lloyd Wright,* ed. Edgar Tafel (New York: John Wiley, 1993), 214.

28. "Here Is Prefabrication's Biggest News for 1957," *House and Home,* December 1956, 117–21.

29. Cynthia Kellogg, "Frank Lloyd Wright's Mass-Produced House," *New York Times,* December 21, 1956, 20.

30. John Peter to Frank Lloyd Wright, January 11, 1957, Wright Correspondence.

31. Examples include "Frank Lloyd Wright Designs New Prefab Home," *Pasadena Star-News,* February 20, 1957; "Frank Lloyd Wright Design for Prefab Is Applauded," *Yuma Daily Sun,* June 8, 1958; "Frank Lloyd Wright Prefab Gets Praise," *Daily Chronicle* (Centralia, Wash.), June 14, 1958; "Frank Lloyd Wright Uses Masonite Siding in Prefab," *Ukiah Daily Journal,* February 15, 1957; "Critics Applaud 'Prefab' by Frank Lloyd Wright," *Weirton Daily Times,* May 8, 1958; "Wright Starts Prefab Homes Construction," *Oxnard Press-Courier,* January 24, 1958; "Critics Applaud 'Prefab' by Frank Lloyd Wright," *Record-Argus* (Greenville, Pa.), June 15, 1958; "Plan New Prefabricated Home," *Salina Journal,* January 23, 1958; "Famed Wright Designs a Prefab House," *Tucson Daily Citizen,* September 28, 1957. Copies of these and others are in the Erdman Family Archives.

32. The stipulation that a professional builder must oversee construction is found throughout the promotional literature. Promotional materials, Erdman Family Archives.

33. *Frank Lloyd Wright Prefabricated Houses Manufactured by Marshall Erdman Associates, Inc.,* pamphlet, 1959, Wisconsin Historical Society, Madison.

34. *Prospectus: The Frank Lloyd Wright Prefabricated House, Manufactured by Erdman Homes,* brochure, undated, Erdman Family Archives.

35. Marshall Erdman to Frank Lloyd Wright, November 11, 1957, Wright Correspondence.

36. Frank Lloyd Wright to Marshall Erdman, November 16, 1957, Wright Correspondence.

37. Promotional materials, Erdman Family Archives.

38. "Why Not Prefabrication," typed text of speech, with introduction by Marshall Erdman, Erdman Family Archives. Also reproduced in Frank Lloyd Wright, *Truth against the World: Frank Lloyd Wright Speaks for an Organic Architecture,* ed. Patrick J. Meehan (New York: John Wiley, 1991).

39. Estimates from Sprague, "Marshall Erdman Prefabricated Buildings."

40. The house stole the local media attention for the parade that year. See "Wright Prefab Joins 'Parade of Homes,'" *Wisconsin State Journal,* June 14, 1959.

41. Mary Ellen Rudin, interview by author, January 2010, Madison, Wis.

42. By the early 1960s, Erdman began specializing in medical buildings, and by some estimates, he built more than two thousand of them in the course of his career. In 1958, prefabricated office buildings already accounted for 80 percent of Erdman's business. See Robert Meloon, "Drive-In Pharmacy at Doctors Park," *Capital Times,* June 19, 1958.

43. John Newhouse, "Builder's 'Mistake' 10 Years Ago Held Key to Doctors Park Idea," *Wisconsin State Journal,* October 4, 1959.

44. Quoted in "Prefab 'Prescription' Offered for Clinics," *Milwaukee Journal,* February 24, 1957.

45. Paul Starr, *Social Transformation of American Medicine* (New York: Basic Books, 1982).

46. Advertisement, undated, Erdman Family Archives.

47. "Prefab 'Prescription' Offered for Clinics."

48. Wright's name appeared in numerous ads and in newspaper articles, including "New Doctors Park Here Is One of over 200 in U.S." (Columbus, Indiana), in Erdman Family Archives.

49. Nearly one hundred of these testimonials survive in the Erdman Family Archives.

50. "Doctors Park, Rockford, Illinois," *Erdman Newsletter,* July–August 1964, Erdman Family Archives.

51. Quoted in John Newhouse, "West Side Center for Doctors Planned," *Wisconsin State Journal,* October 17, 1954.

52. Quoted in "Prefab 'Prescription' Offered for Clinics."

53. On the buildings looking like houses, see Meloon, "Drive-In Pharmacy at Doctors Park"; "Prefabricated Office Buildings Attract the Medical Profession," *New York Times,* March 12, 1961.

54. Advertisement, *Wall Street Journal,* clipping, June 1959, Erdman Family Archives.

55. Quoted in "New Doctors Park Here Is One of over 200 in U.S." This was something Erdman repeated often throughout his career. Also see "No Substitute for Knowledge," *Wisconsin Business Journal,* December 1984, 44. Erdman also took part in a conference at the University of Wisconsin–Madison in February 1993 titled "Planning and Design of Health Care Facilities for the 21st Century." A copy of the lecture he delivered at the conference is in the Erdman Family Archives.

56. "Prefab 'Prescription' Offered for Clinics."

57. Hugh C. Sherwood, "They Prefer PREFAB Medical Offices," *Medical Economics,* September 14, 1959, 122–42. Also see "Prefab Medical Buildings Make Parks for Doctors," *AMA News,* February 23, 1959; "Prefab Offices," *MD: Medical Newsmagazine,* March 1958, 76–77.

58. Marshall Erdman, "Management Blueprint: Door Placement in Exam and Consultation Rooms," *Physician's Management,* November 1963.

59. Anna Vemer Andrzejewski, "Building Privacy and Community: Surveillance in a Postwar Suburban Development in Madison, Wisconsin," *Landscape Journal* 28 (January 2009): 40–55.

60. Erdman's schools and churches were not terribly successful, but he did build some during the 1950s and 1960s. See Moe and D'Alessio, *Uncommon Sense,* 97–100.

61. See "In-House Laminating Cuts Labor Costs," *Wood Digest,* April 1990; "Making Equipment Pay," *Wood Digest,* April 1985; Steve Ehle, "Techline Redefines RTA Furniture in U.S.," *Wood Digest,* February 1992.

# 18

# A Tiny Orchestra in the Living Room

## High-Fidelity Sound, Stereo Systems, and the Postwar House

### DIANNE HARRIS

In "Signal 30," an episode in the fifth season of the popular television series *Mad Men*, several of the main characters attend a dinner party at the suburban home of Pete Campbell and his wife, Trudy. The very prospect of traveling for the party to Cos Cob, Connecticut, causes the Manhattan-dwelling advertising executive Don Draper to declare to his wife, Megan, "Saturday night in the suburbs? That's when you really want to blow your brains out."

In the very next scene, set shortly before Don and Megan arrive at the party, host Pete reveals a recent purchase to his guest Ken Cosgrove: a new stereo console, set inside a gleaming wood cabinet that occupies the entire length of the floor in front of the living room's picture window. With the cabinet's hinged lid open, Pete and Ken peer inside while listening to a recording of a Beethoven symphony:

> PETE: Incredible, right? You expect to open the doors and see a tiny orchestra in there.
> KEN: That would be amazing.
> PETE: And it's a beautiful piece of furniture. It's seven feet long. Wilt Chamberlain could lie down in there.
> KEN: Why would he want to do that?

Both pieces of dialogue—Don's declaration of suburban antipathy, with its violent reference, and Pete and Ken's conversation about the stereo—reveal much about popular American sentiment between 1950, when stereo systems first became readily available to ordinary consumers, and 1966, the year in which this particular episode of *Mad Men* is set.[1] Implicit in the characters' statements is a distinction between, on one hand, a seemingly banal decision to move away from the city, the

305

presumed site of high culture and worldliness, and, on the other, the introduction of
a new and sophisticated technology—the high-fidelity stereo system—in the very
site of the apparently mundane suburban home. Pete's comment about the tiny
orchestra inside the console might well have been uttered by new stereo owners
nationwide at that time. Indeed, advertisements for in-home stereo systems often
did use words and images that emphasized the new technology's capacity to bring
aspects of the symphonic experience into the domestic sphere. Although numerous studies have examined the impact of technologies on the home, particularly
television, radio, and more recent digital technologies, historians have largely overlooked questions about the sociospatial significance of high-fidelity audio systems
for ordinary houses during the postwar period.

In this essay, I intend to answer the following questions: How did the introduction of high-fidelity sound components (including speakers) in the home shape
postwar domestic life? How did the introduction of home stereo systems change
the ways homeowners imagined the relationship of the private, sequestered suburban home to external and largely urban locations? And how did the introduction
of stereo systems necessitate change within residential spaces? In short, what did it
mean for ordinary Americans to command their own tiny orchestras (or bands,
choirs, singers) inside their living rooms?[2]

Mediated sound changed domestic space in at least two ways: physically, as residents reconfigured rooms and furnishings to create optimal listening environments;
and socially, as occupants fashioned stereophilic environments that reflected new
aspirations linked to particular understandings of social respectability and status.
As I will demonstrate, in-home stereos must be considered along with a range of
postwar technologies that connected the seemingly private, secure, and insulated
domestic realm to external and sometimes disturbing events. Stereos—like televisions and radios before them—rendered the home permeable, admitting sonic
transmissions into the sheltered, private home with an immediacy that could be
startling, and even alarming. News and images of urban crime, in particular, could
be transmitted into the suburban home through television with a frequency and
a level of graphic detail not available to previous generations of homeowners. At
the same time, home stereos provided access to sophisticated aspects of urban
culture—symphony concerts and other forms of high- and popular-culture musical
performance—not easily accessible to suburbanites who lived far away from or
could not afford to attend events taking place in urban venues like concert halls and
theaters, urban coffeehouses, or university campuses.

Moreover, Pete's reference to the size of his stereo cabinet in *Mad Men* reveals
how in-home stereo systems prompted a reconsideration of postwar living rooms
and family rooms, the physical spaces where these systems were most often stored

An advertisement for Stephens Tru-Sonic speakers illustrated the notion, frequently summoned by salesmen, that owning a high-fidelity sound system was like having a symphony orchestra in the living room. *High Fidelity,* June 1954, 15.

YOU
ARE
THERE
WITH

STEPHENS
*True Fidelity*
SPEAKERS

**MODEL 206AX**

List price;
206AX 15" coaxial
  16 ohm..........$166.00
  500 ohm..........$179.00

**FEATURES**

★ 7½ lbs. Alnico Magnet

★ Heavy Die-cast Aluminum Frame

★ Low Frequency Cone Resonance—35 c.p.s.

★ Frequency Response 30 to 18,000 c.p.s.

For emotionally satisfying... thrilling new sound sensations, music critics choose Stephens Tru-Sonic *True Fidelity* Speakers. Made by the Nation's number one pioneer in *High Fidelity* reproducing equipment, these outstanding Speakers will give you years of distortion-free listening pleasure.

Producing pure, clear tones of mellow richness, Tru-Sonic Speakers are a creation of advanced design and master craftsmanship. Frequency response is smooth and distortion-free from 30 to 18,000 c.p.s.

*The International Standard. Write for descriptive literature and specifications.*

**STEPHENS**
TRU-SONIC

STEPHENS MANUFACTURING CORPORATION • 8538 WARNER DRIVE • CULVER CITY, CALIFORNIA and/or displayed. Manufacturers, retailers, audiophiles, and ordinary consumers all sought cabinets and arrangements for their new components that would allow for maximum sound fidelity and listening pleasure while still affording a decorous and even status-conferring appearance that was crucially linked to emerging notions of what it meant to be white, middle-class, and a homeowner.[3]

## How Many Postwar Homes Had Stereos?

There is no question that in-home stereos created a major shift in listening practices.[4] Privately owned radios and phonographs had already permitted the enjoyment of technologically mediated listening within the home for decades prior to the midcentury proliferation of in-home stereo systems. But radio listeners had to rely on those producing the programs to select the music they would hear. Phonographs, or "record players," permitted personal selection, but the sound quality for some recordings, projected through monaural systems, left much to be desired.[5] With in-home stereo systems and the increased commercial availability of stereo recordings in the postwar era, hi-fi owners could listen to all kinds of music inside the home, with advanced technology that made the listening experience more pleasurable. Home stereo likewise allowed—for the first time—the repeated listening/ hearing of the same high-quality recording, so the unique specificity of live performance was superseded by the ability to hear a particular performance in the home repeatedly according to the preferences of the occupant(s).[6] Religious music, country music, sound tracks from musicals, sing-alongs, children's music, folk songs, gospel music and hymns—as well as classical and chamber music and jazz—all could be enjoyed anytime, according to whim, and with a new sense of pleasure derived from the perceived authenticity of the sound. Indeed, notions of authenticity were central to high-fidelity's appeal.

But how many postwar homeowners owned high-fidelity systems? The shelter magazine *House and Home* reported in 1954 that "half a million new hobbyists joined ranks of Hi-Fi enthusiasts last year," and by 1955, one hi-fi publication (the increasing numbers of these and their expanded circulation serve as some indication of the growth of public interest in the systems) noted that "High Fidelity at low cost is available to everyone."[7] Additionally, despite the fact that stereo technology had existed since the 1930s, the first commercial recording in stereo was not made until February 1954 (by RCA), a shift that ushered in a broader, general use of stereo in domestic settings by 1958, with a 1959 publication declaring, "The year 1958 will be remembered in America as the year when Stereo arrived."[8]

Amid these emphatic statements, consumer statistics indicate that from October through December 1965, 3 percent of U.S. households were actually purchasing stereos, and 2.6 percent indicated that they intended to purchase them.[9] It seems fair to say, then, that at least in the 1960s, around 2.5 to 3 percent of households were purchasing stereo equipment annually. Hi-fi systems thus remained a somewhat specialized commodity for the fifteen years following the end of the war, but demand and consumption patterns increased steadily for those who were able to afford such luxuries. For middle-class families, hi-fi systems rapidly became objects of desire, important additions to consumer wish lists.

The popular marketing and acquisition of home stereos created a mass audience for music that had not previously existed—an audience that was in many locations but that crucially included those new inhabitants of the ordinary suburban home. By the second half of the 1950s and more surely by the advent of the 1960s, listening to recorded music on hi-fi systems became not only an important part of music culture but also an accepted part of domestic culture, a complementary activity to almost anything else performed at home (domestic labor, recreation, sex, eating, and so on). As one critic wrote in 1961, "The new middle class in the affluent society reads little, but listens to music with knowing delight. Where the library shelves once stood, there are proud, esoteric rows of record albums and high-fidelity components."[10] Listening to music together became one of the most important shared experiences in the home.[11]

But if families regarded this shared music largely as a welcome addition to their daily home lives, musicians and cultural theorists did not all embrace the mass proliferation of hi-fi technology. For example, many performers worried that high levels of home stereo usage would lead to listener passivity and to mass audiences who thought about musical performance as merely superficial entertainment because they could listen to recorded music anywhere, at any time.[12] This became an abiding concern for the Frankfurt School theorist Theodor Adorno, whose writings on the topic began to appear in the late 1930s and continued into the early 1940s. Stemming from his interest in the impact of mass-media technologies on culture and society, Adorno's was a largely pessimistic view. He connected the proliferation of technologies that permitted easy access to recorded music with an encouragement of peripheral engagements with culture that in turn encouraged the development of an aesthetically insensitive public who retreated from the public sphere by listening increasingly to music at home.[13]

Similarly, and importantly for this essay, Adorno and his sometime collaborator Max Horkheimer also critiqued the insubstantial housing being built on a massive scale on the edges of cities in the immediate postwar period. In their well-known text *Dialectic of Enlightenment* they derided large-scale suburban housing developments for the same reasons they critiqued emerging technologies for listening. For them, both trends were linked to mass-production monotony, and they referred to the new housing being built on urban fringes as "flimsy structures" with a "built-in demand to be discarded after a short while like empty food cans."[14] Taken together and as part of their larger Marxist critique of the culture industry, Horkheimer and Adorno's assessment of both mass suburban housing and the proliferation of in-home listening technologies can today be seen as part of an intellectual framework derived from their situated postwar fears about mass culture generally.[15]

Adorno's critiques were totalizing; he imagined all consumers monolithically and stereotypically, and in this he was not alone. However, and as at least three decades of musicology and popular/cultural studies have revealed, Adorno was wrong about some of his assertions. The rise and rapid proliferation of in-home stereos may well have produced a tolerance for Muzak in some, but it also promoted a hunger for a wide variety of musical recordings by family members of all ages and across geographic regions. It stimulated interest in music for an increasing number of stereo owners who could purchase and listen to a variety of music according to their desires and schedules. As we now know, cookie-cutter houses did not produce cookie-cutter lives; similarly, in-home hi-fi systems did not necessarily produce suburbanites with a homogeneous taste for only the most mass-produced, easily understood musical forms.[16]

Instead, aficionados of jazz, classical, blues, rock, and popular music all honed their tastes using home stereos to educate themselves and sometimes to quarrel over selections with their spouses, children, parents, and neighbors, with whom they also discussed new trends, new artists, and the latest technologies for listening. What the in-home stereo system meant for most Americans was the ability to lie on the living room carpet while waving their arms in the air, conducting an imaginary symphony orchestra (or the tiny one in the stereo cabinet); it meant dancing inside or on the patio with friends of any age to a newly acquired LP; it meant sitting in an easy chair with a drink while listening to chamber music or jazz as it filled the room; it meant sitting on the sofa with small children while Burl Ives sang nursery rhymes, or listening to an educational recording of *Peter and the Wolf* aimed at teaching children to recognize the sounds of various musical instruments; it meant being able to play religious music in the home for specific occasions and holidays; it afforded the ability to learn all the words to the songs from the latest Broadway musical through repeated play of a sound track; and it facilitated the creation of specific teen identities when the latest rock-and-roll LP was blasted through the house at top volume.

Stereos generated sociocultural shifts in domestic life, even as they likewise created spatial problems that demanded new solutions. The introduction of stereo transformed the contours of the house, creating spaces that were both literally and symbolically performative. The proper and measured display of the components themselves afforded the shaping of some aspects of identity—status, cultural capital—and the embodied performances that stereo instigated, such as dancing and singing, made household spaces into quite literal realms for sustained performances of specifically imagined identities. Even when contained within the privacy of surrounding bedroom, basement, or living room walls, high-fidelity sound's authenticity could convey that same sense of realism—and therefore of validity—to the various identities listeners might wish to assume through their careful selection of music.

## Stereos and Mobile Privatization

The spatial impact of stereos occurred at multiple scales. One of the surprises of early stereo was that it seemingly brought the outside world directly into the living room: "Railroad trains and jet planes roared through living rooms across the nation; marching bands came crashing through the walls of studio apartments. . . . this new music had a depth and spaciousness that was surpassed only in the concert hall itself." With stereo, the living room suddenly took on a new depth and spaciousness—the small rooms of an ordinary house were made metaphorically larger through the implementation of stereophonic engineering.[17] And spaciousness was a defining feature of the aesthetically and socially "modern" home.[18]

This imagined dissolution of boundaries between spaces, and particularly between the home and the outside world, is one of the key impacts of stereo technologies on ordinary houses, allowing for an invisible gateway between the outside world and the safe, private home. Perhaps the most well-known theorization of technologies' transgression of domestic boundaries is that formulated by Raymond Williams, whose concept of "mobile privatization" summarizes television's particularly suburban fit. Mobile privatization "served an at-once mobile and home-centred way of living," according to Williams:

> The new homes might appear private and "self-sufficient" but could be maintained only by regular funding and supply from external sources, and these, over a range from employment and prices to depressions and wars, had a decisive and often a disrupting influence on what was nevertheless seen as a separable "family" project. This relationship created both the need and the form of a new kind of "communication": news from "outside," from otherwise inaccessible sources."[19]

If, as Lynn Spigel has demonstrated, television "merge[d] private with public spaces," stereo too brought aspects of public culture into the home, but without television's risk of admitting sometimes disturbing visual images, although rock and roll (and some other genres) may have—was sometimes assumed to have—introduced elements of subversive culture in the same way as did some televised images. And just as Spigel asserts that television allowed Americans to enter public and community life at a distance, stereo's auditory realism and sense of "being there" fostered an imagined participation in cultures of music created and performed in distant locations.[20] In short, the home thus came to serve as a site of cultural participation—however mediated—in events taking place beyond its own boundaries.

Thus, rather than compounding a sense of suburban isolation by keeping music listeners at home and out of the urban concert hall, stereos might be viewed as decreasing that sense, because "through the power of sound, the world becomes intimate, known, possessed."[21] In connecting the living room to the outside world, stereophonic sound blurred the boundaries of the home altogether—that is, it narrowed the gap between "in here" and "out there." As Michael Bull has written, "Sound colonizes the listener but is also used to actively re-create and reconfigure the spaces of experience. . . . Sound enables users to manage and orchestrate their spaces of habitation in a manner that conforms to their desires."[22] Given this conception of the relationship of stereos to domestic space, it is not surprising that advertisements for components frequently touted hi-fi systems as being able to "transport the listener and his favorite arm chair into the concert hall or opera house of his choice."[23]

## A New Culture of Listening

If one thing was made clear to those who purchased hi-fi stereo systems for their homes, it was this: the new technology demanded new attention to the spatial requirements that permitted the reception of true, stereophonic sound. Even those who had previously paid little attention to the aesthetic qualities, materials, and dimensions of rooms had to notice such details if they were to optimize their listening pleasure. In most cases, the acquisition of new hi-fi components and speakers required the moving of furnishings in order to accommodate the various parts and, ideally, to afford the maximum levels of aural authenticity. In turn, the stereophile shaped his or her own ability to listen, to cultivate specific cultural attributes, so the reshaping of the house became directly linked with a reshaping of personal identity vis-à-vis the use of this consumer technology. By shaping the private spaces of the home to accommodate the stereo, one might cultivate what Jonathan Sterne has called "a good ear" that would become "a mark of distinction in modern life," one that corresponded "with the emergence of middle class as a salient cultural category" and that was likewise linked to the emergence of a "new sonic age."[24]

Residents, then, in this new sonic age, produced new sonic spaces. Living rooms became "sonic environments"; they were what they had always been—places to gather as a family or alone, to sit on a sofa with friends, to read, or to watch television, among other activities—but with the addition of stereo systems, they also served as newly and literally attuned spaces, environments for specific kinds of perception/reception.[25] Stereo shifted the ways residents used their home environments because in-home stereos created not only new cultures of listening but also new ways of occupying residential space. The living room became a dance floor, a singing space, a private listening laboratory (especially for men with headphones), and a space for the display of technological prowess (again, especially for men through careful purchasing of the best components and through demonstrated mastery of their functions), and thus a site for performing identities.

Moreover, newly affordable high-quality speaker and amplifier systems meant that new volume levels could be achieved with no sacrifice of desirable sound qualities. Small suburban homes with stereo systems could be filled with sound throughout the day, music to accompany the household labor performed daily by women just as it entertained men and school-age children during the evenings and on weekends.[26] Truly, men were the primary purchasers of high-fidelity stereo components and speakers. Women generally spent far more time at home, however, and though scant research exists on their use of such technologies within the home and during the course of their days, little doubt exists that women equally enjoyed listening to music on stereos and that even if they did not, the stereos could occupy children and teens in ways that mattered to women (even if it sometimes proved equally disruptive).[27]

It is certainly true that the development of new acoustical designs, technologies, and materials allowed the greater manipulation and control of sound in some designed spaces in the twentieth century, especially those that were meant for the public consumption of particular aural experiences, such as symphony halls and motion picture theaters.[28] But stereophonic acoustics were of little concern to those constructing ordinary middle- and working-class houses in the postwar United States, since those houses were built quickly and with relatively inexpensive materials, and for audiences who might not easily afford hi-fi components. When aural concerns surfaced in the literature about such housing, they most frequently focused on mitigating the travel of noises between rooms. Open-planned houses, in this period, were frequently criticized for their inability to control the flow of noise from one space to another, with both television and stereo systems frequently cited as the primary sources of the problem.[29] In higher-end, architect-designed homes, hi-fi systems were frequently incorporated directly into the house plans. Dedicated wiring could be installed during the construction phase, along with hidden or camouflaged speakers mounted into walls and special built-in cabinetry designed to house the components. But in more ordinary houses, space for wiring, speakers, and components had to be claimed from preexisting and generally overcrowded spaces.

## MOVABLE UNITS

PLUSH INSTALLATIONS for apartment dwellers often include every basic component for reproducing sound. In this magnificent example of fine cabinet work, there has been installed an AM-FM tuner (with preamplifier), a record player, extended range speaker system, professional tape recorder, with storage space for both records and tape reels.

The tuner and amplifier installations swing forward on a hinged front plate. This arrangement of controls is easily operated from a standing position, and does away with the necessity of either stooping or sitting. When closed, the tuner is completely covered and there is no possibility of idle fingers changing the accurate settings or damaging equipment.

The tape recorder has been mounted in a drawer-like cabinet. This slides forward on ball bearing rails so that maximum usage may be made of the equipment. By closing the drawer when the tape recorder is operating,

all miscellaneous machinery sounds are contained within the cabinet. The speaker then introduces into the room only harmonious sounds from the tape recorder, radio tuner or record player. The microphone is for producing home-recorded tape programs. ∎

MAGNETIC RECORDERS, LOS ANGELES 46

84

A woman displays the magnetic tape recorder in a movable stereo system console. *High Fidelity Home Music Systems* (Los Angeles: Trend Incorporated, 1955), 84.

## The Spatial Imperatives of Domestic Technologies

The placement of hi-fi components and speakers in postwar houses required careful consideration for homeowners and house builders alike. The purchase of a stereo system was for most buyers an exciting acquisition that could stimulate an eagerness to refashion and refurnish domestic spaces for the properly designed and measured display of components—acts that optimized personal and social aspirations just as they maximized sound quality and listening pleasure. Those in possession of such new equipment had to evaluate at least four types of concerns, each of which included a spatial dimension. First, truly ordinary houses for middle- and working-class families frequently included less than fifteen hundred square feet of living space—most Levittown, Long Island, houses encompassed just one thousand square feet. A family of four could easily fill every square inch of one of these houses and still lack adequate storage space. Where then, and how, was this new equipment to be housed? Second, family members required varying degrees of acoustical privacy depending on the sorts of activities they wished to pursue, and that simultaneously necessitated greater or lesser degrees of quiet. Consideration of these diverse needs had to figure into any solutions for placement of stereo equipment. Third, the achievement of maximum acoustical authenticity—what audiophiles call stereo imaging—necessitated specific speaker arrangements within a room.[30] Fourth, possession of stereo equipment conferred status on the owners. For many, accommodation of the stereo within the room was best accomplished when it simultaneously created an aura of class respectability, so decisions about the placement and appearance of components carried the additional weight of status considerations.

Those purchasing stereo equipment in the postwar era faced two options. One was to purchase separate components and speakers—the likely preference of most true audiophiles, who could customize and personally assemble their own systems. This was also, however, the more expensive option. Alternatively, consumers could purchase a stereo console system, one with preselected, preassembled components housed in a cabinet designed to blend tastefully with other home furnishings. In both cases, nearly everyone (including architects, tastemakers such as shelter magazine editors, interior decorators, the manufacturers of components, and stereo retailers) agreed—at least in the earliest years—that the components should remain largely concealed from the occupants of the room to the greatest extent possible. The very existence of a stereo cabinet in a room signaled status; lifting its lid or swinging open its doors to reveal the expensive components might elicit the appropriate "oohs and aahs" of impressed guests. Thus, to conceal the hi-fi was also to create a carefully configured and controlled display that conveyed the cultural capital of the owners. The more surprising or elegant the cabinet's design, the greater the level of

NOW... *Beautiful Cabinets* TO HOUSE THE FINEST

QUALITY HI-FI COMPONENTS *only* $89⁹⁵*

THESE handsome cabinets make hi-fi desired in every home. They're *finished on all sides*...beautiful from any angle. And, at this low price, your complete ensemble becomes inexpensive to own. Select one that matches your furniture and install the components yourself. You can use it as a chairside piece...as a room divider...or anywhere else in the home.

Yes, for finest hi-fi performance at realistic prices see G-E matched components. Ask for a demonstration before deciding on a custom or cabinet installation.

Local dealers in most cities are showing this cabinet. See it as soon as possible or write for the name of a nearby store.

*General Electric Co., Radio & TV Dept., Sec. R5415, Electronics Park, Syracuse N. Y.*

In Mahogany, Cherry, Blond Oak
—same low price!
It matches G-E speaker enclosure!

G-E Speaker Enclosures (Blond, Mahogany, or Unfinished Veneers)...
A1-406 from $50.37* to $59.95*

G-E Dual Coaxial Speaker
Model A1-400 . . . . . . $41.95*

G-E Preamplifier-Control Unit
Model A1-200 . . . . . . $57.95*

G-E Power Amplifier
Model A1-300 . . . . . . $47.75*

G-E Variable Reluctance Cartridges
from $8.57* to $34.74*

G-E Baton Tone Arms:
Model A1-500 (12") . . . $31.95*
Model A1-501 (16") . . . $35.50*

*Subject to change without notice.
Slightly higher West and South.

# GENERAL ⒼⒺ ELECTRIC

A small stereo cabinet manufactured by General Electric. *High Fidelity,* January 1955, 95.

status conferred, so that appropriately "concealing" the components indexed identity as much as did the quality of the sound.

In order to maximize the effectiveness of hi-fi, owners had to place their systems' speakers according to an exacting set of standards. After all, the big idea behind high-fidelity sound was that it added a third dimension—space—to music as binaural recording on twin tracks was directed out at the listener through dual speakers placed in different parts of the room. The objective was to achieve the feeling of space from sound, something that could also be referred to as three-dimensional sound. To this end, stereo publications presented diagrams carefully calculated to assist homeowners in the creation of "sonic balance." Readers were advised not only about the requisite distances for separating speakers but also about considering the impact of sound vibrations on furnishings, including sofas, coffee tables, end tables, and chairs. Danish modern furnishings were thought to be particularly well suited, since the clean lines of the designs would not deaden sound effects as heavier, overstuffed furnishings might do. Similarly, heavy draperies were considered problematic, since they, too, could deaden sound.[31] Although such calculations likely remained beyond the abilities of most stereo owners, the publications made clear that sonic balance could be attained only if the spaces of the home were newly calibrated and carefully arranged. The room that included the speakers was to become, in essence, a stage for an invisible yet stereophonically ideal performance.

To achieve this, some component retailers sold custom systems that were designed either for built-in installations or to fit into fine cabinets produced by well-known furniture manufacturers such as Herman Miller, Dunbar, and Baker.[32] Small independent retailers sometimes collaborated with local cabinetmakers who produced speaker boxes and cabinets for their clients, or as ready-mades for their showroom floors.[33] Custom installations that hid components in artfully designed cabinetry were available to a relative few and appeared more frequently in houses designed by well-known architects for wealthy clients. But the idea that sound could emerge "subtly from a tasteful installation which almost defies the listener to locate the music or its producer" was presented by magazines like *High Fidelity* as an ideal, and as an "audio hobbyist's dream."[34]

Ideally, and as the trade publications and shelter magazines recommended, storage for stereo components was to be designed to blend with the surroundings whenever possible and to become, essentially, invisible—although conspicuously so. If guests and residents were not intended to gaze directly on exposed components, they were intended to infer the components' existence in the room through the clever design of the installation or cabinetry. The 1961 issue of the annual *Stereo* included numerous illustrations, as did similar publications at the time, of new furnishings that could house the components in what the magazine called "four modes:

# *Custom* INSTALLATIONS

At right is a handsome modern installation done by the Olympic Engineering Company of Seattle. Below (left) same installation is shown with cabinet doors opened: note speaker housing above television screen. Below (right) is an ingenous housing for an air coupler and a three-speaker system. It was designed and built by Louis Nodell of Patterson, New Jersey. The cabinetry is a glue and screw construction of three-quarter-inch tongue-and-groove panelling.

Examples of custom-designed cabinetry to accommodate stereo equipment. *High Fidelity,* January 1955, 40.

built in, 'packaged prettily,' a wall to itself, or build around it." Pretty packaging meant housing the stereo system in a console or some other sort of freestanding cabinet. But creating a built-in system that had space for storage of LPs and tapes and could contain the amplifier, turntable, tape recorder, and, if possible, built-in speakers was considered the best option, since it meant that the room itself remained "undisturbed by the inclusion of a component high-fidelity system." *Stereo* also included an illustration of an "entertainment wall" that had "the special virtue of reducing clutter at the least sacrifice of living space."[35] Stereo systems also involved what one publication referred to as "nests of wires" that could cause unsightly tangles. Exposed wiring, common in tenements and more impoverished dwellings, signaled exactly those lower-class identities and was therefore considered unacceptable for middle-class, white homes. Properly designed stereo cabinets and entertainment walls could conceal this sort of apparatus, disguising the conduits that made possible the sound required by "high-fidelitarians" who wished to transform their living rooms into concert halls.[36]

Reducing clutter and maximizing space were of particular importance in the small, ordinary houses constructed in suburban developments nationwide, for both practical and symbolic reasons. As I have demonstrated elsewhere, tidiness and spaciousness were both essential markers of white identities and middle-class status in the postwar era, and built-in furnishings and storage systems played a significant role in helping homeowners attain the ideals prescribed by tastemakers and promoted in mass publications with national distribution.[37] It is unsurprising, then, that trade journals repeatedly advocated the same solutions for housing this new technology in the home. Another article in the 1961 issue of *Stereo* recommended housing hi-fi equipment in a built-in storage wall with folding doors, which "enabled the owner to restore the formal balance of the living room," as though bringing this technology into the home caused an imbalance of some sort. The article noted that doors and lift-up panels could "completely close the system off from view if desired."[38] Such storage or entertainment walls often included the television as well as the stereo system, and the trade publications advised readers to conceal their equipment behind wood doors to avoid the "cold" or "mechanical" appearance of technology and glass (in the case of TV screens) and thus create "an automatic concert without distraction from shining dials or spinning turntables."[39]

In addition to enhancing the tidy, respectable appearance of ordinary houses, cabinets that hid stereo equipment and televisions allowed homeowners to control visual access to precious possessions that likewise conferred particular degrees of status. By restricting visual access to such material goods while simultaneously hinting at their presence through carefully designed cabinetry, homeowners could avoid the crass display of those shining dials and spinning turntables and could instead

The elegant construction above is the work of *Weingarten Electronics* of *Los Angeles, Calif.* The chest to the right of the speaker above is a storage bin for records; the chest to the left of the speaker (pictured close-up at the right of this caption contains changer, audio equipment and tape recorder. The system below (left), built by *R. L. Happ* of *Pass Christian, Miss.*, features a folded Hypex rear loading horn reinforced with concrete. The cabinetry below (middle) was done for *Mr. and Mrs. Robert Gammell* of *Kenmare, North Dakota.* The corner housing below (right) is another design of the *Olympic Engineering Co.*

Examples of entertainment walls. *High Fidelity,* January 1955, 41.

achieve the appearance of personal refinement considered necessary to the attainment of solid, white, middle-class respectability. Just as hiding the visible signs of labor enhanced the ideal of the nineteenth-century pastoral, so rendering technology invisible afforded a fuller sense of its midcentury and suburban counterpart.[40]

However, some industry insiders advocated hiding components for different, if equally powerful, psychological reasons. Noting that concealing equipment in the walls of the house could not be achieved unless the walls were at least sixteen inches thick—a condition seldom found in ordinary postwar houses—author Richard Roberts suggested that homeowners could conceal speakers by hanging tapestries or pictures over them, or they could construct "wall safes" to house the components, with swinging panels that would likewise blend with the rest of the wall. Speakers, he felt, should be heard and not seen, so that

> behind the false front lurks a hi fi system. . . . the maximum psychological effect of stereo reproduction can be achieved only when the source of sound is invisible. . . . When the source is obviously a mechanical-electrical contrivance, the psychological result of looking at it is a degradation of realism. . . . Why flaunt the artificiality of the reproduced music? Why not, rather, play down that aspect of it? . . . If the installation of speakers radically alters the decor of your home, the installation is wrong. Again, this is psychological in its implications. Upsetting the decor of your home, upsetting it to the point where you realize, every time you look at a room, that speakers are hidden somewhere and that those hidden speakers are the cause of the upset, can only serve to lessen your enjoyment of music. You must feel perfectly at home in your listening room; you must not be aware that it is a listening room.[41]

Psychological manipulation, then, creating the sensation of sound that appeared as if by magic and with minimal spatial intrusion or evidence of its sources, was thought to contribute to the experience of true aural fidelity, which likewise conveyed higher levels of social standing to those who could possess or create such authenticity. Visible components detracted considerably from the creation of the sonically situated residence.

Achieving this ideal, however, was not always easy in small houses. As noted above, wall thicknesses seldom allowed the built-in cabinets most publications and retailers advocated. Even where they might have, most homeowners could not afford the construction of such customized installation or had trouble squeezing stereo cabinets and entertainment walls into already-crowded rooms. If a closet was available, it might be converted to house components, but few residents of ordinary postwar houses could spare any of the little storage space provided by their new abodes.

## The Importance of Display

Perhaps as a result of this problem, by 1963 the publishers of *Stereo* began to promote a new "audio way of life," in which the goal was to achieve a domestic setting that was "at once interesting, relaxing, artistic and utilitarian." Although still promoting cabinetry that could contain or disguise equipment, they also touted the aesthetic quality of the components, describing the

> beauty and function [of] a handsome turntable that spins silently atop a marble, or richly grained wood surface; or the control of an amplifier or tuner, gleaming like an abstract sculpture under lamplight and suggesting the wondrous world of musical sound they control. . . . The materials and colors that are available today can change a room from simply a place surrounded by four walls to a setting that is not only acoustically and visually satisfying—but that expresses and exposes an interesting "you" to the world.[42]

Such cabinets then, fulfilled practical requirements, but they also promised a mid-century aesthetic of high-technological wonder, of industrial awe. As their contents glowed and spun, hi-fi cabinets could transform ordinary living rooms into fantastical, futuristic spaces, just as they held the potential to bestow distinction on their owners.

As homeowners struggled to accommodate the new systems in their homes spatially, both they and the trade publishers developed some comical contrivances. One author aimed to solve the spatial dilemma by advocating the use of kitchen cabinets to house components: "Concertos for the cook. Why not put something else in your kitchen cabinets besides pots and pans? Tuner, amplifier, control panel, player and speaker brighten up the daily chores with something slightly more esthetic than soap serials."[43] One *High Fidelity* reader found his own creative solution: unable to find an appropriate cabinet enclosure for his stereo system, he decided, upon consulting his wife, to place the system inside their oven: "It opened in two directions, it would hold all our equipment without bulging, when closed it resembled something else completely. The perfect answer to our problem."[44] Similarly, a 1955 *Popular Mechanics* article featured a design for an intercom and hi-fi system installation adapted from a clothes drying rack, so that the equipment would fit inside a tiny apartment.[45]

In addition to the spatial impact involved in housing stereo components, the new technology disturbed norms related to residential privacy. Stereos certainly afforded new opportunities for social interaction with family members, friends, and neighbors, who could be invited to listen, dance, or simply discuss the virtues of the technology itself. But they also generated concerns about the ability to isolate sound

"The Goldston all-range rollaway," a stereophile's comical solution to hidden storage for components in the average home. *High Fidelity,* June 1954, 15.

within the home. Stereo systems could create beautiful sound quality at high volumes, but the inhabitants of small houses could not always tolerate the invasion of sound into all their residential spaces. Noise control was a common problem in postwar homes, especially those designed with open plans or hard, modern surfaces that did little to muffle sound. Noises generated by appliances, radios, televisions, and stereos often disturbed family members who wished to read or study in other parts of the house. As the occupants of an open-planned house designed by the Berkeley, California, architect Roger Lee stated: "The house makes for great intimacy in living. In fact, no real privacy is possible. When we entertain on any scale, we park our son elsewhere for the night. Since one of us detests the accordion, it is safe for the other to practice only when he is alone in the house. Our son cannot very well have his friends in at the same time we have ours."[46] Stereos exacerbated these problems, leading to family frictions that were common enough to be addressed in popular magazines such as *Life,* in articles with titles like "Little Houses, Rasping Nerves."[47] In the *Mad Men* episode previously mentioned, the scene around the stereo console ends with Pete's wife admonishing him to turn the music down in order to avoid waking their sleeping infant. The new technology brought enormous pleasure and sociality to some, but it could also bring great annoyance vis-à-vis the deprivation of sonic privacy to others.

To solve this problem, one author recommended that "every stereophile have a headset around, if for no other reason than to be able to listen in privacy."[48] Other solutions for the attainment of "sonic privacy" included the installation of speakers that faced both the living room and the outdoor patio (which could, ostensibly, be sealed off from the house); the installation of a revolving television set that could be viewed from two rooms, so that music could be played in one while television was viewed in another; and the use of a remote control unit that would permit tuning from adjacent spaces.[49] Still, these solutions frequently failed because the powers of stereo amplification could easily overwhelm the dimensions of small homes, and families nationwide struggled to study or relax in quiet.

Acoustical privacy also functioned as an important marker of white, middle-class identities. A home in which particular sounds were appropriately contained was a respectable home, distinct from the noisy houses and streets that might be found in poor, overcrowded urban neighborhoods. Many postwar suburbanites keenly recalled the smells and noises associated with prewar and Depression-era domesticity for families who had not yet attained middle-class status. The ability to control the movement and quality of sound—and especially to create a special listening zone for one individual through the use of a headset—directly signaled both the white and middle-class identities quite literally required of owners of postwar suburban houses.[50]

Whether a high-fidelity stereo system was completely concealed within a custom-designed cabinet, accommodated on the shelves of a purpose-built entertainment center, or housed within a console large enough to accommodate a reclining basketball player, the possession of such a system conferred status on the owner. When Pete Campbell lifted the lid to reveal his hi-fi system and imagined the "tiny orchestra" within, he simultaneously revealed his family's production of a suburban identity. If moving to Cos Cob, or Levittown, or any other American suburb in the postwar era brought on an inevitable boredom and anomy so severe as to cause sophisticated urbanites like Don Draper to imagine "blowing their brains out," the tiny orchestra in the cabinet presented an equally sophisticated antidote. Just as mediated sound required accommodation into the physical space of the home, it simultaneously reshaped the cultural space of the house as a place where "dull" suburbanites could cultivate and exhibit their own cultural knowledge—the possession of a "good ear"—through their choice in music. Likewise, the technological prowess of their stereo permitted this respectable cultural achievement within the privacy of their own, safe homes, located at a calculated remove from the perceived turmoil of the city's more diverse populations.

## Notes

The author thanks Josh Kun, Gabriel Solis, and Matthew Thiebault for conversations that advanced this essay. She also thanks Madeleine Hamlin for editorial assistance.

1. *Mad Men* (2007–15) is a television series that portrays a twenty-first-century interpretation of U.S. cultural life in the 1960s.

2. Matthew Thibeault's in-progress research on John Sousa's recordings from the 1920s indicates that consumers were then likewise encouraged to have Sousa's band at their command. My thanks to Matthew Thibeault for this information.

3. On the relationship of ordinary postwar houses to the construction of white, middle-class identities, see Dianne Harris, *Little White Houses: How the Postwar Home Constructed Race in America* (Minneapolis: University of Minnesota Press, 2013).

4. Timothy Day, *A Century of Recorded Music: Listening to Musical History* (New Haven, Conn.: Yale University Press, 2000), 128.

5. The sound quality of many monaural recordings was quite good, even in the early 1900s, and some early stereo recordings were quite poor. Still, certain types of music were particularly hard to capture until the advent of stereo recording. Again, I thank Matthew Thibeault for this observation.

6. Day, *Century of Recorded Music*, 40, 55.

7. *House and Home*, May 1954, 134; "What Is Hi Fi?," in *High Fidelity Home Music Systems* (Los Angeles: Trend Incorporated, 1955), 11, 12. An article in *High Fidelity* in January 1955 noted that the magazine had acquired twenty thousand new readers in the past year. Although such statistics lack reliability, the article does provide some sense of the growth of popular interest in hi-fi and stereo systems. See Roy F. Allison, "Read Well before Shopping," *High Fidelity*, January 1955, 42.

8. G. A. Briggs, *Stereo Handbook* (Idle, Bradford, England: Wharfdale Wireless Works, 1959), 20.

9. U.S. Bureau of the Census, *Current Population Reports: Series P-65, Consumer Buying Indicators* (Washington, D.C.: Government Printing Office, 1966), 6, 10. Census Bureau data indicate that more than a half million radio-phonograph combinations were shipped to retailers in 1955, and that number more than tripled by 1965. U.S. Bureau of the Census, *Historical Statistics of the United States* (Washington, D.C.: Government Printing Office, 1975), 695–96. Data from 1962 indicate that in 1955, close to 400,000 radio-combination units sold, with double that number selling by 1960. U.S. Bureau of the Census, *Statistical Abstract of the United States* (Washington, D.C.: Government Printing Office, 1962), 815. Still, these statistics do not serve as precise indications of stereo/hi-fi system sales. Other surveys of manufacturing and industrial reports exist, but they provide production numbers rather than consumption statistics. My thanks to Mary Mallory, coordinator, Government Information Services, University of Illinois Library.

10. George Steiner, "The Retreat from the Word" (1961), in *Language and Silence* (London: Faber, 1967), 48–49.

11. Day, *Century of Recorded Music*, 58, 59.

12. Ibid., 55.

13. Theodor W. Adorno, *Essays on Music,* trans. Susan H. Gillespie (Berkeley: University of California Press, 2002), 27, 28; Theodor W. Adorno, "Analytical Study of the NBC Music Appreciation Hour," *Musical Quarterly* 78, no. 2 (Summer 1994): 355–56.

14. Max Horkheimer and Theodor W. Adorno, *Dialectic of Enlightenment,* trans. John Cumming (New York: Continuum, 1972), 120.

15. See also Fredric Jameson, "Reification and Utopia in Mass Culture," *Social Text* 1 (Winter 1979): 132; Richard Leppert, introduction to Adorno, *Essays on Music,* 47.

16. For examples of scholarship that reveal the highly varied and rich texture of suburban lives, see Dianne Harris, ed., *Second Suburb: Levittown, Pennsylvania* (Pittsburgh: University of Pittsburgh Press, 2010).

17. Walter G. Salm, *Stereo in Your Home* (Princeton, N.J.: Vertex, 1971), ix, 4.

18. See Sandy Isenstadt, *The Modern American House: Spaciousness and Middle-Class Identity* (New York: Cambridge University Press, 2006).

19. Raymond Williams, *Television: Technology and Cultural Form* (1974; repr., London: Routledge, 2003), 19, 20–21.

20. Lynn Spigel, *Welcome to the Dreamhouse: Popular Media and Postwar Suburbs* (Durham, N.C.: Duke University Press, 2001), 33, 45, 48.

21. Michael Bull, "Thinking about Sound, Proximity, and Distance in Western Experience: The Case of Odysseus's Walkman," in *Hearing Cultures: Essays on Sound, Listening, and Modernity,* ed. Veit Erlmann (Oxford: Berg, 2004), 181.

22. Ibid., 184.

23. Advertisement for Gateway to Music, *Arts and Architecture,* August 1953, 9.

24. Jonathan Sterne, *The Audible Past: Cultural Origins of Sound Reproduction* (Durham, N.C.: Duke University Press, 2003), 94, 95, 335.

25. For more on the creation of soundscapes and their relationship to twentieth-century public architecture, see Emily Thompson, *The Soundscape of Modernity: Architectural Acoustics and the Culture of Listening in America, 1900–1933* (Cambridge, Mass.: MIT Press, 2002).

26. The connection between men and hi-fi has received far more attention than hi-fi's impact on the daily lives of women. For a gender analysis of the impact of high-fidelity systems on residential space, see Keir Keightley, "Turn It Down! She Shrieked: Gender, Domestic Space, and High Fidelity, 1948–59," *Popular Music* 15, no. 2 (1996): 149–77. Keightley's analysis indicates that the world of high-fidelity and stereo was a largely male-dominated one. For another article that makes a similar case, see Marc Perlman, "Golden Ears and Meter Readers: The Contest for Epistemic Authority in Audiophilia," *Social Studies of Science* 34, no. 5 (October 2004): 783–807.

27. Louis Carlat points out that the "high-tech" aspects of radio and stereo initially placed them as male objects, something only men possessed the ability to tinker with and understand. For these technologies to become integrated into the home on a mass-market scale, they had to be packaged to appeal to women too, "recasting radio hardware as a feminine object, and listening as a feminine activity." See Louis Carlat, "'A Cleanser for the Mind': Marketing Radio Receivers for the American Home, 1922–1932," in *His and Hers: Gender, Consumption, and Technology,* ed. Roger Horowitz and Arwen Mohun (Charlottesville: University of Virginia Press, 1998), 116. Technology is now generally understood to participate in the construction of gender identities and in the construction of power. Men have historically been the predominant creators and designers of technology; women have been stereotyped as technologically incompetent. As such, home technologies have sometimes been seen as instruments of patriarchy. See Cynthia Cockburn, "The Circuit of Technology: Gender, Identity, and Power," in *Consuming Technologies: Media and Information in Domestic Spaces,* ed. Roger Silverstone and Eric Hirsch (London: Routledge, 1992), 32, 40, 41, 42. On the importance of stereo for women, see also Sonia Livingstone, "The Meaning of Domestic Technologies: A Personal Construct Analysis of Familial Gender Relations," in Silverstone and Hirsch, *Consuming Technologies,* 118, 123. Timothy Day has also aimed to balance the narrative about stereo being just for men. See Day, *Century of Recorded Music,* 63.

28. Thompson, *Soundscape of Modernity,* 2.

29. See, for example, Betty Jane Johnston, *Equipment for Modern Living* (New York: Macmillan, 1965), 251; Thomas H. Creighton and Katherine M. Ford, *Contemporary Houses Evaluated by Their Owners* (New York: Reinhold, 1961), 61.

30. The term *stereo imaging* refers to the spatial arrangement of sound sources in a room for maximum sound fidelity.

31. For one example, see Salm, *Stereo in Your Home,* 63, 151.

32. See, for example, the advertisement for Gateway to Music, *Arts and Architecture,* March 1950, 18.

33. This was the case with small retailers such as Weingarten Electronics, an operation that sold high-end stereo components and speakers out of a Melrose Avenue store in Los Angeles in the postwar era. Rudolf Weingarten, the proprietor of this operation, was my grandfather, so this information is based on personal observation of his work in the 1960s.

34. "Custom Installations," *High Fidelity,* June 1954, 36, 37.

35. "Stereo Décor in Four Modes," *Stereo,* 1961, 56–57, 70, 71.

36. "Sound Arrangements," *Stereo,* 1962, 39.

37. Harris, *Little White Houses.*

38. "Stereo Blends with the Modern Touch," *Stereo,* 1961, 49.

39. "Home Music Installations," in *High Fidelity Home Music Systems* (Los Angeles: Trend Incorporated, 1955), 33.

40. For more on the connections among built-ins, concealed technologies, and the construction of white, middle-class identities, see Harris, *Little White Houses*, 223–25.

41. Richard Roberts, *Hi Fi and Stereo: A Self-Instruction Guide to Assembly, Installation, and Maintenance in the Home* (New York: Collier Books, 1965), 148, 153, 154.

42. Phoebe Eisenberg, "Stereo Spells Décor: Attractive Settings for 3-D Sound," *Stereo*, 1963, 37, 43, 44. For another example of the promotion of the aesthetic value of stereo components, see Roberts, *Hi Fi and Stereo*, 136.

43. "Home Music Installations," 31.

44. John Goldston, letter to the editor, *High Fidelity*, June 1954, 13, 15.

45. "Sound in the Home," *Popular Mechanics*, March 1955, 164.

46. Quoted in Creighton and Ford, *Contemporary Houses*, 61.

47. "Little Houses, Rasping Nerves," *Life*, September 15, 1958, 60–63.

48. Roberts, *Hi Fi and Stereo*, 93.

49. Jack Lester, "Designing the High-Fidelity Music Room," *Arts and Architecture*, May 1953, 36, 37; advertisement for Gateway to Music, *Arts and Architecture*, May 1953, 7; "Radio, TV, Hi-Fi, Electronics Are Built-In Too!," *Popular Mechanics*, October 1960, 238.

50. For more on this, see Harris, *Little White Houses*, 114, 134, 142, 144–45.

# 19

# Suburban Noise

## *Getting inside Garage Rock*

STEVE WAKSMAN

Why should a high school boy's efforts to redesign his bedroom be considered newsworthy? This is the question that comes to mind regarding a February 11, 1968, article in the *Washington Post* on fifteen-year-old Robert Wilkoff's redesign of his bedroom into what reporter Ruth Wagner termed a "psychedelic den."[1] The son of interior designer William Wilkoff, young Robert transformed his room in the course of a single evening after being pressured by his parents to clean up the mess he had made in their downstairs recreation room, where he and the other members of his neighborhood rock band held their practices. Opting to move the offending materials upstairs to his bedroom, Wilkoff created a space in which posters and cutout magazine photos populated much of the available wall surface and the ceiling as well. Pictured in a photograph accompanying the short article, the walls and ceiling of Wilkoff's bedroom artfully juxtapose images of rock music luminaries such as Paul McCartney with advertising images for the likes of Gilbey's gin; a Campbell's soup can light fixture hanging from the ceiling suggests the young designer-musician's familiarity with Andy Warhol's pop art mixing of disparate cultural elements. Most prominent in the photo, however, is Wilkoff himself, who is shown sitting with electric guitar in hand. An accompanying photo features the young guitarist's amplifier alongside an incense burner, certifying that this teenage den of psychedelic delights is also—and perhaps especially—a space designed for making music, for privately savoring the pleasures of an amplified electric guitar.

When I first located this article about Robert Wilkoff, I was most struck by how much his bedroom reminded me of my own when I was growing up in the suburban town of Simi Valley, California, during the 1970s and 1980s. My tastes were less urbane than the young Wilkoff's appear to have been—there were no trappings of pop art on my walls or ceiling. Instead, there was an analogous dense layer of rock-and-roll posters, featuring an array of bands that together represented my deep affinity for hard rock and heavy metal music produced in the years from the 1960s to the 1980s. Oversized posters of Kiss and Led Zeppelin framed the larger collection of images, which also included Jimi Hendrix (represented twice), the Who, Santana, Def Leppard, Judas Priest, and Iron Maiden, among others. As appears to be the case for Wilkoff, these images were the visual corollary to the principal activities carried out in my bedroom apart from sleeping. Typically, when I was in my room, I was either listening to music or playing my electric guitar—often I was doing both at once. My bedroom, like Wilkoff's, was the site of a distinctly domestic kind of musicking.[2]

It might seem willfully perverse to begin an essay on garage rock with a discussion of music being made in bedrooms. However, as Wilkoff's example shows, there was often a direct line that connected the isolated bedroom musician and the young person playing in a band, rehearsing in a basement, recreation room, or garage. The one was in many ways a precondition for the other, and both types of musicking happened in the home. This basic insight is the foundation for one of the main arguments I want to pursue in this essay: garage rock emerged from the broader process through which rock music, and more specifically the *playing* of rock music, became a part of daily household life. That Wilkoff's band rehearsed in his family's recreation room and not in the garage is an indication of another point of more general significance: the labels "garage rock" and "garage band" are not to be taken too literally. Garage rock was just as likely to be made in basements or other outlying rooms of the house as in garages (and sometimes even in more central locations, like living rooms). This is not to say that the "garage" of garage rock is an entirely arbitrary designation, however. Garage rock's name—formulated in the 1970s as part of a retrospective effort to reevaluate a body of music produced in the middle years of the 1960s[3]—arises from the ambivalent character of the relationship between rock and domesticity, residing at home but not necessarily *in* the house; it also points to the gendered character of rock's domestic life by linking the music to a part of the house typically cast as a site of masculine pursuit.

The "garage" in garage rock also marks the phenomenon as one with strong ties to suburbia. Again, the connection is as much figurative as material. Bands that have been categorized as garage bands hail from a range of locations, urban and suburban alike. Garage rock's most influential chroniclers—1970s rock critics such as Greg Shaw, Lenny Kaye, and Lester Bangs, and latter-day documentarians such as Mike Stax and Alec Palao—have highlighted this regional diversity as one of its defining qualities.[4] Garage rock demonstrates that rock can come from anywhere, not just from major cosmopolitan areas such as New York or London, but from Seattle or San Jose or the Florida Panhandle.

Within the expansive geography of garage rock historiography, suburbia holds a special if peculiarly unspecified place. Not individual suburbs but suburbia in general has been deemed one of the preconditions for garage rock to flourish. Writing in the liner notes to the reissue of the pivotal garage rock anthology *Nuggets* (first compiled by Lenny Kaye and released by Elektra Records in 1972), Greg Shaw encapsulated the prevailing claim about garage rock demographics: "Families were moving out to the suburbs, and Mom and Dad were buying their kids a guitar or a drum kit and giving them a garage, where they could practice their *Play Guitar with the Ventures*."[5] More recent collections dedicated to music from the Los Angeles and San Francisco music scenes of the mid- to late 1960s have extended the logic of Shaw's observation by devoting whole discs to "suburbia" or to recordings from "beyond the city."[6] Suburbia matters to the history of garage rock because it is a location at once real and ideal that demonstrates one of the essential maxims of garage rock historiography: that rock music gave rise to a wide-ranging grassroots movement of young people who sought not only to consume the music but also to re-create it for themselves, even when they resided well outside the orbit of the mainstream music industry.

Why, though, should garage rock matter to the study of suburbia? Efforts to study the cultural life of suburbia have tended to have a strong bias toward visual rather than aural cultural forms. Film, television, and the designs of the houses themselves have more often been the focus of discussion than questions of how suburbia *sounded*, and how its residents used sound and music within their daily lives. Garage rock lets us listen to suburbia at a particular historical moment when the combined impact of British Invasion rock and resulting mass consumption of electric guitars and other musical instruments brought a new kind of noise into suburban homes and communities. Elsewhere in this collection, Dianne Harris (chapter 18) pursues similar ends in her investigation of the high-fidelity stereo system as a part of the mid-twentieth-century suburban home. By her account, there was great pressure to incorporate home stereo systems in such a way that they blended easily with prevailing ideas of domestic order, but the systems also facilitated the experience of "mobile privatization" and made the line separating private home and public space more porous. Garage rock went even further in rearranging key aspects of suburban domesticity. Attending to the ways in which garage bands made the home into a place of cultural production as well as consumption allows us to better grasp how suburbia functioned as an incubator for rock music's widespread diffusion as a cultural practice. The music made in the home, we shall see, was not contained there; rather, it became a vehicle through which the boundaries of suburban domesticity could be expanded.

Writing about the impact of television on American domestic life, Lynn Spigel has argued that the television set commonly displaced the piano as a central feature of the middle-class suburban living room. In the model homes used to sell the postwar version of suburban domesticity, Spigel notes, "the television set moved into the primary living spaces . . . where its stylish cabinets meshed with and enhanced the interior décor. The new 'entertainment centers,' comprised of a radio, television, and phonograph, often made the piano entirely obsolete."[7] This scenario resonates with larger anxieties surrounding mechanical reproduction and broadcast media in the twentieth century. Similar claims were made about the phonograph a half century earlier, with the underlying suggestion in both instances being that as the piano lost ground, Americans were being transformed from active agents of their musical leisure to passive consumers who listened or watched but did not play for themselves.[8]

Where the 1950s and 1960s were concerned, however, a different kind of shift was taking place. The declining centrality of the piano in American domestic life did not signal the disappearance of home-based amateur music making. Instead, it marked a shift of preference among amateur players away from the piano and toward other instruments, especially the guitar. This trend had been simmering for decades but began to truly take effect in the two decades following World War II—decades that, not coincidentally, also saw booming growth in the U.S. suburban population and the construction of suburban communities. A variety of factors contributed to the musical side of these developments. The near-simultaneous rise of rock and roll and the folk revival in the mid- to late 1950s stimulated unprecedented interest in the guitar, and guitar manufacturers such as Gibson and Fender responded with new, aggressive promotional strategies and groundbreaking innovations in design, especially as applied to the electric guitar, which gained growing currency throughout the decade.[9]

By the early 1960s, popular magazines and newspapers in the United States began to note the rising cultural visibility of the guitar. *Time* reported on the new prevalence of the instrument in 1962, informing readers of such signs of the times as the 400 percent increase in guitar sales at Eddie Bell's Guitar Headquarters in Manhattan during the past ten years and the current enrollment of some four hundred guitar students at the University of California at Berkeley.[10] More suggestive was a *Los Angeles Times* article from the same year by composer Elmer Bernstein, who claimed that contrary to fears that the proliferation of television and high-fidelity stereo systems would undermine domestic musical performance, "the great refinements in passive music—automatic record players, high fidelity, tape, motion picture dimensional sound and stereophonic sound—proved to be the instigators, not the deadeners, of home music."[11] One of Bernstein's informants, the manager of a large retail instrument store in Hollywood, opined: "I can sum up the current trend in musical instruments in one word—guitars. . . . Whole families come in and buy guitars. There must be family guitar combos all over the city."[12]

Such observations proliferated substantially in 1965. The intervening years had seen the folk revival continue to grow in its impact and youthful appeal, especially due to the mounting popularity of Bob Dylan. The Beatles (and the broader British Invasion of which they were a part) also had an important effect, dating from their February 1964 appearance on *The Ed Sullivan Show*. As the phenomenon termed "Beatlemania" by the national press took hold, guitar sales boomed. The first week of January 1965 brought news of the Fender guitar company's sale to the Columbia Broadcasting System (CBS) for $13 million, an event that both the *New York Times* and the *Boston Globe* took to be a landmark in the evolution of the guitar industry.[13] *BusinessWeek* offered a statistical breakdown of the guitar's rising stature, claiming, "Since 1960, sales [of guitars] have jumped from 420,000 units and $22-million retail sales to 1,065,000 units and $95-million retail sales."[14] Meanwhile, *Esquire* placed especial emphasis on the electric guitar as the driving force behind such swelling sales figures, presenting the instrument's capacity for noise as a powerful lure for teenage players.[15]

*Esquire*'s Peter Vanderwicken highlighted a further tendency that both stimulated guitar sales and resulted from them: young people could increasingly be found not just playing their instruments in isolation but also playing them in combination with others. That is, they were forming bands—the kinds of bands that would earn the designation "garage band" a decade or so later. Vanderwicken interviewed fifteen-year-old Bill Newman, a student at the Hotchkiss School in Connecticut who took up the electric guitar under the influence of his older brother and played in a band for fun and to make some extra money.[16] Writing in the *Washington Post* in September 1965, Nan Randall estimated that there were at least one hundred semiprofessional teenage bands in Washington, D.C., and the surrounding areas, and profiled seventeen-year-old drummer Rick Miller of local group the Chordones, from District Heights, Maryland. Describing a visit to the group's rehearsal space in the basement of Miller's home, Randall observed, "The listener has the feeling of being caught in the middle of an immense stereo speaker. The decibels are deafening."[17]

Within the next year or two, Randall's surprise at the rising tide of teenage music making would seem quaint, and the numbers that she reported to document such activity would be strikingly overshadowed. A March 1967 *Boston Globe* story on the phenomenon suggested that, according to a Denver booking agent, there were more than three thousand teenage rock-and-roll bands in the state of Colorado alone;

likely many more such bands in Massachusetts, taking the state's population into account; and more than three hundred thousand nationally based on information collected by the American Music Conference in Chicago.[18] These figures prompted the story's writer, Frederick Pillsbury, to exclaim that "there never was anything like the teenage band craze," a sentiment that seemed to be shared by a growing range of observers.[19]

Pillsbury also provided one of the most detailed and valuable overviews of such activity, viewed from the perspective of the greater Boston area, documenting the workings of two vital institutions—the battle of the bands and the teen nightclub—that emerged in conjunction with the rise of teen rock bands. Both settings established bridges between amateur and professional status for young musicians and provided a kind of public sphere in which these bands could find spaces to play outside the home and come into contact with audiences made up of their peers. The band battles documented by Pillsbury had grown not in Boston but in the South Shore town of Weymouth, where they began in 1963 as the creation of a member of the local Junior Chamber of Commerce, John Agnew Jr.; they soon evolved to have a statewide and even a national component, with twenty-seven states due to sponsor similar contests in 1967 and a national final to be held in Boston.[20] As a representative nightclub, Pillsbury presented the Surf in Nantasket Beach, another South Shore location, where auditions for new bands occurred weekly, drawing a continual stream of young hopefuls seeking a chance to play onstage for the club's capacity of eighteen hundred teenagers. Club owner William Spence, described as a Harvard Business School graduate, offered a vivid assessment of the conditions that made his club a success, as Pillsbury summarized:

> "A few years ago," said Spence, "you couldn't give away a live band." Records were the big thing then, but today's bands play the same music the kids hear on the records, which are the source of 99 per cent of their music. Most of the teenage band members are, to use Spence's term, "uneducated musicians" . . . and they learn the latest songs by listening to them over and over on the radio or the phonograph and then laboriously picking away until they have them down cold.[21]

Such were the terms whereby, according to Pillsbury, a "listening generation" was turning into a "playing generation," a formulation that matched Elmer Bernstein's assertion that the tools of "passive music" had become the instigators of a renewed impulse to make music, loudly, actively, and sometimes publicly.

If we return to Robert Wilkoff in his "psychedelic den," we are reminded that these public performances went hand in hand with considerable private effort. Yet the home's importance as a crucible of music making should not be understood as a strictly private affair. As historians of suburbia such as Lisa McGirr have shown that the home could be a key site of grassroots political organizing, so too was the domestic setting a site of musical activity that had both public and private dimensions.[22] Here the garage assumes importance as a part of the house that is not completely "inside," a space that mediates between the home and the surrounding neighborhood and so could be alternately private, public, or some combination thereof. Unlike the basement, an "underground" space that tends to have limited access to the outside, the garage is a point of exit and entry. Its utility as such comes through in this description by Tommy Ratchford, who worked as vocalist with the Pensacola, Florida, group the Laymen from summer 1966 to spring 1967. Ratchford recalls the garage where the Laymen practiced, attached to the home of his bandmate Bill Motley:

> Motley had converted the garage at his parents' house into a music/practice room by lining the walls and ceilings with egg carton dividers and placing several layers of carpet on the floor. He had a record player all connected to speakers scattered about for listening to new material and the garage door opened up for easy access and exit for the gear.[23]

The garage here becomes an ideal listening and performance setting, the egg cartons and carpet serving to damp the echo of the presumably unfinished space while the stereo equipment allowed the band members to concentrate on learning new material from the shared act of listening to favorite or popular records. Just as important, the oversized door of the garage allowed the band members to load in or out easily without having to travel through the more lived-in—and securely private—sections of the house.

That this aspect of the garage had more than practical importance can be gleaned from the recollections of Michael Isenberg, who spent his high school years playing in teen rock combos in Pekin, Illinois. Discussing his band the Mods, in which he sang and played guitar as a young teenager, Isenberg recounts:

> Although we started out practicing in [drummer] Rick [Durrand]'s parents' basement, in the summer we moved our gear into the garage. The level of excitement you could get back then just practicing was amazing; it would only be minutes before everyone in the neighborhood was crowded around the garage to watch. It was a new deal back then. The Beatles opened a floodgate and people weren't used to seeing kids with guitars. If you could play at all people were amazed and if you sang as well it was like winning the girl lottery.[24]

Isenberg further elaborates on the thin line between rehearsal and concert as he discusses the growth of the local rock scene:

> The band scene in Pekin, Illinois was growing like a weed. All sorts of bands started to spring up, practicing in their garages on nice days to get attention and a fan base. The different neighborhoods that had bands in them had a sort of "our band is better than your band" allegiance, though really everyone loved most all of the bands anyway. It was very like admiring your hometown sports team.[25]

Whereas Lynn Spigel has described the suburban living room in the age of television as a "home theater," following from Isenberg's account of his youthful music making, we can observe that the garage functioned as a different kind of home theater in these instances.[26] Unlike television, which brought aspects of the outside world into the domestic setting, the garage-as-theater projected a home-based performance outward, allowing others in the neighborhood to participate. One could locate in this theater the basis for a kind of community, but any community that may have derived from garage rock was defined as much by whom it excluded as by whom it bound together. This is because, also unlike television, which was promoted in connection with an idealized version of family togetherness that Spigel terms the "family circle," the garage embodied the fragmentation of space along lines of age that suburban architecture encouraged. Like a teenager's bedroom, the garage could function as a space apart from the rest of the family for the home's young residents, but one that also facilitated the effort to reach beyond the house rather than withdraw into it.

It is hard to know just how common the kind of experience described by Isenberg was. I have found few other accounts that so clearly depict the garage as an intensely localized analogue to more squarely public performance venues like the teen nightclubs described above. However, there is a tantalizing piece of photographic evidence that both supports Isenberg's account and gives further cause for curiosity. The image appears on the cover of a 2000 reissue of recordings by Parma, Ohio's the Alarm Clocks, one of the hundreds upon hundreds of 1960s era bands who released lone singles in their careers as recording artists and otherwise passed into obscurity until rediscovered by the sonic archivists who have given garage rock its enduring reputation.[27] In the photo, the three members of the Alarm Clocks appear performing on guitar, bass, and drums. The drummer and his set are within an open garage; standing in front of the garage space, on either side of the open door, are the guitarist and bass player, whose amplifiers appear just outside the garage behind them. Most strikingly, they have an audience. Since the photo is taken from within the audience, it is impossible to know just how many were watching this particular garage show, but we can see six listeners, with the photographer making seven. Perhaps the most unusual detail is the apparent age of those watching and listening: four of the six look to be not teenagers but small children, under ten years of age. Was this a typical garage rock audience when the music appeared in its neighborhood habitat? Was garage rock not so squarely a teenage phenomenon as has been widely thought, but something with a broader and younger sort of appeal? The evidence is far from conclusive, but it indicates that whoever was present, garage rock functioned in such instances as a unique hybrid of private pastime and public spectacle.

To offer more of a close-up perspective on the lives of such bands, I want to turn to a final example. Children of the Mushroom was a band formed in March 1967 in Thousand Oaks, California, as an offshoot of an earlier band called the Captives. My interest in the band stems from geography: Thousand Oaks is next to Simi Valley, where I was born and raised. Both towns are suburbs on the southeastern edge of Ventura County, adjacent to the northern boundary of Los Angeles County. Children of the Mushroom was part of a surprisingly thriving local rock scene that arose in Ventura County in the middle and later years of the 1960s that also included another Thousand Oaks band, California Grassfield, and the Simi Valley band the Humane Society. Drummer Dennis Christensen Swanson and other members of Children of the Mushroom began keeping a blog in 2005 to help musicians of that place and time reconnect and share memories, and so the group's doings are better documented and more accessible than those of many comparable regional bands from around the United States. Children of the Mushroom issued only one "official" record in its time, a single featuring the songs "You Can't Erase a Mirror" and "August Mademoiselle," which enjoyed a small measure of chart success and has since become something of a collector's item.[28]

As members of first the Captives and then Children of the Mushroom, Swanson and his bandmates—including guitarist Jerry McMillen—did in fact do most of their rehearsing in a garage.[29] While they do not seem to have used the garage as a performance venue in the manner of Michael Isenberg's Mods or the Alarm Clocks, the semiprivate character of the garage helped them discover a new member, keyboardist Bob Holland. In Swanson's words:

In December of 66 the Captives were practicing in the garage at my house (we played so loud with Al's Fender amp & Jerry['s] Vox amp) when a kids [sic] with glasses rode up on his bike & stated he wanted to be in the band. So we went over to Bob Holland's home & he proceeded to make our jaws drop when he sat down [and] played The House of the Rising Sun, with a bass line on foot pedals.

We told him we wanted him in the band. He came with a new Vox keyboard & Silvertone amp.[30]

In the larger community, the members of the Captives and later Children of the Mushroom received particular support from the Conejo Car Wash, where several local musicians worked. Swanson remembers: "Since our bands didn't generate the funds for us our job there allowed many of us to buy equipment & cars. Along with the hard work we were able to keep up with all the band & girl gossip."[31] Asked where they tended to perform, the band members describe a mix of area high schools, recreation centers and household parties. Jerry McMillen lists "high school and teen dances, free concerts, outdoor festivals, Battle of the Bands, flower happenings," adding that "we received invitations to play all over Ventura County and beyond." One of the band's biggest shows was at the local California Lutheran College (now California Lutheran University), where they played on a bill that also featured the band Sweetwater, who would appear at the landmark Woodstock rock festival in 1969.[32] The few concert flyers posted on Swanson's blog bear out the existence of such a county-based regional circuit, with one flyer advertising a concert at Newbury Park High School, another promoting a show at the Agoura Teen Center, and a third announcing the appearance of a clutch of local bands (the Bleu Forest, the California Grassfield, and the Union Bookstore, along with the Mushroom—as Children of the Mushroom began to call themselves) at a "free outdoor rock festival" at Steckel Park in the town of Santa Paula.

Conventional wisdom might lead us to believe that if the suburbs were home to a significant amount of rock-related musical activity, those young suburban players would still have had to travel to the surrounding cities to get any real exposure or be part of a genuine scene. Pop culture historian Domenic Priore pursues this line of argument in his detailed account of the history of rock on Hollywood's Sunset Strip in the mid-1960s. Although he pays considerable attention to the efforts of musicians from the greater Los Angeles area—and includes a brief discussion of Children of the Mushroom—he also portrays the Strip as the central urban space where the diverse local strains of Southern California rock would eventually meet. As Priore claims: "It has always been natural for people to congregate in the center of a city. Suburbs offer no cultural content, so the youth of post-war LA made the Sunset Strip their public epicenter."[33] There is much truth to this perspective, and indeed the story of Children of the Mushroom bears it out to a degree. For the band's lone recording session in a professional studio, the members had to caravan to the Hollywood recording studio dubbed Nashville West, a small independent studio that had also been used by one of their biggest influences, the psychedelic, proto-metal band Iron Butterfly.[34]

Yet the story of Children of the Mushroom also demonstrates that suburban rock groups of the 1960s did not have to make their way into the city to find places to play outside the home. According to the recollections of the band's members, there were plentiful places to play within the boundaries of Ventura County, a county that has no single metropolitan center, being defined rather by its proximity to Los Angeles. High schools, teen centers, and public parks—these were the places where a kind of public sphere emerged for suburbia's young residents, motivated by their desire to play, listen, and dance to rock music. Moreover, bands like Children of the Mushroom and their hundreds upon hundreds of counterparts spread across the United States, proving the wrongheadedness of Priore's suggestion that suburbia lacked cultural content. Rather, garage rock might instead be perceived as one of suburbia's most significant indigenous cultural forms.

While public space in the suburbs has typically been depicted as homogeneous and highly subject to private control—the suburban shopping center standing as a paradigmatic development—garage rock provides a different lens through which we might consider the interrelationships between public and private leisure in suburbia.[35] In this connection, the garage emerged as a space that was itself not fully private and that functioned at times as a sort of home or even neighborhood theater where the noise of youth could begin to draw wider notice. Yet the blurring of the boundaries between public and private experience went further than that. Here again the comparison with television is instructive. Radio and recordings, mass-media forms parallel to television, typically motivated even the most solitary music making that happened in the home. All of these forms of media brought significant elements of the outside world into the home, but television in the 1950s and 1960s did not give rise to a comparable impulse among viewers to re-create televised content for themselves or for others. Aspiring rock musicians blurred the lines between amateur and professional performance, and they used the home as a launching pad for music making that often moved into more broadly public arenas but also already had something of a public character even when situated at home. In doing so, they exhibited the degree to which public and private spaces and modes of performance were not strictly separated but were instead deeply implicated with one another. It is not just that domestic garage rock performance was influenced by music that circulated widely and publicly, but that garage rock was often driven by the aspiration to make music publicly even while playing it privately.

Garage bands of the 1960s made rock into an intensely localized form. Bands of suburban, urban, and rural youth did not just passively absorb and consume music produced from afar—they sought to reproduce that music for themselves. Sometimes, perhaps most of the time, their efforts amounted to little more than pale imitations of the recorded "originals," but on occasion they gave rise to work of surprising originality in which the existing terms of rock music were not radically reinvented but were creatively rearranged. In this, rock music assumed a status something like the suburban landscape as architectural historian John Archer has analyzed it: a "tabula not-quite-rasa on which to undertake multiple and diverse acts of individuation."[36] Like the suburban homeowners discussed by Archer, garage rock players used the resources they acquired (guitars, drums, amplifiers, and records) to ends that were far from predetermined. That so much of this music was made in suburbia indicates that what many critics have taken to be the dark underside of the suburbs—the selling of a dream of plenitude and self-realization accessible through acts of consumption that ultimately promote homogeneity—had a crucial flip side. Garage rock disturbed the peace of suburban consumption even as it resulted from consumer habits, and it demonstrated that in the suburbs, buying music and making music went hand in hand.

## Notes

1. Ruth Wagner, "Bob Psychs His Room," *Washington Post,* February 11, 1968, E2.
2. The term *musicking* here is taken from Christopher Small's important work, in which the term connotes a focus on music as performed social practice, as opposed to the emphasis on music as fixed artistic work that characterizes so much musicological scholarship. See Christopher Small, *Musicking: The Meanings of Performing and Listening* (Hanover, N.H.: Wesleyan University Press, 1998).
3. I should clarify that I am mainly concerned with garage rock as a phenomenon of the 1960s. There has been a notable garage rock revivalist movement active since the 1980s that has adopted and to some degree redefined the connotations of the term. For a study of more recent trends in garage rock, focused on Detroit, Michigan, see Eric James Abbey, *Garage Rock and Its Roots: Musical Rebels and the Drive for Individuality* (Jefferson, N.C.: McFarland, 2006).
4. Greg Shaw edited the pivotal rock fanzine *Who Put the Bomp!*—later renamed *Bomp!*—which ran from 1970 to 1979 and arguably did more than any other single publication to define and document the garage rock phenomenon. Much of the content of *Who Put the Bomp!* has been reprinted in two recent overviews: Suzy Shaw and Mick Farren, eds., *Bomp! Saving the World One Record at a Time* (Pasadena, Calif.: Ammo Books, 2007); Suzy Shaw and Mike Stax, eds., *Bomp! 2: Born in the Garage* (La Mesa, Calif.: Bomp/Ugly Things, 2009). Lenny Kaye published widely as a rock journalist in the 1970s and assembled the classic anthology of garage rock *Nuggets*, referenced below, before joining as a guitarist with singer/poet Patti Smith to form the Patti Smith Group. Lester Bangs was one of the most distinctive and outrageous voices in 1970s rock criticism until his death in 1982; some of his most important writing on garage rock can be found in his collection *Psychotic Reactions and Carburetor Dung*, ed. Greil Marcus (New York: Alfred A. Knopf, 1987). Mike Stax began publishing the fanzine *Ugly Things* in 1983 and has been central to the revival of interest in documenting the history of garage rock that has taken root in the past three decades. Alec Palao is a music writer and record producer who has overseen the reissue of several anthologies of music from the 1960s, with a particular emphasis on music of California.

5. Greg Shaw, "Sic Transit Gloria . . . : The Story of Punk Rock in the '60s," in *Nuggets: Original Artyfacts from the First Psychedelic Era, 1965–1968* (Los Angeles: Rhino Records, 1998), 19. Shaw's use of "punk rock" here gestures toward the complex interrelationship between "punk rock" and "garage rock," a topic that is beyond the scope of this essay. For more on this subject, see Bernard Gendron, *Between Montmartre and the Mudd Club: Popular Music and the Avant-garde* (Chicago: University of Chicago Press, 2002), 232; Steve Waksman, *This Ain't the Summer of Love: Conflict and Crossover in Heavy Metal and Punk* (Berkeley: University of California Press, 2009), 50–66.

6. *Love Is the Song We Sing: San Francisco Nuggets, 1965–1970* (Burbank, Calif.: Rhino Records, 2007); *Where the Action Is! Los Angeles Nuggets, 1965–1968* (Burbank, Calif.: Rhino Records, 2009).

7. Lynn Spigel, *Make Room for TV: Television and the Family Ideal in Postwar America* (Chicago: University of Chicago Press, 1992), 38.

8. On the reception of the phonograph, see Mark Katz, *Capturing Sound: How Technology Has Changed Music,* rev. ed. (Berkeley: University of California Press, 2010). For more on the changing position of the piano in American life in the early years of the twentieth century, see Craig Roell, *The Piano in America, 1890–1940* (Chapel Hill: University of North Carolina Press, 1991).

9. On changes in postwar popular music and the advent of rock and roll, see Charlie Gillett, *The Sound of the City: The Rise of Rock and Roll,* rev. ed. (New York: Pantheon, 1983); Philip H. Ennis, *The Seventh Stream: The Emergence of Rocknroll in American Popular Music* (Hanover, N.H.: Wesleyan University Press, 1992); Reebee Garofalo, *Rockin' Out: Popular Music in the U.S.A.,* 5th ed. (Boston: Prentice Hall, 2011). On the folk revival, see Robert Cantwell, *When We Were Good: The Folk Revival* (Cambridge, Mass.: Harvard University Press, 1996). On the rise of the electric guitar as a commercial and cultural force in American music, see Steve Waksman, *Instruments of Desire: The Electric Guitar and the Shaping of Musical Experience* (Cambridge, Mass.: Harvard University Press, 1999).

10. "String 'em Up," *Time,* January 5, 1962, 46.

11. Elmer Bernstein, "Young People Learning Music by Doing, Not Just Listening," *Los Angeles Times,* November 11, 1962, A3.

12. Quoted in ibid., A7.

13. Clare M. Reckert, "C.B.S. Acquires Guitar Concern," *New York Times,* January 5, 1965, 54; "What's Your Pleasure, Baseball or Guitars?," *Boston Globe,* January 7, 1965, 37.

14. "Guitars Hit a Cashbox Crescendo," *BusinessWeek,* May 8, 1965, 155.

15. Peter Vanderwicken, "The Big Noise," *Esquire,* July 1965, 39.

16. Ibid., 38.

17. Nan Randall, "They're Beating Out a New Tempo," *Washington Post,* September 12, 1965, F29.

18. Frederick Pillsbury, "The Playing Generation Is Really Plugged In," *Boston Globe,* March 5, 1967, B6–B7.

19. Ibid., B7.

20. Ibid., B9.

21. Ibid., B11.

22. Lisa McGirr, *Suburban Warriors: The Origins of the New American Right* (Princeton, N.J.: Princeton University Press, 2001).

23. Tommy Ratchford, "Pensacola Groups of the 1960's," 60sgaragebands.com, accessed December 9, 2014, http://www.60sgaragebands.com. The website 60sgaragebands.com, which is largely the work of rock historian Mike Dugo, contains one of the most extensive archives of original interviews and historic recordings by regional rock bands of the 1960s available.

24. "Michael Isenberg and the Pekin, Illinois Scene," 60sgaragebands.com, accessed December 9, 2014, http://www.60sgaragebands.com.

25. Ibid.

26. Spigel, *Make Room for TV,* 99–135.

27. Alarm Clocks, *Yeah! Savage 1966 Ohio Garage Raunch!* (New York: W. W. Norton, 2000).

28. "You Can't Erase a Mirror" was listed in *Billboard* magazine as a "best leftfield happening" in March 1968, when it stirred significant interest after being picked up for airplay on a radio station in El Paso, Texas. *Billboard* applied the designation "best leftfield happening" to "a record by a new artist or one who hasn't had a hit recently that is getting most requests and sales in [an] area." "Programming Aids," *Billboard,* March 23, 1968, 28.

29. Details regarding the band's history come from an interview by Mike Dugo with Swanson, McMillen, and bassist Al Pisciotta posted at the web archive Beyond the Beat Generation, an adjunct of 60sgaragebands.com, http://home.unet.nl/kesteloo/childrenmushroom.html.

30. Quoted in Klemen Bleznikar, "Children of the Mushroom Interview with Dennis Christensen Swanson," It's Psychedelic Baby!, September 3, 2011, http://psychedelicbaby.blogspot .com.

31. Dennis Swanson, "Phil Hareff Reminiscing at Band Tree III August 2009," Thousand Oaks Rock Bands—Stories of Our Times, September 3, 2009, http://bandtreereunion.blogspot .com.

32. Dugo, interview with Children of the Mushroom.

33. Domenic Priore, *Riot on Sunset Strip: Rock 'n' Roll's Last Stand in Hollywood* (London: Jawbone Press, 2007), 254.

34. Dugo, interview with Children of the Mushroom.

35. On the mall or shopping center as the linchpin of the suburban public sphere, see Lizabeth Cohen, *A Consumers' Republic: The Politics of Mass Consumption in Postwar America* (New York: Vintage, 2004), 257–89.

36. John Archer, *Architecture and Suburbia: From English Villa to American Dream House, 1690–2000* (Minneapolis: University of Minnesota Press, 2005), 337.

# 20

# The Complex

## Social Difference and the
## Suburban Apartment in Postwar America

MATTHEW GORDON LASNER

In 1959, the *Los Angeles Times* published a series of articles on hundreds of small new apartment complexes going up in the city's South Bay district. This section of town, straddling the San Diego Freeway between Los Angeles International Airport and the Port of Los Angeles, had remained semiagricultural until World War II and the arrival of airframe contractors. In the 1940s and 1950s developers filled much of the area with modest low-slung tracts of detached houses. But by the late 1950s, the *Times* noticed "a building boom never before seen": "Everywhere you go . . . you are greeted by construction of new apartment houses." Low-rise and medium density, with parking lots and landscaped common spaces, they were creating "a new look for the area," a departure from the sea of single-family stucco and grassy lawn.[1]

Underlying the trend, the reporter speculated, was a shift in living preferences. Rather than buy houses inland, where space and land prices still accommodated new low-cost subdivisions, families, he suggested, were making new choices. Turned off by the declining air quality and intense summer heat, they were opting for places closer to the ocean with "cool ocean breezes and [a] comparatively smog-free climate," even if this meant an apartment. A second factor identified was proximity to the major aircraft and missile plants—that is, families were trading American Dream houses for shorter commutes.[2]

In reality, few families chose South Bay apartments for these reasons. In fact, few chose apartments at all. The surge, rather, was the result of social and economic shifts that stimulated two robust new market segments for housing beginning in the fifties and early sixties: well-pensioned "oldsters" enjoying comfortable, independent retirements; and, especially, a burgeoning cohort of well-educated and -employed singles, young men and women living out on their own before marriage. These

343

Venetian Isle Apartments, 13926 Cordary Avenue, Hawthorne, California, circa 1959. A generic wood frame and stucco box, the complex announced itself with an exotic name, decorative signs, and stone trim. A swimming pool in the first of two interior courts (not shown) was visible from the street through plate-glass front doors. Gates at the parking area (shown open, at left; perhaps added later) offered residents a measure of security. Photograph by the author, 2012.

relatively novel kinds of households neither wanted nor needed single-family houses. The apartments, which promised a carefree and convivial atmosphere without long-term commitment, catered to them.[3]

## The Complex Culture

The rise of postwar garden apartments of the type visited by the *Times* was both a social and a physical phenomenon. As recently as the forties, "unattached" people— whose ranks, one sociologist imagined in 1947, were characterized by the never married as well as by immigrants, "homeless men," traveling salesmen, and prostitutes— clustered in city centers, much as they had done since the nineteenth century. They made their homes mostly in single-sex hotels, YMCAs, rooming and lodging houses, and spare bedrooms. Those who were older and unattached might live with adult children or in dedicated institutions such as sanatoriums and rest homes.[4]

High city housing costs meant relatively few individuals, before or after the war, could afford to maintain homes of their own, let alone in up-to-date buildings. Indeed, only the most privileged among them had ever had their own places. Cities saw many apartments for small households, especially in the Roaring Twenties, but overall they were rare, even in the largest, richest centers like Manhattan.[5]

As the ranks and financial resources of the unattached and elderly grew after World War II, and once the postwar housing emergency subsided, developers began to recognize these groups as important clients. Unlike before the Great Depression, however, the bulk of new housing for them was concentrated not in rented rooms with collective housekeeping but in apartments, which offered complete self-contained homes. An equally big change was that in lieu of city-center apartment *houses* production shifted to *complexes*: lower-density groups, often with multiple buildings arranged on a parklike campus, the physical form of which was defined more by voids—around, within, and sometimes below (for parking)—than by mass.[6]

A major advantage of this type was cost: garden-apartment complexes could be built and rented (or sold) for less than city-center buildings with no sacrifice of privacy, amenity, or comfort. Peripheral sites were, by definition, less valuable than

Encino Royale, 4733 Haskell Avenue, Encino, California, 1958–59; CBS Construction, developer. Like other suburban building types (and unlike apartment houses, in the form of vertical masses rising from the sidewalk), complexes were defined physically and visually by voids, including those for swimming pools, courtyards, front and side setbacks, and driveways. The residences (forty one-bedroom and twenty two-bedroom apartments in this San Fernando Valley complex), parking (top right), common facilities, and management offices enclosed these common spaces. Rendering by C. Ruffino, circa 1958. Courtesy of University of Southern California, on behalf of the USC Libraries Special Collections.

central ones. Construction was also cheaper, since complexes were low- or mid-rise and therefore exempt from rigorous fire codes. Like postwar nuclear families, older and younger households found they could afford more, and better-quality, shelter in peripheral sections like the South Bay.[7]

Of yet greater importance than cost was culture. Lower-density edges were where more and more postwar singles and seniors preferred to live. Ordinary families may not have shifted to apartments in the 1950s as imagined by the *Times*, but smaller, older, and younger households were rapidly embracing suburbia. Two reasons, as the newspaper suggested, were fresh air and access to jobs. Also critical were anxieties about race, crime, and physical safety in the context of accelerating migration of black and Hispanic families to city centers. Among the first mass-market gated communities in the United States, in the late fifties and early sixties, for example, the preponderance were large-scale multiple-family complexes.[8]

More generally, the appeal was that by midcentury, middle-class Americans of nearly every cohort understood suburbia, with its autocentricity, visually controlled environments, physical privacy, and proximity to nature, as the up-to-date way to live. As one tenant outside Atlanta explained, he chose his 1960s complex because he liked the rental manager, the apartment looked out on a river, and there were "horses in a field next door."[9] A contemporary survey found that what suburban tenants valued most in their homes apart from "guards and other protective devices" were "recreation facilities" and "panoramic view[s] of hills or water."[10] And as an urban planner specializing in the study of the "new garden apartment" concluded, the type was thriving because "the qualities that people desire in a residence—open space, tranquility, privacy, security, recreation—are to be found in suburbs in greater abundance then elsewhere."[11]

## Suburban Difference

The rise of the complex, which by the twenty-first century constituted a third of housing in U.S. suburbs, represents an important but overlooked turn in the evolution of the American metropolis.[12] Since the nineteenth century suburbs have been synonymous with marriage, child rearing, and the detached house.[13] As one man reported in the 1930s, "I lived in Greenwich Village till I married. Then I needed a kitchen so I moved uptown in Manhattan. When the first baby came we moved to the suburbs. I suppose we'll go back to the city when they are all grown up."[14]

Over the past generation, as the United States has become majority suburban, new realities have come into focus: suburbia as a rich and varied social and physical terrain, home to the poor as well as the affluent, black as well as white, new immigrant as well as native-born. As manifest in work by Jodi Rios (chapter 12), Willow Lung-Amam (chapter 13), Trecia Pottinger (chapter 2), and others in this volume

Riverbend Club Apartments, 6640 Akers Mill Road Southeast, Atlanta, Georgia, 1966–69; Lincoln Property Company Number 9 (principals: Trammell Crow, Ewell G. Pope Jr., Frank Carter Jr.), developer; Richard Vignolo of Lawrence Halprin and Associates, site planning; Jerry Cooper of Cooper, Salzman and Carry, architect. A chief appeal of the complex was access to nature. Riverbend, with architecture that embraced a contemporary rustic language, was built on sixty-five wooded acres along a picturesque curve of the Chattahoochee River and included wooded nature trails, a pine grove, and a lake. Rendering by Cooper, Salzman and Carry. Courtesy of Jerry Cooper.

and elsewhere, new narratives have emerged, and scholars have begun to explore ideas of suburbia as a place of difference as well as conformity, as the site of ethnic tension and assimilation, and as a natural home of American Dream houses but also of shopping, leisure, and work.[15]

For all the popular and scholarly interest in the multiplicity of suburban lives and land uses, however, in one fundamental respect we continue to imagine suburbia much as we did in the mid-nineteenth century: a space, above all else, for social reproduction. Mainstream suburban architecture and neighborhood planning, from the grassy lawn to the McMansion, with their emphasis on physical, social, and visual isolation and control, reflect this priority. So too does the cultural currency of common suburban social stereotypes, from the organization man to the soccer mom.[16]

Yet just as department stores, office buildings, African Americans, and China-towns have joined the white middle class in suburbia, so too have other kinds of households: younger and older families, single people, divorced families, and, as Tim Retzloff documents in chapter 4 of this book, gay men and lesbians. By the millennium suburbia housed more identities and offered more choices than conventional city centers, with their extremes of racialized poverty on one hand and hypergentrification on the other.

This chapter introduces some of these other suburban lives through other suburban architectures. Although physical form is an imperfect proxy for social mixture, by and large need shapes design. Many widows, single professionals, and childless gay men live in single-family houses; many nuclear families live in apartment and "townhouse" complexes. As a rule, however, physical diversity follows social. And it was the multiple-family complex, with its greater range of unit sizes (including small sizes), freedom from the burdens of physical and yard maintenance, unique mixture of privacy and community, and greater capacity to accommodate itinerancy, that best accommodated difference. In the space permitted, I will introduce the first generation of mass-market complexes, which were built between the late 1950s and early 1970s, and examine the lives of some of their tenants.

My chief argument is simple: in the postwar United States, suburbia became home not just to a majority of families; it became the *preferred,* and most frequent, home of nearly all other Americans too. This idea that Americans chose suburbia is contentious. For decades, scholars and pundits have emphasized the ways in which government and business directed housing behavior toward specific, often conservative, ends. They have suggested that tax codes, modern systems of mortgage underwriting, and the antiurban whims of policy makers precluded metropolitan patterns from responding to social change and diverted growth from cosmopolitan centers to the privatized periphery.[17] I am skeptical of such claims.[18] To the contrary, I believe the complex reveals diversity and flexibility in housing. More important, it suggests the all but universal appeal of the suburban environment in this era.

## Precedents and Prototypes

Physically and, to some degree, socially, the postwar complex represented the culmination of a century of experimentation. Suburbs had long catered to middle-class families, but never exclusively. In several cities philanthropic developers built courtyard complexes for workers in outer sections.[19] In Southern California bungalow courts were built for seasonal visitors but also for workers and single women.[20] In metropolitan New York a range of innovative multiple-family types appeared at the beginning of the twentieth century in places like Bronxville, in Westchester County. In the 1920s this trend accelerated, with apartment colonies appearing in suburban sections of every larger U.S. city. Many tenants preferred suburbia but could not afford to buy a whole house given available financing. Others, especially older, younger, and smaller households, had little use for houses.[21] As one suburban builder reported, his tenants were "women and older people who cannot maintain their own properties or who do not want to tend furnaces or climb stairs."[22]

Although little housing of any type was built during the thirties, the New Deal included provisions crucial to the expansion of the complex after World War II. Generations of housing reformers had frowned upon the "congested" city apartment as un-American and hoped to see government encourage families of ordinary means to live at lower densities at the urban periphery. The most radical proposals envisioned a full third of the nation rehoused in low-rent suburban garden-apartment complexes financed by the federal government. Political compromises, however, reduced this program to a small system of inner-city public housing for the very poor.[23]

Public housing was accompanied, however, by a provision for "large-scale" housing in the National Housing Act of 1934. This established the Rental Housing Division at the Federal Housing Administration (FHA), which operated by helping developers of high-quality, moderate-rent apartments secure financing from private lenders. Some projects were done in city centers, including many in elevator buildings. But this type had been greatly overbuilt in the twenties. Moreover, it was expensive to construct. Instead, the agency directed attention to lower-cost suburban variants that better met reformers' social goals as well as new public tastes. In 1935, FHA staff helped pioneer a new kind of "garden apartment": a complex, patterned on a small handful of experiments by architects Clarence Stein and Henry Wright, of two- and three-story walk-up buildings arranged around spacious green courts as on a college campus. The type proved immensely popular. Applications for leases far surpassed capacity, even as city-center buildings languished. Scores of FHA projects, with tens of thousands of units, were built in the late thirties; hundreds of thousands more went up during the war and amid the housing crisis that followed. By the early fifties the American apartment had become suburban.[24]

## The New Demographics

Through the early postwar period the typical garden-apartment dweller was a middle-class family awaiting a house. As production of single-family tracts caught up to demand by the mid-1950s, most left. This was especially true outside metropolitan New York, where, by contrast, high housing costs, Jewish communalism, and robust tenant-directed housing laws like rent control made multiple-family living a more frequent long-term choice.[25]

New demand for suburban apartments, however, came from new kinds of households, including those of "oldsters" and young professionals. The postwar period saw rapid expansion of both groups as part of a larger long-term shift in how, and with whom, Americans lived. The nuclear family had replaced the extended family as a norm in the early twentieth century. In concert with rising wealth, better education, and birth control, household size had decreased dramatically. At the same time, consumption of housing soared for most Americans, in both quantity and quality. These trends continued after World War II.[26]

More crucially, increasing numbers of people were living on their own, independent of family and institutions of collective living. The elderly were living longer and enjoying more robust pensions, including Social Security benefits. Meanwhile, a relaxing of social codes freed young men and, especially, women to enjoy an extended postadolescence. Marriage rates, divorce rates, and ages of marriage and childbearing ebbed and flowed, but by the 1960s the overwhelming trend was toward liberation of the individual. Rising wages, falling production costs in housing, and the surge in white-collar employment that accompanied the rise of the service economy further stimulated the trend toward living alone.[27]

As these changes were unfolding, the nation's center of gravity shifted toward suburbia and the Sunbelt. Older city centers, disorderly before the Depression, became drab by the fifties. With the stigmas of obsolescence and decay came stigmatized populations, especially poor African Americans migrating from the rural South. The concentration of racialized poverty, in turn, intensified social dysfunction. Middle-class singles and seniors began to join the exodus to the metropolitan edge. The number of singles in suburbs nationally nearly doubled in the sixties (the total suburban population, by comparison, grew by less than 40 percent). In the Washington, D.C., area, nearly half again as many singles lived in Maryland and Virginia as in the District by 1970; in Boston half the apartments outside Route 128 were occupied by singles, half of whom were under age thirty.[28]

## Resort Environment

Singles and seniors had housing needs that were different from those of the nuclear families who had long dominated the market for new housing. Early complexes, like many single-family subdivisions, included schools and playgrounds; some had pedestrian greenways to protect children from automobiles. Retirees, by contrast, required space for social activities; for them leisure was paramount. For younger people it was sex. For both this meant greater emphasis on shared social spaces than on private ones. Developers jettisoned the generic garden-apartment idea for new types, including the retirement complex and the "adult" or singles (by the mid-sixties, "swinging singles") complex for young professionals. Both barred children.

Programming was critical to the identities of these new dwelling types. Senior communities were engineered to enrich residents' lives at an important moment of transition. Out of the workforce and living in a new place—often a new region—tenants needed things to do and new friends to do them with. Builders who anticipated this dynamic pioneered the idea of the "active retirement" community. The first was Sun City, Arizona, announced in 1959. An equally influential prototype was Leisure World in Orange County, California, begun in 1961. These kinds of complexes were structured around shared facilities for activities such as golf, tennis, lawn bowling, and shuffleboard and had expansive clubhouses. Some included medical clinics, libraries, and classrooms for university extension courses. Streets were made safe for residents to travel by golf cart. Homes were designed for easy upkeep. Life resembled that in a resort, and the atmosphere was festive and invigorating, while also unequivocally suburban.[29]

Sun City, Arizona, 1959–61; Del Webb, developer. "Wake Up & Live!" with the Sun City Merry Makers in a Memorial Day parade. To attract retirees and single people, complexes promised tenants conviviality, in part through programming that offered a new hybrid of resort and suburban living. Sun City, the first master-planned large-scale complex built specifically for older families, marketed itself as an "active retirement" community. Photograph by Ralph Crane/Time & Life Pictures/Getty Images.

At complexes appealing to postadolescents enjoying historically high wages with historically few family obligations, conviviality was equally essential. Young men and women busy with careers (many recently relocated to new towns for jobs) also found themselves lonely, especially in an era when other kinds of suburban community institutions, such as the megachurches Charity R. Carney describes in chapter 15 of this volume, were still nascent.[30] Halfway between "a campus for single people" (as one resident put it) and a cul-de-sac, the complex served as post-baccalaureate, coed fraternity house.[31]

If the raison d'être of conventional suburbia was social reproduction (child rearing), that of adult complexes was reproduction. Alongside fern bars and discos, they came to fulfill the crucial social role that matchmakers and church dances had done for earlier generations, albeit with large quantities of beer and, by the sixties and seventies, drugs. "Living in an apartment house," declared the *Los Angeles Times* as early as 1959, "is not only a source of shelter but a new social outlet." In particular, the article continued, apartment houses had "blossomed into good hunting grounds for marriage seekers."[32]

Especially important in this endeavor was the pool. As the *Times* explained, the pool was "a must for modern apartments. And not a small one, at that. It must be big enough to hold a bang-up swim party for all the tenants."[33] Nights and weekends, it continued, "the tenants find themselves camped around the swimming pool. It's not unusual to see practically every tenant bringing food out at dinner time and participating in a potluck."[34] Tenants socialized away from the complex, too, organizing ski trips and hikes.[35] But the pool served as the primary stage for the "close association of all the tenants," where "everyone gets to know one another during hot week ends."[36]

By the sixties and seventies it was not uncommon to find complexes with multiple pools—even in the Northeast and Midwest—along with saunas, gyms, snack bars, and tennis courts. Club facilities, sometimes including pools, also appeared in city-center and high-rise buildings, but it was in low-slung districts where the emphasis on physical culture, the body, and the outdoors was most evident. In cosmopolitan centers such as Manhattan and Chicago bachelors represented by figures like Hugh Hefner lived (or aspired to live) in high-rise pads and took out single "girls" like Helen Gurley Brown to supper clubs. In the Sunbelt and in suburbia tenants prioritized informal poolside get-togethers with bathing suits and barbecues.[37]

Unfortunately, not everyone was at the party. Early tenants at Atlanta's leading complex, for example, recall no African American neighbors. Although I have found no evidence to suggest suburban complexes were more segregated than city apartment houses or other kinds of neighborhoods, homogeneity of race, as of class and life-cycle stage, was clearly a hallmark.[38]

South Bay Club, 20900 Anza Avenue, Torrance, California, 1965; R&B Development, developer; Robert H. Skinner of Ternstrom & Skinner, architect. Tenants and a refrigerator full of beer at a private house party in one of the complex's apartments. Complexes offered young adults an environment free of the moral guardianship of older dwelling types like the single-sex residential hotel, as well as the private spaces necessary to experiment with new, more liberal social norms. Photograph by Arthur Schatz/Time & Life Pictures/Getty Images.

South Bay Club, Torrance, California. A defining feature of the complex was shared space for recreation and socializing, and a defining feature of complex life was the impromptu get-together in and by the pool. Tenants got to know one another around pools and hot tubs, where it was easy to shed inhibitions. Complex design arranged apartments around these recreational spaces, further encouraging interaction by enticing tenants to join the fun. Photograph by Bill Ray/Time & Life Pictures/Getty Images.

## Designing for Difference

In basic physical form the first complexes for seniors and singles differed little from earlier garden apartments. Well into the 1960s many were barracks-like in site plan, with simple structures of wood frame and stucco (or brick veneer, depending on the region) with mass-produced aluminum-frame windows. They were distinguished from wartime examples chiefly in their use of decorative trim and richer landscaping.

As the first baby boomers left home in the late sixties and early seventies, robust competition for their affections—and those of their parents—prompted many improvements. The sixties saw ever greater attention to common spaces like pools and clubhouses, while older garden-apartment plans evolved into row-type "townhouses," such as the ArdSpring Condominiums discussed by Pottinger in chapter 2 of this volume, which offered more individuality and privacy for each unit. By the seventies a variety of more playful—sometimes to the point of disorienting—formulas emerged, with units arranged either as apartments or as row houses in

Il Pompeii Apartments, 3655 Artesia Boulevard, Torrance, California, 1963; CalProp Investments (principal: Victor Zaccaglin), developer. Most postwar complexes comprised repetitive groups of simple buildings clad in painted stucco (or, east of the Mississippi River, brick), with aluminum-frame windows. Prototypes built for families during the post–World War II housing emergency often resembled barracks. To cater to singles and seniors in the more prosperous early 1960s, developers softened economical construction with landscaping. Typical elements included flowering ground cover, trees, and curvilinear footpaths. Photograph by the author, 2013.

small clusters connected by networks of pedestrian paths. Suburban multiple-family housing in this era became one of the most exciting fields in American architecture and urban design.[39]

Advancements were also made in the planning of individual units. Early garden apartments had been imagined for conventional kinds of households: couples (one bedroom, one bath) and young families (two bedrooms, one bath). These arrangements worked for seniors but not for singles. Young men in professions like aerospace engineering could afford to rent places alone, but almost everyone else had to share, with two, three, or even four unrelated adults in a single one-family apartment.

To accommodate this relatively novel dwelling practice while upholding middle-class standards for personal space, storage, and hygiene, landlords began including extravagances previously unimagined in mass-built multiple-family housing, such as powder rooms and walk-in closets.[40] By the late sixties a whole new unit type appeared, the double-master or "super two-bedroom," which featured a yet more radical plumbing luxury: a full bathroom for each bedroom.[41]

These adjustments were especially helpful to women. Women earned far less than men, and, even in the age of *Ms.*, they tended to have more concerns about living on their own, for reasons of both physical safety and propriety.[42] (Landlords also addressed this issue in nonarchitectural ways, through lavish landscaping, which suggested attentive management, and by employing women as resident managers and activity directors.)[43]

## The Complex Evolves

After its efflorescence in the sixties and seventies the complex entered a more mature phase. Senior communities remained popular while becoming less exuberant in design and programming and more modest in scale. Early critiques prompted developers to spend more generously on architecture and site planning. This, coupled with overproduction in the seventies followed by a poor economy, all but hobbled the format for many years. In the eighties and nineties, however, it revived, despite the popularity of alternatives such as aging in place and the emergence of the NORC (naturally occurring retirement community).[44] Half a century after they first appeared, early examples like Sun City and Leisure World remain stable while new ones, like the fictional Heron Bay Estates discussed by Martin Dines in chapter 6 of this book are thriving.

The adult complex, by contrast, all but disappeared, replaced by new kinds of all-purpose, all-age suburban multiple-family developments, mostly in the form of townhouse groups or, since the nineties, well-equipped mid-rise buildings like the Orange County Palazzo and "Texas doughnut" types, which included elevators, parking decks, and other embellishments that broadened their appeal to a larger range of households beyond twenty-somethings.[45]

A proximate reason for the withering of the singles complex was revisions to the Fair Housing Act in 1988 that outlawed prohibitions against children in housing, with the exception of senior communities.[46] More important were cultural and demographic shifts. The number of young people fell in the yuppie eighties and even more in the Generation X nineties. These smaller cohorts, resentful of living in the shadow of the baby boom and facing diminished economic opportunities, never aspired to dedicated complexes. To the contrary, many saw the idea as artificial. Meanwhile, middle-class Americans, especially young adults, became increasingly interested in city-center living. Gentrification dated to the 1920s and had gained momentum—and much attention—in the sixties and seventies alongside

Sorelle Apartments at Lindbergh, 2399 Parkland Drive NE, Atlanta, Georgia, 2009. In the 1980s and 1990s, after a decade of experimentation, complex design grew more restrained and standardized. Prevailing physical forms included the townhouse and the mid-rise elevator building. By 2000, a common variant became the Texas doughnut; courts were occupied, in part, by multistory parking decks, giving access to units directly from parking spaces. At Sorelle Apartments, one of the two main courts contains parking and the other the pool. Photograph by the author, 2011.

the explosive rise of the complex. But only in the nineties did the city-center countertrend became mainstream.[47] Well into the new millennium many young people continued to prefer suburbia to the city center, but the emphasis on the edge was less complete than for the preceding generations.[48]

## Epilogue: Old Complexes, New Difference

Given their rapid cultural obsolescence, the first wave of mass-market complexes—especially those for singles—may have had their most enduring impact in the relationships commenced poolside, and their offspring. But these projects have had another important legacy: as filtered, or secondhand, housing for new groups, including the kinds of families once all but excluded from suburbia.

By the eighties and nineties metropolitan poverty had become exacerbated by the decentralization of jobs on one hand and racialized resistance to affordable housing in suburbs on the other. It was precisely at this moment, however, that twenty-somethings of the sixties and seventies became marrieds-with-children and moved into houses. Cast off by yuppies, these zones of youthful white privilege transformed into homes for new, highly diverse populations, becoming enclaves for economically marginal groups, including African American and new immigrant families.[49]

This reoccupation of complexes with new groups of difference has not been simple, or uncontested. Lack of public transit and facilities for pedestrians has

Royale Apartments, 3593 Buford Highway Northeast, Atlanta, Georgia. Complexes were designed for tenants with automobiles. Those without must negotiate a difficult urban landscape often lacking in sidewalks and crosswalks and serviced infrequently by public transit. Livery shuttles (dollar vans) augment public bus service, while pedestrians force unpaved pathways along landscape buffers. Photograph by the author, 2011.

proved a challenge for tenants without cars. Where zoning allows it, some apartments have been repurposed as corner stores. Swimming pools threatened unsupervised children, prompting many complexes to drain them. Lawns and courts have given over to slides and swing sets.[50]

These changes have struck some as a loss. In the 1990s, as one complex underwent the first of two multimillion-dollar renovations to accommodate "playgrounds, school buses, and families," it was reported that "for baby boomers . . . they might as well be tearing it down." For longtime tenants and, especially, nostalgic former tenants, the alterations, which included conversion of the clubhouse into a leasing office, "turned a good thing bland."[51] But for new tenants, the refashioning of these spaces offered a critical opportunity to begin to realize their own American Dreams. From L.A.'s South Bay to Houston to Boston, complexes became crucial sources of low-rent housing and, in many places, new ethnic villages. Viva the complex.

## Notes

1. Herbert Jay Vida, "Building Boom, Bay Story: Vacant Lot Today—an Apartment House Tomorrow," *Los Angeles Times*, July 19, 1959, A10. On southern Los Angeles County, see Greg Hise, *Magnetic Los Angeles: Planning the Twentieth-Century Metropolis* (Baltimore: Johns Hopkins University Press, 1997); Becky M. Nicolaides, *My Blue Heaven: Life and Politics in the Working-Class Suburbs of Los Angeles, 1920–1965* (Chicago: University of Chicago Press, 2002); D. J. Waldie, *Holy Land: A Suburban Memoir* (New York: W. W. Norton, 1996).

2. Vida, "Building Boom."

3. These clienteles have rarely been discussed in histories of the postwar United States. For their treatment in studies of the prewar era, see Paul Groth, *Living Downtown: The History of Residential Hotels in the United States* (Berkeley: University of California Press, 1994); Joanne J. Meyerowitz, *Women Adrift: Independent Wage Earners in Chicago, 1880–1930* (Chicago: University of Chicago Press, 1988); Howard Chudacoff, *The Age of the Bachelor: Creating an American Subculture* (Princeton, N.J.: Princeton University Press, 1999).

4. Arnold M. Rose, "Living Arrangements of Unattached Persons," *American Sociological Review* 12, no. 4 (August 1947), 431. On seniors, see Norman D. Ford, *Norman Ford's Florida: A Complete Guide to Finding What You Seek in Florida* (Greenlawn, N.Y.: Harlan, 1954).

5. Elizabeth Collins Cromley, *Alone Together: A History of New York's Early Apartments* (Ithaca, N.Y.: Cornell University Press, 1990); Matthew Gordon Lasner, *High Life: Condo Living in the Suburban Century* (New Haven, Conn.: Yale University Press, 2012), chaps. 1–2.

6. Lasner, *High Life*, chaps. 3–5; John Chase and John Beach, "The Stucco Box" (1983), in John Chase, *Glitter Stucco and Dumpster Diving: Reflections on Building Production in the Vernacular City* (New York: Verso, 2000); Anne Vernez Moudon and Paul Mitchell Hess, "Suburban Clusters: The Nucleation of Multifamily Suburban Areas of the Central Puget Sound," *Journal of the American Planning Association* 66, no. 3 (Summer 2000): 243–64.

7. Carl F. Horowitz, *The New Garden Apartment: Current Market Realities of an American Housing Form* (New Brunswick, N.J.: Center for Urban Policy Research, Rutgers University, 1983), 36–41; Chase and Beach, "Stucco Box."

8. On concerns about safety, see Charles Bethea, "Hoochie Koo," *Atlanta*, November 2009, 98; Robert Schafer, *The Suburbanization of Multifamily Housing* (Lexington, Mass.: Lexington Books, 1974), 106; Charles E. Dole, "Single Persons Seek Housing Identity and Avoid 'Singles' Pitch," *Washington Post*, February 8, 1975, E44.

9. Fred Pape, quoted in John McCosh, "The Remake of Riverbend," *Atlanta Constitution*, May 9, 1992, B1.

10. Schafer, *Suburbanization of Multifamily Housing*, 119.

11. Horowitz, *New Garden Apartment*, 35.

12. Data from Paul Mitchell Hess, "Rediscovering the Logic of Garden Apartments," *Places* 17, no. 2 (Summer 2005): 30.

13. John R. Stilgoe, *Borderland: Origins of the American Suburb, 1820–1939* (New Haven, Conn.: Yale University Press, 1988), 98; John Archer, *Architecture and Suburbia: From English Villa to American Dream House, 1690–2000* (Minneapolis: University of Minnesota Press, 2005), chap. 4; Robert Fishman, *Bourgeois Utopias: The Rise and Fall of Suburbia* (New York: Basic, 1987); Kenneth T. Jackson, *Crabgrass Frontier: The Suburbanization of the United States* (New York: Oxford University Press, 1987), introduction, chaps. 3–5.

14. Quoted in George A. Lundberg, Mirra Komarovsky, and Mary Alice McInerny, *Leisure: A Suburban Study* (New York: Columbia University Press, 1934), 175–76.

15. For an overview, see Andrew Blauvelt, "Preface: Worlds Away and the World Next Door," in *Worlds Away: New Suburban Landscapes*, ed. Andrew Blauvelt (Minneapolis: Walker Art Center, 2008). See also Kevin M. Kruse and Thomas J. Sugrue, eds., *The New Suburban History* (Chicago: University of Chicago Press, 2006).

16. Examples of innovative suburban histories that still privilege the house include Hise, *Magnetic Los Angeles*; Nicolaides, *My Blue Heaven*; Kevin M. Kruse, *White Flight: Atlanta and the Making of Modern Conservatism* (Princeton, N.J.: Princeton University Press, 2005); Matthew D. Lassiter, *The Silent Majority: Suburban Politics in the Sunbelt South* (Princeton, N.J.: Princeton University Press, 2006); Archer, *Architecture and Suburbia*; Richard Harris, *Unplanned Suburbs: Toronto's American Tragedy, 1900–1950* (Baltimore: Johns Hopkins University Press, 1996); Andrew Wiese, *Places of Their Own: African American Suburbanization in the Twentieth Century* (Chicago: University of Chicago Press, 2004).

17. Jackson, *Crabgrass Frontier*; Lizabeth Cohen, *A Consumers' Republic: The Politics of Mass Consumption in Postwar America* (New York: Alfred A. Knopf, 2003); Thomas W. Hanchett, "The Other 'Subsidized Housing': Federal Aid to Suburbanization, 1940s–1960s," in *From Tenements to the Taylor Homes: In Search of an Urban Housing Policy in Twentieth-Century America*, ed. John F. Bauman, Roger Biles, and Kristin M. Szylvian (University Park: Pennsylvania State University Press, 2000).

18. For arguments offered by other skeptics, see Herbert J. Gans, "Urbanism and Suburbanism as Ways of Life," in *People, Plans, and Policies: Essays on Poverty, Racism, and Other National Urban Problems* (New York: Columbia University Press, 1991); Mary Corbin Sies, "North American Suburbs, 1880–1950: Cultural and Social Considerations," *Journal of Urban History* 27, no. 3 (March 2001): 313–46; David Steigerwald, "All Hail the Republic of Choice: Consumer History as Contemporary Thought," *Journal of American History* 93, no. 2 (September 2006): 385–403; Archer, *Architecture and Suburbia*; Robert Bruegmann, *Sprawl: A Compact History* (Chicago: University of Chicago Press, 2005); Blauvelt, "Preface."

19. Richard Plunz, *A History of Housing in New York City* (New York: Columbia University Press, 1990); Roy Lubove, "I. N. Phelps Stokes: Tenement Architect, Economist, Planner," *Journal of the Society of Architectural Historians* 23, no. 2 (May 1964): 75–87.

20. Dolores Hayden, *The Grand Domestic Revolution: A History of Feminist Designs for American Homes, Neighborhoods, and Cities* (Cambridge, Mass.: MIT Press, 1981), 237–50; Stefanos Polyzoides, Roger Sherwood, and James Tice, *Courtyard Housing in Los Angeles* (Berkeley: University of California Press, 1982).

21. John Taylor Boyd Jr., "Garden Apartments in Cities, Part I," *Architectural Record* 48 ( July 1920): 52–74; John Taylor Boyd Jr., "Garden Apartments in Cities, Part II," *Architectural Record* 48 (August 1920): 121–35; Plunz, *History of Housing in New York City*, 117–21, 204–5; *Architectural Record,* apartment house issue (March 1928); Lasner, *High Life,* chaps. 2, 3, 6.

22. Herbert Emmerich, "The Problem of Low-Priced Cooperative Apartments: An Experiment at Sunnyside Gardens," *Journal of Land and Public Utility Economics* 4, no. 3 (August 1928): 233.

23. D. Bradford Hunt, "Was the 1937 U.S. Housing Act a Pyrrhic Victory?," *Journal of Planning History* 4, no. 3 (August 2005): 195–221; Gail Radford, *Modern Housing for America: Policy Struggles in the New Deal Era* (Chicago: University of Chicago Press, 1996); Alexander von Hoffman, "The End of the Dream: The Political Struggle of America's Public Housers," *Journal of Planning History* 4, no. 3 (August 2005): 222–53.

24. Laura Bobeczko and Richard Longstreth, "Housing Reform Meets the Marketplace: Washington and the Federal Housing Administration's Contribution to Apartment Building Design, 1935–40," in *Housing Washington: Two Centuries of Residential Development and Planning in the National Capital Area,* ed. Richard Longstreth (Chicago: Center for American Places, 2010); Joseph B. Mason, *History of Housing in the U.S., 1930–1980* (Houston: Gulf, 1982), 67–69; Hanchett, "Other 'Subsidized Housing'"; Larry R. Ford, "Multiunit Housing in the American City," *Geographical Review* 76, no. 4 (October 1986): 360–407; Schafer, *Suburbanization of Multifamily Housing,* 6–7.

25. On transience, see Marvin Caplin, "Trenton Terrace Remembered: Life in a 'Leftists Nest,'" *Washington History* 6, no. 1 (Spring/Summer 1994): 62–63; Ellen Dunham-Jones and June Williamson, *Retrofitting Suburbia: Urban Design Solutions for Redesigning Suburbs* (Hoboken, N.J.: John Wiley, 2009), 32–33; William H. Whyte Jr., *The Organization Man* (New York: Simon & Schuster, 1956). On New York, see Lasner, *High Life,* chap. 4; Deborah Dash Moore, *At Home in America: Second Generation New York Jews* (New York: Columbia University Press, 1981), 15–16, chap. 2.

26. Mason Doan, *American Housing Production: A Concise History, 1880–2000* (Lanham, Md.: University Press of America, 1998); Dowell Myers and John Pitkin, "Demographic Forces and Turning Points in the American City, 1950–2040," *Annals of the American Academy of Political Science* 626, no. 11 (November 2009): 91–111; Horowitz, *New Garden Apartment,* chap. 1.

27. Eric Klinenberg, *Going Solo: The Extraordinary Rise and Surprising Appeal of Living Alone* (New York: Penguin, 2012); Loretta Lees, Tom Slater, and Elvin Wyly, *Gentrification* (New York: Routledge, 2008), 92–93; Horowitz, *New Garden Apartment,* 23–33.

28. Schafer, *Suburbanization of Multifamily Housing,* 115; Mason, *History of Housing in the U.S.,* 77–78; Jay Mathews, "Suburbs and Single Person," *Washington Post,* July 20, 1972, F1. On stigma, see Loïc Wacquant, *Urban Outcasts: A Comparative Sociology of Advanced Marginality* (Cambridge: Polity Press, 2008), chap. 6.

29. Judith Ann Trolander, *From Sun Cities to the Villages: A History of Active Adult, Age-Restricted Communities* (Gainesville: University Press of Florida, 2011); Lasner, *High Life,* chap. 6; John M. Findlay, *Magic Lands: Western Cityscapes and American Culture after 1940* (Berkeley: University of California Press, 1992), chap. 4; Paul O'Neil, "For the Retired, a World All Their Own," *Life,* May 15, 1970, 45–50.

30. On loneliness, see Mathews, "Suburbs and Single Person." On singles complexes, see Matthew Gordon Lasner, "Swingsites for Singles: New Housing for New Households in Mid-century America," *Places Journal* (October 2014), http://www.placesjournal.org.

31. Bill Domenico, quoted in Bethea, "Hoochie Koo," 97.

32. Herbert Jay Vida, "It's Friendship: Apartment House Offers Dweller Both Shelter and Social Outlet," *Los Angeles Times,* July 26, 1959, CS3. See also Vida, "Building Boom."

33. Vida, "Building Boom." On pools, also see Horowitz, *New Garden Apartment,* 18–19.

34. Vida, "It's Friendship."

35. Vida, "Building Boom."

36. Vida, "It's Friendship."

37. Elizabeth Fraterrigo, "The Answer to Suburbia: *Playboy*'s Urban Lifestyle," *Journal of Urban History* 34, no. 5 (July 2008): 747–74; Bill Osgerby, "The Bachelor Pad as Cultural Icon: Masculinity, Consumption and Interior Design in American Men's Magazine, 1930–65," *Journal of Design History* 18, no. 1 (2005): 99–113.

38. Bethea, "Hoochie Koo," 98; McCosh, "Remake of Riverbend."

39. On design of Southern California complexes, see Chase and Beach, "Stucco Box"; Matthew Gordon Lasner, "Own-Your-Owns, Co-ops, Town Houses: Hybrid Housing Types and the New Urban Form in Postwar Southern California," *Journal of the Society of Architectural Historians* 68, no. 3 (September 2009): 378–403. On design more generally, see Lasner, *High Life,* chap. 5; Doan, *American Housing Production,* chap. 5.

40. Derek Thompson, "How Roommates Replaced Spouses in the 20th Century," *Atlantic,* September 3, 2013, http://www.theatlantic.com; Vida, "Building Boom"; Vida, "It's Friendship."

41. Peter C. Papademetriou, "Magnificent Fountains, Beautiful Courtyards," in *Culture and the Social Vision,* ed. Mark A. Hewitt, Benjamin Kracauer, John Massengale, and Michael McDonough (Philadelphia: Graduate School of Fine Arts, University of Pennsylvania, 1980), 132–33.

42. Vida, "Building Boom"; "How an Apartment Builder Taps the Young-Singles Market," *House and Home,* September 1969, 98–101.

43. David Goldberg, "Man of Action," *Atlanta Constitution,* February 22, 1999, 1E; "Much More than Garden-Type Apartments," *BusinessWeek,* March 14, 1970, 146–47; Kent Hansen Wadsworth, "Brand Marketing Apartments," *Journal of Property Management,* March–April 1997, 44–49.

44. Fredda Vladeck, "Aging in Place: Shaping Communities for Tomorrow's Baby Boomers—Naturally Occurring Retirement Communities (NORCs)," in *Baby Boomers: Can My Eighties Be Like My Fifties?,* ed. M. Joanna Mellor and Helen Rehr (New York: Springer, 2005); Michael E. Hunt and Gail Gunter-Hunt, "Naturally Occurring Retirement Communities," *Journal of Housing for the Elderly* 3, nos. 3–4 (1986): 3–22.

45. On the Texas doughnut—a typology that includes a multistory parking deck within one of the complex courtyards—see Brian O'Looney and Neal Payton, "Seeking Urbane Parking Solutions," *Places* 18, no. 1 (2006): 40–45.

46. On the impact of the Fair Housing Act, see "Metro in Brief," *Atlanta Constitution*, October 30, 1991, E2. For a broader discussion of the exclusion of children in housing, see, for example, Gretchen Walsh, "The Necessity for Shelter: States Must Prohibit Discrimination against Children in Housing," *Fordham Urban Law Journal* 15, no. 2 (1986): 481–532.

47. On the history of gentrification, see Suleiman Osman, *The Invention of Brownstone Brooklyn: Gentrification and the Search for Authenticity in Postwar New York* (Oxford: Oxford University Press, 2011); Lees et al., *Gentrification*. On tension between revived interest in city living and the popularity of the complex, see Horowitz, *New Garden Apartment*, 43n13.

48. Gregg Logan, "RCLCO Forecast: Does the Housing Market Still Want the Suburbs?," *The Advisory*, April 30, 2012, http://www.rclco.com.

49. Dunham-Jones and Williamson, *Retrofitting Suburbia*, 30–33, 89–90; Susan Rogers, "Superneighborhood 27: A Brief History of Change," *Places* 17, no. 2 (Summer 2005): 36–41; Roy Vu, "Retaining the Home Not the Homeland: The Significance of Vietnamese Ethnic Identity in Houston's Village Communities" (paper presented at the Fourth Biennial Conference of the Urban History Association, Houston, November 5–8, 2008); Drew Kane, "Immigrant Communities: Transforming the Buford Highway Strip," in *Building Metropolitan Atlanta: Past, Present and Future*, ed. Jonathan Lerner (Atlanta: Atlanta Chapter of the Congress for the New Urbanism, 2010), 54–56; Chenoa A. Flippen and Emilio A. Parrado, "Forging Hispanic Communities in New Destinations: A Case Study of Durham, North Carolina," *City & Community* 11, no. 1 (March 2012): 1–30.

50. "Blueprint America Special Report: Crossing the Line," video, PBS, July 23, 2010, http://www.pbs.org; Dunham-Jones and Williamson, *Retrofitting Suburbia*, 30–31; Rogers, "Superneighborhood 27"; Hess, "Rediscovering the Logic of Garden Apartments," 33–34; Moudon and Hess, "Suburban Clusters," 251–53.

51. McCosh, "Remake of Riverbend."

# 21

# The Outdoor Kitchen and Twenty-First-Century Domesticity

BEVERLY K. GRINDSTAFF

The credit-rich late twentieth and early twenty-first centuries allowed for the rise of a broad spectrum of new consumer habits. In suburban America, homeowners realized newly enabled tastes in lavish professional, owner-designed, and do-it-yourself (DIY) remodeling projects. Chief among their architectural and interior design modifications was the "outdoor kitchen," an amorphous, wall-less room with varying dimensions, appliances, and functionalities sited in what one owner-designer identified as "the previously underutilized space of the backyard." By 2009, this new room had been installed in more than a million American households; by 2012, it had survived the Great Recession and related housing crisis to become a feature the National Association of Home Builders (NAHB) reports is requested by one in three prospective suburban homeowners. Currently free of restrictive traditions, the outdoor kitchen is determined by and gives form to diverse but intersecting discourses of homeownership, changing gender relations, televised programs that fuse celebrity and the act of cooking, the "obesity epidemic," and the elevation of food from mere nutrition to a source of novelty and entertainment. The outdoor kitchen is a new arena of suburban sociodomestic performance, the built environment of the contemporary American Dream.

## "The Kitchen Can't Be Contained Anymore"

In the late nineteenth-century Manhattan described by Edith Wharton's *Age of Innocence*, social standing was measured—and generated—by the elaborate ceremony of the formal dinner. The "heavy brown-stone palaces" of the New York elite were activated by the engraved invitation, hothouse gloxinias, and expensive food prepared by hired chefs and distributed on fine china by professional servers. The entire social ritual elevated the animal necessity of eating into a grand choreography of manners and status that progressed in accordance with season and gender from reception hall to drawing room, dining table, and various libraries and studies for cigars, gossip, and flirtation.[1] The kitchen remained the unseen mechanism at its core.

The early twenty-first century found the kitchen not merely visible but moved into central focus. In 2003, the Builder's Choice national survey of home builders, contractors, and architects featured the kitchen in three of the top ten residential trends. (The survey has been hosted since 1981 by *Builder* magazine, flagship publication of Hanley Wood, the leading supplier of national housing market data.)[2] *Builder* editor Boyce Thompson explained that the "family kitchen," trend number five, is "where families entertain; it's where they spend quality time together. We're seeing more kitchens designed for activities" unrelated to food preparation, such as homework, television viewing, and laundry folding. "Wetrooms," ranked eighth, marked a similar change to residential space. These plumbed adjuncts "pop up all over the house" such that "cabinets, sinks, and mini-refrigerators are showing up in family rooms, master suites, libraries, and basements."[3] The assigned functionality of other rooms gave way as household commissariat proliferated throughout the home. A 2002 *Time* cover story noted the demise of the living room and concomitant emergence of the kitchen as symbolic center of both house and family:

> The kitchen can't be contained anymore, so it blends into that large live-eat-play space often called a great room, which connects through glass doors to the outside space. . . . The idea is to allow family togetherness and personal space at the same time, meaning never having to reach a consensus about what to do together.[4]

The propensity of these "live-eat-play" spaces to continue their sprawl was represented by trend number four, the "great outdoors." This general category defined a broad array of features and "inspired outdoor architecture" intended to facilitate "great indoor/outdoor relationships."[5] The concept is best described by a 2007 testimonial from a contented homeowner in Oceanside, California:

> We bought this house [in 2001] when it was new and the backyard was a blank slate. With three-quarters of an acre, there was plenty of space to create a yard that had the feel of a nice resort with room to entertain outdoors but that still flowed together. [My husband] and I knew we wanted to cook and eat outdoors, so we built an outdoor kitchen with a barbecue, side burners, a rotisserie, a sink and a refrigerator. The kitchen also has a serving counter that can seat 15 on bar stools, though the yard can hold many more.[6]

This is the outdoor kitchen. With more than one million installed in American backyards by 2009, this wall-less room has supplanted the barbecue of past suburban weekends with weather-resistant, multiple gas-line-fueled rotisseries, braziers, and cooktops; stone-lined bread kilns; restaurant-quality refrigerators and beer coolers; and plumbed sinks and dishwashers. Calise, a leading supplier of outdoor appliances, markets the patented Modular Island System of stainless steel components that can be configured "1.9 million possible ways." The description on its website is couched in the rhetoric of individualization and self-empowerment, announcing, "Whether it's a do it yourself project, or assembled and finished by our Mod Squad™ it's fast, easy, and FUN for you to create the outdoor kitchen of your dreams."[7] These modular combinations of infinite suppleness are arranged in accordance with the unique tastes of individual designer-homeowners, most of whom require professional assistance with plumbing, wiring, and other aspects of construction. Those new to the dream find ample instruction in Home & Garden Television (HGTV) programs and online features and magazines as diverse as *Ebony, House Beautiful,* and *Trailer Life.* Examples range from the relatively modest ten-by-ten-foot DIY installation in Vermont ("a state known more for snowfall than for cookouts") featured in *Fine Cooking* to elaborate versions incorporating built-in sound systems, high-definition televisions, and home theaters.[8] One newswire reported on a retired Las Vegas businessman who "spent $200,000 on his backyard,

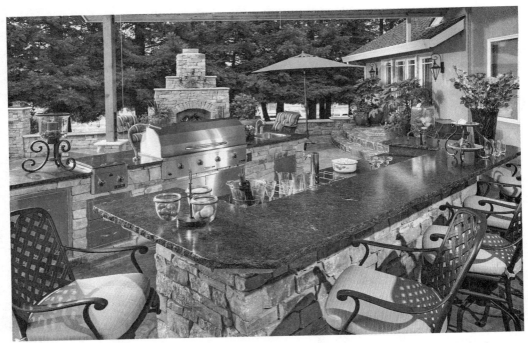

The outdoor kitchen by Galaxy Outdoor LLC. This model features a granite-topped cooking island and a second island with a wet bar. Photograph by Bruce Spangrud; courtesy Galaxy Outdoor LLC.

reconfiguring the swimming pool and making room for bubbling fountains and a waterfall, a full kitchen with a fourteen-foot barbecue island, a slate and cement deck, and a thirty-seven-inch plasma television." The man pronounced the result "perfect for hosting outdoor dinner parties."[9] Regardless of scope, the outdoor kitchen allows the homeowner to perform the entire ritual of the social dinner, from initial greeting to cooking, serving, and entertaining.

The often fantastic projects of the early twenty-first century are now poised to become a stock feature of luxury and suburban single-family housing. Supporting data abound. The National Association of Home Builders is a Washington, D.C.–based trade association whose 235,000 members design, finance, and construct an estimated 80 percent of all new American housing units.[10] In 2006, NAHB projections for typical single-family luxury homes of 2015 included two stories and more than four thousand square feet, as well as outdoor "rooms" outfitted with sinks, refrigerators, grills, and cooking islands, all joined by fireplaces, televisions or audio equipment or both, and pools or home spas. While tempered by the lingering housing crisis, demand for the outdoor kitchen has proved resilient at both luxury and average price points. Indeed, it may well have become a standard residential feature. As asserted in 2012 by the Food Channel, a website dedicated to food-based entertaining and other social activities:

> Who would have thought we needed kitchens outdoors? For grilling, perhaps— but a full kitchen, complete with covered patio, granite-counter prep area, sink, mini fridge, rotisserie, stove top, and TV? They are becoming the new home essential. Expensive, yes, but people are justifying it by continuing to stay home more, entertaining more, and doing it in style.[11]

That same year saw the debut of the NAHB "New American Home" Outside Kitchen, proposed as a standardized format for new-build outdoor kitchens at the annual International Builders' Show. Its gleaming assemblage of stainless steel appliances closely conforms to the modernist architecture and materials of the house itself, its sole flaw the sleek perfection that stands against the endearing and not-infrequent clumsiness of its owner-designed counterparts.

Professionalized goods and services have kept pace with the growing trend. Domestic goods manufacturers increasingly offer exterior equivalents of standard lines, and homeowners' escalating expectations are fulfilled by specialized interior designers, landscape architects, and architects. "My gosh, basically now anything you have in your indoor kitchen, you can have outdoors," says Leslie Wheeler, spokeswoman for an association of manufacturers, dealers, and retailers of hearth, patio, and barbecue products. The outdoor kitchen is "beyond a trend," she adds.

The NAHB 2012 "New American Home" Outside Kitchen at the International Builders' Show in Winter Park, Florida. Phil Kean Designs. Photograph by James F. Wilson; courtesy of National Association of Home Builders.

"It is now a lifestyle, an easy way to entertain family and friends."[12] These are not purely subjective advantages. In December 2011, *Builder* reported that a well-executed outdoor kitchen adds as much or more value than an indoor kitchen remodel. A year later, it announced that a "thoughtfully conceived outdoor living space . . . can make the difference between selling a home and not."[13] The current dearth of formal criteria allows for successful partial and accretive installations that (relatively) inexpensively contribute desirable livable space.

## What to Make of This New Type of Room?

The doubling of the American kitchen is not without irony. The outdoor kitchen emerged as the home kitchen in general was falling into disuse or undergoing modification for other family and communal activities. For example, in 2001, 40.5 percent of American households cooked on average only "once a day," and by 2004, 29 percent of all meals were consumed in restaurants. Data vary, but by 2009 up to 75 percent of all nonrestaurant meals and snacks, including those consumed in the home, were precooked, ready-to-eat, and other forms of convenience food and food products.[14] Clearly, the outdoor kitchen did not arise in response to contemporary cooking needs. Spatial redefinition is, of course, a constant of the modern residence. The American dining room is a nineteenth-century creation, a designated space that supplanted seventeenth- and eighteenth-century customs of taking meals in rooms that supported sleeping, storage, and various other non-food-related household functions before it, too, gave way to the eat-in kitchens and living and dining room combinations of the twentieth century.[15] But outdoor kitchens, wetrooms, and "family kitchens" do not yet appear related to traditional expectations placed on designed domestic space since the early twentieth century. Not the least of these is the linked act of cooking and eating *en famille* that anthropologist Bronislaw Malinowski placed against the satisfaction of mere animal appetite. As he noted in *A Scientific Theory of Culture* (1960):

> Some physical apparatus for eating is used, table manners observed, and the social conditions of the act carefully defined. It would be possible, indeed, to show that in every human society and as regards any individual in society the act of eating happens within a definite institution. . . . *It is always a fixed place, with an organization for the supply of food or its preparation, and for the opportunities of consuming it.*[16]

The "smooth working" of social and built apparatuses of food is "as indispensable to the biological performance as the placing of food into the individual's mouth, mastication, salivation, swallowing, and digestion."[17] In contrast, shelter magazine *Domino* celebrates flowing, decentralized home layouts for allowing the possibility, in the encouraging terms of a subheading, of "eating wherever, whenever."[18] The outdoor kitchen is one of these decentralized forms, and it has a direct correspondence with the deregulated dietary habits that currently justify converting backyard family playgrounds into extended dining rooms.

Architectural theoretician Fred Scott writes that built domestic forms are created "in response to the needs, habits and desires of a particular age."[19] The first large-scale change in dedicated rooms appeared in Enlightenment-era France. Here, nonelite luxury and its built outgrowths of convenience and comfort were fostered in deliberate preparation for the coming industrial age. Voltaire, Diderot, and other philosophes introduced and explained new patterns for a consumer-based national culture.[20] Glorification of "material excess" inspired a dazzling array of new desires, attitudes, and customs, which in turn inspired new designed spaces and objects, each with its own name, assigned purpose, and associated private and social behaviors. One major change focused on food consumption as long-standing admonitions against gluttony were supplanted by broad calls to the French people "to adjust their diet to their circumstances." Cultural historian Daniel Roche explains that wealthy and bourgeois Parisians responded by supplementing an existing "wide range of items such as eggs, butter, cheese, sugar, coffee, wine, spirits, cider and beer" with fresh fruits, vegetables, and herbs; high-quality domestic meat and dairy products marked with their sites of origin; imported spices, chocolate, and tea; and other "sophisticated, costly, and exotic ingredients." Kitchens changed in direct response to heightened attention accorded to food and its preparation. In 1715, the open hearth so defined the kitchen that iron frying pans, grills, tripods and cooking hooks, copper cauldrons, and casseroles joined tin dishware in constituting a full fifth of the average household inventory. By 1780, the open hearth as site of both heating and cooking gave way to the greater efficiency of the stove, and once-vital heavy cookware and utensils were supplanted by lighter, less expensive stoneware and ceramic goods better suited to the elaborate preparations of pâté, fricassee, rissole, and bouillon. Wealthier bourgeois homes sported a proliferation of "egg cups, bowls, coffee makers, sugar bowls," and other dedicated utensils for new foods, techniques, and domestic habits.[21] The kitchen thus constituted a collective fixed point that gave stability and meaning to new varieties of foodstuffs, their preparation, and the surrounding constellation of emerging customs and newly essential accessories. That the most literal act of consumption took place within the private residence mitigated lingering religious and social inhibitions against material excess. As Voltaire explained, "One can live with luxury in his house without ostentation, that is to say without adorning oneself in public with a revolting opulence."[22]

Change in the function, form, and social use of the twentieth-century residential American kitchen is amply documented by works ranging from Maud C. Cooke's *Breakfast, Dinner, and Supper; or, What to Eat and How to Prepare It* (1897), a late nineteenth-century manual of etiquette and hygienic food handling, to the theoretical explorations of Ellen Lupton and J. Abbot Miller's *The Bathroom, the Kitchen, and the Aesthetics of Waste* (1992).[23] In broad strokes, the rational household movement of the early 1900s displaced fin de siècle emphases on taste, morality, and decoration and professionalized the predominantly feminine control of production and consumption. During the 1910s and into the interwar period, kitchens changed in response to "household engineering" modeled on factory efficiency and promoted as a means of maximizing productivity within the home. The key proponent of this movement was Christine Fredericks, whose *The New Housekeeping: Efficiency Studies in Home Management* (1913) reduced kitchen work to sequential processes of "preparing" and "clearing away."[24] Fredericks proposed the "efficiency kitchen," a small (ideally ten feet by twelve feet) white room with icebox, preparation table, stove, serving table, sink, and china and dish closets "set in right relation to each other and the processes they develop." This kitchen's standardized arrangement provided a "steady track from icebox to dining-room" and back, and increased efficiency by eradicating features of earlier, overlarge kitchens such as sitting rooms, lounges, sewing spaces, flower pots, and all other elements "unrelated to the true work of the kitchen, which is the preparing of food."[25] It was a spare, efficient space that accommodated one person and her sequential performance of necessary tasks.

The reception of scientific household management as it supplanted Victorian rooms and practices is recorded in the popular *Inside the House of Good Taste* (1915, 1918). This book as a whole asserted that a home should express its inhabitants' personalities, instructing readers that the "living-room must be made for entertaining as well as for every-day life," while bedrooms were where women could most freely express individual tastes through decor. The kitchen was a notable exception. It was to have rational arrangements of shelved cabinets, sanitary porcelain sinks, washable Sanitas wall covering, and an overall rigorous asepticism that called for such extremes as a "double-acting door" and pantries installed between kitchen and dining room that together blocked the sights, sounds, and smells of cooking food from those awaiting the "good dinner [that] works the daily miracle of a man's existence." Processes of preparation were wholly separate from the social and familial rituals enacted within the dining room. Yet the keen enthusiasm for the precise and controlled spaces defined in architect Watson K. Phillips's chapter "The Modern Kitchen and Its Planning" is countered by the author's boyhood sense memory of his grandmother's sprawling country kitchen and its now-obsolete checkered oilcloths, cistern, wood box, and earthen root cellar that offered a magical glimpse of open sky.[26]

While hygienic advances ushered in by Fredericks remain codified at municipal and federal levels, admiration for the efficient kitchen began to flag as early as 1929. "The day of the white laboratory-like kitchen is past," announced an Iowa State College Extension Service booklet on home management.[27] In its stead came forms determined by the large-scale construction and automated convenience that characterized the post–World War II housing boom. Inexpensive and rapidly made postwar suburban housing abandoned traditional layouts and introduced multipurpose, hybrid rooms designed, in part, to keep construction costs low. The kitchen moved from the back of the house to become "a U-shaped work space equipped with appliances and gadgets," separated by a low counter from a living room that similarly assumed additional roles as study, dining room, parlor, and playroom.[28] The kitchen remained efficient but was now startlingly visible and imbued with a new flexibility of purpose and the progressive consumptionism of 1950s America. As in the earlier example of France, the altered kitchens of single-family suburban homes coincided with correspondingly massive changes in national living patterns and accommodated new domestic technologies, disposable products, and packaged foods.[29]

In the current era, veteran interior designer Troy Adams's own outdoor kitchen negotiates contemporary emphases on individualization and long-standing efficiency ideals.[30] At ten feet by thirty feet it is small for the type, and photographs by no less than the great Julius Shulman, best known for his iconic images of Case Study Houses, make clear that it is outdoors only when recessed sliding doors constituting the back wall of the house are pulled open. Refined interior materials (red enameled lava stone, soapstone, glass, bamboo) join rusticated slate tile and redwood on the exterior; partially sunken river rock demarcates where "room" becomes simply yard. Adams's remodel incorporates long-standing discourses of modernist functionality, practicality, and hygiene. His kitchen is effectively sealed against dirt, weather, and wildlife when not in use, and appliances remain largely in the house proper, the sole exception an alfresco dining table fitted with a gas fire pit. It also conforms, up to a point, to the work triangle set forth by industrial designer Henry Dreyfuss's *The Measure of Man* (1959). Following Dreyfuss, proper kitchen design has long called for "a small triangle from refrigerator to sink to stove to refrigerator. The sum of this work triangle is under twenty-three feet. The triangle should not be interrupted by traffic flow."[31] Adams doubles the formula—increased size is apparently a critical element of the outdoor kitchen—to create two distinct triangular pathways anchored by a central cooking island. The designer invokes the form's organizing metaphor in announcing, approvingly, that these overly long dimensions require "hiking across the kitchen for everything."[32] More important, they transform the semienclosed kitchen into a long, shallow stage, its center point a dynamic focal point for guests seated both indoors and out.

   Adams's variation presents a stylish update of what postwar developers of suburban housing marketed as "California living" as well as an eminently practical "indoor–outdoor experience" invoked through material and siting.[33] The same attention to modernist efficiency informs the crisp architectural precision of the 2012 National Association of Home Builders model for the "New American Home." One wonders, however, if these variants adequately manifest the individual, often unruly impulses that define the form itself. Design historian Penny Sparke attributes change in interior design to an ongoing dialectic of taste and efficiency, the latter of which carries "the potential to homogenize taste and eliminate individuality and difference." Efficiency, utility, and standardization are set against "those alternate principles [of] taste, beauty, and irrationality" that, in this case, find expression in backyard stove tops and all-weather dishwashers accessorized by spectator seating, fire pit dining tables (where one can "roast marshmallows after a feast"), waterfalls, and other imaginative features and redundancies that transform the processes of preparing and clearing away into play, discovery, and delight for cook and diner alike.[34] The desires of this particular age must necessarily be examined within their own gloriously inefficient parameters.

SPECIAL KITCHEN SECTION

148/ **a kitchen designer's kitchen**
How L.A. designer Troy Adams used his skills to maximize his own diminutive kitchen.
*Text by Amy Albert*

154/ **find your range**
Before you buy your next stove, make sure you've asked yourself these five questions.
*Text by Amy Albert*

156/ **get a grip**
Beautiful drawer pulls and knobs give kitchens an instant—and inexpensive—upgrade.
*Produced by Kim Wong*
*Text by Amy Albert*

a kitchen designer's kitchen /148

JULIUS SHULMAN AND JUERGEN NOGAI

HAVE A QUESTION ABOUT A RECIPE, OR A COMMENT? Call Reader Service at 323-965-3633, or contact the editorial offices: *Bon Appétit*, 6300 Wilshire Boulevard, Los Angeles, CA 90048. FOR SUBSCRIPTIONS AND CHANGES OF ADDRESS, call 800-765-9419 (515-433-5019 from outside the U.S.A.) or send e-mail to: subscriptions@bonappetit.com. PRINTED IN THE U.S.A.

Troy Adams's outdoor kitchen. Photograph by Julius Shulman and Juergen Nogai, originally published in *Bon Appétit*, April 2008, 148. Reprinted by permission of Julius Shulman Photography.

## Dreams of Twenty-First-Century Suburbia

Consumer desire and individualism encoded as dream is at the very heart of American attitudes toward homeownership. "Every man has within him at least one house and one garden which, were he able to create them, would doubtless bring him Nirvana," Richardson Wright explained in the foreword to *Inside the House of Good Taste*. "It's his dream house and his dream garden, the sort of garden that he will make when he gets enough money . . . whatever the size or wherever the place, it will be his, his alone."[35] This language persists in the postwar "kitchen of tomorrow," "dream kitchen," and "miracle kitchen."[36] Manufacturers such as Calise rely on similar phrasing.

The American Dream, like all others, can be analyzed. This was the goal of early motivation research into consumer response to the symbolic meanings of design. Postwar manufacturers used companies such as Social Research, Inc., founded in 1946, to explore consumer values, behaviors, and choices and generally "uncover the ways that design in mass-produced goods conveyed social assumptions that were widely understood."[37] The operating conviction was that the intangibles of consumer psychology are as valid as more overtly tangible aspects of modernist functionality. A variant maintains that the "mundane movements and moments that comprise homemaking encompass a whole suite of entanglements between object, subject, agency and space. Objects and their acquisition, use, placement and value are thus mutually constituted, relationally governed by both production and consumption."[38] Similar tactics can be used to explore key associations and factors that are enacted in specific features of the outdoor kitchen.

The most consistent feature of the outdoor kitchen is the cooking island. This typically plumbed and wired component anchors the installation and serves as its central focus while in use (recall the Oceanside example ringed with bar stools and Troy Adams's central preparation area). In this it echoes the kitchen island, which similarly serves as a fixed point within indefinite interior space and expands rather logically into a "favorite spot for eating and hanging out" and the de facto center of indoor family life.[39] But the function of this familiar form expands in critical ways when transferred outdoors. Here the cooking island gives definition and purpose to indeterminate exterior space, arranges people into the physical form of togetherness, and draws collective attention to the real-time processes of cooking. It activates the backyard as a room dedicated to food and sociability.

The cooking island also fundamentally establishes the host-cook as focal point for family and guest diners. That this admirable intimate connection between cook and family, or host and guests, is the driving logic of the feature is documented on blogs, Facebook pages, and other sites by owner-posted photographs of professional and homeowner-designed installations. These images rather consistently show cooking-island seating abutting range tops, set directly behind massive hinged grill covers, and in general paying little heed to diners' proximity to high heat, open flame, smoke, running water, sputtering oil, and other unfortunate facts of working kitchens. This complete reversal of earlier design strategies that minimized sensory awareness of the kitchen (not to mention standard safety considerations) is in complete conformity with contemporary expectations that the pleasures of dining will include some degree of culinary theater. A 1999 survey of open kitchens in restaurants, campus food courts, health care facilities, and commercial venues found that up to 80 percent operated "in full view of customers" to entice appetites and reinforce perceptions of freshness. The larger goal was visual entertainment, however; as the report concluded, "Food is theater, the audience is seated and waiting, so bring on the chefs!"[40] Industry journals note the growing popularity of food *as* theater. "Mongolian barbeques invite diners to select fresh food items while chefs prepare the meal on large flat grills; glass kitchens . . . permit patrons to view their meal being prepared over open fires and in brick ovens; and sushi and teppanyaki restaurants feature Japanese chefs showing off their skills."[41] Visual and experiential stimuli take precedence over the meal itself, a phenomenon to which reporter A. Elizabeth Sloan awards the tongue-in-cheek title "eatertainment." Writing of diners who flock to the House of Blues, Dave & Buster's, and Elvis Presley's Memphis (theme restaurants, a trend pioneered by the Hard Rock Cafe, which opened in 1971), Sloan notes, "Table-side Internet access, comic books, and stock car racing themes are some of the latest permutations expanding the definition of *eatertainment*. All of these successful business ventures tap into a particular interest in the population."[42] Restaurant designer Frederick Brush's summary is more succinct: "Going to a restaurant is like attending a play."[43]

Structuring twenty-first-century culinary display through the outdoor kitchen island raises the question: How, precisely, is the host-cook to regale family, friends, and guests with "theater associated with the culinary arts"?[44] One readily available model extends the postwar transference of domestic labor from servants to housewives and concomitant merging of once-enclosed kitchens into adjoining living and dining spaces. These changes occasioned the reframing of kitchen work as a highly visible pleasurable, public, and "fun" activity women performed in view of husbands, children, and guests.[45] Contemporary kitchens as a whole now serve as the social core of the home, with outdoor kitchens offering especially rich sites of potential familial and semipublic entertainment. Homeowners have access to a ubiquitous flow of appropriable habits presented through television and its technological sister, the Internet. Behavioral shifts modeled by scripted television programs and so-called reality shows have changed popular perceptions of cooking from a domestic, feminine-gendered chore into acts of exciting, even exhilarating, creativity. Chief among these is Food Network, a cable channel launched in 1993 that now draws more than 1.1 million American viewers to its nightly programming alone. It has 100 million coverage-area homes, more than 9.9 million monthly users on its unique website, and a subscriber base of 1.5 million for its *Food Network Magazine*.[46] Its programming has given rise to network and cable imitators and is disseminated and perpetuated by social networking sites such as FoodBuzz and its 4,245 food-oriented blog partners. Where Julia Child demystified haute cuisine for American homemakers, celebrity chefs Emeril Lagasse, Bobby Flay (host of *Throwdown with Bobby Flay*), Mario Batali, et al. are today adulated as paradigms of culinary showmanship.[47] These men present an accessible model of cooking whose critical reconfiguration of (heterosexual) masculine activity coincides with that of the outdoor kitchen. "Culinarily, I try to be correct," Lagasse stated in a 1998 interview. "It's not like I'm bastardizing my craft. . . . What I'm trying to do with the people is connect and say, hey, this isn't rocket science."[48] (In the same article, *Food Arts* magazine founder Michael Batterberry mused that the *Essence of Emeril* show "smacks a little bit of the wrestling ring or the roller derby.")[49] That Lagasse's exuberant "Bam!" became a late-1990s catchphrase is a measure of the far reach of these programs and of their strong male personalities' demonstration of how to transform food preparation into a solid hour of entertainment. Demographics enter into coverage as well. Guy Fieri, the bowling shirt and board shorts–clad host of *Guy's Big Bite*, a show targeted to Gen-X viewers, "puts the party together" for his "posse" on a set equipped with a full bar, big-screen television, pinball machine, pool table, and orange race car–themed refrigerator.[50] Host, show, and set follow the playful logic of themed restaurants and the outdoor kitchen.

The outdoor kitchen and, not coincidentally, Food Network emerged as Americans began viewing cooking as an admired skill and household food preparation became more evenly undertaken by men and women. As the outdoor kitchen becomes more prevalent and more widely used within the home, its focus on theatricality will surely fade. One area in which it likely will change is in its relation to gendered domestic roles. The outdoor kitchen is an ambivalent space to which users and guests alike bring conflicting understandings of built form and gender. It rejects easy binaries, and in doing so accommodates novel recombinations that adjust for contemporary circumstances. One of these may well reject the long-standing assumption that Mother will take care of the cooking. In a 2009 study, Rebecca Swenson explored gendered assumptions of "doing dinner" in Food Network programming. In addition to the spectacular shows hosted exclusively by male chefs, Swenson examined equally prominent cooks Rachael Ray, Ina Garten, Giada De Laurentiis and Nigella Lawson. She found that their shows demonstrate how to meet the daily challenges of preparing food for family members, and in the process they "cod[e] cooking as a fulfilling act of love and intimacy done for others."[51] These women also typically appear unaccompanied on sets designed to resemble home kitchens or within their actual kitchens to enhance their intimacy with the home viewer.[52] This model of performative nurturing offers host-cooks of both sexes less an alternate model for entertaining than an additional element, one fully resonant with outdoor kitchen goals of togetherness and quality family connection.

The outdoor kitchen is yet to have its Edith Wharton, herself an interior decorator, emerge to make sense of it. The language used in describing it takes on shadings of exploration, as in the do-it-yourselfer's description of setting his kitchen in the underutilized space of his backyard. It is also infused with a sense of adventure and perhaps lawlessness as well, for outdoor trends largely skirt municipal codes covering remodeling and new construction. There is no need for a range hood if the entire unit vents to open sky, and formal legal regulations and aesthetic guidelines governing these new spaces have yet to fully emerge. It is precisely the lack of definition that accounts for the proliferation and imaginative combination of kitchen-like features contained within each of these exterior quasi-rooms. Further, the early twenty-first-century kitchen is less the isolated and strictly gendered work space of prior eras than an increasingly demarcated open territory, the outdoor kitchen marking its ultimate migration from the house altogether. As a design trend, the outdoor kitchen and parallel emergence of amorphous, interconnected rooms signals both the continuation and the dissolution of the modernist principals of good design. These spaces mark the upper limit of the open-plan layout that characterized postwar American homes and eliminated areas viewed as old-fashioned by prospective homeowners; however, they differ in favoring subjective tastes and even symbolism over utilitarian or practical needs. Then, as now, these combined living and dining or, alternately, kitchen and dining spaces allowed for freshly imagined ideals of family togetherness.[53] The outdoor kitchen is appropriate for an era marked by real and virtual alienation, an exuberant bricolage that responds to and gives pleasure to fragmented lives. It is the built environment of interactive design, the latest iteration of the American Dream.

## Notes

1. Edith Wharton, *The Age of Innocence* (New York: D. Appleton, 1920).
2. Boyce Thompson, "Make No Mistake: Residential Design Is Evolving Rapidly, Thanks to a Brisk Market for New-Home Sales," *Builder,* October 1, 2003. Acquired by Hanley Wood in 1981 and launched as *Builder On-Line* in 1996, *Builder* is "the number 1 source for industry news and product information." See "History," Hanley Wood, accessed October 27, 2009, http://hanleywood.com.

3. Thompson, "Make No Mistake."

4. Bill Saporito, "Inside the New American Home: Humble No More," *Time*, October 14, 2002, 64.

5. Thompson, "Make No Mistake."

6. Carrie Wilhite, quoted in Amy Gunderson, "Living Here: Outdoor Entertaining; Rooms without Walls," *New York Times*, May 25, 2007, F4.

7. Calise website, accessed March 18, 2008, http://outdoorkitchenconcepts.com.

8. Lisa Waddle, "A Kitchen That Goes All Out," *Fine Cooking*, June/July 2007, 54.

9. June Fletcher, "Giving Up on the Outdoors—Elements Take a Toll on Pricey Backyard 'Rooms'; Fire Ants in the TV," *Wall Street Journal*, June 28, 2007, 1.

10. "NAHB Study Profiles Home of the Future," National Association of Home Builders, newswire release, IBS2007-10, 2006. Founded in 1942, the NAHB is affiliated with more than eight hundred state and local home builders' associations, and its members are "involved in home building, remodeling, multifamily construction, property management, subcontracting, design, housing finance, building product manufacturing and other aspects of residential and light commercial construction."

11. "#9 Food Trend for 2012: Social Cooking," Food Channel, December 2, 2011, http://www.foodchannel.com.

12. Quoted in Ruth Bashinsky, "Finding a Home with an Outdoor Kitchen," *Newsday*, May 14, 2012.

13. Amy Albert, "10 Top Design Trends of 2011," *Builder*, December 2, 2011, http://www.builderonline.com; Amy Albert, "10 Top Design Trends of 2012," *Builder*, December 3, 2012, http://www.builderonline.com.

14. "Cooking Trends in the United States: Are We Really Becoming a Fast Food Country?," Energy Information Administration, November 25, 2002, http://www.eia.doe.gov; Karen Goldberg Goff, "Shall We Gather in the Kitchen? Preparing Meals Can Be Family Activity," *Washington Times*, March 30, 2003, D1.

15. Elizabeth C. Cromley, "Transforming the Food Axis: Houses, Tools, Modes of Analysis," *Material History Review* 44 (Fall 1996): 10.

16. Bronislaw Malinowski, *A Scientific Theory of Culture, and Other Essays* (New York: Oxford University Press, 1960), 94–95; emphasis added.

17. Ibid., 97.

18. Ariana Speyer, "Live the Dream," *Domino*, March 2009, 97.

19. Fred Scott, *On Altering Architecture* (London: Routledge, 2008), 152–53.

20. See Grant McCracken, "Diderot Unities and the Diderot Effect," in *Culture and Consumption: New Approaches to the Symbolic Character of Goods and Activities* (Bloomington: Indiana University Press, 1988), 118–29.

21. Daniel Roche, *France in the Enlightenment* (Cambridge, Mass.: Harvard University Press, 1998), 614–16, 624–26, 615.

22. Quoted in Michael Kwass, "Ordering the World of Goods: Consumer Revolution and the Classification of Objects in Eighteenth-Century France," *Representations* 82 (Spring 2003): 95.

23. See Maud C. Cooke, *Breakfast, Dinner, and Supper; or, What to Eat and How to Prepare It* (Philadelphia: J. H. Moore, 1897); Ellen Lupton and J. Abbott Miller, *The Bathroom, the Kitchen, and the Aesthetics of Waste* (Dalton, Mass.: Dudley Press, 1992).

24. Christine Fredericks, *The New Housekeeping: Efficiency Studies in Home Management* (New York: Doubleday, 1913), 47. The book arose from Fredericks's "The New Housekeeping" series published in *Ladies' Home Journal* (1912), as did her later *Household Engineering and Scientific Management in the Home* (Chicago: American School of Home Economics, 1915).

25. Fredericks, *New Housekeeping*, 49–51.

26. Mary McBurney, "The Essentials for Making a Living-Room Livable," 3; Agnes Foster, "Creating Personality in Bedrooms," 97–98; Agnes Foster, "Distinction in Dining-Rooms," 50; and Watson K. Phillips, "The Modern Kitchen and Its Planning," 122, all in *Inside the House of Good Taste*, ed. Richardson Wright (1915; repr., New York: Robert M. McBride, 1918).

27. Cited in Andy Warhol, Bill Stumpf, and Nicholas Polites, "Julia's Kitchen: A Design Anatomy," *Design Quarterly* 104 (1977): 6.

28. Avi Friedman, "The Evolution of Design Characteristics during the Post–Second World War Housing Boom: The US Experience," *Journal of Design History* 8, no. 2 (1995): 139.

29. Warhol et al., "Julia's Kitchen," 8.

30. Amy Albert, "A Kitchen Designer's Kitchen," *Bon Appétit,* April 2008, 151.

31. Henry Dreyfuss and Associates, *The Measure of Man and Woman: Human Factors in Design,* rev. ed. (New York: John Wiley, 2002), 61. This book is a revised edition of Dreyfuss's *The Measure of Man* (New York: Whitney Library of Design, 1959).

32. Quoted in Albert, "Kitchen Designer's Kitchen," 151.

33. See Paul Adamson, *Eichler: Modernism Rebuilds the American Dream* (Layton, Utah: Gibbs Smith, 2002). As Adamson notes, "California living" appeared in 1950s and 1960s advertising campaigns to describe the "access to nature, the virtues of modern technology, and the informality engendered by the open plan" characteristic of modernist suburban housing developments (163).

34. Penny Sparke, *As Long as It's Pink: The Sexual Politics of Taste* (London: Pandora, 1995), 87; Jessica Dickler, "5 Killer Outdoor Kitchens," CNN Money, accessed February 5, 2013, http://money.cnn.com.

35. Richardson Wright, foreword to *Inside the House of Good Taste,* iv.

36. Warhol et al., "Julia's Kitchen," 8.

37. Shelley Nickles, "More Is Better: Mass Consumption, Gender, and Class Identity in Postwar America," *American Quarterly* 54, no. 4 (December 2002): 586n65. Nickles cites SRI founder Burleigh J. Gardner's *Women and Advertising: A Motivation Study of the Attitudes of Women Toward Eight Magazines* (Chicago: Social Research, Inc., for Hearst Corp., 1954); and Lee Rainwater, Richard P. Coleman, and Gerald Handel, *Workingman's Wife: Her Personality, World and Life Style* (New York: Oceana, 1959), iv–xiv, 219–36.

38. Louis Crewe, Nicky Gregson, and Alan Metcalfe, "The Screen and the Drum: On Form, Function, Fit and Failure in Contemporary Home Consumption," *Design and Culture* 1, no. 3 (November 2009): 322.

39. "Kitchen Accomplished!," *Good Housekeeping,* November 2009, 111–12.

40. William Eaton, "Trends in Kitchen Design," *Foodservice Equipment & Supplies,* December 1999, 23–24.

41. A. Elizabeth Sloan, "It's Eatertainment!," *Food Technology* 53, no. 5 (May 1999): 22.

42. Ibid.

43. Quoted in Patricia Brooks, "Restaurants du Jour: Heavy on the Décor," *New York Times,* March 21, 2004, 17(CN).

44. Eaton, "Trends in Kitchen Design," 23.

45. Cromley, "Transforming the Food Axis," 19.

46. "Food Network Drew Record Viewership in 2012," news release, Scripps Networks Interactive, December 12, 2012, http://scrippsnetworksinteractive.com; data compiled by Nielsen Media Research.

47. A measure of the stature of Lagasse, Flay, and Batali is their appearance in an episode of *Iron Chef America* filmed at the Obama White House in late 2009. See "White House to Host 'Iron Chef' Food Fight," *San Jose Mercury News,* November 5, 2009, 2(A).

48. Quoted in Amanda Hesser, "Under the Toque; 'Here's Emeril!' Where's the Chef?," *New York Times,* November 4, 1998, 1(F).

49. Quoted in ibid.

50. Rebecca Swenson, "Domestic Divo? Televised Treatments of Masculinity, Femininity and Food," *Critical Studies in Media Communication* 26, no. 1 (March 2009): 46.

51. Ibid., 41, 44, 45.

52. Elizabeth Nathanson, "As Easy as Pie: Cooking Shows, Domestic Efficiency, and Post-feminist Temporality," *Television & New Media* 10, no. 4 (July 2009): 315, 321–22.

53. Sparke, *As Long as It's Pink,* 177.

# AFTERWORD

MARGARET CRAWFORD

Suburban studies is an exciting field, still in development. With more than half the population of the United States now living in suburbs, scholars have finally acknowledged the importance of suburbia, not just as a problem but as a dominant fact of American life. Suburbanization can no longer be considered merely "sub" to a centrally defined "urban"; rather, it is an actual form of urbanization, with its own dynamics, that over the course of the twentieth century expanded to dominate the American landscape. But, as the editors of this volume point out, clearly defining what *suburban* means is difficult. Today many millions of people are living suburban lives, but analyzing and communicating the nature and meaning of these lives remains a challenge for scholars.

One reason for this difficulty is the surprising multiplicity and diversity of suburban environments, institutions, and experiences. Like some of the best books about suburbs, such as *Holy Land, My Blue Heaven,* and *Second Suburb,*[1] this collection emphasizes this growing complexity by replacing generalizations with local specificity. Focused and empirical, the twenty-one essays in this book make an important contribution to the growing corpus of writing about suburbs that, through detail and particularity, challenges stereotypes. Collectively, this approach demonstrates the enormous disparities among various suburbs. These disparities include such obvious features as size, location, demographics, history, and physical form. Suburbs can be rich or poor, near or far from the city, enormous or tiny. Fremont, for example, covers ninety square miles, while Pagedale, like most of St. Louis's Normandy suburbs, occupies just over one square mile. If some suburbs remain exclusively white, others, like Pasadena and Ardmore, have significant minority populations, still others are almost completely African American, and yet others are increasingly populated by Asian and Hispanic immigrants. Beginning in the 1960s, housing typologies such as garden apartments and townhouses, and then high-rise rental apartments and condominiums, offered important alternatives to the single-family house. Today, as families and finances continue to change, illegal garage apartments and rented in-law units add invisible density to suburban single-family neighborhoods.[2]

All of these factors and more have shaped equally divergent ways of life in suburbs. The stories defy many popular and scholarly depictions. Perhaps more important, they often contradict each other, undermining the easy generalities so prevalent in discussions of suburban life. If, for instance, gay men and African Americans organized to defend their rights in the suburbs of Detroit and Philadelphia, and if the Junior League in Pasadena began to welcome minority women, then other, more conservative factions from New York suburbs joined forces to defeat the state's proposed Equal Rights Amendment. Even within racially homogeneous suburbs, residents defined race and space in conflicting ways. In the all-black suburb of Pagedale, residents who equate "suburban life" with middle-class respectability have tried to control behavior they associate with urban ghettos. *Second Suburb* describes how Levittown's white residents, when faced with the first African American family to move into the neighborhood, took violently opposed stands.

Charting the complexity, contradictions, and even paradoxes contained within suburbs, these accounts suggest that *difference* may actually be the defining characteristic of suburbia, rather than the sameness consistently attributed to it. In fact, currently, in an inversion of conventional wisdom, cities are becoming more homogeneous while suburbs grow more diverse. In widely varying circumstances, suburban people of different races, classes, religions, genders, and sexual orientations, acting according to a broad range of politics and values, live highly divergent lives.

These differences are further complicated by the continuous changes that suburbs have undergone over the past century. If the original impulse for incorporation and regulation in Riverside, Tuxedo Park, and other nineteenth-century "bourgeois utopias" was to avoid the uncontrollable changes that were continually remaking American cities, it has become clear that this early strategy has been successful only in a very small minority of elite suburbs. And even there, success has been limited. An intact physical fabric can mask significant social and cultural transformation. In San Marino, Los Angeles's richest suburb, wealthy white residents are currently being replaced by wealthy Asians. This population shift has produced so much social tension that the city felt the need to establish an "Ethnic Harmony Commission."[3] Change can also be partial. My own hometown of Bethesda, Maryland, has seen its downtown develop from a sleepy crossroads into a high-rise corporate center while most of the area's leafy residential streets have remained untouched. Although some residents bemoan the changes, others are thrilled to have subway stops and high-end restaurants, shops, and services at their doorsteps.

Even canonical postwar housing tracts, often characterized as the epitome of mass-produced monotony, demonstrate disparate patterns of change and stability. A quick look at real estate ads for houses in Levittown, New York, reveals this suburb's extensive culture of home remodeling. Since 1949 continuous additions and modifications have rendered the original Cape Cods and ranch houses almost completely unrecognizable. In contrast, most of the facades in Lakewood, California—a suburb of the same vintage as Levittown—remain remarkably unaltered, and a surprising number of Lakewood's original residents and their children continue to live there, perhaps accounting for the town's new motto, adopted in 2004: "Times change, values don't."[4] But of course values do change, and social change is often particularly visible in suburbs. In the 1980s Detroit's suburban gays needed to band together to fight police abuse and discrimination; in contrast, since 2000 same-sex couples have been a common and accepted sight in the suburbs of large cities. Popular culture reflects these new values, as in the gay wedding between two of the main characters recently featured in the popular suburban sitcom *Modern Family*.

## Voices, Habitation, and Imaginaries

What does this mean for suburban scholarship? In the face of overwhelming complexity and constant change, it is tempting to generalize or attempt to identify patterns or models. But I would argue for a move in the opposite direction, toward accumulating even more detail through ever more fine-grained accounts of specific cases and local stories. This book takes an important step in that direction, enriching our understanding of suburbia by accumulating rather than distilling knowledge. At the same time, much remains to be discovered. How can we zoom in for close-ups that capture the everyday experiences of suburban life? How can we understand how such experiences add up over of the course of a day, a week, a year, or a lifetime? How can we identify the multiple ways in which suburbanites attain, conceptualize, and exercise agency in the course of living their lives? How can we decipher the mixed and often contradictory motives underlying people's actions? How do these individual choices and decisions shape both the conceptual and physical dimensions of suburbia? The only way to answer these questions is to get even closer to the suburban lives we study. We do not need to abandon our scholarly methods in order to incorporate more suburban voices and experiences and attitudes into our scholarship. Toward that end, I want to highlight three very different but equally promising topics of research that could offer suburban studies richer and more detailed narratives of individual and collective lives.

The first is the individual voice. Incorporating first-person narratives such as those found in ethnographies, oral histories, memoirs, and interviews can significantly expand the explanatory power of suburban research. Books such as *My Blue*

*Heaven* and *Second Suburb,* by combining historical scholarship with memoirs, interviews, and oral histories, add depth and texture to our understanding of suburban life. Residents' accounts of not only important moments, like the decision to buy a house, but also everyday occurrences provide illuminating glimpses into ordinary yet meaningful lives. Multiple accounts of the same event, told through personal recollections, complement historical documentation, but the contrasts between different individuals' perspectives and memories raise important questions about what close-up and faraway perspectives can contribute to historical interpretation. Juxtaposing these competing accounts and multiple voices reveals significant gaps between what scholars assume and what suburbanites perceive and experience. Recognizing these differences—which can undermine our expectations—can serve as a useful correction and thus open up new avenues for further investigation.

The repository of suburban stories available to scholars is rapidly increasing, partly due to the rebirth of storytelling as a popular medium. Although programs such as *This American Life*—National Public Radio's most downloaded podcast— and live storytelling slams rarely promote themselves as specifically suburban, many of the stories told in these venues take place, not surprisingly, in suburbs. These curated forms of personal narrative are currently being supplemented by more broad-based forms of public history such as StoryCorps, an enormous oral history project that has now collected forty-five thousand interviews, stored at the Library of Congress. StoryCorps and similar initiatives offer scholars raw material as well as methods and opportunities to engage with residents to create meaningful public histories grounded in suburban places and experiences.

Habitation is another potent theme. Investigating both the ways in which people live in particular places and the houses in which they live can tell us far more than studying either one by itself. Studying the single-family house—probably the most investigated topic in suburban history—in terms of ongoing habitation as well as basic design reveals a complex and nuanced spatial order. Typically depicted and usually attacked as an exclusively private realm, the suburban house can also be understood as a highly malleable boundary between the residents and the larger world "outside." For example, Dianne Harris and Steve Waksman describe the house as a complex layering of spatial zones in which public and private mix according to the residents' interests in listening to and playing music. Most suburban houses were not designed with music in mind, of course, but the growing availability of consumer goods such as stereo systems, electric guitars, and amplifiers has effectively altered the nature of suburban spaces—and boundaries. Music, carefully selected according to individual tastes, breaches the walls of the house, bringing aspects of urban culture usually found in public venues into suburban environments, to be listened to alone or shared with family and friends. Similarly, rock bands practicing in the basement or the garage transform these spaces into semipublic venues that attract friends, neighbors, and passersby.

Even the teenage bedroom, often imagined as a solitary refuge, may not be all that isolated. In some cases listening to and playing music is the first step toward more public and semipublic forms of performance in these supposedly private spaces. In recent years, for example, it has become common for teenagers to post pictures and videos of themselves in their rooms on YouTube and other social media sites—platforms that are accessible to millions of viewers. Or, to note another example, as more and more people telecommute or run businesses from their dining tables or garages, nearly every room in the house can potentially take on a public character. Similarly, as Ursula Lang demonstrates, the yard is not always a barrier. Minneapolis gardeners, proud of their handiwork, often welcome admiring neighbors or curious strangers into their yards.

The penetrability of these different private/public domestic zones shifts according to time, with maximum openness at particular moments, such as during garage band rehearsals, or on Halloween, when front yards and porches and doors become accessible to costumed trick-or-treaters. The maximum inversion of public and private occurs during the quintessential suburban event, the garage sale. For the duration of a day or even a weekend, the front or side yard transforms into a public space, open to all. Personal items and household goods that once resided in private places—in closets, drawers, attics—are placed on the lawn or driveway, where any passing stranger can examine them and even purchase them.

Habitation also reveals the ways in which housing production and consumption interact, an increasingly important theme in suburban studies. One key register of consumer agency is the ability of individuals to use mass-produced commodities to suit their own particular purposes. Several chapters in this book demonstrate the complexity of possible relationships among producers, designers, and consumers. In certain cases these roles can even be reversed; as Trecia Pottinger shows, Ardmore's African American residents organized to initiate and construct housing typologies appropriate for their social and spatial needs. As suburbs evolve over time, habitation marks change in both the public and private spheres. Martin Dines shows how Pam Conrad's children's stories document the accumulation of layers of experience, memory, and meaning in Levittown, New York. In an essay published in 1995, Annmarie Adams describes how large the gap can be between intention and actual use, detailing a single California family's experience in their modernist Eichler Home. Almost totally undermining the house's design concepts, the family kept the curtains drawn across the glass walls, arranged furniture to re-create conventional room-like configurations, and used the garden atrium for storage.[5] By examining the house from both outside and inside, Adams reveals how widely divergent generalized intentions and specific habitation can be.

Finally, suburban imaginaries can clarify the ways in which individual experiences coalesce into collective representations. Identifying the urban imaginaries of iconic cities has become a staple of urban scholarship over the past decades. Typically a city's imaginary is a highly selective mental construction composed of collectively shared representations of its space, history, and culture. A mixture of everyday experience, popular representations, political discourse, and historical memories, imaginaries are both material—acknowledging the specific conditions that shape the city—and fanciful, based on existing representations and the city's intangible "atmosphere." Their composite nature allows them to contain both "truth" (empirically verifiable facts) and fiction (invented stories) and to highlight certain places and qualities while disregarding others. Repeated and shared over time, these selective images—or "mental maps"—acquire a life of their own; they can be celebratory, as in descriptions of New York, or abject, as in the case of Detroit.

In contrast, most scholars have interpreted such collective mental constructs about suburbs negatively, often portraying them as mere ideology or "false consciousness." They assume that those who choose to live in suburbs do so because they have unwittingly bought into myths of nature, community, and homeownership. Popular culture has imposed other, equally reductive, constructs on suburban life, imagining it as conformist, alienating, and socially impoverished. Suburbs in general have often served as convenient stand-ins for larger social concerns, such as the role of women, consumerism, and, most recently, public health and environmental crisis.

Such generic concepts are far from the highly specific process of "memory work" that Paul J. P. Sandul identified in Orangevale, California. Orangevale's suburban imaginary, literally rooted in its agricultural past as a citrus colony, is made up of a multilayered set of physical and mental associations. In addition to the rural past, these include images of early settlement, small-town flavor, and community coherence, constructed and communicated through yearly events, local organizations, building preservation, and history books.

An architect friend, charged with designing a Metro rail station for a Los Angeles suburb, discovered that Chatsworth residents overwhelmingly favored what they called "the Western Ranch style." They saw themselves not as suburbanites but as the inheritors of a place where there had once been ranches, cows, and horses. The fact that several of these ranches were owned by movie studios and used as sets for westerns just added another layer of meaning to their suburban imaginary.

Such imaginaries, however far from the current "reality" of a place, serve important functions for residents. First, they construct and codify the specificity of different suburbs. Their selective use of symbols, places, and activities incorporates change into easily accessible narratives of popular history, easily shared meanings that shape individual identities and add perspective and temporal depth to the daily lives of the inhabitants. Critics might see these imaginaries as limited, but the images they convey are often more than clichéd narratives such as those about New York or Paris, still circulating in spite of the fact that the majority of their populations now reside in their suburbs.

All of these stories underline the diversity of suburban realities and imaginaries. They demonstrate how confronting the human experiences of suburbia through careful observation, research, and analysis can expand and deepen our understanding of their multiple meanings. This greater awareness of suburban lives will inevitably challenge many accepted facts and interpretations. Moving in close, looking and listening attentively narrows the distance between scholar and subject. This can help correct the a priori assumptions and critiques that many scholars still bring to suburban topics. The closer one gets to the lives of suburban residents, the more difficult it is to believe that they are simply unwitting prisoners of larger economic and political imperatives, even if their agency, like everyone's, is bounded by constraints of all kinds. Focusing on lives and subjectivities can also address one of the lingering dilemmas of suburban studies: the continuing dependence on the urban "other." It is difficult to study suburbs without responding to the extensive literature on urban topics or reacting to the stated and implied attacks on suburbs contained in its city-centric perspectives. By investigating and understanding what is meaningful about suburban lives, suburban studies can move out of the shadow of the city and become as complex as its subject.

## Notes

1. D. J. Waldie, *Holy Land: A Suburban Memoir* (New York: W. W. Norton, 1995); Becky M. Nicolaides, *My Blue Heaven: Life and Politics in the Working-Class Suburbs of Los Angeles, 1920–1965* (Chicago: University of Chicago Press, 2002); Dianne Harris, ed., *Second Suburb: Levittown, Pennsylvania* (Pittsburgh: University of Pittsburgh Press, 2010).

2. Vinit Mukhija, "Outlaw In-Laws: Informal Second Units and the Stealth Reinvention of Single-Family Housing," in *The Informal American City: Beyond Taco Trucks and Day Labor,* ed. Vinit Mukhija and Anastasia Loukaitou-Sideris (Cambridge, Mass.: MIT Press, 2014), 39–59.

3. Merlin Chowkwanyun and Jordan Segall, "How an Exclusive Los Angeles Suburb Lost Its Whiteness," CityLab, August 27, 2012, http://www.citylab.com.

4. "About Lakewood—Established 1954," City of Lakewood, California, accessed December 22, 2014, http://www.lakewoodcity.org/about.

5. Annmarie Adams, "The Eichler Home: Intention and Experience in Postwar Suburbia," in *Gender, Class, and Shelter,* ed. Elizabeth Collins Cromley and Carter L. Hudgins (Knoxville: University of Tennessee Press, 1995), 164–78.

# CONTRIBUTORS

**ANNA VEMER ANDRZEJEWSKI** is professor of art history at the University of Wisconsin–Madison and codirector of the Buildings–Landscapes–Cultures Ph.D. companion program. She is author of *Building Power: Architecture and Surveillance in Victorian America* and is writing a book on Marshall Erdman and the post–World War II building industry.

**JOHN ARCHER**, professor of cultural studies and comparative literature at the University of Minnesota, works on the spatial, ideological, and cultural history of suburbia. His prize-winning book *Architecture and Suburbia* (Minnesota, 2005) examines the history of suburbia from its genesis in late seventeenth-century Enlightenment England to its manifestation as the ideal of the American Dream.

**HEATHER BAILEY** is the historic preservation grants specialist for History Colorado, the State Historical Fund, leading the western field office in Durango, Colorado. She documents the history of underrepresented communities and resources, conducts fieldwork, and assists communities with ongoing use of their historic places.

**GRETCHEN BUGGELN** holds the Phyllis and Richard Duesenberg Chair in Christianity and the Arts at Valparaiso University, where she studies the intersections of the sacred and the material in religious spaces and in museums. She is author of *Temples of Grace: The Material Transformation of Connecticut's Churches, 1790–1840* and *The Suburban Church: Modernism and Community in Postwar America* (Minnesota, 2016).

**CHARITY R. CARNEY** is author of *Ministers and Masters: Methodism, Manhood, and Honor in the Antebellum South*. She teaches history at Western Governors

University and is working on a book-length study of the history of the modern megachurch.

**MARGARET CRAWFORD** is professor of architecture at the University of California, Berkeley, where she teaches the history and theory of architecture, urbanism and urban history, and studios on small-scale urbanity. Her research focuses on the evolution, uses, and meanings of urban space. She is author of *Building the Workingman's Paradise: The Design of American Company Towns* and editor of *The Car and the City: The Automobile, the Built Environment, and Daily Urban Life* and *Everyday Urbanism*.

**MARTIN DINES** is senior lecturer in English literature at Kingston University London. His research focuses on the suburbs in Anglo-American writing, queer domesticities, and the connections among national identity, space, and sexuality. He is author of *Gay Suburban Narratives in American and British Culture: Homecoming Queens* and coeditor (with Timotheus Vermeulen) of *New Suburban Stories*.

**ANDREW FRIEDMAN** is assistant professor of history at Haverford College. He is author of *Covert Capital: Landscapes of Denial and the Making of U.S. Empire in the Suburbs of Northern Virginia*.

**BEVERLY K. GRINDSTAFF** is associate professor of design history at the San José State University School of Art and Design. Her research interests focus on the construction of identity through design, popular culture, and display. She is writing a book on midcentury American interior design.

**DIANNE HARRIS** is professor and director of the Illinois Program for Research in the Humanities at the University of Illinois at Urbana–Champaign, where she teaches courses in architectural and urban history. She is author of *Little White Houses: How the Postwar Home Constructed Race in America* (Minnesota, 2013) and editor of *Second Suburb: Levittown, Pennsylvania*.

**URSULA LANG** is a geographer interested in contemporary environmental politics and in the intersections of practice, everyday life, and built environments. She earned her Ph.D. in geography at the University of Minnesota and studied architecture at the University of California, Berkeley.

**MATTHEW GORDON LASNER** is assistant professor of urban affairs and planning at Hunter College, where he teaches courses in North American and global urbanism, housing, and the built environment. His research concerns the production of metropolitan space in the United States, with a focus on the relationships among design, social change, the market, and the state. His first book, *High Life: Condo Living in the Suburban Century,* examines the social and architectural history of owner-occupied multifamily housing in the United States and was awarded the 2013 Cummings Prize by the Vernacular Architecture Forum.

**WILLOW LUNG-AMAM** is assistant professor of urban studies and planning at the University of Maryland, College Park. Her research focuses on issues of social inequality and diversity as they relate to the design of cities, urban policy, and planning practice. She is writing a book on Asian immigration in Silicon Valley suburbia, looking at place-making and politics of development in the region.

**BECKY M. NICOLAIDES** is a research scholar at the UCLA Center for the Study of Women, specializing in the history of American suburbanization. She is author of *My Blue Heaven: Life and Politics in the Working-Class Suburbs of Los Angeles, 1920–1965* and coeditor (with Andrew Wiese) of *The Suburb Reader.* She is working on a book about social and civic transformation in postwar suburban Los Angeles.

**TRECIA POTTINGER** is program director of the Bonner Scholars Program at Oberlin College and a Ph.D. candidate in American studies at the University of Minnesota. Her research examines nineteenth- and twentieth-century black suburbanization on Philadelphia's Main Line.

**TIM RETZLOFF** is a lecturer with the Center for Gender in Global Context at Michigan State University. He completed his Ph.D. in history at Yale University with a dissertation that examines how suburb and city shaped gay and lesbian life in postwar metropolitan Detroit.

**JODI RIOS** taught architecture and urban design at Washington University in St. Louis and now conducts interdisciplinary research on race, racism, and marginalized suburbs at the University of California, Berkeley. She has published on transdisciplinary research and transformative pedagogy, and her design work has received many notable awards.

**PAUL J. P. SANDUL** is assistant professor of history at Stephen F. Austin State University, where he codirects the public history program. He is author of *California Dreaming: Boosterism, Memory, and Rural Suburbs in the Golden State.*

**CHRISTOPHER SELLERS** is professor of history at Stony Brook University, where he studies the histories and contemporary legacies of cities, suburbs, environmentalism, and inequality. He is author of *Crabgrass Crucible: Suburban Nature and the Rise of Environmentalism in Twentieth-Century America* and is now writing on the historical relationships among suburbanization, race, and environmentalism around Atlanta.

**DAVID SMILEY** teaches at the Graduate School of Architecture, Planning, and Preservation at Columbia University. A practicing architect and historian, he edited *Redressing the Mall: Sprawl and Public Space in Suburbia*. His book *Pedestrian Modern: Shopping and American Architecture, 1925–1956* (Minnesota, 2013) elucidates the unrecognized mutual significance of store and shopping center design to modernist architectural and urban tenets in the United States.

**KATHERINE SOLOMONSON** is associate professor in the School of Architecture at the University of Minnesota. She is author of *The Chicago Tribune Tower Competition: Skyscraper Design and Cultural Change in the 1920s*, recipient of the Alice Davis Hitchcock Award from the Society of Architectural Historians. She is researching the changing building cultures and social practices that produced new urban and suburban landscapes along the route of the Northern Pacific Railway in the nineteenth century. She coedits the book series Architecture, Landscape, and American Culture for the University of Minnesota Press.

**STACIE TARANTO** is assistant professor of history and women's studies at Ramapo College of New Jersey. She is writing a book on conservative women and family values during the 1970s.

**STEVE WAKSMAN** is professor of music and American studies at Smith College. He is author of *Instruments of Desire: The Electric Guitar and the Shaping of Musical Experience* and *This Ain't the Summer of Love: Conflict and Crossover in Heavy Metal and Punk,* which won the 2010 Woody Guthrie Award for outstanding book on popular music from the U.S. chapter of the International Association for the Study of Popular Music. He is coauthor (with Reebee Garofalo) of *Rockin' Out: Popular Music in the U.S.A.* and coeditor (with Andy Bennett) of *The SAGE Handbook of Popular Music.*

**HOLLEY WLODARCZYK** completed her Ph.D. in comparative studies in discourse and society at the University of Minnesota, where she teaches cultural studies. Her dissertation explores environmental goals and values related to contemporary American suburban communities, homes, and lifestyles as articulated in popular media, visual arts, and marketing materials. She has published on suburban photography and popular culture and is working on a visual history of Twin Cities suburban development.

3